During the test I noticed Billie leaning forward in his chair to look over the answer sheet of Wendy in the row ahead.

"Do you know, Billie," I said, "that curiosity killed the cat?"

"Not our cat," said Billie. "The Cow sat on it."

searching
writing

chpt. 9

HAYDEN WRITING SERIES

ROBERT W. BOYNTON, *Consulting Editor*

searching writing

a contextbook

KEN MACRORIE

Professor Emeritus of English
Western Michigan University

HAYDEN BOOK COMPANY, INC.
Rochelle Park, New Jersey

The author would like to thank the proprietors for permission to quote from copyrighted works, as follows:

MAYA ANGELOU: from *I Know Why the Caged Bird Sings*, © Maya Angelou. Permission to reprint granted by Random House, Inc.

MICHAEL J. ARLEN: from "Surprised in Iowa; Surprised in Nam," *New Yorker* (May 7, 1979). Reprinted by permission.

HOWARD BLUM: "Relatives Told the Sad News at a Firehouse," *New York Times*, August 3, 1978, © 1978 by The New York Times Company. Reprinted by permission.

DONALD H. GRAVES: "Balance the Basics: Let Them Write," *Papers on Research about Learning*, © 1978 by the Ford Foundation. Reprinted by permission.

CHRISTOPHER LEHMANN-HAUPT: from a review of Tom Wicker's *A Time to Die*, *New York Times*, March 6, 1975, © 1975 by The New York Times Company. Reprinted by permission.

BARRY LOPEZ: from *Of Wolves and Men*, © 1978 by Charles Scribner's Sons. Used by permission.

Library of Congress Catalog Card Number 80-14425

4   5   6   7   8   9   PRINTING

83 84 85 86 87 88   YEAR

preface

ANYONE CAN LEARN to search and write in a way that furthers thought and reflection, that builds and sees. For several years a number of college and high school teachers around the country have been refining a process we call *I-Search,* and our students have become excited carrying it out.

I search. That's the truth of any inquiry. Re-search doesn't say it, rather implies complete detachment, absolute objectivity. Time to clear the miasma and admit that the best searchers act both subjectively and objectively and write so that professionals and the public can understand their searches and profit from them. Time to get down to the basics, which are not footnotes, but curiosity, need, rigor in judging one's findings and the opinions of experts and helping others test the validity of the search.

For many decades high schools and colleges have fostered the "research paper," which has become an exercise in badly done bibliography, often an introduction to the art of plagiarism, and a triumph of meaninglessness—for both writer and reader. As a teacher I've helped bring about such inane productions myself. Now I look forward to reading I-Search Papers because they tell stories of quests that counted for the questers and they're written in a way that catches and holds readers, as examples in this book make evident.

When students arrive initially on a college campus, they're overwhelmed by the foreignness and size of the place. The professors seem to come from a different world. In strange vocabularies they rain new knowledge and theory upon these young people, who feel alienated at the very time when they need to become attached. Now they must make responsible decisions about how to manage their money, time, sex life, eating, recreation—all without the counsel of the people they've grown up with. In classes, the experiences in textbooks and lectures belong to others. Students are expected to see the relevance of this material to their new lives, but their old lives are seldom allowed into the discussion, and half-people learn poorly. So most of them feel diminished and frightened in unfamiliar and hostile territory. A bad place to begin a new life.

If, in the first weeks, freshmen write I-Search projects in which they examine and respect their experience and needs, school becomes a place where initiative and self-discipline are developed instead of passivity.

• • •

I've called this a *contextbook* for several reasons.

Contrary to most school research papers, the I-Search comes out of a student's life and answers a need in it. The writer testifies to the subjective-objective character of the project. The paper is alive, not borrowedly inert. Writing it, many students for the first time find that writing is a way of thinking, of objectifying an act that has counted for them. As the sentences go down on the page, they become both finished statements and starting points for reflection and evaluation. The passages grow with thought. And the thought is not just about the writers' searches but also about how readers will respond to the words that report and complete them. The enterprise is not self-centered. That term misrepresents an activity in which people are pursuing what counts for them through interviewing and reading authorities while writing papers to be read by their peers. Because they talk to experts, they feel an obligation to them. The experts are Others, but others who have helped, who take on size and importance and must be properly acknowledged. There's an alternation or balance here between objectivity and subjectivity that I call Moebian—a term I discuss at length in Chapter 2.

In the more than four years of classes that lie behind this book—not only mine but those of other teachers—I had always in mind the need to bring the context of the student up against the context of authorities; but not until I began writing did I see that most textbooks present only the conclusions, the abstracted or generalized findings of experts, detached from the experience in which they were formed. And this for students who are novices in the field and often have never encountered its data or theories in any form. Reading such textbooks is not only difficult but discouraging. The discoveries of the experts seem to be delivered by genius or the touch of God, and so students come to feel that they never could make such discoveries themselves. The expert is up there and they are down here taking notes. But if they were to see the experts at work—finding needs in their own lives and answering them, working brilliantly, working stupidly, making mistakes, stumbling into profitable answers—they would understand the true nature of productive women and men, and would come to believe that they might become such people themselves. In this contextbook I've presented some of the experience out of which the best ideas and productions of experts have arisen.

•   •   •

This contextbook discusses spelling and punctuation in their historical context, as systems created by human intelligence, weakness, inconsistency, and confusion, not as works of perfection to be memorized as Holy Writ under the threat of divine punishment. The program in this book is devised to bring about what Benjamin Franklin and others in the 18th century called *countenancing*. In his plan for the academy that eventually became the University of Pennsylvania, Franklin suggested

> That the Members of the corporation make it their Pleasure, and in some Degree their Business, to visit the Academy often, encourage and *countenance* the Youth, *countenance* and assist the Masters, and by all Means in their Power advance the Usefulness and Reputation of the Design; that they look on the Students as in some Sort their Children, treat them with Familiarity and Affection . . .

Among the meanings *The Oxford English Dictionary* gives for this verb are: "to favour . . . sanction, encourage, 'back up', bear out a person." *Searching Writing* is designed to countenance students as searchers and writers, and to help them countenance others.

One of the messages of this contextbook is that no individuals learn by giving back to authorities the accepted word the authorities have given them. The two must meet, bringing with them their own experiences and searches, their own effort and commitment. Students can accomplish wonders if they don't allow themselves to be benumbed and bedumbed by the Lecture-Test System. They need to escape this conventional closed circle. This is a breakout manual.

Because it's a new kind of book I can't say all the places in which it might be used, but these are possibilities:

1. In a semester course in college English that's complete in itself and asks students to write two I-Search Papers.
2. In one of the semesters of a year-long freshman English program.
3. In a year's course in freshman English that has traditionally included literature and a research project.
4. In the beginning course in any field or discipline, or in a general education course that introduces students to research. To start students in history, social science, or science, for example, with *Searching Writing* would enable them to become writers instead of jargoneers, and to retain and increase their natural human curiosity and initiative in searching.
5. In a club outside school formed by persons of any age who meet

regularly to share responses to their own experiences and ideas, and put them up against those of accepted authorities.

This book was designed for people of college age and older, but exceptional teachers may use it with younger students. It treats library materials with a sophistication beyond most high school students, but a judicious, selective use of the section entitled "Looking in the Cupboard" will make the book useful to persons of less than college age.

Suggestions for teachers, or leaders of non-school groups, appear at the end of the book.

• • •

In the last four years, many teachers have asked students to write I-Search Papers and have shared the results with me. To them and others who have countenanced this project and improved upon my notions, I say thank you. Most helpful have been Doreen McFarlane and Jean E. Smith of Bunnell High School, Stratford, Connecticut, and Linda Floyd Kennedy of Rochester, New York, who sent me such first-rate papers.

I'd like also to thank the following teachers: Larry Levy of Delta College, University Center, Michigan; Larry Rudner of Lakeland College, Sheboygan, Wisconsin; Doug Nietzke of Illinois State University at Normal; Richard M. Lebovitz of Cape Hatteras School, Buxton, North Carolina; Chris Honoré of Northgate High School, Walnut Creek, California; Amy F. Pace of the University of Georgia at Athens; Sharon Graville of Belleville Area College, Illinois; Helen Heaton, Ginny Kirsch, and Mary Croft of the University of Wisconsin, Stevens Point; Joe Inners of Suffolk County Community College, Long Island, New York; George Felton and Alan Govenar of the Columbus College of Art and Design in Ohio; Des Margaris of the Havre Public Schools in Montana; Dick Adler of the University of Montana at Missoula; Sam Watson, Jr. of the University of North Carolina at Charlotte; Bill Aull of Parkland College, Champaign, Illinois; and others whose names I regret to say I don't have in mind or at hand at the moment.

My thanks to Joyce T. Macrorie and Ronnie Groff for their concerned and thoughtful criticism of this manuscript, and most of all, to Robert W. Boynton for shepherding this book from inception to final form.

K.M.

Santa Fe, New Mexico

contents

A writer is a person whose best is re-leased in the accomplishment of writing. . . . He does not necessarily think these things—he does not, that is, think them out and then write them down: he writes, and the best of him, in spite even of his thought, will appear on the page even to his surprise, unrecognized or even sometimes against his will, by proper use of words.

WILLIAM CARLOS WILLIAMS

part one
writing
every
day

Almost everybody interposes a massive and complicated series of editings between the time words start to be born into consciousness and when they finally come off at the end of the pencil or typewriter onto the page. This is partly because schooling makes us obsessed with the "mistakes" we make in writing.

PETER ELBOW

chapter 1
free
writing

THE HUMAN MIND is a connector, it puts things together. That's the sort of instrument it is. When pressures become heavy it may break down and refuse to connect things, scattering and fragmenting what it perceives and remembers. But ordinarily, it will work for you like a fan sucking in leaves and then blowing them in the direction you point it. The mind's your wind, so it can do what the other wind out there—which you don't own—seldom does. Tell it what direction you'd like it to blow, and watch what happens.

In the last fifteen years, a number of teachers around the country and their students have been amazed by what happened when people wrote fast for ten to fifteen minutes without worrying about grammar, punctuation, or spelling, and concentrating only on telling some kind of truth. When you write freely, losing yourself in trying to tell truths, you'll often find yourself and others. But if you allow yourself to play the game of trying to look good, you'll probably write junk, like this:

1

This is an interesting little exercise—write freely—whatever comes to mind—Well, here goes. Got up late this morning—alarm clock trouble. Never did like to get up. School is pretty exciting on the first day—new kids—new teachers.

Don't know why mom and dad worried so much about me going off to school this year—I wasn't worried. I can handle it, I'm sure. I'm interested in improving my mind as well as having fun. I believe in the training of one's reasoning abilities. Some of these chicks in this class are pretty smooth —especially that blonde over there—I think she's looking at me, just as I've been looking at her. Oh well, my hand is getting tired, and I ought to sign off. I'm thinking that my next class is math, which is a subject I've always had trouble with.

That piece of free writing is not free; it's self-conscious. A person who concentrates on truthtelling and then writes as fast as he can whatever comes to mind will *naturally* say more about his alarm clock than this writer did, more about the exciting people he met on the first day, more about how Mom and Dad acted worried. He'll bring them alive.

When you begin a sentence with tongue or pen you don't know what words will finish it for you. I say "finish it for you" as if someone or something other than your conscious mind is in charge, and that's often the truth of the act. Psychologists and linguists don't know yet how the brain manages to store words, or perhaps whole phrases or clauses, and then release them at the right time. We all know moments when the brain is not working for us, when we reach for words and they aren't there, when language won't flow. But we can set up situations conducive to flow.

> . . . the story, the essay, and even something so apparently inconsequential as a book review (I mean one which is approached with seriousness), is already there, much in the way that Socrates said mathematical knowledge was already there, before a word is ever put to paper, and the act of writing is the act of finding the magical key that will unlock the floodgates and let the flow begin.
>
> NORMAN PODHORETZ

Look at this piece of genuine free writing:

2

I remember it happened on July 11 at 11:29. It was in the fire log of *The Muskegon Chronicle* because gas poured all over the street. There was a car waiting to turn left into a store parking lot, an old green car. I slowed down because the traffic had cleared and I figured she'd turn. But she just sat there so I stepped on the brake—boy did I step on the brake—all the way to the floor and nothing happened. I barreled into the tail of her car. There was no noise and everything moved very slowly. The glass sort of sparkled as it flew in front of my windshield. At last everything was still—I held fast to the steering wheel and kept repeating, "My God, I don't believe this happened." After a few seconds I got out of the car and an old friend who'd been driving right behind me asked if I was all right. I was, but that stupid old woman in the other car just sat there with gas pouring out all over. I went to her car and helped her out and into the store to sit down. All the way there she kept repeating that her son would have to be called in Grand Rapids, he's a lawyer, you know. She was o.k. after she sat down for a few minutes. I made all the necessary arrangements for my car to be towed and called my insurance agent and the lady I was going to have a job interview with. The police finally got there and asked me what happened. I told him I thought my brakes had gone out. He looked at me skeptically as one looks at a small child telling a foolish story. But he went and looked at my car, checked the brakes and came back sheepishly saying that he thought I was right. We went through all the questions and answers—the whole time both the policeman and I being informed that the old lady's son is a lawyer in Grand Rapids. She never did understand no fault insurance and still thinks I'm a crazy, young kid driver that purposely put her rear bumper into her back seat.

JULIE BISHOP

Julie's account is stronger than writing number 1 because she writes honestly of her feelings and shows herself wavering. Like many professional writers, she puts us there in the event and presents the reader with conflict.

When you write truths freely you'll find that in small and large ways you use the strategies of professional writers, without thinking of them. For example, notice the way this free writer employed sound effects:

3

Skydiving is one of the most unbelievable things you can do for yourself. It's a thrill that compares to nothing you've done before. Four people cramped in a tiny single-engined plane, knees knocking partly because of the plane's rocking motion and partly because you're scared. You are sitting on the trembling metal floor, feeling extremely bulky, with the chutes strapped to your back and your stomach—oh, let's not mention the stomach.

You're perched on the edge of the doorway, your feet dangling out of the plane, being grabbed and pulled by a vicious 110 mph wind. You lean your head out and look down. The wind and the view are too much and you draw your head back in. You place one hand on the wall of the plane on each side of the door and scoot forward until you are teetering on the border between sitting and falling. One more inch forward and you're gone. You push off hard. Wind. Start counting to five. You must always remember to count. More wind. No noise, except wind. It grabs at your jumpsuit so powerfully you swear it will be ripped right off. The ground is so far away, but yet so near. Oh, forgot to count. Has it been five seconds?

Ah! The chute opens with a sound like someone is shaking the hell out of a very large bedsheet. You get a mild reassuring jerk, and there you are.

No sound. No wind. Just you. What a view.

You're absorbed so much in the view you forget a bit about the landing. No turning back now. Bend your knees. Look straight ahead, not down. Oh God, you'd love to look down, but you aren't supposed to. You look down anyway. You scare the hell out of yourself and look straight ahead again. You hit the ground, roll a bit, and smile.

RYAN NAGY

An editor would probably say to this writer, "Drop your first two sentences and change the *you* throughout the piece to *I,* because you're obviously telling your own experience. But having made those suggestions, the editor would probably praise the writing. It sounds right. It puts the reader in the action. Much of the expression is gripping, as it should be. In remembering, the writer allowed himself to be pulled into the experience again. Note the dramatic action words in the first four sentences of the second paragraph: *perched, dangling, grabbed, pulled, lean, draw, scoot, teetering, sitting, falling.* The last three sentences also superbly control sound:

Oh God, you'd love to look down, but you aren't supposed to. You look down anyway. [That quick, four-word sentence is perfect there.] **You scare the hell out of yourself and look straight ahead again.**

And now, hard sounds—appropriately—in these words:

You hit the ground . . .

And the shortness of the roll:

roll a bit . . .

And the suddenness of realizing you're all right, in these words:

and smile.

In our fifteen-year observation of seminars conducted in colleges and high schools around the country we've found that listeners or readers respond positively to writing that employs rhythms skillfully. And negatively to writing that's stiff, awkward, rhythmless. That's not a surprising finding, but we were surprised to realize that the writers who achieved strong effects through rhythm or other techniques of sound had usually achieved them unconsciously. When praised for an artistic effect they frequently said, "What?" and listened with amazement to what they had written.

> *Anyone who breathes is in the rhythm business . . .*
>
> WILLIAM STAFFORD

∞ **DOING ONE:** For twelve minutes write as fast as you can whatever comes to mind. Don't worry about spelling, punctuation, or grammar, or what you think a teacher might want you to say. Write as fast as you can and still be legible. Don't stop. If at any point, you can't think of what to write, look in front of you—at the wall, window, ceiling, whatever—and start describing what you see. You'll find you're soon thinking yourself into a chain of sentences that belong to you. Say to yourself, "What goes down here is going to be truth of some kind, nothing phony, nothing designed to make me look good."

Some people presume that when they're asked to do free writing they're supposed to meander and maunder around in gibberish and later everyone in the seminar should say, "Oh, I think that's just beautiful," like doting parents asking strangers to praise their baby for the way it slobbered at the dinner table. A person asked to do free writing on the first day of school once wrote:

4

I think first of all that free writing is kind of a crummy trick to get us all to write. I think high school students should

be able to organize their thoughts into cohesive units of expression rather than sloppy streams of consciousness. I spent last year on independent study trying to organize, organize, and now I have to get suddenly disorganized.

An understandable reaction, but from someone who hasn't yet learned that our unconscious selves often organize things better than our conscious selves. Both can organize. It's good to let the unconscious do its spontaneous, often brilliant, job and later let the conscious self do its rational, logical job if needed. Frequently we can write our way into "cohesive units of expression." We start cold and warm to it, as this free writer did in writing her way into the understanding that she was in love.

5

A couple of months ago—it doesn't seem possible—he was too arrogant, too untouchable. He even had the nerve to tell me I acted like a child sometimes. The fact that I did didn't matter to me. He was just wrong and I was right, of course. I said it would never work so let's just forget it— you're not worth the effort.

He didn't hear, so now we're here. We went away for a while and saw things that I'd never have enjoyed alone— some were elaborate, such as an off-Broadway musical, and some were simple, like the beautiful lake-shore. Talking wasn't always necessary, but when we did, it was fine and we both heard.

We laughed so hard in the cab at the cab driver's stories and then the driver who tried to rip us off. Another one told us we looked like movie stars and we laughed harder. This guy even recited some of his own poetry for us. We ate and drank so much and loved every bit of it.

Almost a new world is opening up for me even in this small town of Michigan; so many things I never thought were fun before or exciting. It has to be him because I've done them before.

If you're free-writing well, you'll concentrate so hard on truthtelling and write so fast you'll put yourself into a kind of trance, like that state between waking and sleeping at night (or sleeping and waking in the morning) when a gaggle of good ideas or memories comes together for you. But if you can't find a topic you feel right with, do as I said earlier, look in front of you and start writing about what you see. You'll be writing sentences that make sense and they'll flow into each other with the logic of mind or feeling.

Most of the free writing I'm presenting here centers on the writers' own experiences. That's because they've been asked to write truths, and the truths they know best are their own. So they turn to them, not to someone else's experience or knowledge. Some persons—the same who fear free writing may be just mucking around in mud puddles— think that in free writing one must confess his sins or search for his true self. The "Who Am I, Really?" School. When you're telling truths, you're not pretending to carry out a dramatic self-analysis. You're putting truths down and watching where they go.

> *Oh, I suppose everyone continues to be interested in the quest for the self, but what you feel when you're older, I think, is that—how to express this—that you really must* make *the self. It's absolutely useless to look for it, you won't find it, but it's possible in some sense to make it.*
>
> MARY MCCARTHY

We become ourselves, not by asking who we are, but by playing, working, at things we care about, standing up to storms when they dump on us. Writing is one kind of work or play, and free writing is one of the best because it finds for us genuine voices, in which we can speak with authority.

You may have noticed that in free writing in this chapter some writers use mainly common words, like those we hear in the kitchen —*this guy, fine, ripped us off*—and others use more unusual words— *proffered, insidious,* and *matter* [in the medical sense, meaning pus, a discharge from an infection or irritation]. That makes no difference. If the words belong to you, you'll use them naturally and accurately. But when you forget truthtelling you're apt to try to show off with words you only partially know, and that's almost always fatal to a piece of writing. Don't allow yourself to become self-conscious about vocabulary. Use the words that come to you. If later, with the help of others in the seminar, you find that some of those words were weak or imprecise, you can change them just as professional writers do with the help of their editors.

Concentrate on truthtelling while writing freely as fast as you can without worrying about errors or what other people will think. Then show your best writing to them. That's the time to worry about what they think of your work. In this seminar you'll get from them not ridicule but the sort of help Mother gave when you were learning to speak.

When the best passages of free writing are read aloud in your group, your job as a countenancer will be to act like Mother. Comment on what you like in the writing. If it contains things you don't like, or think weak, refrain from commenting about them. What you say must be honest, but you don't have to say everything you feel. This truthfulness on your part will help the other writers and increase the truth in your next writing. You've probably heard the saying that one lie breeds another; in seminars we've found that one truth breeds another. Later, the response sessions will be opened up to negative remarks and suggestions for improvement.

When I first asked people to do free writing, I thought they would do best when alone in quiet places; but in the last fifteen years of observing seminars, I've found that the best free writing is usually done in the company of others. Apparently when a group of people sit down together with the expectation of writing well, they affect each other. If they concentrate on truths, a silence takes over the room, its surface ruffled only by the scratch of pens or pencils. Perhaps that sound, along with the fast, uninterrupted act of making letters on the paper, puts some people into that twilight state in which experience and thoughts flow steadily through their pens and pencils. The voices in their heads speak, and the writers take dictation as fast as they can. Some people are so controlled that in the space of an allotted ten or twelve minutes they start writing with what others would call a grabbing beginning to a story and round it off neatly with a perfectly ending sentence.

∞ **DOING TWO:** After reading the paper "Dad," in the chapter on "Truthtelling," or listening to it read aloud by someone else in your seminar, do a free writing about someone you're related to. Again, concentrate on truths and write as fast as you can, not worrying about grammar, spelling, punctuation, or vocabulary. Twelve minutes.

> *The writer must be able to feel words intimately, one at a time. He must also be able to step back, inside his head, and see the flowing sentence.*
>
> DONALD HALL

People want to write. The desire to express is relentless. People want others to know what they hold to be truthful. They need the sense of authority that goes with authorship.

DONALD H. GRAVES

chapter 2
loopy
learning

NOW THAT you're into free writing—which reveals powers most people don't know they have—I'd like to show you where this book is coming from and where it's going to take you, or more accurately, where you're going to take it.

A few years ago, anxious to find how young children would perform if they wrote for each other and helped each other improve their papers, I visited a fourth-grade class once a week for two months. The students were squirming puppies, into everything in the classroom, talking and shouting to each other across the rows, planning what they would do next time they were freed of their chairs, loudly whispering taunts and gibes about how they would best each other on the playground, creating or damaging relationships. That energy harnessed could heat the homes of America, I thought, and if I could make it flow into the act of writing down here in fourth grade, it would melt the difficulties of teaching writing in high school and college.

So I asked the kids to write freely and concentrate on truthtelling. Most were still worried about forming letters that would satisfy a teacher's eye and wrote too slowly to break up the ice floes and get the river running. But I excerpted the best passages from the papers, ignoring a few that could only embarrass the authors, and presented them to the class, saying we would read them aloud and I wanted some honest responses.

For the first couple of meetings "only praise, please—if you don't like the writing, don't say anything." I asked that someone read the first excerpt, and hands shot up all over the room. I had chosen Debbie's paper to be read, and Richard to read it.

> One day when I was five I was staying at my grandma's house and the phone rang. It was my mom. She was in the Borgess hospital and said that she had a boy and they named it Lonnie. I was so excited I kept asking what color of eyes does he have? What color of hair? Then she had to get ready to come home. I kept begging my grandma, "Come on, get ready," and finally we went. We had left early that day so my grandma said, "Why don't we stop at Kindleberger Park?" I played on the slide and swings and then I wanted to go to my house and so we did. When we got there I saw my brother. He was cute and I got to hold him, but now I am ten and he is five and I wish in a way he wasn't my brother because he is a little snot.

"All right," I said. "Did anyone like that? Were there certain things in it that you liked as Richard was reading it?"

Hands again, about seventeen out of the thirty kids were waving a hand. "OK, Keith."

Keith dropped his hand and said excitedly, "Can I have mine read now?"

"Keith," I said, "I'm trying to get people to react to the paper that was just read."

More squirming and panting and hands shooting up in the air. "All right," I said, pointing at a boy waving his hand near me. "What did you like about it?"

"Would you read mine next?"

When I finally located a child who would speak of the writing, she said, "I thought it was great. Can I have mine read next?"

> *Above all, a living thing wants to* discharge *its energy . . .*
>
> FRIEDRICH NIETZSCHE

The commenting and editing sessions then and later flopped. After several weeks, I accepted the egotism because I found it in all my relations with the kids. When I walked in the door as recess was ending, the first boy into the room grabbed my arm and said, "Mr. Macrorie, would you look at the rock I brought today?" and pulled me over to the window to see it. On my way, I was yanked the other direction by a girl saying, "Come over here! I want you to see the picture I painted yesterday." And so it went, the room suffused with egos, kids not saying, in effect, "I'm better than Clare or Jimmy," but "Look at me. Don't pay attention to them because if you do, you won't have time for me."

Later I asked a seventy-year-old retired teacher about my experience. "To be expected," she said, "third- and fourth-grade kids are like that." I was shaken by the discovery and went back to what the philosopher George Herbert Mead had said in *Mind, Self & Society* in 1934:

> The self has the characteristic that it is an object to itself . . . We can lose parts of the body without any serious invasion of the self. . . . [The self] . . . is a reflexive . . . can be both subject and object.

Keith and Debbie were in the early stages of developing selves.

How powerful are these drives to assert ourselves, to become persons in our own right! You can see them at work in Debbie's free writing. She chose to report how eager she was to see her new brother but pleased to interrupt the journey of recognition to play on the swings at the park. The passage reveals her ambivalence, her flashing curiosity about this new creature, and then her admission that finally, at five, he's a snot. In these years when Debbie is trying to establish her self, not only as a power in the family, but as an entity in the larger society, Lonnie is in the way. As long as others are considering him, they can't be considering her.

Debbie's struggling. If she doesn't sometimes win at home and school, she won't exist for the others or herself. She's right to be selfish. In the next three years or so she'll rapidly become a person and can afford to think more about the performance of others. I'm not sure whether she would gain from a quicker becoming. Maybe if I had been more patient with Debbie's class and spent more time with them in what I call "The Helping Circle," they would have matured faster. I should say the circle is not really a circle—although in physical fact I place the chairs in the round—but a one-sided loop, with each *I* and *The Others* both on it, flowing into each other. You can understand the relationship if you make a Moebius Loop, or Strip. Cut a half-inch strip down the side of a sheet of typing paper, give one end a twist, and scotch-tape the ends together so it joins like this:

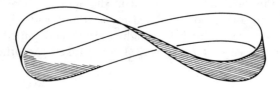

At any one point along the Loop there are two sides—for the *I* and *The Others*, for subjectivity and objectivity, or any other set of polar opposites. If you press the point of your pencil on the Strip and pull the paper along, you'll find that the line eventually runs into itself. Two sides, but in the long pull they become each other.

The Moebius Strip is not a simple loop of the kind we made chains out of in kindergarten, with two sides that never flow into each other:

In 1821 the British poet Percy Shelley wrote:

> A man to be greatly good, must imagine intensely and comprehensively; he must put himself in the place of another, and of many others; the pains and pleasures of his species must become his own.

To make that act a habit is central to becoming mature and human. But most of us teachers have given students only half the materials for this transformation. We've lectured them about The Others and their achievements, but we haven't given this culture to them so they can make it part of themselves. We've put it out there and thought that was enough, forgetting how much our own school experience was an act of forgetting. And we haven't encouraged or allowed students to bring themselves, with their experience and abilities, into the act of reading and discussing the experience of the authorities. Shelley said man "must put *himself* in the place of another." That *himself* is an achievement itself. Whatever your age, you're an accumulation of experiences, a working creature of many abilities, although not always of those that school traditionally centers on. This self, which is you, must be allowed to appear in class or it can't be put in anyone else's place.

The principal reason education doesn't "take" better than it does is that it's a closed loop, with the knowledge and experience of experts on one side and no way for it to flow into or over to the other side, where in darkness—unarticulated, unreflected upon, unused—lie the knowledge and experience of students. The discipline of real learning consists of The Self and The Others flowing into each other.

I've written this book to present one way in which people in school or outside it can get on the Moebius Loop. I call it *The I-Search Paper*. It enables people to become instrumental because it begins with truth and need. All through our lifetimes we're becoming ourselves. By the time we're in high school or college we're capable of doing much more than Debbie and Keith when they raised their hands and said, "Now can I have my paper read?" They needed to have their papers read. We all need to have our papers read. But no more than we need to have the papers of The Others read to us. We can be authors reading authorities while we are becoming authorities ourselves—however limited and naive. *Authorities*, from the Latin *auctoritas*, with opinions, able to make decisions, and to employ power.

No one can give other persons knowledge, make them think or become curious. Knowledge must reside in a person or it is not knowledge; and even if that person accumulates it, without use it is—what else could it be?—useless. Ralph Emerson wrote of using knowledge:

> It was dead fact; now, it is quick thought. It can stand, and it can go. It now endures, it now flies, it now inspires. . . .

Until persons become curious, start thinking, do something with their knowledge, there is no such thing as curiosity, thinking, or use of knowledge. These activities don't exist in the abstract but in individuals, who then become alive. It's that sort of liveness which this book encourages.   *Feb 29*

AN I-SEARCH PAPER

In the last four years other teachers around the country and I have been challenging students to do what we call *I-Searches*—not Re-Searches, in which the job is to search again what someone has already searched—but original searches in which persons scratch an itch they feel, one so marvelously itchy that they begin rubbing a finger tip against it and the rubbing feels so good that they dig in with a fingernail. A search to fulfill a need, not that the teacher has imagined for them, but one they feel themselves, one that would please Emerson because it endures and flies.

Although you won't be I-Searching for several weeks or writing a report of your adventure, I want to show you an I-Search Paper so you'll have a sense of what you're preparing to do as you continue free writing. I present this one in the form in which it was first written, before the writer received editing help from members of his seminar or the teacher. Looking at this first draft you'll see the truth of its making and not believe the paper is so perfect that it's beyond your powers.

> *He who never makes mistakes makes nothing.*
>
> ERIC PARTRIDGE

THE CAPTIVE WOLF

Kirk Moll

i. INTRODUCTION

When I asked the question, the answers were always the same: they will turn on you, you can't train them, or simply you're crazy. Why such reactions? Other people own lions, bears; Lincoln Mercury even owns a cougar. But when I asked the question: Hey guy I've always been interested in owning a wolf, do you think I would have a hard time finding one and training it? there was usually some negative response. For the last 7 or 8 years, I've been thinking about trying to get a wolf as a pet. For a while, I was kind of turned off at keeping an animal that is naturally wild captive. Then a couple of years ago, I saw a special on the tundra timber wolves in Alaska. The animals are being shot from helicopters by the Department of Natural Resources (DNR) to keep the pack numbers down. The DNR likes to try to keep the ratio of wolves per square mile to moose and elk per square mile at a number that they can both survive at. When the wolves begin taking too large a toll on the moose and elk herds, the DNR shoots them to keep nature's balance. This theory seems rather valid to me but I still feel capturing them and transporting them to an area that has a low wolf population would be worth the cost and time it would take to do so. I was instructed to write my introduction knowing only what I had known prior to my research. One of the things I have known is that there is a *Red Book* by Harry A. Goodman that lists the present status of endangered species (1972). The book lists the timber and gray wolves as vulnerable. Although Alaska is bountiful with wolves, it still seems senseless to me that the DNR, of all groups, are shooting an endangered species. There are roughly 6,300 wolves in all of North America and Canada. They are spread out as follows: 2,000–3,000 in Alaska, the same number in the Northern Canadian regions, 200–300 in Minnesota, and 20–30 in Isle Royale, Michigan. These figures are quite low when you consider that the wolf is adaptable to almost any climate in North America. The figures grow even lower when you realize that the only enemy the wolf actually has is man. The other animals cannot keep the wolf from becoming extinct; only man can undo what he has already done.

Now you may be thinking why the hell does he want to keep a wolf captive after that big ecology speech he just handed me? The answer to this is I would like to own one so I can show it to people, take him to schools and talk a little about the wolf so people can see just what they will lose if some measures are not taken. It seems to me that it might do a little good; at least it beats those "Save a Whale" t-shirts. There is another reason and that is I personally have always wanted one for a pet. The same as most people want a dog or a cat—I have always wanted different pets. When I was little, I found a baby squirrel and trained him (he lived in our house for quite a while). Then when I was around 12, I almost conned my parents into buying a monkey. So having a pet wolf as a pet will be no big surprise to anyone I've known for a while—I've been talking about it for years. I kind of hope this fascination for wild animals leaves me when I get old, for at this pace I will want a grizzly for my 60th birthday.

Since I don't know where I will be living for the next couple of years, I don't think I will be able to get the wolf until then, but it is important for me to find out about this subject now because it may take a couple of years to obtain one for all I know. *For all I know,* that is the biggest reason I'm writing this paper because there is too much I don't know.

ii. SEARCHING

After starting my search, I learned a couple of facts about the Detroit zoo. Number one is they used to have a couple of wolves but have none at the present time. The second was they seem to have no knowledge about where the hell their animals go after leaving their zoo. I called the zoo when I was home in Detroit, only to hear a recording saying peanuts were 50¢ and parking a dollar. At the end of the tape, they gave me a number to call for more information. With hope, I dialed the number. The man who answered thought the zoo had some wolves a couple of years back, but he wasn't sure, he also didn't know anyone I could talk to about the subject or what happened to the wolves the zoo used to have. After hanging up the phone, I had a great sense of gratification knowing that he was the right man for "information." I remember in high school that a lady came to our Biology class with her pet wolf. I called my old biology teacher and got the lady's number. I tried calling her for the duration of the weekend, but there was never an answer. It was now time to go back to Kalamazoo so it looked as if the rest of my search would be conducted there.

When I got back to Kalamazoo I decided to go talk to the head of the Science Department here at Western. He was a nice guy who knew nothing at all about wolves, but assured me that a professor under him would. I went to his room. His office hours were posted on the door. I copied them down and left. The next day I called him and he told me to walk over to see him. He said he would be in his room. It was about five degrees below zero that day and as usual the wind was blowing in my face on the way there. (The wind blows in four directions in Kalamazoo.) When I got there he was not in his room as he told me. (I had third degree chill burns over 90% of my body and I was damned if I was going to turn around and walk right back.) I started a new search "stalking the wild professor." I asked five other professors and finally found him in a lab room down the hall. I went in the room and there sat Western's foremost expert on outdoor sciences—what a joke that was. He looked at me as if I was crazy when I asked him if he knew any wolf breeders. He did not really know any more about wolves than the head of the science department or at least he came on that way. I think he really wasn't concerned about what I had to say as he never lifted his eyes from the science magazine he was reading. I finally gave up and left.

iii. FINDING

After quite a few more dead ends, I finally resorted to just asking anybody if they knew of any wolf breeders or anyone who owns a wolf. I must have asked over 50 people and gotten over 50 no's. I was telling my story to a girl down the hall and to my astonishment she said, "My neighbor at home breeds wolves." (She lives in South Haven, Michigan; about a 45-minute drive from Kalamazoo.) The next day I called the woman. She told me she no longer breeds wolves. She was very enthusiastic about wolves though. She still owns a couple of wolves now. About six months ago she had a bad accident with a ½ husky-½ wolf. The animal had been sent to an attack school and was not yet fully trained when the incident occurred. The lady told me that she was choking on some food and the other people there were trying to help her. "I literally turned blue," she said. When the dog saw her, he didn't recognize her and attacked. He ripped deep gashes into her face and took a piece of her rear the size of your fist. The woman spent four hours in surgery and said she is fine now. She blamed the whole thing on that attack school though, not the viciousness of the dog. I was very impressed with the deep love for the wolves she had, especially after her accident. She told me that wolves are much smarter than dogs and are much more receptive toward you. "They know your emotions at all times. You can't train a wolf, you can only show them how you want them to behave." That last line had a real impact on me; she went on to explain that the wolf is too smart to be trained. He looks at that as an insult to his intelligence. You have to show them how you would like them to behave and if he doesn't do it, give up because they are like people—they do what they want to sometimes. But by the way, she had said, "you can't train a wolf, you can only show them how you want them to behave." I had already known exactly what she meant. There was another thing she told me that I knew would have never come out of the books I had read. She said, "The wolf will respond to you, his owner, as he looks at you as his family and expects you to treat him the same. You should be the one to teach him and be the only one to." The wolf she owns she feeds scraps to only from her plate. In return her wolf will walk up to her when she is sitting somewhere and drop some of his food on the lady's lap, as a gift to the lady for sharing her food with the wolf. "It is very important not to turn the food down because the wolf will be very hurt at this and might not come by you for days," she said.

Although this lady no longer breeds she told me of a deputy sheriff in Berrien County (south of South Haven a few miles) who still breeds. I thanked the lady for all the information and she told me to make sure and come see her wolves. This lady had been a lot more informative than the foremost authority at Western—that was for sure.

I called the sheriff's department and got hold of this man the lady had told me about. I was totally amazed at the way he spoke. He sounded like a dittoed copy of the woman! He had the same praise and admiration for his wolves as the lady had for her wolves. He said that his wolf knows him better than his wife does. "That wolf can look at me and he knows if I am mad, happy, or indifferent. If I am mad he doesn't come near but if I am not, he knocks me over. He gets a big kick out of being able to knock me down." The man told me that in play he can hit the wolf as hard as he wants but if the wolf is bad, he would never hit him because the wolf, like any animal you hit, might turn around and bite his arm off. If he yells at him the wolf will cower (they hate it when their owner is mad at them). Both the man and woman told stories the same way. Every negative story they had about their wolves ended up on a positive note.

I asked him about some facts now, wanting to get right down to cost and so on. He told me that his wife had talked him into having one more litter of cubs (this will be the third) and he expects them to be born right around Easter. He usually only sells them to people he knows, but he said if I wanted one to call him when I was sure and I could have one. The price would be $75, the other woman said she sold hers for $125 and mostly to just friends so this seems like a very good price. In Michigan, you can't own a purebred wolf, you can own a ⅞ wolf though. The way you obtain this is to have a pure wolf mate with a husky. The DNR figures that a husky is part wolf and that makes up the percentage to obtain ⅞ wolf. An easier way is to have two ⅞ wolves mate and this is what will happen in this case. In the wild only 4 or 5 cubs survive birth out of 8 or 10. This is a kind of nature's balance that assures that the ones who live shall survive the wild. With the help of the breeder, usually all the cubs survive. Wolves have a hard time in birth. The mother often crushes them or cuts their umbilical cords too short. It takes a wolf up to 24 hours to have a litter, not like a dog. After 3 weeks, the breeder separates the cubs from their mother. The cubs get too attached to their mother after this time, they also develop teeth and cause the mother pain. Cub wolves are not like puppies; they mature much faster. Their eyes are open at 8–10 days and they can eat food with the consistency of oatmeal at 11 days. Although the cubs mature physically fast, they don't mature psychologically until they are two years old.

The man told me the background of his two wolves. I felt it important to put this in because it not only tells you about what the cubs will look like, but gives you some data on wolves in general.

The female is a timber wolf (timber wolves are second in size to only the tundra wolf which runs wild in Alaska and the Northern Canadian Region). She is a little small for a timber wolf; the female weighs around 80 pounds. She is part malamute, and her coat is a brownish gray. The male is a brush wolf (brush wolves are smaller than a timber wolf). He, on the other hand, is big for a brush wolf and weighs around 100 pounds. He is part husky and has a little coyote in him; his coat is black and white. A ⅞ wolf (as these two are) are considered a dog as far as licenses go, their shots are the same as dogs too. It costs around $3–$4 a week to feed an adult wolf. Their diet consists of chicken necks, heart, liver, canned dog food, and vegetables.

iv. CONCLUSION

The man's wolves sound very healthy and the temptation to get one at that price is hard to cope with. I think though, that it wouldn't be fair to me or the wolf for me to take him at this time. I will wait until I am going to live somewhere permanently. The woman breeder let her personal wolf have freedom of her house and I am sure to a degree I will too, but the wolf needs room to run in order to be healthy. I never was too crazy about zoos—they are good for people as a learning situation, but I always felt them somewhat unfair to the animals. I wouldn't want to have to keep a wolf in a zoo-type situation. I am going to have to switch schools pretty soon as Western doesn't have a major in zoology or a veterinarian program, so I will have to at least wait and see what school I will end up at. If I owned a house and some land maybe then I could swing owning a wolf while I attend school, but again this is purely speculation.

What I have learned about wolves, the laws, and facts has been very important to me. But the thing that I really learned about was the enthusiasm people have about their wolves. That one thing has made up my mind for me; the people that own wolves are happy with them.

People just don't get that excited over their cat or something. "The wolf will teach you things you never noticed before," the breeders said. That seems very important. You can always do a better job at something if what you are doing gives you something back. Right now I don't think I can give enough back to the wolf as far as room to run, but who knows, I have until Easter to figure out a way that won't tie me or a wolf down.

References

Book	Author
Manifesto on Wolf Conservation	U.S. Wildlife Dept.
The Wolf (1970)	David L. Mesh
Canis Lupus (1974)	David L. Mesh
Captive Wild	Lois Crisler
Red Book	Harry A. Goodman

∞ **DOING THREE:** Do another twelve-minute free writing about someone you're related to. You may choose another person than you wrote about before, or if you feel the urge, continue to write more about the first person you chose.

> *While on the Thayer expedition* [to Brazil in 1865] *I remember that I often put questions to* [Agassiz] *about the facts of our new tropical habitat, but I doubt if he ever answered one of these questions of mine outright. He always said, "There, you see you have a definite problem. Go and look, and find the answer for yourself."*
>
> WILLIAM JAMES

It is not pomp or pretension, but the adaptation of the expression to the idea, that clenches a writer's meaning:—as it is not the size or glossiness of the materials, but their being fitted each to its place, that gives strength to the arch. . . .

WILLIAM HAZLITT

chapter 3
throwing
back
the
engfish

WHEN ASKED TO WRITE papers that others will judge, many Americans are terrified. You may say it's stupid for people to be afraid to write their native language which they've already mastered in speech, but remember that many teachers make writing an exercise in punishment and embarrassment. That isn't their intention, but they do it nevertheless.

In fourth grade you were probably drilled on grammatical points like the difference between *who* and *whom* before you were ready to make such distinctions. The things you had to write about were not usually yours, and when they were (for example, "How I Spent My Summer Vacation") you knew the game was to write with the fewest possible errors and to use a lot of Teacher-Words that suggested you had a large vocabulary. It wasn't to tell truths that counted for you. If it had been, you might have written of that summer vacation when you and Linda shoplifted a doll from J.C. Penney's, and when you were caught, Linda whispered, "You fart! I told you to wait until that old lady went by!" Strangely, most of your teachers weren't interested in truth, that elusive spirit who steadies us so when we have her by the hand.

Most of your teachers used the Errors Approach, the opposite of Mother's method of teaching her child to talk. When teachers hammer away at errors, they stop the flow of words in their students. And worse, when they ask students to write in situations where they won't be communicating—because their audience is teacher and she already knows what they'll be saying—they destroy the function of writing.

> *Writing is a form of discipline, in the best sense of that word, that has been turned into a form of punishment. A castor-oil syndrome plagues writing from the first grade through the university: "It's good for you." Punishments in the form of compositions and mechanical writing exercises are still not uncommon in the classroom. "Write a hundred times, 'I will not chew gum in school.'"*
>
> DONALD H. GRAVES

The result of such training is that people learn to write *Engfish*, a name one of my students gave to the say-nothing, feel-nothing, word-wasting, pretentious language of the schools. Here's a paragraph of it written by a student of mine years ago.

> For the most part, time plays a very important role on this campus. It tells us the orders of the day. A class begins at a certain time and ends at a predetermined place on the clock. We at Western Michigan University have begun to make out our orders for next year. The orders are the predetermined times of the classes that we must take in order to graduate.

[That passage is not set in boldface type—like most student writing in this book—because it's an example of weak writing.]

That pompous paragraph says no more than that classes are limited in time, and students filling out schedules should remember this fact. I'm not sure why the student wrote such an empty paragraph. High school classes are also limited in time. Perhaps the writer meant to point out that he had never before been required to take responsibility for making his class schedule, but that's not the way the statement came out. Probably he wanted to sound educated in one of his first college classes. He had noticed that professors use a lot of abstract and general words, so he wrote generally on the subject of time. You can't find a more abstract subject than that. And he worked into his paper Teacher-Words like *important* and *role*. He tossed in *predetermined* twice, where it didn't make much sense. No one—teacher or student—wants to read such dull stuff, but students go on writing it and teachers go on accepting it because they don't know how to get out of the rut.

Not only do schools unwittingly encourage you to write Engfish, but they prepare you to write it in a future occupation. In such professions as law, insurance, science, and government, complaints against Engfish have been made for centuries. Waggish names have been given to such language: *fustian, balderdash, bombast, governmentese, gobbledygook.* Presidents and prime ministers and presidents of great corportations have appealed to persons working under them to simplify and clarify their language. During the Second World War, President Franklin D. Roosevelt complained that a writer directed office workers to "terminate the illumination" rather than to "turn out the lights."

> *A common farmer shall make you understand in three words,* that his foot is out of joint, *or* his collarbone broken, *wherein a surgeon, after a hundred terms of art, if you are not a scholar, shall leave you to seek. It is frequently the same case in law, physic, and even many of the meaner arts.*
>
> JONATHAN SWIFT, 1720

Here's a passage from a newspaper notice written by a utilities company and addressed to its customers. [The name of the company has been changed.]

> Monthly hearings will be held before the Western Public Service Commission for the purpose of considering authorization to permit Citizens Power Company to reflect in monthly billings to its customers charges or credits for changes in appropriate items of expense associated with purchased and net interchange power from a base cost included in previously approved rate levels.

These words may make sense to the persons who wrote them and might hold up in court, but in effect the writing is fraudulent. When I read this announcement, I didn't understand it, and I was one of the customers the company was legally required to inform of what I'm guessing might be a rise in my monthly electrical bill.

The writer of that announcement by the utilities company was probably a lawyer of the breed that Professor Fred Rodell of the Yale Law School wrote about in *The Virginia Law Review* (Vol. 23, No. 38, 1936). He had no sympathy for legal Engfish. "The average law review writer," he said, "is peculiarly able to say nothing with an air of great importance. When I used to read law reviews, I used constantly

to be reminded of an elephant trying to swat a fly." Rodell deplored
the lack of humor in law review articles:

> It does not matter that even in the comparatively rare in-
> stances when people read to be informed, they like a dash
> of salt along with their information. They won't get any
> seasoning if the law reviews can help it. The law reviews
> would rather be dignified and ignored.

"The law," said Rodell, "is a fat man walking down the street in a
high hat. And far be it from the law reviews to be any party to the
chucking of a snowball or the judicious placing of a banana-peel."
After that poke at the unfunny legal writers, Rodell said, "The best
way to get a laugh out of a law review is to take a couple of drinks
and then read an article, any article, aloud. That can be really funny."

The cottony language Rodell condemned we all use at times. During the Watergate hearings, when a collection of superb, habitual
liars sat before the microphone, the country heard dozens of high-
sounding empty phrases, like "at this point in time" (meaning "now"),
"as far as (something or other) is concerned," and all sorts of dodges
like "It became apparent—." Rodell scores members of his profession
for such language.

Examples of Engfish are everywhere in the work of professionals. A
sports reporter writes:

> If the field is snow covered and slippery, the advantage
> could tip to Plymouth Salem's side, since the Rocks have a
> much larger team in the weight department.

If he hadn't been so anxious to impress readers with his language, he
would have written simply:

> . . . since the Rocks have a much heavier team.

If you become a sports writer, a business researcher, or an M.D., I
hope some day you'll help improve the writing in your field. Perhaps
you could say something like what Professor Rodell said to his colleagues in the law:

> Maybe they [the law reviews] will come to realize that
> the English language is most useful when it is used nor-
> mally and naturally, and that the law is nothing more than
> a means to a social end and should never, for all the law
> schools and law firms in the world, be treated as an end in
> itself. In short, maybe one of these days, the law reviews will
> catch on. Meanwhile I say they're spinach.

That we should go to school to learn pretension is a mockery; for there we're supposed to study what the English critic Matthew Arnold called "the best which has been thought and said in the world," and people are supposed to be pursuing truth. But students feel the pressure of all those new thoughts and words and attempt to use unfamiliar language for the sake of showing off instead of saying something. A citizen writes this letter to his local newspaper, for example, parading his vocabulary because he feels the pressure to sound educated when speaking to the university community:

> May I add an addendum to the "Blizzard of '78" book, which you have just closed. I wish to express admiration for G——— P———, a young man who noted human activity which he perceived to be improper and had the courage to do something about it. In so doing he risked abuse and vilification. Our nation suffers from a critical shortage of the character strength demonstrated in this incident.

O.K., fella, we now are aware you know the words *addendum, abuse,* and *vilification,* but we have no notion of what G.P. did that was so admirable. *Human activity* and *character strength*—phew! Come off those abstractions and tell us what G.P. did.

The same pressure is felt by college freshmen, seniors, and graduate students. They become so awed by the abstract language of textbooks that some of them use it even when they're writing about their own families. Here's an example from a composition course:

> . Each morning, before leaving for school, I habitually check the temperature outside. I secretly hope that the cool weather will warrant the wearing of my Grandfather's winter jacket because this is my favorite object.
>
> One of the reasons that it is my favorite object is that it reminds me of my Grandfather and all that he meant to our family, obviously, I am somewhat sentimental. I often look at his picture and wonder what he would say, or I will look through his memories and try to predict his actions. There is one picture in which he wears the jacket and appears quite rugged.
>
> The rugged appearance of the jacket seems to be the vogue style. Because I have always been abreast of current trends in fashion, the jacket with its short-waisted and very full appearance gives my body the rough-and-rugged look of a Northern woodsman. Young men are trying to identify with this caliber of man.

The woodsman symbolizes all of the qualities of the admired man who carved America out of the wilderness. The
qualities that provide him with this envied status are
strength, to fell trees; peace of mind to be alone for days at
a time, and endurance, to cope with the weather.

The northern woodsman would like this jacket because it
provides a great protection from the wind and cold weather.
The reason for this factor's appeal to me might be best
conveyed by the comfort that is portrayed by the image of a
woodsman huddled in the warmth of a blanket next to a
roaring campfire on a cool evening.

However, of late, I noticed that the hues of a campfire are
spreading to the trees now and the evenings are getting
cooler. With the drop in temperature I have donned my
Grandfather's jacket—proud-looking, smart, and very warm.

If you're used to reading Engfish in school, you may have thought
that "Grandfather's Jacket" was a pleasant enough little piece of writing, but consider it again. A great idea to look at a photograph of
Grandpa in his favorite jacket and let it call up memories of the old
man—but the writing is ridiculous.

"I habitually check"? You've already said "Each morning," which
takes care of the notion of *habitually*—drop that word. "I secretly
hope"? Why use *secretly*? If you're hoping and you don't tell anyone
about it, that's hoping. Would it be the revelation of a great secret to
tell someone that you want cool weather so you can wear your grandfather's jacket? Leave out *secretly*.

"One of the reasons that it is my favorite object . . ." You just
said it was your favorite object in the preceding sentences. Words,
words, words—you're using a lot of them and getting nowhere. You
end paragraph 2 with *rugged* and start paragraph 3 with it, and yet
you never let us see the jacket or your grandfather. Is it leather? wool?
Shows signs of wear? Bright red like a hunter's jacket in Michigan? You
do say it's "short-waisted" and has a "very full appearance," but I don't
know what that last phrase means. You mean "baggy"? And then
you're back to calling it *rugged* again. You say you "look through his
memories" but you don't let us get one look at Grandfather, except
that he wears a "rugged jacket," whatever that is.

In the third and fifth paragraphs your words sound foolish. "The
vogue style." What does *vogue* mean?—what's *in style*, doesn't it? So
you don't need both those words. "I have always been abreast of current, trends in fashion." That doesn't sound like a rugged woodsman
talking. And then you say that "The northern woodsman would like

this jacket because it provides a great protection from the wind and cold weather." Watch out! Do you think we're two-year-old readers? It would be some poor rugged jacket if it didn't do that.

> *Don't, Sir, accustom yourself to use big words for little matters.*
> SAMUEL JOHNSON

We all write Engfish at times, even when we don't believe in doing it, but we have an obligation to give our readers something better. It's an abomination we should be making fun of, in both its spoken and written forms. In his many years in the United States Senate, Mike Mansfield stood out because he spoke "normally and naturally" as lawyer Fred Rodell advocated. When Senator Mansfield became Ambassador to Japan, at an embassy staff meeting one of his staff members said: "Mr. Ambassador, it would take me several hours to adequately outline the full detailed ramifications of this policy." Andrew Malcolm of *The New York Times* reported that

> The Ambassador from Montana puffed on his pipe once or twice and replied, "I don't think you could do it if you had several years."

∞ **DOING FOUR:** Find three examples of Engfish—anywhere, in magazines, newspapers, books, signs, or student writing. Bring them to your group and share the best one with the other members.

∞ **DOING FIVE:** Do another twelve-minute free writing about someone you're related to. If you're at the end of the week, from all the free writings you've done inside and outside class choose the one you like best, expand it, improve it, and bring it to your first meeting next week for response from the others.

*I often accuse my finest acquaintances of
an immense frivolity; for, while there are
manners and compliments we do not
meet, we do not teach one another the
lessons of honesty and sincerity that the
brutes do, or of steadiness and solidity
that the rocks do. The fault is commonly
mutual, however; for we do not habitually demand any more of each other.*

HENRY THOREAU

chapter 4

truthtelling

MANY FAMOUS WRITERS have advised
younger writers to try hard for truths. Strange that we haven't given
weight to the advice of those persons most apt to know what makes
good writing. The novelist Ralph Ellison, who wrote *Invisible Man,*
said that he learned wing-shooting from reading the short stories of
Ernest Hemingway: "When he describes something in print," said
Ellison, "believe him even when he describes the process of art in
terms of baseball or boxing; he's been there." And Henry Thoreau of
Massachusetts, author of *Walden,* which continues to be published in
edition after edition all over the world, said in his Journal for December 6, 1859 ". . . the one great rule of composition—and if I were a
professor of rhetoric I should insist on this—is to *speak the truth.*
This first, this second, this third."

In seminars we've found that trying to tell truths makes an astounding difference in writing. Sentences become stronger, sprout wings.
Sure, sometimes people think they're telling truths when they aren't.
They misremember a date or get a fact wrong when they have no intention of misleading others. And there are white lies that are sometimes better told than truths. And we don't always agree on what is a
truth. And fantasies need to be told, but I say they should arise from
truths or take us back to them. We live a short time on earth and
need to keep in touch with it and ourselves. The effort toward truth—
we can know when we're making it—puts a charge in our writing.

28

We don't have to write Absolute Truths—whatever they are. Or argue in the abstract about what truth is. All we have to do is say to ourselves: "Nothing's going down on this paper that's phony or pretentious. I'll check my facts. I'll try to put down real feelings."

Truth can be dangerous—injure persons or call a writer to court to answer a libel suit. But in the seminars we've found that writers can refrain from telling everything they know is true and still release their language powers—if their holding back some of the truth is to protect someone's feelings or make sure no one is publicly injured.

If truth has such power, why don't we have more writing of it in school? I think because truthtelling is killed or maimed by (1) The Errors Approach, (2) grading, and (3) the giving of too many instructions about how a piece of writing should be put together. "Use a topic sentence." "Write three paragraphs and develop each by a different method—argument, example, and analogy." "End your paper with a summary." In a conversation we would never think of giving such instructions to a friend about to speak. If we did, they would probably destroy or block the unconscious flow natural to composition of words into sentences and longer statements.

Here's a paper about a father written in one of the seminars—to show you a truthful writer in action:

SO SMOOTH

I spent a good part of my eighth summer hugging my knees on the front steps, watching Sherry and my sister Laurie ride their bikes up and down the street. I toyed with the idea of going in and telling Mom that Laurie was riding in the street again, but decided no. It looked so smooth and fast. But I had seen Laurie's skinned knees and I was a coward. In third grade and not knowing how to ride a bike.

Mom, finally driven mad between my desires and cowardice, decided to teach me. Sherry and Laurie signed up as consultants. As they all held up the giant bike, I clumsily clambered onto the seat and sat, a mile from the ground, clutching the handlebars.

"What d'I *do*?" I whined.

"Just work the pedals, honey," Mom said.

"Hey, don't be so scared," Sherry yelled as they began to push me down the sidewalk. "Your dad'll flip his wig when he comes home from work."

They were pushing faster now, running behind, holding the fender. I was concentrating on the pedals rising and falling independent of my feet when the bike began to wobble.

I looked back: Mom, Laurie, and Sherry were watching me.

"Help! Help! How do I stop?" I screamed.

"Steer, steer!"

The bike swerved onto Mr. Buckaloo's lawn, and slowing on the grass, pitched over on top of me.

"C'mon! Get up and try again," Sherry said.

"Why'd you guys let go?" I cried.

"That's the way you gotta learn," said Sherry.

"C'mon, honey, you're not hurt," said Mom.

Sherry looked disgustedly at my tears. "Your dad'll never flip his wig now," she announced.

When Dad came home he said, "I'll take you out after supper and we'll go try on that big blacktop at Greenwood."

As we headed toward the school the light was fading. Dad walked the bike as I hurried along beside him. When we reached the blacktop, he parked the bike, swung me up under my arms and sat me squarely on the seat. Everything fit—feet on pedals, hands on handlebars. He firmly took hold of my hands and the handlebars with his smooth strong hands and kicked up the stand. Running slowly, he began to push the bike in a circle around the blacktop. It was giddy, rolling so fast so far from the ground. I looked down and saw the blacktop spinning away and looked quickly back up. Better to concentrate on keeping on the bike.

Now we were circling faster and I was leaning in naturally with the pull of the bike. It was so easy, just gliding along. The bike seemed to want to go around in this circle with no help from anyone. Dad was running along behind, touching the fender lightly to give it a nudge now and then. My feet were part of the pedals and I kept leaning in, turning the front wheel ever so slightly to the left to keep me in the circle.

In a flash, I saw Dad standing off to the side. I was riding with no help! The wind was rushing into my face, ballooning my jacket out behind me. I glided to a stop, feeling like a pro.

"See if you can ride straight in a line toward me," Dad called. Of course! The bike and I were friends. Dad was beaming. "Let's head home," he said; and I turned and pushed off, still coltish on my wobbly new legs.

ELIZABETH KING

In any human action, expectations are crucial. What you expect of yourself and think your readers expect of you makes the trunk and leaves of your writing grow in a certain direction. To the seminar writing program discussed in this book, students may bring along expectations they had in other school experiences. When a teacher says try for truths, they believe that means bare your soul and say something shocking. Confess your secret sins. They're perhaps remembering a teacher they once had who lived for shock alone. But in this program, "Try for truths" means what it says. If the truths are no more than that Dad helped you learn to ride a bike when Mother, sister, and Sherry didn't, that's what's expected of you—the deeply felt truth of that experience.

But notice how far down into her truth Elizabeth King got, and what that effort did to her writing. Like most writers in the groove of truthtelling, she doesn't waste words. What you've read is the third draft of her paper. When the second draft was read in the seminar, listeners said that a conversation Elizabeth had written between her sister and herself near the opening of the story should be omitted because it kept the reader from experiencing quickly Elizabeth's ambivalent feelings (attraction and fear) about riding a bicycle. So she cut that out. What remains is concentrated. Instead of saying, "I was eight years old and it was summer," Elizabeth says, "my eighth summer." Three words instead of nine. Instead of "I was fascinated by the thought of riding a bicycle and often I sat on the front steps watching eagerly and jealously . . ." she says, "hugging my knees"—three words instead of twenty-two, and we know how anxious she was. One reason the paper wheels along so fast is that it contains little or no wasted repetitions. She could have written, "It was a big *bike,* and it seemed an even bigger *bike* to me because I was so little. They were all holding the *bike* up for me. I climbed up on the *bike* with a great deal of trouble and sat on the *bike* seat." Instead she wrote: "As they all held up the giant bike, I clumsily clambered onto the seat." (The next draft might well eliminate "clumsily," because "clamber" means to climb clumsily.)

∞ **DOING SIX:** Do a twelve-minute free writing on some incident in your childhood that struck you hard.

• • •

Since 1964 we seminar teachers have known that the effort toward truthtelling improves writing, but we're just beginning to understand or guess why and how it does. For example, apparently when people try to write truths rather than show off, their memories begin to work so well that they become immersed in the facts they're relating and can hardly keep up with the flow of words being supplied to their fingers. They're not stalling or hunting for things to say, so they don't repeat words weakly. When we try to manipulate words, we have to make constant conscious decisions about what to say and how to say it, so that we lose that unconscious stream of words so refreshing to our readers. The effort to tell truths places us in the world we're think- ing about. We lose ourselves and our egos, as the feelings and sights of that world take over. It's a positive miracle, and we might as well profit from it.

Once a person begins writing in the truthtelling groove, she seldom uses trite phrases and clichés. Fresh expressions come to her. Note Elizabeth's ending. She doesn't say, "I felt weak in my knees" or "I still had butterflies in my stomach," but rather, "I turned and pushed off, still *coltish on my wobbly new legs.*" With that comparison of bicycle wheels to human legs (called a *metaphor*), she stated the es- sence of the act of riding a bicycle. It involves learning to move on a new set of legs, and they have thin feet, are round, and turn, and are not attached to us as firmly as our true legs. But if we balance our- selves properly on them, they will take us truly where we want to go.

The effort to tell nothing but truths in every line gives us wheels as writers. We can glide faster than we ever thought we could. One brave shove from the curb gets us going. Do you remember that feeling when you first started riding—that you could do things you couldn't do before, and yet you were not completely in command of the vehi- cle? As Elizabeth put it so truly, "I was concentrating on the pedals rising and falling independent of my feet . . ." You could move faster than you ever had on your feet, and yet you knew you could crash harder than if your own feet were running you somewhere. New pos- sibilities. You could ride downtown and back, or over to Sue's house in one-quarter the time it used to take you. But scary. Writing truth- fully is much the same. It will take you places in yourself or with others that you never realized existed, although they were right there all the time. That's what I mean when I say you can write your- self into understanding.

> *The process of writing heightened a re-*
> *membered experience. It developed a way*
> *of seeing.*
>
> DONALD H. GRAVES

I find truthtelling easier if I let myself feel I'm sinking down to a lower level as I write. Sometimes at the typewriter I close my eyes and think "Nothing but truths," and type that way, opening my eyes only when I think I'm probably at the end of a line. It's frightening to let truth take over, but remember—the great advantage of writing over speaking is that when you've put the words down, you can edit them, censor them, or throw them out before showing them to anyone else—if you feel the need. Here's another piece of writing done in a seminar, by a married woman with children. She's remembering her father, who didn't help her learn to ride.

DAD

He sits hunched over in a padded rocking chair continuously drumming his tobacco-stained fingers on its arms while he watches T.V., whether it's turned on or not. He never smiles, rarely speaks. When he gets up from the chair to search the refrigerator for beer, he makes a noise like a horse's neigh, "Uh-huh-huh-huh."

My father. I'm not sure he even knows who I am. He's sixty-nine but looks ninety. His skin is like soggy leather—grayish red with yellowed bumps between his intricate spider web of wrinkles. The lower lid of his right eye droops, exposing a bloodshot eyeball with a cloudy blue iris. No teeth. White, prickly whisker stubs sprout from his face and meet with coarse, matted hair at ear level.

I don't like to look at him—I hardly ever do. He looks like the life he's led. Every misdeed is etched on his troll-like face, but his blank eyes betray the senility which has terminated his cruelty. He is a hollow devil now.

I was born when he was in the service, and I was a year and a half old the first time he saw me. Mom said I was afraid of him—screamed and tried to get away when he held me. Maybe that's why he didn't like me. I was a defiant stranger demanding my share of love and attention from "his" wife.

The first memory I have of him is when I was four or five. My little sister and I were standing in the doorway of the diningroom watching him sway back and forth in his chair, eyes closed, a half-full glass of beer on the table before him. Then he toppled off his chair onto the cold linoleum floor, never even waking up. It sounded like the floor would fall through to the basement but he just lay there, heaped on the linoleum until Mom came running, jostled him awake, and led him upstairs to bed.

He used to smoke in bed when he was drunk and catch their mattress on fire. It was covered with sooty black holes where ashes had fallen. When Mom had to go to work nights to help pay the bills, I used to lie awake in my room worrying that he'd set his mattress on fire and burn the house down with us trapped inside. That's why I learned to crawl out my bedroom window onto the roof and down the side of the house. I taught my sister to do the same.

He never did the things my friends said their fathers did. I guess the nicest thing he ever did was to come home drunk and throw his change all over the floor for my sister and me to pick up. But he canceled even that out by breaking into our piggy banks when he needed beer money. Sometimes he'd leave a slip of paper with I.O.U. however much money he took on it, but as the years went by he stopped leaving the I.O.U.'s and just took the money. He used to play jokes on us occasionally. Like one Christmas when he placed huge thorny rosebush branches under the tree and told us they were from Santa Claus. Or when we'd discover dolls under the tree with cigarettes in their mouths.

He never hugged us or said he loved us. The only time he purposely touched us was to spank us and then his face would turn purple and his eyes would bulge like they were going to pop out of his head. He hit hard and we screamed loud because the louder we screamed the sooner he'd stop. Mom didn't interfere when he spanked us. She knew it'd make him worse, so she kept quiet but those spankings hurt her. She loved us as he didn't. We didn't get spanked often, though. We learned to stay out of his way. When he came into a room, we left. If he was already there, we wouldn't go in.

But we couldn't avoid him at mealtime. He didn't like us to talk during dinner and would get furious if we'd giggle at the table. We tried so hard to stop—we could see he was getting mad—but then one of us would look at the other and start to choke on a giggle. Dad would explode, his voice booming that he was going to "shove our plates down our goddamn throats." Then Mom would get mad and let us eat in the livingroom, leaving Dad to devour his meal in solitary.

One time when Mom had an argument with him, she got her coat, rushed out the door, and drove off, leaving my sister and me with Dad. I never left the window all the time she was gone. I stood there, peering into blackness, my heart pounding every time I saw a pair of headlights coming down the road. Two hours later she returned and when she saw what a trembling wreck I was she never left us alone with Dad again. Whenever she got mad, she either stayed home or took us with her.

For a while we had a dog—a lively, wiggling, wavy-haired spaniel named Molasses. During the hot weather he'd get some sort of fungus around his tail which would cause his hair to fall out and make him scratch incessantly. We put medicine on it but it still itched and Molasses would drag his rear across the rug to scratch himself. Dad decided to put the dog out of his misery and beat him to death with a wrecking bar. He'd already buried him in the backyard by the time Mom and we kids got home, but our next-door neighbor told Mom what had happened. She was nearly hysterical when she told Mom how he'd missed Molasses' head and struck him across the middle of his back. Yipping, the dog ran and hid under the porch until Dad dragged him out and finished bludgeoning him to death.

One spring my brother found an orphaned raccoon in the woods and brought her home. He raised her as a pet. She was delightful to watch as she performed acrobatics on the clothesline. One day Coonie got loose in the house and when Dad chased her she hid behind the refrigerator and wouldn't come out. He reached in to grab her but she bit his hand, so he got the wrecking bar and finished her off right where she was.

He didn't seem to feel any guilt after killing these animals. To him they were "just animals." He used to brag how he'd learned in the army to break a dog's jaw by grabbing hold of his upper and lower jaws and twisting them.

One summer he won a couple of baby ducks at a carnival and brought them home for my sister and me. When my sister's duck died, he remarked, "We can't have only one duck" and snatched up my duck, took it outside, and smashed it against the sidewalk. We didn't get any more pets—except a parakeet who stayed in his cage.

As we grew older we couldn't have slumber parties or friends stay over night, because of Dad. He made a rule that we could talk on the phone for only five minutes. "Anything that can't be said in five minutes ain't worth saying." He'd actually time us and if we went over our allotted five minutes he'd push down the button to disconnect us, no matter whom we were talking to.

When I got a part-time job in high school and spent the money I'd earned on a stereo, he became so enraged I thought he was going to chop it into kindling wood. Until I got a place of my own I could play it only when he wasn't home.

I asked Mom why she never divorced him. She said she was afraid what would happen to him—that he would drink himself to death and it would be her fault for turning him out. Besides, she needed money to pay bills and when Dad worked he'd give her two-thirds of his paycheck, keeping the other third for beer money. When he didn't work a full week (which was often) he kept the same amount for himself and Mom got whatever was left.

He called his beer "Hadacol" after a tonic he'd seen advertised on T.V. I can still see the rows of empty beer bottles lined up beside his chair in the living room. There'd usually be twelve or sixteen of them from one night's drinking. If you bumped one, it would start a chain reaction of clattering bottles toppling over, with the thin amber liquid dribbling from a not quite empty bottle onto the carpet.

Only one thirty-two ounce bottle stands beside his chair now. That's all the doctor says he can have, and Mom controls all the money. He lives only for that moment at 3:00 p.m. when Mom counts out seventy-two cents after he's asked for the hundredth time in his plaintive, childlike voice, "Can I get me a Hadacol?"

KRISTIN ROLLA

"Dad" is such a tale of cruelty that I changed the name of the writer to protect her parents and relatives from embarrassment. Listening to the story, I wondered if Kristin hadn't left out incidents that showed the good side of her father. Most portraits suffer when they depict a person as all bad or good. I asked Kristin if she wanted to add anything that would present a more rounded character. "No," she said, "I'd like to keep it just like it is. I'm not bitter about him. He hasn't wrecked my life, but I don't want to add anything."

A year later I asked Kristin to visit another class and talk about how she came to write this piece. I read the paper aloud. At the conclusion, one listener said. "Was he really like that?" Another replied, "Sure, can't you tell that was the truth?" And the first speaker said, "Oh yeah, it had to be the truth. Nobody could have made up things like that." After hearing the paper and listening to Kristin tell how one memory had opened up another, the members of that class did the best writing they had done all semester. I invited them to write at the level of truthtelling Kristin had reached, and many were able to do that.

*Educated people, in my opinion, must
satisfy the following conditions: . . . They
are pure in heart, and fear a lie as they
fear fire. They do not lie, even in trifles.
A lie is humiliating to the listener, and
it debases the speaker in his own eyes.*

ANTON CHEKHOV

When for the first time in her life Kristin decided to put down what her father was like, she unlocked a torrent of words and memories, in details that convince readers: "break a dog's jaw by grabbing hold of his upper and lower jaws and twisting them." Over the years in the seminars we've found that much of the best writing effects come to writers as gifts. If you force writing, saying as you compose a paragraph, "Now I'm going to use specific details to illustrate this person's character," the postman probably will leave nothing for you. Empty mailbox. You can't go out there and stuff it with old letters and get what you want. You have to wait for the delivery.

I'm not saying that all good writing is delivered to a writer free, while she sits in a trance. At times the effort to tell truths doesn't pay off and you're left with sentences that waste words, stumble, overstate, and bore the reader with triteness. When that happens you may be able simply to throw the writing away and start over. But if you haven't time to do that, you'll have to become highly conscious and revise the work, cutting all the waste and phoniness and adding better expressions where you can.

If you've never written a long piece of writing about someone or something you're snagged on, as the writer of "Dad" did, you may not know how much the act of writing is thinking, and leads to new understandings. It's like planning a trip or building a cabin. A person says to himself, "I have to get some things down on paper before I really know what I'm going to do." One proposed stop on the trip or partition in the cabin leads him to new notions, additions, subtractions, relationships, purposes. When he sketches out the floor plan for the bathroom, he may see that a pantry can be easily constructed next to it, and perhaps he's encouraged to add other rooms. Soon he hasn't got a cabin but a house. And with a house in mind, his lot in the far woods is no longer right for his purposes and eventually he drops the whole notion of spending summers there and and decides not to build a vacation place but to move north and live year-round in surroundings he loves. Writing can be like that when you're being commanded by urges to speak meaningfully for yourself. When you do that, you often speak meaningfully to others as well.

In part, writing is designing or planning; in part, it's watching things happen and discovering meaning. A Moebian act. When I began this book I intended to write a textbook presenting the experience of many students and teachers in I-Searching, but as I wrote, it turned into something new—a contextbook. My cabin became a house.

In this course you don't have to start with failure and the agony of trying to resurrect a dead body of writing. You'll begin in the best circumstances for using your unconscious language powers. The first move is to try to tell truths. The second is to begin your course as a writer freely writing as fast as you can, without worrying about punctuation, spelling, or grammar, so that you release your already learned powers of language.

"You release your powers"—that's what truthtelling so often enables a person to do. Apparently when a writer says to himself, "I'm not going to fake it. I won't pretend to own more words, knowledge, experience, or feeling than I do," he feels secure, and then he's freed to assert all his powers. Truthtelling makes you feel confident and comfortable. It's a way of countenancing yourself. Benjamin Franklin said, "A lie stands on one leg, truth on two."

For a while, the pretender may live thrillingly, but eventually his words lose force. They and he sicken, and people stop listening. Try giving yourself over to truthtelling. Then you won't fear a listening or reading audience because you'll know they can't show you up. To their questions you'll always answer what you truly know. No need to fear the questions to come. You can't betray yourself, because available to you always are the words, "I don't know," or "I was wrong," or "I don't think I should say anything about that right now."

> Persist, only persist in seeking the truth.
> Persist in saying you do not know what
> you do not know, and you do not care
> for what you do not care for. . . .
>
> RALPH EMERSON

∞ **DOING SEVEN:** Write another twelve minutes freely on an incident in your childhood, the same one as before, or a different one.

∞ **DOING EIGHT:** Read aloud the free writings you've done this week and make whatever changes your ear asks for.

I believe in impulse and naturalness, but followed by discipline in the cutting.
ANAÏS NIN

chapter 5

cutting wasted words

MOST PEOPLE resent listening to or reading more words than necessary. The principle of least effort. We admire persons who can do a job without fuss. Wasted motion irritates or infuriates us because at bottom we know we're going to die at seventy or ninety and we want to make good use of the time we have left.

Cutting out wasted words in a writing is a highly conscious part of the act of writing. We listen to the voice in our head dictating the sentences or we force the words onto the page. Once on paper they no longer seem to be a part of us the way they were earlier. Yet they are an extension of us. Where do *we* leave off and our words on the page begin? If we write a letter, are we traveling from California to New York to greet our friend? Yes and no. We are the letter and we are ourselves in California—a Moebian loop again.

Once our sentences stand on paper we can more easily step back, detach ourselves, and look to improve them. One way is the read the sentences aloud. Then they sound as if someone else wrote them, and it's easier to criticize foreigners than ourselves. Another way is to ask someone to read our writing aloud to us, so we can become more objective about it. Professional writers (people who get paid for writing) ask professional editors (people who get paid for reading writing) to read their writing and suggest improvements. In the seminars you can get the help free.

WORLD'S BEST DIRECTIONS WRITER

As we turned to the elevator on the third floor of the Business Associates Building at 1115-20 Horace Street, we saw the scratched black letters on the frosted glass of the window to the right: "Edward Zybowski—Best Directions Writer in the World." We let the elevator go down without us.

Mr. Zybowski was willing to talk to us, he said, because at the moment he was stuck. "I've got 45 words for a label and I've got to get it down to 25."

As he spoke, he lifted the rod that held his paper against the typewriter roller and squinted at the words. He was ordinary-looking, about forty, the black hair at the back and sides of his head emphasizing the whiteness of the balding front part. Except for his face: it was kindly but looked mashed in.

"Not kicking about copy they gave me," he said. "Never do. More copy, more challenge to cut it till you wouldn't believe it was possible. That's what keeps customers comin' to me."

"We don't want to keep you from your work . . ."

"That's O.K. I'm stuck. No use worryin' and worryin' over a label. Don't think consciously about it for a few hours when you're stuck. Then suddenly your unconscious comes through for you—wham! There it is. Needs only final touches. No ulcers for the writer that way."

"Inspiration?" we ventured.

"Inspiration! That's a literary myth. Purely a matter of the unconscious memories and tips your mind has stored up. Then they spill over.

"This job's more than just writing," he said. "Deciding position and size of type very important." He picked up a brightly colored jar lid. "Ad on top for radio program, see? Where's the direction? On side of lid where you put your fingers to open it. Why there? Most logical place in the world."

We read the instructions printed in blue along the fluted edge:

AFTER OPENING, KEEP IN REFRIGERATOR
DO NOT FREEZE

"You're opening the jar," he said, "and you see the word OPENING. Stops you, doesn't it? Same thing appears on other side of lid. Don't ordinarily believe in presenting any direction twice, but got to here. So important—food'll spoil if you don't follow these directions."

"We're just curious, Mr. Zybowski. What is difficult about writing a direction like that? Seems the only way one could say this idea."

Mr. Z. looked affronted for a second, then smiled. "Yeah, no one can see it at first. And that's really a compliment to me. Shows I did it the simplest and most natural way it could be done. Now take this jar-lid direction—copy came to me like this:

" 'When stored at normal refrigerator temperature this food will retain its taste, lightness, color, and value as a food product; but when exposed to air or kept at freezing temperature will suffer a chemical change which may render it unfit for human consumption. It is therefore recommended that it be kept at refrigerated temperature when not being used. However, it may be stored at room temperature safely if the lid has never been removed.'

"I get that essay on the 'subject, figure I got a space a half an inch high around the lid, and a damned important direction. So I write:

AFTER OPENING, KEEP IN REFRIGERATOR
DO NOT FREEZE"

Our respect for Mr. Z. was growing. "You must be quite an expert on the English language," we said.

"I hate to put it this way," he said, "but I think I know more about English usage than 90 percent of the college teachers in the country. And also how to use English—that's a different thing, you know. Under the how-to-use part, for example, there's this business of adjectives. The college experts who think they're up on the latest, say don't use adjectives. They got it from Hemingway, they claim. I read all the books and magazines on English, too. Almost never learn anything from them. When you got a space half an inch square facing you and an important idea to get across, you learn something about language. What was I going to say?"

"You were speaking of not using adjectives."

"Yeah. They say don't use 'em. In a way they're right. Adjectives are usually weak as hell." Without looking, he pointed to the wall behind him where hung a half-letter-size

sheet of blue paper framed in black. "That one up there,"
he said, "has no adjectives. Shouldn't have any. It's true you
should use 'em sparingly. But take this tea-bag carton." He
pulled a box from a desk drawer. "After I told 'em how to
make hot tea on the left panel here, then I say: 'For *perfect*
iced tea, make hot tea and steep for 6 minutes.' The word
perfect is a selling word there—plug. I don't like to write
any plug angles into directions. Leave that slush to ad-
writers, damn their lyin' souls. This business of mine you
can be honest in. Givin' directions is really helpin' people,
educatin' them."

We could see Mr. Z. was in the first glow of a long speech,
but we wanted to find out how he wrote directions. So we
interrupted. "We can see that it is an honorable occupation
in a dirty business world. Would you mind telling us more
about this tea-bag label? You said you used no adjectives
except for *perfect,* but in the hot-tea instructions we see the
words *warmed* teapot, *fresh, bubbling,* boiling water."

"Glad you mentioned it. Easy to misunderstand. You see,
warmed teapot is what you've got to use, one of the important tricks of tea-making. So *warmed* isn't an idle little de-
scriptive word thrown in. It's the kind of teapot you've got
to use or else you don't get first-rate tea. And the same way
with *fresh.* I hate a word like that usually because it sounds
like those damned ad-writers' slush. You know how you always see the word on the package when you buy five-day-old
stale cupcakes in a grocery store. But when used with water,
the word *fresh* means something. When water stands around,
it loses a lot—loses, to be exact . . ." He reached for a chemical dictionary.

"Oh, don't bother," we said. "We know you're right
there."

"And *bubbling,*" he said, pushing the book back in the
case behind him. "I'm sure you know there are many different stages of boiling, and 'bubbling' identifies the stage we
want."

"Yes, so in that sense of basic meaning, you don't consider
these words adjectives," we said.

"Right," he said, beaming with satisfaction as he leaned
back in his chair. "One point those modern English teachers
are straight on: use active verbs whenever possible. I use
'push,' 'lift,' 'scoop,' 'unscrew.' Never say anything like,

'The turn of the cap is accomplished by a twist.' " He smiled. "I would say, 'Twist cap to left.' "

"We'll have to go soon," we said. Mr. Z. looked crestfallen. "Could you show us the direction that you consider your masterpiece?"

"Well," he said, "there can be only one masterpiece done by any one artist. I couldn't pick which is best. I try not to let any of 'em get out of this office till they're at least pared to the minimum. They may not always be brilliant, but they gotta be the minimum or they don't go out."

"How about that one in the frame? Any special significance in putting it on blue paper?"

He stood up and unhooked it from the wall. "Blue paper, use it for all final O.K.'d directions, so as not to make a mistake and let one of the earlier versions—call them scratches —get out when there's a better one been done." He held the frame out to us. "This one, I'll admit, is pretty good."

We read:

> IF TOO HARD-WARM · IF TOO SOFT-COOL
> PEANUT BUTTER SOMETIMES CONTRACTS
> CAUSING AIR SPACE ON SIDE OF JAR
> THIS MAY RESULT IN A WHITE APPEARANCE
> WHICH IN NO WAY AFFECTS QUALITY OR TASTE.

"I like this one," he said, " 'cause no adjectives and no plug. First line there got the concentration of a line from Milton's *Samson,* my favorite poem."

We noticed the adjective *white* before *appearance,* but knew now that it wasn't an adjective to Mr. Z. and, for that matter, to us any more. "Why so little punctuation?" we asked. "One period at the end and then only two hyphens in the first line."

"Glad you asked," he said, wiping his forehead with a handkerchief. "Damnedest thing, punctuation! Spent years mastering American English punctuation when I started this business. Had to know it first but all along thought I wouldn't use it much." He picked up the framed direction from the desk. "Didn't either.

"Now first of all, you see these words," said Mr. Z.

> "BUTTER SOMETIMES CONTRACTS
> CAUSING AIR SPACE

Ordinary punctuation usage says comma before 'causing,' but I take care of that by ending one line and starting another. Never need punctuation when eye has to stop and move over and down to a new line. In first line I use hyphen instead of dash because public doesn't know hyphen from a dash anyway. Hyphen saves space, and, when you don't use both in same copy, you don't need to differentiate between them. Remember, my context for a direction is not a chapter or a book or even a page, just the round top of a jar lid or one side of a package. Sometimes no other words except the direction. No chance for confusing with antecedents or references several pages before. And thank God! No footnotes! I won't allow any asterisks. Every explanation's gotta be complete in itself."

"How about that middle dot in the first line?" we said.

"Oh, that? I'm proud of that middle dot. Easier to see than period. A better stop really. We ought to use 'em in all writing, but you know the power of convention in usage. And this particular middle dot is in center of eight words, four on each side, with equal meaning and importance. A really logical and rational mark here, don't you think?"

We had to agree. "Anybody can see it's a very intelligent job of direction writing," we said. "There is only one thing that seems inconsistent with what you have said today."

"What's that?"

"After 'CAUSING AIR SPACE ON SIDE OF JAR,' you say 'THIS MAY RESULT.' It seems that the 'THIS' is a waste of words. Couldn't you say 'CAUSING AIR SPACE ON SIDE OF JAR AND RESULTING IN A WHITE . . .'?"

"Good point," said Mr. Z. "A really fine point of the trade. I'm glad, though, you didn't object to 'THIS' and say it is a vague reference. Anybody can see the reference is perfectly clear. But I'll tell you why I used the 'THIS.' Gettin' to be a pretty long sentence, that one. And if you say RESULTING,' you have to look back to be sure what the relationship is between 'RESULTING,' and 'CAUSING.' In a sense it would be no vaguer than 'THIS' in its reference, but in reality it would be harder to follow because that kind of parallelism is not in common everyday speech use. But the 'THIS' construction is. Remember my audience is everybody. A lot of those everybodys really don't read, so you gotta talk, not write, to 'em."

"What would you say is the secret of this job, if there is one, Mr. Zybowski?"

"Funny thing," he said, "but I've thought that over a lot and come to an awfully egotistic conclusion. The secret is the same as for writing a great book or doing anything else that really gives something to people. That is to learn to put yourself in the other guy's place."

We knew nothing to say to such a statement. "It's been a pleasure," we said, getting up.

"Come in again. Sure enjoyed talkin' to you," he said.

As we got to the door, he looked up from the typewriter. "I forgot to tell you one other thing about this peanut-butter direction. Notice last phrase: 'IN NO WAY AFFECTS QUALITY OR TASTE.' That's the time I beat the ad-writers at their own game and still didn't misrepresent anything or slush the customer. The way I put it, it's a statement of fact, yet a subtle idea creeps into customer's mind that the quality and taste of this butter is exceptionally good. This time language did even more than it was expected to do."

"Goodbye," we said, shaking our head in wonder as we closed the frosted-glass door. We believed the words on it now.

What Zybowski said about writing directions is true for all writing. Be clear. Say things precisely. Repeat words or ideas only when the repetition scores. Expect your readers to figure out your meaning without a deluge of words. Don't childishly explain things that don't need explanation:

Fair tomorrow (Monday) with slight warming trend in the west.

Your readers know it's today right now. It always is. Either *tomorrow* or *Monday* will do the job, but not both, please. Yet certain occasions and purposes may dictate explanation. In this book my policy has been to explain key terms about writing but usually not to give the meanings of those few words I think some readers may not know. Those they may look up in their dictionaries.

Because many English teachers write in red ink "rep" for "repetition," some students infer that repetition is an error in school writing. But it can be a powerful writing device. Here's an excerpt from a free writing:

I like short sentences. **And I almost always read long sentences. I dislike them. No, I can't stand them sometimes.**

> **Make me have to go back and re-read them. Make me a**
> ***slow*** **reader. I'm afraid someone will see my** ***slow*** **eyes and**
> **think I'm dumb.** *I like short sentences.*

Good repetitions. I would explain why but then I'd be treating you
as a dumb reader, and that's one of Zybowski's no-no's.

It's natural for human beings to repeat words for emphasis. "Get
out of here! I said get out of here!" But it's also natural for them to
become stuck on a word they don't want to emphasize. Something
about the way the brain gets hung up on a word, as a finger gets stuck
on the same piano note and keeps hitting it monotonously.

What's the difference between emphasis and monotony? Mostly
meaning. And behind that is the principle of repeat-and-vary. Ask
any songwriter. (How powerful is our unconscious—I find myself writing short sentences so you won't have slow eyes!) *One two* can be
repeated once without boring your reader—*one two, one two.* But if
you're going to do it a third time, you better vary it—*one two, one
two, one two three.* I think Zybowski would agree with that.

As I was saying, speakers and writers get hung up on a word or a
sound. The TV announcer says, "Violence occurred during the demonstrations at the peak of the wall poster campaigns. In Peking . . ."
Those *peek* sounds aren't working there. A writer says, "Childhood
was a *hard* time for me. I was *hardly* ten when I became ill with
pneumonia." Poor repetition. All listeners and readers unconsciously
pick up on repetitions and wonder rightly if there's a reason for the
hard—hardly there? A second's reflection tells them no, but a second has interfered with meaning. In long pieces of writing our unconscious sometimes gets so snagged on a word that our readers groan.
That's why we must write on the Moebius Strip, putting down what
the writing voice dictates and then later looking at our sentences
and listening to them as if—as Samuel Butler said—we were our own
worst enemy.

Here's a good paper written in one of the seminars that shows a
student and teacher failing to communicate. Yet it stammers over the
word *class,* which I've italicized to show how excessively a writer can
repeat a word without noticing. There was no title on the paper; I'll
call it "Cutting Class."

CUTTING CLASS

> I had moved from Detroit to Westway Hills during Janu-
> ary of the 10th grade. Arrangements were made for me to
> attend the girls' school in Earlville. I wasn't sure I would
> like going to school without seeing guys roaming through

the halls, but I didn't want to attend the public school because it was very large.

I was introduced to my teachers and began my *classes*. I had the basic *classes* like English, Math, Biology, History, and Gym. All my *classes* seemed fairly decent and the teachers appeared friendly. All but my English teacher, anyway.

I had been attending my *classes* and found that I was lost in my English *class*. One day I asked a girl what we were supposed to be doing. Very quickly she replied, "I don't know." I thought to myself, "Gee, that's great. She's been here from day one and she has no idea what was going on in *class*." I decided the best thing to do was to ask the nun.

After *class*, several people gathered around her desk and I patiently awaited an opportunity to speak. She looked at me now and then but when I started to talk, she turned away. I was beginning to get angry with Sister Dolores. When there was only a few of us left in the room, I tried again. This time I was able to say, "Sister, would you mind explaining what we are doing in *class*?" She looked at me, having no special expression on her face, sort of a stoned face. She didn't say anything and looked away.

I walked away angrily into the hall. My body movements didn't let on that I was upset but I said to myself, "What a bitch! What the hell does she expect me to do? I don't need this grief from her."

I found out that we were allowed ten absences from each *class* without penalty. On the eleventh absence we were supposed to get called to the office and take a note home to our parents. Each time we were absent from *class*, our name was to be sent to the office.

I don't think my name was ever sent to the office by Sr. Dolores because nothing was said when I had my eleventh absence. I was disappointed that my plan had flopped. I thought for sure that someone would want to know why I had skipped my English *class* so often. Nothing happened. My new plan of action was to approach the dean of students.

"Sister Carol?"

She looked up from her desk and replied, "Yes?"

"Hi, I dropped in because I have skipped my English *class* eleven times and nothing has been done about it." She looked at me as though she wanted to laugh. Surely she must have thought me crazy.

"Why haven't you been attending *class*?"

"Well, I went a couple of times but then I couldn't figure out what we were doing in *class* and the schedule didn't help. When I asked Sister Dolores what we were doing, she merely ignored me. I then proceeded to ignore the *class*."

Contemplating the situation, Sr. Carol said, "That doesn't sound like a very mature way to handle the problem." I thought to myself, "So what? I don't have to act maturely. I'm a student. This woman probably thinks that I don't know what the word means."

Looking in her eyes, I replied, "That's the way it goes."

I was getting the feeling that in spite of the fact that I was being apathetic toward the whole situation, she was humored by my straightforwardness. How many people would be so foolish as to turn themselves in, plus show little or no respect in the presence of the sole person that would determine my fate?

We went over my schedule that I received in *class* and she assured me that she would talk to Sr. Dolores. I left her office and went to my *class*.

I could see that Sr. Dolores and I wouldn't get along very well. She would look at me with an angry expression. Maybe I had gotten her into trouble. We never said anything to each other about the sessions I had missed, and she only called on me when she thought I was not paying attention in *class*.

A friend of mine had Sr. Dolores for homeroom and a few weeks after I reattended *class*, Sister Dolores said to Mary Ann, "I hope that girl doesn't plan on attending college. She's not college material." Mary Ann told me what was said and the following day I confronted the teacher in the hall.

The hall was empty and quiet. Sr. Dolores was on her way to the office when I stopped her. "Hey, what's this about me not being college material?" She was dumbfounded. I went on to say, "I just want to let you know that I am going to college and I am going to do well. Good day." I left her standing there but I was too angry to feel bad about what I had said.

For the rest of the term I only talked to her when she asked me questions in *class*. It was clear that we weren't friends.

That's twenty uses of the word *class,* and even two uses of it wouldn't be powerful because the writer wasn't trying to emphasize that word. Yet the repetition implies otherwise.

After I wrote those lines immediately above, I realized I had wasted words myself. Since I had been talking earlier about *class* and italicized it, I didn't need to explain to my readers that it is a word. That's a writing weakness I call *Namery,* giving a name to something that the reader doesn't need named. I wrote: *two uses of it.* You know I was talking about uses *of it,* meaning *class,* so I can write merely *uses.* Then my sentence loses four words but no meaning. Here's my revision:

> That's twenty uses of *class,* and even two uses wouldn't be powerful because the writer wasn't trying to emphasize that word.

The twenty uses are unsettling. Maybe the writer is trying to do something subtle with that word? Not so here, but the suspicion has been planted.

As a helping editor you can suggest ways of cutting some of the repetitions of *class* in that paper. At times the word *course* might be substituted for *class.* Of the second paragraph Zybowski would probably say, "If you write that all your classes seemed fairly decent, we know that you had begun them and you don't need to tell us that. You could remove all uses of *class* in that second paragraph if you said":

> I was introduced to my teachers. I had the basics like English, Math, Biology, History, and Gym. All the courses seemed fairly decent and the teachers appeared friendly. All but my English teacher, anyway.

One of our frequent habits in speaking and writing is to end a sentence with a word and start the next one with the same word:

> Mary Ann told me what was said and the following day I confronted the teacher in *the hall. The hall* was empty and quiet. . . .

You've done that dozens of times and so have I. The writer might better have said:

> . . . I confronted the teacher. The hall was empty and quiet

and we readers would take for granted that the confrontation took place in the hall. Watch for such repetitions: "It was my brother Sam. Sam was . . . "Sam—Sam" sounds ridiculous. The second *Sam* can be supplanted with *he.* That's what *he's* and *she's* and *they's* and *it's* are for—to take the place of names.

Behind these changes I've suggested is the fact that good writers remember that most of their readers are intelligent. They can put one and a half and two and a half together and get four.

Before I leave that classy paper about Sister Dolores, I must say that a great writer like Shakespeare or Charles Dickens sometimes sprinkles one word through a long passage and the emphasis works. In *King Richard II*, Shakespeare many times repeats the word *flatter,* and in *Macbeth* often repeats forms of the word *do* or *deed,* but for good reason. Here's Dickens introducing the subject of his 800-page novel *Bleak House*—the Court of Chancery in London. He's making fun of it. His *fog* spreads in the direction he wants it to go.

> Fog everywhere. Fog up the river, where it flows among green aits and meadows; fog down the river, where it rolls defiled among the tiers of shipping and the waterside pollutions of a great (and dirty) city. Fog on the Essex marshes, fog on the Kentish heights. Fog creeping into the cabooses of collier-brigs; fog lying out on the yards and hovering in the rigging of great ships; fog drooping on the gunwales of barges and small boats. Fog in the eyes and throats of ancient Greenwich pensioners, wheezing by the firesides of their wards; fog in the stem and bowl of the afternoon pipe of the wrathful skipper, down in his close cabin; fog cruelly pinching the toes and fingers of his shivering little 'prentice boy on deck. Chance people on the bridges peeping over the parapets into a nether sky of fog, with fog all around them, as if they were up in a balloon and hanging in the misty clouds.
>
> Gas looming through the fog in divers places in the streets, much as the sun may, from the spongey fields, be seen to loom by husbandman and ploughboy. Most of the shops lighted two hours before their time—as the gas seems to know, for it has a haggard and unwilling look.
>
> The raw afternoon is rawest, and the dense fog is densest, and the muddy streets are muddiest near that leaden-headed old obstruction, appropriate ornament for the threshold of a leaden-headed old corporation, Temple Bar. And hard by Temple Bar, in Lincoln's Inn Hall, at the very heart of the fog, sits the Lord High Chancellor in his High Court of Chancery.

That's powerful British repetition, published in 1853. Twelve years earlier Ralph Emerson wrote an American essay called "Self-Reliance," from which I quote this famous paragraph. Note the repetitions:

A foolish consistency is the hobgoblin of little minds, adored by little statesmen and philosophers and divines. With consistency a great soul has simply nothing to do. He may as well concern himself with his shadow on the wall. Speak what you think now in hard words and to-morrow speak what to-morrow thinks in hard words again, though it contradict every thing you said to-day.—"Ah, so you shall be sure to be misunderstood."—Is it bad then to be misunderstood? Pythagoras was misunderstood, and Socrates, and Jesus, and Luther, and Copernicus, and Galileo, and Newton, and every pure and wise spirit that ever took flesh. To be great is to be misunderstood.

Emerson repeated the words he wanted to pound into his readers: *consistency, speak, hard words, to-morrow, misunderstood,* and then once again—*misunderstood,* which he had something surprising to say about. Note that he didn't say that to be misunderstood is to be great but rather that to be great is to be misunderstood.

You can see that repetition may be good or bad. When you care about what you're saying, you'll unconsciously write strong repetitions. Let them stand. But when your pen or typewriter is stammering, let the writing cool a while and go back and cut out the weak repetitions. But first be clear, even if that requires stupid-sounding repetition.

Fifteen minutes after I wrote that last remark I stopped to eat lunch, picked up *The New Yorker* Magazine for May 7, 1979, and read this passage on page 154 from Michael J. Arlen's article, "The Air":

I note that I have just written the words "shocked," "outraged," and "astonished" in order to avoid repeating the word "surprise" too many times, but surprise is what I meant. In some ways, surprise is a much weaker and younger or less elevated emotion than, say, shock or outrage. Shock pertains to trauma, and outrage is a form of rage, outer-directed; at any rate, it is an emotion that comes from knowing where one is. The man who curses the gods usually knows where he stands, and doesn't like it. Surprise, however, is the small voice that says, "Gosh, how did I get here? How did this happen to me? Where am I now?"

[Are you beginning to think about how writers should acknowledge their sources? Since I gave all the information you would need to find Arlen's article in the library if you want to read more of it, I won't need to cite the magazine in the List of Sources which appears at the end of this book.]

∞ **DOING NINE:** Choose the best free writing you've done and edit it for wasted words and weak repetitions. Bring both versions to the seminar.

In this book I'm trying constantly to demonstrate that writing is both an unconscious and conscious activity. When a voice takes over your writing, and it's an eloquent one, all you need do is take dictation as fast and accurately as you can. But when things go wrong up there and the voice stutters, you'll find your sentences clumsy and verbose. Sometimes that's because you didn't know what you wanted to say—weren't ready to start writing yourself into a thought. And other times because for some unaccountable reason the voice deserted you. When you believe the thought is down there in a maze of poorly expressed sentences, one expedient is to cut and cut and cut, so that you'll be able to see if there's a flower growing beneath all the underbrush. Be ruthless. Attila the Hun.

∞ **DOING TEN:** Choose one of the worst papers you've written—free writing or otherwise—that you think may have some solid thought in it, and cut it in half. To do that you'll have to cut not only a few words in almost every sentence, but whole sentences, and maybe whole paragraphs. Resolve: nothing stays that isn't absolutely necessary.

As you're cutting try to be a reader. What is special or precious to you as a writer but might not be to a reader? Cut that. This is cutting off an arm? Not a real one, but an artificial one like the one Harold cut off while his mother was watching in the movie *Harold and Maude*. If your sentences are unwieldy and artificial, chop them out. After the chop you can always pick the arm up and attach it again if the loss seems too great.

∞ **DOING ELEVEN:** Take the writing you cut in half and see if you can cut the revision in half. You can learn things that way.

> *They may not always be brilliant, but they gotta be the minimum....*
> EDWARD ZYBOWSKI

*. . . I have shown to the reader the steps
of the process by which I have come to
my conclusions. Instead of requiring him
to take my version of the story on trust,
I have endeavored to give him a reason
for my faith. By copious citations from
the original authorities, and by such critical notices of them as would explain to
him the influences to which they were
subjected, I have endeavored to put him
in a position for judging for himself,
and thus for revising, and, if need be,
reversing the judgments of the historian.
He will, at any rate, by this means, be
enabled to estimate the difficulty of arriving at truth amidst the conflict of tes-
timony; and he will learn to place little
reliance on those writers who pronounce
on the mysterious past with what Fonte-
nelle calls "a frightful degree of certainty,"—a spirit the most opposite to
that of the true philosophy of history.*

WILLIAM H. PRESCOTT, Preface to
*The History of the Conquest
of Peru,* 1847

part two
i-searching

Where there is curiosity, a mouse may be caught.

LU PO HUA

chapter 6
the
i-search
paper

LOOK at a two-year-old grabbing books off a shelf, seeing how they open, ripping pages, finding out how they taste. Not much different from a kitten first time out of his box. Apparently we're all born curious.

Inside or outside school, research should be like that, but usually it isn't. As I write, I'm looking at a term paper "study aid," one of those masterpieces of dull directions. "What Is a Term Paper" is the first line—no question mark after that question, so I guess I'll take 5 percent off the grade. "A term paper is the written result of diligent research into a particular subject." That's the answer. I can't wait to start, nothing I like better than to be *diligent*—one of those words you never hear but from a schoolteacher's lips. "The writer utilizes what others have written, and organizes this material into a new, original product." Original! School term papers that are written from the directions in English composition textbooks or study aids are the most unoriginal writings the world has ever seen. What grinds me about these directions I'm looking at is their hypocrisy. I know the authors don't mean to misrepresent, but they've never thought in a large way about what they're doing. This study aid is jazzed up by illustrations: for example, a girl lying in bed on her stomach, bare legs waving abandonedly in the air. She's peering at a book propped against a pile of other books and a file box, as if she's giving a male student in the snack bar a come-on, and yet on the next page the instructions say:

> Use clear and competent prose. Be restrained, impersonal,
> objective, and factual. Avoid expressing personal opinion
> and feelings.

As a teacher I've been that hypocritical without realizing it. I thought
I was helping students learn to use the library and master the forms of
research reporting. I had been told that people have to know them in
order to get through college, graduate school, and make a go of a
profession. Now I realize that other teachers and I have given so many
instructions to students about the form and length of papers that
we've destroyed their natural curiosity. They don't want to grab books
off the shelf and taste them.

I think of how my wife consumes books while searching for something. Several years ago, I was given a sabbatical leave from my university. She and I decided to spend it in another country. Africa
sounded exciting, so she ate nine books on Africa and wrote a friend
who had spent several years there studying the songs of different
countries. We read the newspapers for every mention of Africa. Eventually we concluded that too many people were reporting that
traveling there was dangerous or awkward because of wars and in-
surrections. Joyce found that such a long trip would be exorbitantly
expensive for our family of four—I would be getting only half pay
during the year's leave.

So the next possibility was Mexico, closer, less expensive, and I had
always wanted to go there. But where should we live when we got
there? Like most ignorant North Americans, I thought Mexico was
altogether flat and hot. Reading books from the library, Joyce found
that in many parts it was mountainous. That meant we could pick
our climate, according to height. But what city? She phoned two
friends who had recently visited Mexico. They told her of other local
persons who had just returned. These people suggested other books
Joyce might read. They knew which ones in the library were out of
date or gave false pictures of the country. We watched the newspapers
and university bulletins for announcements of talks or films by authorities in Mexico. We were zeroing in on our choice.

Joyce thought that the ideal for both of us, and our daughters,
aged ten and thirteen (although I must admit we thought more of
ourselves than of them), would be the city of Oaxaca, capital of the
state of Oaxaca, far south, just before Mexico turns tail up into
Yucatan. There the temperature is 60° to 80° throughout the year—
lots of sun, a rainy season (but only thunderstorms conveniently
short and in late afternoon). I like ruins and Joyce needed to see
people in villages doing crafts. We read that in sight of Oaxaca stand

the remains of Monte Alban, a mountaintop ceremonial city that goes back to about 700 B.C. In the valley of Oaxaca and on its slope nestle dozens and dozens of Indian villages, many of which specialize in a craft. Joyce had checked out other more metropolitan cities and also isolated provincial places. Twenty-eight books and a dozen informants helped us choose Oaxaca.

All that searching was fun for Joyce. She brought home each armful of books excitedly and opened them with anticipation. She does the same sort of search when she needs a new vacuum cleaner. When I thought of her habit of searching, I asked myself, "Why couldn't school research be like that?" So I asked a number of college and high-school teachers around the country if they'd like their students to try such I-Searching. Kirk Moll's paper in Chapter 2 of this book is one that was done in a college class. Such papers have meant a great deal to the people who have written them. The writers felt as excited as Joyce did searching our trip to Mexico, but these searchers found the job more difficult because they had to break themselves of the habit of writing for teacher and in Engfish. In I-Search classes they were asked to write papers that counted for them, and in such a way that they would count for others in the class also, including the teacher.

What a good lifetime habit I-Searching would be. Not just a casual, one-glance investigation, but a thorough search like those Joyce customarily makes, like that which Kirk Moll made about procuring and keeping a wolf, or like that made by Kathy Stacknik in the following paper:

COULD I BECOME A FIREFIGHTER?

Kathy Stacknik

My mother had heard a woman was recently hired as a firefighter in Noonan, a city nearby. I thought I would talk to her to get an idea of how I might like working as a firefighter. I started my search at the Noonan City Hall Personnel Department and received a Firefighter Applicant Information Sheet. Listed at the top are seven unwaivable qualifications. Number five read:

> Eyesight—not worse than 20/40 uncorrected and must be corrected to 20/20.

My vision is 20/200 uncorrected. Well, that's the end of my "Eyesearch." Fortunately I started early enough to pick another topic. During the weekend I sponged around, but didn't come up with any great ideas, so I settled for a good one. I decided to find out why the eyesight stipulation was important. I wasn't too enthused but restarted my search.

Wondering if the volunteer firefighters required the same qualifications, I called William Vormer, Chief of the Xavier Volunteer Firefighters.

"All we require is that you pass a good physical and are able to handle the work load."

The men are not paid professionals, and each individual helps to the best of his ability. I thanked Mr. Vormer and called the Noonan Fire Department. I was connected to Lieutenant Kenney and asked him to justify the strict vision requirement.

"Well, for one thing you've got to be able to see what you're doing, and another, you can't wear glasses under a Scott Air Pack." He explained firefighting is an extremely physical job. A lot of instant moves are made and glasses do fall off. When operations are measured in seconds, fumbling for a pair of glasses wastes too much time. "Scott" is a trade name, the air packs are self-contained breathing apparatus. The mask seals around the entire face and together with the tanks must be on and adjusted in less than thirty seconds. The air packs are used where heavy accumulation of smoke occurs, as in a basement fire. Ventilation is poor and smoke and heat are trapped at head level.

I was interested in learning more. I could tell Lieutenant Kenney was pleased, by the way he answered my questions completely, making sure I understood. I felt at ease and was about to ask if I could make an appointment but he made the suggestion first. We agreed on Monday morning at 9:30.

"I'll keep the whole morning open. If you're here from 9:30 a.m. to 12:00 noon, it's ok." I was impressed.

When Monday morning came around it was gray, I was tired and didn't feel like going. I wanted to dress grubby and be comfy, but I felt I should look nice. I put on my green pantsuit, mascara (mouth closed), lipstick, and left one half hour early. I wasn't worried about finding the station, but parking downtown is such a pain I wanted to make sure I had enough time to walk if necessary.

As it turned out, I parked across the street and walked in early.

"Katherine?"

"Yes, hi, I'm early."

"That's ok, just come right in."

He cleared a chair, offered me coffee, and sat down to finish his. I asked general questions. Fire causes, prevention, and safety, and about training.

"Here—" He handed me a copy of the annual report. "This will take care of the statistics and later on I'll let you talk to our Training Officer. Dunn's a little overbearing, but you'll like him."

I was looking forward to Dunn. Overbearing people can be trying but they keep me awake.

Lieutenant Kenney was anxious for me to see the entire station and began at the dispatching room. "If time and transportation permit, I'd like to take you to one of the oldest single-engine fire houses, built in 1907." We squeezed in with a four-plug switchboard, dispatcher, and tape recorder. Every call is taped. This serves as a record to check on an address or a voice. People fooling around calling in false alarms are prosecuted by voice prints made from the tape. "We throw the book at them." On the switchboard are four "hot lines," one each from an ambulance, Civil Defense, police, and Mid-State University. Mid-State has its own fire crew and is immediately notified of any fires on campus.

The downtown station (#1) is the largest, with ten firefighters, three officers, and three equipment operators for the engine, ladder truck, and mini-pumper. The mini-pumper carries its own water and is used for small fires. The engine was the newest but I couldn't tell. They all looked new. I don't think there was a fingerprint anywhere. The undersides are the same way; in fact, the whole station is spotless.

Hard-hats and coats are piled on the trucks, with boots nearby. We passed the kitchen where the men were having coffee. I peeked in and caught a few men peeking back.

I saw the equipment room and where the hoses are hung to dry, then on up the stairs to the dorms.

Not far from the stairs was the first of four fire poles. I looked down and expected to see the floor below, but saw instead a covering around the pole. A man on his way to the ground floor demonstrated how the covering opened with his weight. It reminded me of a blood cell going through the tri-cuspid valve in the heart. I almost asked if I could slide down.

There are three dorms, a lounge (a pole in each), a shower, and a locker room. The officers have double or triple occupancy with a private bath. Everything looked pretty sterile, no carpeting or pictures on the wall, not even in the lounge.

"Any particular reason why there aren't pictures?"

"Rank has its privileges."

"But the officers don't have them."

"They don't because they don't let the men."

Sounded like military logic.

Night gear consists of black fire pants pulled down over knee-high rubber boots. The combination is placed about six inches from the middle of the bed.

"When the alarm goes off you jump into your boots and pull up on the suspenders."

"What do the men sleep in . . ."

He looked at me like it was a dumb question.

". . . their clothes?"

"It all depends on the weather."

"You mean all they have on sometimes is their boots and firepants?" I took his grin to be "Yes."

Back on ground floor the lieutenant introduced me to the secretary and told her I was interested in becoming a fireman.

"Can you slide up the pole? That's a requirement."

After a few minutes we were on our way to the old fire house. I felt important riding in the officer's red squad car with a big red N.F.D. on the door. Incidentally, fire equipment is gradually changing from red to a mid-spectrum greeny color. Experts claim the new color can be seen better.

As we drove, Lieutenant Kenney gave a quick rundown of a typical week at any fire station.

Men arrive at the station in street clothes, change into fatigues, and line up for roll call at 7:00 a.m. At 7:30 they receive orders and have coffee. At 9:00 a.m. the men are asked what they want to eat for lunch and dinner, changes in orders are announced, if any, and maintenance work is started. Daily duties are varied from station to station, but each week the trucks are completely cleaned, top and underside. Floors are washed and waxed, apparatus is checked and cleaned, even drains in the garage are flushed of sand. The men take turns cooking all the meals for one week each. At 1:00 p.m. the men will engage in some form of training, either book work or going over new procedures. Fridays and Saturdays are yard work and catchall days. On Sundays the men do what they want.

With the summary completed, the lieutenant called in to report his position at Station #3. Two engines are kept but one is reserved as a spare. The cement floor showed signs of grease and oil from the days this station was responsible for mechanical repairs on all the equipment. The stables were long gone and the hay loft was converted into a mini basketball court.

As I handled the railing and climbed the creaky stairs, I thought of my grandmother's house. Three firefighters and one officer lived here. We found the firefighters in the lounge. I was introduced and we talked a while. They asked how I'd like living with a minimum of three men.

"How would you like living with a woman?"

It was ok with them as long as she pulled her weight, something the men were sure a woman couldn't do. Maybe they have a valid point.

Could I move a refrigerator blocking a door? What if my buddy collapsed, would I have time to go for help, or should I take him out myself, risking both our lives? The fire isn't going to wait for me to make up my mind.

I think I could carry 50 feet of empty hose, only 45-50 pounds, but dragging one filled with water is 35 pounds heavier and harder to handle.

"We're closer than husband and wife, don't argue half as much, and get twice as much done. At home you can walk out on your wife. Not here, you have to stay."

Already I was imagining myself avoiding the shower room and dressing in a corner. How would I react to men running around in the nude and to listening to their foul language and crude stories?

"What would you do if some man climbed in bed with you?"

"I don't know. Hit him over the head with my boot?"

"I'm just telling you, these are the hard, cold facts. It will happen. The divorce rates among firemen and policemen are two of the highest."

The lieutenant checked his watch. We had to head back. He kept teasing about living with the men, but encouraged me to apply. One woman was accepted but withdrew before she was told to report for duty.

"You'd know who'd really bitch? The wives. There's no way in hell my wife is going to let me sleep in the same room with another woman."

There would have to be modifications made, if for that reason alone. The lieutenant didn't think so. He seemed to enjoy the idea of possible static in this direction.

I finally met Dunn. He had to be some place in fifteen minutes but said he'd help out. We leafed through the training manual, watched sections of video tape, and waded through transparencies. He was especially proud of the transparencies. I'm embarrassed to admit I felt like a babysitter going through crayon drawings. "Oh, that's nice. My, how clever. A coronary infarction, you say."

"It looks like my fifteen minutes are up."

"That's ok. I can talk to Howard later." Dunn wasn't overbearing. He was sweet and knew what he was talking about, as did everyone I met. I was exposed to the best.

I'm glad my vision is poor. Otherwise I'd feel obligated to apply. I started my search knowing I couldn't be a firefighter but found more reasons than poor eyesight, thanks to everybody.

I realize I didn't go into detail concerning the equipment or the techniques of actual firefighting. Most of this knowledge comes from experience. I have included a copy of the Department of Fire Annual

Report, 1975, and Firefighter Applicant Information Sheet. These two sources answer many questions in capsule form. The annual report gives a brief history of the Fire Department's growth and an idea of happenings during the year.

I thought the search was a success. I learned something and had fun in the process.

Sources

1. Department of Fire Annual Report, 1975, Noonan, Michigan.
2. City of Noonan, Firefighter Applicant Information Sheet.

Interviews

3. William Vormer, Chief of Volunteer Firefighters, Xavier, Michigan, March 24, 1976.
4. John Kenney, Lieutenant, Service Division, Noonan Fire Department, Noonan, Michigan, March 23, 29, 1976.
5. Ed Dunn, Training Officer, Noonan Fire Department, Noonan, Michigan, March 29, 1976.
6. Other firefighters, Noonan Fire Department, Noonan, Michigan, March 29, 1976.

(Names of cities and firefighters have been changed to protect against injury or embarrassment. Although these named sources are therefore not valuable to someone who might want to ask further questions, Kathy and I thought the men might get in trouble with their wives or superiors if this report were issued with real names.)

That paper by Kathy Stacknik and the one by Kirk Moll on the captive wolf are rigorous—the writers kept digging, were not easily satisfied. They didn't stop with the first person they interviewed. They had in mind exactly what they needed to know and went after it. Both papers are lively reading because the searchers reveal their feelings in a way that creates suspense and helps the reader judge the validity of the writers' perceptions and judgments. They did little reading of books or documents, but the answers to their questions probably couldn't have been found in publications. The writers had only a few hours each week for seven weeks to do all the searching and writing. In carrying out an I-Search you'll sometimes find that you have to spend a lot of time arranging interviews and getting to where they're going to take place. Professional researchers often take several years to complete a piece of research. If you're attending school or working at a job not connected with your searching, you don't have that kind of time, so you shouldn't expect to produce a paper as lengthy and comprehensive as a professional's.

Before you begin the smaller tasks that will help prepare you to write an I-Search Paper of the caliber of Kathy's and Kirk's, you need to have an idea of what you're preparing to do. Here's a quick summary of what the searching and writing for an I-Search Paper may include. All the points here will be taken up in more detail in succeeding chapters.

> *Until you are ready to change any minute, you can never see the truth; but you must hold fast and be steady in the search for truth.*
>
> VIVEKANANDA

SKETCH OF I-SEARCHING

Allow something to choose you that you want intensely to know or possess. Maybe it's a stereo record or tape player that's right for your desires and pocketbook. Maybe it's a motorcycle. Or the name of an occupation or technical school best for your needs. Or a spot in the United States or a foreign country you'd enjoy visiting this summer.

These are only a few suggestions to inform you that for a change you're being asked to investigate something you're interested in that will fulfill a need in your life rather than a teacher's notion of what would be good for you to pursue.

Walk around for a couple of days letting yourself think of what you feel you need to know. At night when you're beginning to slide off into sleep, and in the morning when you're coming out of sleep, let your mind receive possible topics. Keep a note pad and pencil beside your bed. Scientists have discovered that these periods are the most productive of good ideas, when one leads to another, and the connections between them are solid and real. Don't be satisfied with something you can do that seems proper for school. You're in command here, and there must be a payoff for *you*.

1. Once you've got a topic, take it to class or the group you're working with, tell the others how you became interested in it, and ask them if they can help you—tips, names, addresses, phone numbers of experts, whatever.
2. Find experts or authorities. Ask them where to locate the most useful books, magazines, newspapers, films, tapes, or other experts on your topic.
3. Look at or listen to this information and these ideas. Note down what may be useful to you.
4. Before you interview people who know a lot about your topic, think about the best way to approach them. Through another

person who knows them? Directly, by telephone or letter? Find out what their lives are like. When would they be most apt to have time and inclination to talk to you? Do you need an introduction of some sort from others?

5. If you're largely ignorant on the topic you're going to ask them about, they may resent your taking up their time; for they'll probably get less than you do from an exchange. Know something of the topic before you talk to them. And don't approach them like this: "I'm sorry to bother you. I know you're a very busy person, and don't have time to talk to little people like me. . . ." If that's true, why are you talking to them? "Because I'm assigned to do it" won't do as an answer this time because now you're investigating something you need to know. If you were an expert or authority, how would you like to be approached by a novice? People like that are usually busy or they wouldn't have become experts. Often they enjoy helping others because they get a chance to talk about what they love; but they don't like to waste time, and one of the best ways to do that is talk about wasting time.

6. If you're worried that experts may not be able to spare you time, begin by asking them where you might look for information and advice on your topic. Then if they don't want to talk at length with you, or haven't time, they can refer you to others.

7. Test the statements of experts against those of other experts. Actually, we're all constantly evaluating experts in our lives. We try to find out how right they've been in the past. If as children we asked Johnny how to build a tree house, we did so because we had heard he was the principal builder of one in the lot next door. We asked the other kids if he was good at it. What's his reputation? You can do the same in your I-Search. Consider whether the expert is rated highly by her peers. Does she publish in reputable publications? What company or institution does she work for? Does one thing she says seem to uphold another?

8. Consult both firsthand sources (people who talk to you about what they're doing, or objects and events you observe on your own) and secondhand sources (books, magazines, newspapers, or people who tell you about what others have done). Remember that experts are persons who know a lot about something. They need not hold an official position or be a certain age. Your roommate may be the best authority on skiing in your area.

Lay aside all conceit. Learn to read the book of nature for yourself. Those who have succeeded best have followed for years some slim thread which has once in a while broadened out and disclosed some treasure worth a life-long search.

LOUIS AGASSIZ

FORM

In short papers, introductions and summaries are bulky and unnecessary. A good way to organize an I-Search Paper is simply to tell
the story of what you did in your search, in the order in which everything happened.

You needn't tell everything (that you got a drink at the park fountain or a stomachache at Tony's Cafe on your journey—unless food
and drink are your topics). The happenings and facts crucial to your
hunt—they should appear in your report. Remember how Kathy Stacknik omitted many facts about firefighting that she found: she told
only those which caused her to make her decision and feel right
about it.

If you wish, you can divide your paper into four parts, like this:

1. What I Knew (and didn't know about my topic when I started
   out).
2. Why I'm Writing This Paper. (Here's where a real need should
   show up: the writer demonstrates that the search may make a difference in his life.)
3. The Search (story of the hunt).
4. What I Learned (or didn't learn. A search that failed can be as
   exciting and valuable as one that succeeded).

Your language and style should belong to you. As you think of
your search and topic, maybe you feel formal or informal—makes no
difference. Write the way that seems natural, as long as you don't
write in Engfish.

DOCUMENTATION

The purpose of footnotes and bibliographies (lists of publications
consulted by a writer) is to help readers assess the reliability of a
search and to keep clear when the writer is speaking and when his
sources are being quoted. Also they assist a reader who may get so
interested in the topic that he wants to check further himself; they
tell him where to go so he won't have to do all the hunting the I-
Searcher did in order to find a good authority.

For short papers, footnotes (notes at the foot of a page) aren't
appropriate as documentation. What makes sense is "back-notes" that
appear at the end of a paper. If readers need to know while they're
reading who published a book mentioned on the first page of a paper,
or its date, they can look to the list of sources at the end and find
out. Footnotes were invented for books and long research papers that
are made up of sections or chapters. At the end of such a book or
paper a complete list of all the works used is customarily included,

in addition to the footnotes in each chapter. This bibliography allows readers to get an overview of the sources and authorities consulted by the author. But what a lot of work! Each source appears at least twice in the book, as footnote and item in the bibliography.

Footnotes are hard to type because a writer has to have enough room at the bottom of each page for them. Printers hate footnotes—more chance for mistakes. Many professional publications don't use them but simply list the sources at the end, each one numbered so it can be keyed in the text in this way: (5:31), which means "You'll find what I've mentioned or quoted from by looking up page 31 in the source numbered 5 in my bibliography or list of sources, which appears at the end of my paper."

Such documentation will help the reader who wants to know when a source is published. An 1891 book on airplanes is not as experienced and authoritative as one written in 1980. And who published a source may be significant—a handwritten booklet on airplanes written by your fourth-grader cousin is a different kind of source from a volume in the Time-Life science series.

This chapter has presented an overview of the I-Search project. More detailed material on the process appears in subsequent chapters.

> *So history, namely change, has been mainly due to a small number of "seers,"—really gropers and monkeyers—whose native curiosity outran that of their fellows and led them to escape here and there from the sanctified blindness of their time.*
>
> JAMES HARVEY ROBINSON

I think that we may detect that some sort of preparation and faint expectation preceded every discovery we have made. We blunder into no discovery but it will appear that we have prayed and disciplined ourselves for it.

HENRY THOREAU

chapter 7
a topic choosing you

AN I-SEARCH PAPER requires courage and patience in arranging to interview people, as well as what detectives and news reporters call "legwork." But it's a natural activity; if you let a genuine need or desire grab you, you'll find people helping so much that you become embarrassed. They'll do that because they sense how much you care about what you're looking for and because like all human beings they enjoy telling someone else what they know.

What do you need to know these days? Stand outside yourself every once in a while and check what the fingers of your mind are scratching. That's how you'll locate the itch. Maybe it's a small thing like deciding what to do with the large amount of money a relative gave you for Christmas or graduation. Here's Elizabeth King with such a gift in hand, thinking that she had always wanted to take pictures more seriously but never had a good camera. She felt that a paper which would require several hours for five weeks of the semester should be on a more profound topic, but she let herself look for a camera because she had a need to find one right then. The notion that something she did in school might be immediately useful to her life had shocked her, but she was intelligent enough to give in to it.

A CAMERA RIGHT FOR ME

Elizabeth King

"What do you want for a graduation present?" my mom asked. I hadn't even thought about graduation, let alone a present, but that's my mom—always ten months ahead of time. "How about a good camera?"

"Sure." It sounded exciting, but photography had never progressed beyond 120 Instamatics for me. The only contact I had had with 35 mm. cameras was in high school when I had a boyfriend who did some photography for the school newspaper. He had shown me some of the basic workings of a 35 mm., but that was five long years ago.

Mom naturally told me to investigate and choose the kind of camera I wanted. I floundered around until my friend John brought me a copy of the *Consumer's Guide to Buying Photographic Equipment* from the bookstore where he worked. The jargon about "Eye-level pentaprism, accessory angle finder, dioptic adjustment lenses, fresnel lens, and microprism screen range finder" was Chinese to me, but I did manage to gather that they considered the Canon FTb a "best buy" in its price range. Knowing nothing but this, I got my first investigative break when I was putting up signs in Sangren Hall and saw the ad:

> CANON FTb camera
> 35 mm. SLR
> Black body—case & strap
> FD 50 mm. 1:1.8 s.c. lens
> $230.00 excellent condition

I was reluctant to call, knowing as little as I did, but John said he had a friend, Dave Lon, who was a real camera expert and that he'd call him to ask if he'd look it over.

When I called the camera owner to ask if I could take it to have a friend appraise it, he was reluctant, saying he'd been "ripped off before." I finally got him to agree and ended up bringing over my flute as collateral. He was very nice once we got over there, though, and said I could forget about leaving the flute.

Dave was just opening up the Miller's Ice Cream Store in West Main Mall when we arrived. He handled the camera like a pro, I noted enviously (earlier at the owner's house he had handed me the case to put the camera in and I didn't know how; he ended up putting it in himself after I tried to shove it in upside down). Dave took it apart (I was scared to death he'd drop the lens), clicked and twisted and examined, and ended up saying it was in good shape. He praised Canon's lenses, saying they were one of the top lines in the whole business. But he also thought the price was a little high and went on to make some general critical comments:

"This is an all-black body. They look real nice but cost you about $20.00 more. Just for a little paint. And even then, the acids in your fingers wear it off after a few months of use.

"This case is nice but I never use mine. You only need a bag to carry everything in; film, lens caps, other lenses and stuff. This is going to drive up the price too—they cost about $50.00.

"The lens on this camera is a 1.8, which is about normal. But if you're not going to invest in other lenses right away then you should get a 1.4, which is more versatile."

Although he owned a whole army of cameras, he began to praise one made by Olympus, the OM-1. "It's very small and light. Olympus makes great lenses too. It's a really good camera for the money."

I eventually decided against the used Canon for a variety of reasons, including the price, the frills of black paint and case, the lack of a warranty, and the 1.8 lens. However, I was really intrigued by the OM-1 and decided to investigate both the Canon and the OM-1 further.

I went to Manfred's, a camera store with a reputation for excellent discount prices and pushy sales clerks. It was a busy Saturday morning and I looked over the glass cases filled with every conceivable kind of photographic equipment. Eventually my turn came up and I found myself talking to a heavy-set man in his late 50's who, by the business-like suit and general air of laziness he wore, appeared to be Mr. Manfred, the owner. He was somewhat vague and bored by my questions about the OM-1, but took one out of the case for me to inspect. I picked it up, imitating Dave, and found it light and compact, fitting beautifully in my hands. I briefly mentioned the Canon line and he lighted up like West Main at dusk.

"Now look at this! For the $330 you'd pay for an Olympus with a 1.4 lens you could get this new line Canon, the AE-1; it's a new generation of camera. All run by a little computer. Just set your film speed and it adjusts everything else automatically—aperture, shutter speed, everything."

"That doesn't sound too challenging. I mean, I'd rather do all that myself," I said.

"Hey, tell me, does your car have an automatic transmission?"

"No."

Pause. "Well, do you realize you're in the eleven percent minority that doesn't?"

I smiled.

He went on. "This camera also has attachments for a power winder for continuous shooting and an automatic electronic flash. Just plug them in here . . . and here, and they're all run by the computer. This is the hottest-selling camera we've ever had."

"Well, how much is all this?"

"Listed price for the camera—$413. Our price—$299.95."

"How can they manage to sell such a complicated camera so cheaply?"

"It's forty percent electronically made—much cheaper to manufacture."

I hefted the AE-1. "It's pretty heavy compared to that OM-1."

"How do you think they made that so light? They cut down the walls forty percent. How else do you make a Caddy into a VW?"

He gave me a glossy brochure on the AE-1. I had to ask for literature on the OM-1. As I said goodbye he said, "And Canon makes the best lenses in the world!"

Whew! What a supersalesman! He really wanted me to buy that AE-1, no doubt hoping I'd also buy the extra $200 worth of attachments if needed to become a complete system. The literature he gave me didn't tell me anything except how new and wonderful both cameras were—company propaganda. I began to compare the cameras:

CANON AE-1

$299.95 with 1:1.8 lens

$339.95 with 1:1.4 lens

OLYMPUS OM-1

$269.95 with 1:1.8 lens

$309.95 with 1:1.4 lens

CANON PROS

- good price for such an advanced camera
- excellent lenses
- capability to expand into a more complex system if I got more serious

OLYMPUS PROS

- very light weight
- excellent lenses
- good camera at a lower price
- simplified—more my style

CANONS CONS

- heavy
- too automated for me
- expensive to expand

OLYMPUS CONS

Am I getting as much camera for the money?

Meanwhile I also did some reading in *Fundamental Photography* magazine, which helped me through the basic terminology. It doesn't seem relevant here, but briefly, I learned how to load and unload film, what shutter speeds, f-stops, and film speeds were, and generally how to use a camera on paper. I discovered the reason a 1:1.4 lens was more desirable was that it could open up farther, allowing more light to pass and thereby enabling a photographer to work in darker settings. I also found out that photography is basically a pretty simple matter these days because cameras are so advanced. It mainly depends on your interests to determine how complicated you want to get.

Conclusion

I decided to stay simple, and therefore decided on the Olympus OM-1. The Canon was impressive but too heavy and complicated. I wanted a good, light camera with good lenses, and I think I've found it in Dave's suggestion. Ideally I'd like to get one with the 1:1.4 lens, but it *is* my parents' money and I'm sure I could get along just as well with a 1:1.8.

When I first started looking at cameras, it wasn't too wholeheartedly, mainly because I couldn't afford the time away from school work. This I-Search Paper gave me the perfect opportunity to work on it. I feel good about the choice I've made. The OM-1 really suits what I wanted in a camera.

Sources

1. *Consumer's Guide to Buying Photographic Equipment.* I read this before I began the I-Search so I neglected to write down the publication information. I tried to get it back but my friend tells me that it's now out of print.
2. *Fundamental Photography Magazine,* Petersen Publishing Company, various issues, 1976.
3. *Photo Equipment: Buyer's Guide Reports,* ed. Michael L. Green, DMR Publications, Vol. III, no. 13, 1976.
4. Interviews with Dave Lon and (I assume) Mr. Manfred or one of his better-dressed older clerks, November 1976.

This paper is not weighty, but it weighed enough for Elizabeth, just as the camera did. The search was challenging, for she did the essential things: she learned from a salesman but didn't let his word dominate her. Through a friend she met a camera expert who had no advantage to gain by recommending one camera or another—an unbiased authority. She read a little about cameras, but not so much that she became dizzy with new information. She thought about everyone involved in the matter, including her parents, who were putting up the money. She could have made a more thorough search, one that in the scholarly world is significantly called "exhaustive." But she was already tired that semester from a multitude of chores and commitments both personal and academic, so she restricted the project wisely. Small as it was, it tested her and extended her powers of estimating the validity of statements made by so-called authorities.

The I-Search project is designed to give you lifetime skills in listening, interviewing, reading, quoting, reporting, and writing in a way that others will profit from and enjoy. No matter how small a question you're asking, you can make the project teach you many skills. Improve your thinking. And pay off with a wolf in your house or a camera in your hand.

The words of other people—which ones are to be trusted? Which are worth passing on to others? And your words—which ones will both catch and hold readers and then enlighten them? Buying a camera may be a small event, but these questions are large and essential as long as you live.

What should *you* choose to search? I can't say enough times that this is the wrong question. Rather ask, "What's choosing me? What do I need to know? Not what I believe will impress others, but what keeps nagging me?" It needn't be a new, momentary need or itch. Maybe it's an old one that you've had for years but never got round to scratching. A teacher at the Columbus College of Art & Design, where all students major in commercial or fine art, asked students in a composition class to write I-Search Papers. He wrote me:

> One student had always wanted to be a ballerina—she grew up mad that her mother had never sent her to have lessons. Ballerinas were her ideal self: she loved their grace and beauty and femininity. She wondered if what she thought of them was what they were. So she interviewed a few dancers, saw *The Turning Point* (a good movie about people in ballet), and read some books. She learned about one-sided, over-pressured athletes with feet so bruised, banged up, and bent out of shape that they sometimes had trouble walking. She's glad she's an artist. I enjoyed the paper.

If in your paper you're asking a question like "Should I be a ballet dancer?" the answer *no* can make the search as valuable to you as the answer *yes*. You may have spent years worrying and dreaming about the possibility of taking a long trip down a road that's not for you.

Finding a right one immediately and instinctively is most enjoyable, but in matters that you've messed around with for years, often a process of elimination will slowly ease your mind.

> *My books. I never make them: they grow; they come to me and insist on being written, and on being such and such. I did not want to write* Erewhon, *I wanted to go on painting and found it an abominable nuisance being dragged willy-nilly into writing it. So with all my books— the subjects were never of my own choosing; they pressed themselves upon me with more force than I could resist. If I had not liked the subjects I should have kicked, and nothing would have got me to do them at all. As I did like the subjects and the books came and said they were to be written, I grumbled a little and wrote them.*
>
> SAMUEL BUTLER

If you're going to write two I-Search Papers in this program (a good idea, because a person often needs a second time around before she gets the knack of something), then you ought to make the first one smaller and less ambitious than the second. Maybe you'll have four or five weeks for the first and seven for the second. Whatever, the first I-Search might be modest in scope, like Elizabeth King's quest for a camera or the adventure Pat Philbin records in this I-Search Paper:

COULD I BE A DISC JOCKEY?
Pat Philbin

The constant repetition of the same routine causes a person to try and change his drab ways. I've been here for almost seven months, and I find myself going through the same boring routine. It's time I got involved in other things than school work.

My interest in the radio is relatively new. I am more interested in the actual broadcasting than the technical aspects of the radio. I want to know if I am cut out to be a disc jockey. I was never good at making speeches. What kind of person does it take to slur, stutter, and gag the weather out over the air? One with a lot of nerve. I wonder if I am a person with that kind of nerve.

The only way to find out the above was to actually try it. The idea was challenging. The closest contact I have to any radio station is a friend who works for WRLR, AM a couple times a week. Sam takes his radio show as seriously as he does his partying. He said I could sit in on his show if I wanted to. I jumped at the invitation. I felt if I saw how it was done I might get up enough nerve to try it.

It was a cold January night when Sam and I walked up to the offices of the Student Services Building. I wondered if it was all worth it. The most important thing he said was to always keep calm, never get thrown out of whack. I wondered what that meant. We arrived not too soon, my ears were frozen. The rooms were downstairs on the ground floor. Each wall was covered with records. It was like the Detroit Library. I was surprised at how little equipment was involved in the actual broadcasting. There were two turntables that were worn down and turned sort of funny. When I asked why the turntables were so ragged, he informed me that this was the AM station, and the FM station, I guess, was second-classing it. The microphone protruded from a panel in front of the desk chair. The panel was rather plain, just a few dials and lights. There were a couple of buttons that started the turntables. Over to the left was a panel of tape players. They were used to play certain songs that were not on the forty-five records.

His show started at 9:00 and we were about ready to start. The first thing he did was to find records and place them on the turntables. He then would place headphones on to listen to the record start. Once he had heard the record (or song) start he would turn the table off and spin the table backwards to find the spot where the song begins. This was done so that on the air it would begin right away and there would be no long moment of silence. I was more nervous than he was and I was only there to watch. He was very smooth and clear from the sound of the speakers that conveyed his voice. He could turn the room speakers off and play another record while the audience listened to the original one. This was how he kept the records following after each other. The records were color keyed. Green was oldies but goodies. Yellow was mellow. Red was your rock and roll. He had a chart that told him what he should play. It all seemed so simple until he had to do the weather.

> Partly cloudy today and increasing clouds—rather, increasing chance of snow. Temperatures in the high teens.

He started laughing after he finished and I couldn't hold back either. He said he was trying to edit the thing because it was too long, but he got mixed up. He said he usually takes a good shot of whisky before the show and the stronger the better. It sounded like good advice.

The show went pretty good from then on. I'd pick out the records and he would introduce them and tell who they were done by. He would often hesitate when the record was over, trying to remember which group went to what record. Every so often he got them wrong. It was over before I knew it. He was on for three hours. After the show he took me over to the United Press International printer. That's where they get all their news. It seemed as if it would never stop printing. The paper was piling up on the floor. He said because the station manager was there he wouldn't be able to let me read the weather. It looked as though I wasn't going to get my chance for a while.

My next step was to find something out about the stations at Central Southern University. The school has two stations. WRLR, AM-FM, and WCEN, FM. I got hold of the chief engineer of WCEN first. His name is Dirk Home. In a short conversation he told me the basics of the radio station. WCEN, FM is 104.1 on the dial. FM stands for frequency modulation. They broadcast off of 50 kilowatts. This, he informed me, is more powerful than WRLR's 40 kilowatts. He said the differences between AM and FM stations were that frequency changes during output but that power output is constant. AM stations' output changes. He said that FM doesn't have noise problems and it has better fidelity. He said that WCEN was licensed with Washington as a public radio station, nonprofit. He said that WRLR was run mostly by students while WCEN was run by the school. He said that in order to broadcast, you must get a third class radio permit. I asked if this took any experience; he said that all one had to do was pass the written test. I thought that to be a bit strange. He reminded me that WCEN has a wider mixture of music. He said that it was a fine arts station, but it also broadcasted football and hockey games.

WRLR was more to my liking. The people were more my age and the music was bearable compared to the classical on WCEN. There I talked to Monty Pullen, who was a disc jockey for the station. He said that it was pretty late to get started this semester but to come down sometime before spring term and they would set me up. He said that you didn't need a license for the AM station because it was a nonprofit organization. The director there requires it for the FM disc jockeys. I've found that if I want to do it, all I have to do is go through the system; but the system takes time. I left for the spring break with not much hope of getting on the radio relatively soon.

The break brought my roommate and I to Boston for some rest and relaxation. We stayed with an old high school buddy at a small college called Brickwood (enrollment 1,200). Norm was involved with the radio and did the news at 6:00 p.m. He said that I could come and watch. Sensing that I might get my chance, I tagged along. The room was like a news room you see on T.V. It had a long table with four microphones on it adjusted to mouth level. It even had a sign that flashed "On the Air" above the window. There were clip boards filled with the UPI printouts of the day. Norm asked if I'd find some sports stories that sounded interesting. I looked through all of them and found about six stories. Norm started the news by stating that he had a special guest.

> Good evening, this is Norm Beeler, and with me tonight is Patrick Philbin from Idlewood, Michigan, to give you the latest in sports.

It was news to me, but this was my big chance. He went on with the news as I frantically tried to read the articles again before he was done. I was a nervous wreck. What if I said something wrong? My heart felt queasy and it was pumping hard. He was on his last article and he sounded so good. It was almost my turn. I picked up my first article. It was about Central Southern making it into the NCAA basketball playoffs. I was just about to start when Norm informed me that there was a commercial on now; but that I was going on in sixty seconds. I watched the clock. It was moving too fast to suit me, 5-4-3-2-1. The light flashed above the window "On the Air." Oh, my God, I thought. My throat wouldn't work . . . and then finally,

> In sports today, Central Southern gained a berth in the NCAA tournament by defeating Miami of Ohio at Miami.

I was doing it. I couldn't believe it. I went on to talk about the Pistons and the Lions and Mark Fydrich. I thought about how stupid it was to be talking about Michigan teams. I was in New Hampshire. Norm passed me a note saying I was reading too fast. I took it as a compliment. I wanted to get done fast. I did fine until the end. I was so glad to be done.

> . . . leaving the Lions for the Cowboys, and that's all for forts.

Oh my God, I said, "forts" instead of "sports." It didn't matter. I was done. Norm had trouble closing out because of my blunder. Even with the mistake, I felt I could do it again, and I wanted to do it again so I could get it right. All I had to do was go through the process of becoming licensed. I proved to myself that all it takes is a little nerve. I had that nerve. It turned out to be a great way of breaking up a daily routine. Not once did I think about other things. Yes! A great way to break up a boring routine.

Sources

1. Beeler, Norman, WXXL newscaster, Brickwood College, East River, New Hampshire, March 1977.
2. Todd, Sam, WRLR, AM disc jockey, Central Southern University, Idlewood, Michigan, February 1977.
3. Home, Dirk, WCEN, FM Chief Engineer, Central Southern University, Idlewood, Michigan, March 1977.
4. Pullen, Monty, WRLR, FM disc jockey, Central Southern University, Idlewood, Michigan, February 1977.

[NOTE: Names of persons, radio stations, and schools have been changed to prevent embarrassment or injury.]

Pat's I-Search Paper is full of little grammatical and stylistic slips that he could have caught if he had read the paper aloud before finally typing it up. As I remember, he was absent on editing day, when another student would have helped him catch some of these things that an author misses because he's too familiar with what he's just written. For example, in the paragraph beginning "My next step . . ." he uses the words "He said" seven times. Once he begins to tell the story of his getting on the air, his style picks up, events move swiftly, and tension builds. You can see that the memory of those exciting moments gave him an appropriate voice in which to tell of them.

When the paper was read to the seminar, it scored, I think because at times it was light and humorous, and it told a story of courage. Like the hero of Homer's *Odyssey*, Pat took on a fearful challenge in order to get where he wanted to go.

You may wonder what this paper is doing in this book when it reports no reading on Pat's part, no investigation in libraries, as is characteristic of school research papers. The point is that books and magazines would probably not have helped Pat. He could have faked the whole thing and listed a number of printed sources on the topic of disc jockeying or announcing, but he knew it was supposed to be a truthful report.

Usually consulting printed materials as well as live experts or authorities is helpful in a search because writers have time to remember, reflect, and put together what they know. In print they can give you an hour, or many hours, of words. When you read their sentences, you don't interrupt them in the middle of their busy work day. If Pat had searched in a library, he might have been lucky enough to have stumbled on a book or article that recorded an experienced disc jockey's first days on the job, and thus extended and deepened the knowledge he gained in his own trials. But the chances were slim for such luck. Pat took considerable time to do his on-the-spot search, and he had only five weeks of the course (about 15-20 hours) in which to ask questions, visit radio stations, write several drafts of his paper. That the search was valuable to him and fascinating for the other members of the seminar is undeniable.

In the seminars I hoped my students would learn a great deal about using libraries in at least one of their I-Searches, but the first requirement remained—to carry out a search that answered a genuine need in their lives. The time to learn a technique is when you need to use it. School ordinarily works on the opposite assumption: that you should learn all the techniques in preparation for a day when you might use one or two of them. This is a way to cram and forget, to develop the habit of learning what is seldom if ever used.

When you write a first-rate I-Search Paper, you'll not only be developing a useful lifetime habit and carrying out an intellectual task, but you'll also be getting experience in writing the sort of account often published in magazines and books these days. More and more, editors are ignoring the old essay and article forms. Readers are buying magazines and books which tell stories of experience rather than present reports that consist mainly of abstracted or generalized points and statistics accompanied by an anecdote or two. For example, the book *Widow* by Lynn Caine (New York, William Morrow, 1974, and in paperback by Bantam Books, 1975) tells the story of the death of a husband and the several years following it in which Ms. Caine as a widow learned to live alone with her children. Such a book puts tragic experience into a context readers can imagine themselves in, and explains and teaches more than an article that summarizes the experiences of many. To generalize and quantify such experience may deprive it of its essential reality and sometimes render it misrepresentative or meaningless.

How many false alarms do fire stations answer in a year? What are the reasons the alarms were turned in? With what consequences to the firemen and inhabitants of the city? Answered in statistical or generalized fashion, these questions mean little, but when found in the whole context of individual firemen's lives on the job, as they are in Dennis Smith's *Report from Engine Co. 82* (New York, Saturday Review Press, 1972, and in paperback by Pocket Books, 1973), the answers to these questions arise out of experiences which readers feel and thus will not forget. At times we need to look at generalized and comprehensive surveys of human action—for example, if we're planning large industrial or municipal projects—but readers are seldom moved to understanding or action by reports that ignore people in the context of their lives and work.

The book *Friendly Fire* (New York, G. P. Putnam's Sons, 1976) tells the story of C. D. B. Bryan's search to find why the mother and father of a young man killed in Viet Nam were so upset that they ran an advertisement in a newspaper about his death. In writing this I-Search, Bryan revealed a great deal about war, the military mind and methods, and the nature of obsession. He was so truthful in his quest that it became exceedingly painful for him, but the story is rich with meaning, and unforgettable. In 1979 it was presented, again in an honest version, as a three-hour television movie.

I'm talking about these professional records of experience not to suggest that you can match them in a paper that takes only ten to thirty hours of your time, but to suggest that they're natural human productions. To relive one of the crucial experiences of your life, or to search for the answer to a pressing question, is to think through it, to give it a structure that will probably reveal its significance. If you do it well, others will profit from it.

Here's another such professional job, the record of an experience not unlike Pat Philbin's search "Can I Be a Disc Jockey?" In this case-history, Joyce T. Macrorie, the woman who searched out where our family should live in Mexico, asked the question: "Can I become a jeweler while I'm here in Oaxaca?" [By the way, Oaxaca is pronounced *Wah-hah-kah* and the name of the god in the title below, *Zee-pay-low-tek*.] This article was not written in school, but it is related to the I-Search Paper, as I will show after you've read it.

A GIFT FROM XIPELOTEC

Joyce T. Macrorie

We were living in Oaxaca, Mexico, in a rented house—two daughters sprung from their schools but studying, a husband on a sabbatical writing leave from his university, and an artist without studio. My 2,000-pound etching press was home in Michigan.

I drew. I tried a few woodcuts. I read. I knitted while I read, knowing we already owned enough sweaters. I shopped in the spirit of people who drink. Leisure overflowed on me.

I had brought two bequeathed diamond rings with me to have made into earrings. American friends recommended the jeweler Jorge

Garcia Mendez. "You'll have to wait, but when he does a job he does it right. His only problem is too many customers. If he tells you a week, plan on four."

I had expected a prosperous store. Jorge's shop was a converted gatekeeper's room guarding the entrance to an old house wedged between commercial buildings. *Don* Jorge stood behind a scarred glass counter, a fortyish man chatting with another, elbows plunked, body bent in a pose suggesting he had all day.

"Good afternoon," he said, smiling near-sightedly. Both men looked at me and waited. I stammered through Spanish, encouraged by both men supplying gestures. The *maestro* made a sketch, measured the stones, and gave me a receipt. "They will be ready next Friday," he said surely.

The Monday after the next Friday I went to see *Señor* Garcia Mendez. I thought I'd nudge him. "Are my earrings ready?"

"How not?" he said haughtily. "I promised Friday didn't I?" And here it is, um," he peeked over his shoulder at the wall calendar, "Here it is Monday." He tucked his chin in so his face flattened, then smiled radiantly. Opening a drawer in his work table, he pawed squirrel-fashion through small boxes, tissue-paper scraps, and bulging envelopes with notations on the outside. He stuck a divining finger down in the middle and extracted a tissued lump. Turning his lips in toward his teeth and pinching the package gently, he said, "Ah, sí," and opened the paper to reveal the completed earrings.

I held each one up reverently, examining the workmanship. He put both hands on the counter, flat, and rocked back and forth, beaming as he watched. I heard myself blurting, "Could I work for you as an apprentice? I've made jewelry before but most of it was simple or cast." I held up my seal ring, one of two I had made for my husband and me when we got married.

"You want to work in this *taller*?"

I nodded.

"Well." He paused, his head bobbing heavily while he thought. "Once an American *señorita* worked in another shop here in town."

That takes care of tradition, I thought. But no.

"All she wanted was to spend a week or two learning typical filigree. She was a fine jeweler."

No good, I thought, sagging.

He paused again, looking at his hands, the counter top, sideways at me. Then he lifted his shoulders, smiled into my face, and said, "*Cómo no?*"—Why not?" We shook hands on six hours a day, five days a week, for a year.

• • •

The next morning I arrived at a boarded-up shop. I stood in the pale sun shivering, nervous. Soon a boy unlocked the side door and went in. I heard sweeping and humming. I opened the door quietly. Black dust swirled and resettled on the boy and benches as he flicked a bunch of feathers three inches above all the surfaces. "I'm the new apprentice," I said.

He stopped flicking and looked me over. "Come in." He went on cleaning. When he finished, he sat down at one of the benches, pulled out a drawer, and began working, whistling.

I went outside.

Soon another young man arrived on a bike. He wheeled it carefully past me into the hall and entered the studio.

The sun warmed up, traffic increased, people filed in and out of the bakery across the street buying bags full of good smells. I thought about another cup of coffee, of going home and forgetting this nonsense. Then Jorge arrived, breathless, scurrying up with a black doctor's bag in one hand, the other outstretched to shake mine. "Oh, I'm late on your first day. *Que lástima*. Forgive me. Come in, come in."

He introduced me to Felipe and Pablo who each shook my hand and smiled widely as though seeing me for the first time. Then we set to work. "We will share this first project, you understand? That way I can show you how we use the equipment and you can show me how much you already know." Jorge said this confidently, ready to be impressed with the quality of my craftsmanship. Sweat ran down the inside of my arms.

We started three gold rings set with jade. In less than two days we had them finished. In that short time I convinced *Don* Jorge of my sincerity, my diligence, and my lack of experience. He bought silver for me to learn on.

Within a week I realized that the *maestro* had been very early the first day, not late. It was his custom to arrive around eleven, after everybody else had been there two hours. He always came in breathless, acting late even though it was his more-or-less regular time. Partly he felt harried from searching out parking for his burden and pride—an old Plymouth. Partly, it was his self-image to be rushed, always a step behind, a minute off, a date removed. He made up for it with charm. As he entered, he grinned at us, rolled his eyes heavenward, implying that we should be glad he had made it.

•   •   •

The second week *Don* Jorge came in carrying a clean, folded muslin towel. He looked disgustedly at the several grimy shop towels and said, "This is for you," shaking his finger in the Mexican gesture that serves all negating purposes. Wag-wag, "Don't thank me, it isn't right for you to use the dirty towels we men use," and wag-wag, "Don't let those guys use it." Every day I took it home to wash so he could see I knew how to accept an honor.

A few days after the towel gift he puffed in at 11:30, put his jewelry out, started working, and then said, "Soap!" From his sweater pocket he took a small bar of soap wrapped in a picture of palm trees around a lagoon. Printed over the inevitable full moon was "California Night." Imported. Ceremoniously he put it on my bench top. The rest of the shop used detergent out of a plastic bag nailed to the wall. It did a better job but detergent was common and I, evidently, was a lady.

My Spanish prohibited full technical explanations from *Don* Jorge. Instead, he gave lucid demonstrations and waited for me to understand the reasons after the logic had come clear in the work. Starting me on my first filigree chain after the jade rings, he showed me how to measure and cut small pieces of wire. "Put them against the thumb nail like this," tap, tap, "and then hang on to that end tight while you cut. Be sure you hang on tight and get them exactly the same," he said.

It was difficult to make them the same length, and a few fell short; but I used them anyway. As the bending and curling progressed, the slight variations increased geometrically. I spent hours trying to create filigree squiggles perfectly alike after starting with unalikes. Next time I held very tightly and made them exactly the same.

At Christmas time I worried about presents for the men—something small so as not to embarrass them, not too personal but appropriate. I asked a friend coming from the States to bring a red sweatshirt for Felipe. After ridiculous agonizing I settled on shaving lotion for Pablo and for *Don* Jorge a bottle of liquor. The most pedestrian, obvious, therefore safe, choices. I wrapped them the day before Christmas Eve and took them to the shop the next morning. When I arrived, Pablo and Felipe were both working heads down. I put the packages on their desks, over to one side, not saying anything. They didn't say anything either. I stuck *Don* Jorge's bottle beside his chair on the floor where he would see it but customers wouldn't.

"What's this?" Jorge asked when he came in. He shook the bottle.

"It's from the *Señora*," Pablo said.

"Ahhhhh," said *Don* Jorge, putting it in his black bag.

My initial surprise that we should work on Christmas Eve evaporated in the heat of that frantic day. Last minute sales, jewelry engravings that couldn't wait, and sweaty rushing in and out to the bank for gold—run, Felipe, to Mrs. Cohen with this cross. I sat in my corner, working slowly on silver, feeling out of pace with the rest of the gold-buying city.

Finally the 2:30 news came on the radio. We started putting things away for dinner and *siesta* hours. *Don* Jorge stuck his head into the work-shop from out front and shook his finger at me.

"Don't leave yet," he ordered.

Pablo and Felipe smirked while they put the files in the rack, picked litter from the floor in unusual tidiness. I rearranged my already neat bench drawer and played with the habitual studio litter on top. Again *Don* Jorge stuck his head into the work-shop, this time trying to be dignified but succeeding only in looking embarrassed. He cleared his throat and began. "*Señora Hoysay* (Joyce) . . ." He stopped. He looked at Pablo and Felipe, who turned away smiling. "This . . ." He stopped again. Then firmly he said, "*Señora Hoysay,* this present is from Pablo, Felipe, and me. *Feliz Navidad.*" He put a tiny package down in the litter.

Now I was embarrassed, realizing it was partly the need to respond to my gifts that had blown the shop into a spatter of activity. I couldn't think how to say they shouldn't have done it. I realized almost immediately that wasn't right anyway. According to their custom they should have. So I thanked them and left, taking my unopened gift and red face out into the three o'clock sun.

Christmas morning I opened the present from the *taller,* reading aloud the hand-lettered card splendid with *Don* Jorge's engraving script. Inside, lying on a cotton bed, was the god of jewelers—Xipelotec —duplicated from the original Monte Alban Tomb Number Seven jewel. Nose ring, ear and chin bells dangling, the tiny face looked at me from a filigree pin bar. The entire piece was exquisitely done in eighteen karat gold. I held it up for everyone to see, my chin wobbling, tears filling my eyes.

"Oooooh," Karin said admiringly. Then looking at my face, she asked, "What's wrong, don't you like it?"

"Karin, she loves it, can't you tell that?" Lisa said.

"Well," said Ken, "this just shows what they think of you down at the shop. And you're always talking about being in their way and getting on their nerves."

Wiping my nose I said, "This just shows that we should be careful about giving gifts to Mexicans—they reciprocate so hard."

In January I myself completed six silver Xipelotec faces for the shop and was feeling smug if not original. Karin came down to buy one and walk me home for dinner. On the way she told me, a propos of nothing, that she bet Jorge had let me apprentice because he couldn't say no.

"Why do you say that?" I asked, hurt.

"Well, when I ask Teresa (our housekeeper) what kind of pop she wants, she always says she doesn't care. And when I give her grape she says 'thank you' but she doesn't drink it. I don't give it to her any more. But she's never told me she didn't like grape."

"I don't see what that has to do with Jorge," I said.

"Mo-om—it's the same as when you ask a Mexican how to get some-place. They always tell you where to go even when they don't know, just so they won't make you feel bad."

I knew exactly what she was talking about.

•   •   •

About the time I wore out the California Night soap and started washing up with detergent, Jorge realized I wasn't going to discourage. He bought a small bellows, torch, and gasoline bottle for me alone. Hooking it to my bench, he said, "A friend of mine has women work-ing for him. He says the big bellows hurt their legs. This small one is better for you." I wasn't fooled. I knew the small torch would keep me off the big one where my slowness had sometimes queued up all three men.

With me fixed to my bench, the nine-by-twelve shop was as tightly fitted as a travel kit: two double work benches, a table, the buffing machine, torch, water and acid baths, a stump sprouting anvils, and right in the middle—its handles sticking out wickedly—the decrepit rolling mill where flat stock and wire were made. Two doors opened into the room, one from the hall and the other from the store where Jorge's bench and display case held in their stomachs to let the store front fold open and shut. We were crowded, but I was part of the kit.

In the big glass display case Jorge kept gold jewelry for sale, dusty leather watch bands, odds and ends of string, and all of the previous years' receipt books. The top shelf alone maintained a semblance of display. Sunk in the wall behind the big show case was another glass-fronted box about the size of a bathroom cabinet. It was full of scrap paper Jorge hoarded for sketches and estimates. Just before Christmas he had bought red construction paper and announced he was going to decorate. Business turned frantic and nothing happened.

The first part of February Jorge got sail up for the Christmas project. He emptied the glass cabinet of its nesting materials, papered the back, rigged up a wire, and hung or pinned my silver jewelry against the dark red. We all went out on the sidewalk to look at the effect. Pablo and Felipe wall-eyed the display, smoking and smacking each other while they wondered, I'm sure, what new and startling thing Jorge would do next. First a woman apprentice and now deco-rating. Jorge picked up the junk from the cabinet, looked distractedly for some place to put it, and stuffed it in with the receipt books on the bottom shelf of the big case.

•   •   •

In the fiber-board partition dividing the showroom from the work-room, Jorge had drilled numerous peep-holes at different heights. They weren't big enough to be noticed from out front but through them we could see who was tapping the counter or shuffling quietly, waiting. In the months I worked, I never figured out the criterion for who was kept waiting long, longer, longest. It didn't depend on money. Some starchy Oaxaca matrons waiting patiently for the *maestro* might have been dismayed had they known he was buffing a cross for an Indian who wouldn't be back until next week's market day.

Jorge muttered, "I'm coming," and went on buffing or showing me how to bend the shapes for a Spanish chain. Lacquered fingernails out front tattoed, I shook, and Jorge calmly whispered, "Now you do it." My bent wire took on tortured angles and Jorge sweetly showed me again, never understanding that North American sensibilities can't ignore people who want to do business.

The inside of the workshop was dark, the walls blackened by smoke and soot. Often the acid fumes made us cough until we opened the hall door. Then the draft extinguished my starter lamp and I couldn't solder until the air had cleared enough to shut the door. Most of our dirt and dinge came from the tiny coal-oil starter lamps and inefficiently burning gasoline torches. Delicate, barely visible smoke from our collective fires curled up to patina the walls eight hours daily, six days a week. We worked under sixty-watt overhead bulbs hanging like yellow fruit from the black reaches of the ceiling. We squinted and rubbed our eyes, stepped outside to stare at the building across the street or at the blue slit of the sky. The work was hard on everyone's eyes, but Jorge's nearsighted pair was the most shopworn.

•   •   •

One day Jorge decided to teach me Oaxaca-style lost wax casting. He built a charcoal fire in the studio's portable brazier. When the heat was steady and fierce we poked the tin-can flasks cozily under a red glowing blanket and watched as the first trickle of wax hit the coals.

After an hour, waxy smoke fuming out of the cans began to make us dizzy. Jorge set the brazier in the hall where a draft from the street door to our neighbor's patio made short work of the burn-out. Each time we checked the cans we pretended not to notice our neighbor and her maid standing in the pall on their balcony, staring angrily down at us. Until the last time.

When Jorge decided the flasks were ready to pour full of gold, he stood straight, swiveled his torso toward the balcony and bowed. "Good morning, *Señorita*, lovely morning, Your health is good?"

"What? Oh yes, thank you, *Don* Jorge," she replied, bowing and putting her hand to her hair. Jorge bowed again, hooked a translucent orange-hot can out of the fire on the tip of the caster and carried it with dignity into the *taller*.

In March Felipe announced that he was leaving for a truck-driving job with his cousin. When, unbelieving, I asked why, he said, "I don't want to go blind," and his eyes filled with tears. He drove truck for three weeks and then came back, grinning and twisting in embarrassed pleasure at our welcome.

Most days Jorge didn't have trouble but sometimes he hesitated before a medal to be engraved, took off his glasses, rubbed his eyes, and put the work away, sighing. He engraved all the sales for a large shop owned by *Señora* Cohen, from whom he also bought metal and stones. Sometimes she came over to chide him about an order. "*Don* Jorge, *Señor* Mortadela has been waiting for two weeks. He's in the shop now and he's angry. Maybe I better take it back to him, heh? I'll wait here while you do it." She was imperious, rich, and dependent on Jorge's superior craftsmanship to maintain her edge on the competition.

Jorge sighed again, fumbled in the litter for the bracelet, heated up the lacquer stick, and sharpened his tools. Then with Mrs. Cohen watching—her breath sucked in and held so as not to disturb the genius—Jorge commenced. He printed the name and date on a scrap of paper, studied it with his lips held between his teeth in speculative position; and digging the tool directly into the metal, he began the first serif of what would be a perfect italic inscription.

A single earring came in for duplication. For three months it sat on Pablo's bench with the files and clippers. One day Jorge picked it out and said, "I have to make this right away. The owner goes to Mexico City tomorrow and she wants to take it with her." With that, he began melting gold and when I left two hours later he was fitting the tricky hinge that distinguished this design from any other I had seen.

"That's such a handsome earring," I said, "why don't we make some more for the shop?"

"Oh, I don't think so for this shop," Jorge said. "This design is typical of Mexico City, not Oaxaca."

And that was the end of it, I knew.

•　　　•　　　•

As the spring progressed, I outfitted myself with the necessary hand tools for a small one-woman shop. I also splurged on a new version of Jorge's ancient wire-forming mill, and he made me an impossibly dangerous whirlygig caster like his. Jorge approved each purchase, aiming me away from the tacky, suggesting money-savers.

In July he began giving me formulas, whatever he thought of— ratio of sulphuric acid to water for cleaning metal; how to make sterling and solder from fine silver; how to make karat and colored golds from pure gold; what to use for gold plating. He was cutting me loose.

In late July he came in at 10:30 one morning. Unheard of hour. "I think you should buy some silver, maybe, so you can get started right away when you get home. I don't think suppliers can be trusted to hurry." This from one of Oaxaca's most unhurried men. "Come."

We walked to *Doña* Cohen, the dragon, the source.

"I knew you were back there in the shop," she said, pouncing on my hand. "I've known it all year. Well, did you learn anything?" Without pausing she turned to Jorge. "Is she any good at all?"

"She is good enough to do her own business. You see"—he leaned confidentially on the counter—"she was an artist to begin with, a *professora*! Yes!" he said, to her raised eyebrows. "She will make her own designs now, not mine."

Mrs. Cohen took that in easily, then turned to me. "Is he any good as a teacher?"

"He's mean," I said, rolling Little Eva eyes. "He beat me without stopping—and for nothing!"

She blinked, jaw askew. Then she began laughing. "Wonderful! And now you know everything. 'Beat me without stopping,' Oh, that's comical." While she measured lumps of fine silver she laughed and repeated "He's mean," shaking her head and snorting each time she looked at poor Jorge.

•   •   •

The last week in July I finished the sets of earrings and chains I had worked on for two months. On the last walk home from the shop, I envisioned transforming it. First I would buy a new milling machine, then a casting machine. But nothing could be done. Money was beside the point. Only so much meddling can be endured by proud people.

I settled on buying a graduated array of shiny dapping tools to re-place the worn set used every day in the *taller*. I would deliver it to Jorge's home as my family and I started on the way out of town toward the border. That way he would be unable to reciprocate with another gift he couldn't afford to buy.

The *maestro* met us at the door. "Oh, good. I was afraid I hadn't finished in time," he said, as though the meeting had been planned. "'Here!" He held out a full-sized soldering outfit complete with leather bellows, brass torch head, and the traditional two-liter peach jar for the gasoline. He had fabricated every part from odds and ends, from junk. It was fit for years of hard use and beautiful enough for a museum.

Jorge rubbed the leather bellows fondly, pinched the inner-tube top to show its toughness. "Here, look—see? I put a *centavo* for the valve handle so you might think of Oaxaca and the *taller* from time to time."

Through my tears I couldn't see the *centavo*. Jorge fumbled for a handkerchief, flipped it out, and just as I reached for it, blew his nose loudly into it and wiped his eyes. We shook hands five or six times, Mexican-fashion, stumbling to the car. "Say goodbye to Pablo and Felipe," I said, "I wish I could have buffed the graduation rings."

"When you come back to Oaxaca there will always be something to buff."

Both of us smiled. It had worked out all around. Once.

That report of a search was published in *The North American Review* for winter, 1976. Originally the story was much longer. When Joyce submitted it to the magazine, the editor replied that he would like to use it but had space for an article only two-thirds as long. At first, Joyce said, "I can't cut it that much. I'll forget the whole matter." But I prevailed upon her to take this opportunity, and together we cut it by a third. As usual, in such cutting some lively things were lost; but overall, I think the story became more attractive to most readers because it was short enough to entice them to begin it.

Usually when we "write up" an experience, we "think it through" more fully than before. The flow of other experiences (which we call *time*) has intervened and given us what we call "distance" upon the events. The act of putting words on paper makes us think of the order of events and their significance. I'm not saying that either *Friendly Fire* or "A Gift from Xipelotec" is an I-Search Paper, but both have a lot in common with such an enterprise. Neither C. D. B. Bryan nor Joyce was assigned the job of writing an experience, and I-Searchers in school are. But the professionals and the students both let their topics choose them. They were doing searching writing. The stories of truthtelling searchers are among the oldest and most basic creations of human beings. They involve curiosity and reflection. They teach the searchers and others who read the accounts not only about the activities centered on but about the ways of human perception, about objectivity and subjectivity and the difficulties of coming to firm judgments about complex matters.

In my estimation Pat Philbin's I-Search Paper is not as strong, full, or stylish as Joyce's story; but his experience was briefer, he had less time to reflect upon it, and he had had little experience in this kind of writing. In his first two paragraphs I wish he had told more about his feelings and reactions as a boy to listening to disc jockeys. I suspect he had had experiences and daydreams that helped prepare him— as Thoreau said—for the day when he realized he was interested enough in disc jockeys to spend the time and energy to find out whether he had the courage to go on the air himself. Joyce was thirty-nine years old when she wrote of her search, Pat eighteen or nineteen. I think his search was exciting and significant, to the members of his seminar as well as to him. The paper has spirit. It was not written by a drudge.

> *At a lyceum, not long since, I felt that the lecturer had chosen a theme too foreign to himself, and so failed to interest me as much as he might have done. He described things not in or near to his heart, but toward his extremities and superficies. There was, in this sense, no truly central or centralizing thought in the lecture. I would have had him deal with his privatest experience, as the poet does.*
>
> HENRY THOREAU

∞ **DOING TWELVE:** Write freely for twelve minutes on, into, or about the topic that has chosen you for your I-Search Paper. Let your mind go anywhere. This writing doesn't have to serve any direct purpose. It could be the first entry in a journal you keep for several years, as Thoreau did. It helped him understand his world.

Source. A support or underprop. Ob-
solete.
Source. The act of rising on the wing.
Obsolete.
Source. The rising of the sun. Obsolete.
Source. A spring; a fountain.
*Source. A work etc., supplying informa-
tion or evidence (esp. of an original
or primary character) as to some fact,
event, or series of these.*

OXFORD ENGLISH DICTIONARY

chapter 8
locating
sources

THE WORST PLACE you can begin your
search is at the card catalog in the library. Go to people. They're alive
this year, up to date—and the books listed in the file drawer cards
aren't. They can't be because librarians need several months to buy a
book and "catalog" it by entering it in the accession record and filing
a card for it. The titles of books seldom reveal which one is best for
your purposes. Some volumes may be too difficult for you to read
and some too simple for your needs.

If you speak with experts on your subject, you'll usually find that
they are also experts on the "literature of the field." They've made
themselves familiar with printed matter on your topic and can advise
you what to read for your special purposes. Over many years they have
been comparing one authority against another, while you have only a
few hours for that task. They know which authors are most knowledgeable, which are to be trusted. The books and magazines on the topic
say things, but can't be asked further questions.

Until you've written a true I-Search Paper and seen how the other
members of the class and persons in your community can help, you
won't believe what expertise is available in the town where you're

living. I'll always remember a student who wanted to write a research paper on the United States mediation effort in Indonesia in the late 1940s. When he turned in his rough draft of the paper several weeks before the final one was due, I noticed that all his sources were magazines and newspapers. He had talked to no one, and yet the president of the university, who had just returned from a mission as chief mediator of the conflict between the Indonesian people and the Dutch colonial government, lived about two and a half blocks from our classroom. That was in Chapel Hill, North Carolina. I said, "John, why don't you talk to President Graham? He knows more about your subject than anyone else in the world."

"I couldn't do that. I'm just a little freshman. He wouldn't have time for me."

John couldn't have been more wrong. Six months earlier I had wanted to discuss a civil rights matter with Frank Graham and had gone to his office to ask for an appointment. I remember his secretary saying, "When would you like to see him?"

"When would *I* like to see *him?*" I replied. "Isn't the question when does he have time to see me?"

"No," she said, "you name a time and if he's free I'll put you down for it." I did that and she said, "O.K., 3:00 tomorrow afternoon."

As I got to the door, I turned back. "Don't you have to have my name?"

"No," she said. "Dr. Frank is willing to meet with anyone who wants to see him. The man who cuts the lawn out there often comes in and chats with him."

It was ironic that John was so sure that this man wouldn't see him—one of the most approachable leaders in the country. Not every person you'd like to talk to about your topic is going to be that easy to see. You must find out. If you're looking for good sources, you'll probably be surprised to find they're available and accessible right in your neighborhood.

The I-Search project is designed to help you get first to living, speaking sources. After you have a topic, you'll be expected to come to class and say what it is. You announce your topic and tell briefly how it came to choose you. Then the teacher goes round the circle and calls on each member of the class to see first if he or she knows of anyone who's an expert on your topic or can tell you someone who is, and second, if people have read books, magazines, newspapers, or anything else that might help you or lead you to good sources. This takes time, and will not only help you but show everyone how much knowledge resides in any group of people. If the class or group is large, the teacher or director may have to break the group into smaller sections after one go-round in order to give people a chance to help fully. If that is done, a list of chosen topics can be posted somewhere so that people in another section can get in touch with searchers they know they can help.

What makes this Source Day, or Days, valuable is the willingness of group members to speak out. Perhaps what you know about a searcher's topic seems insignificant or trivial, but one thought may lead to another and soon together the group members may find helpful sources for the searcher. You're part of the other people's search. This is a collective session, one that will reveal to you the powers of a group, if you'll let it. The word *search* comes from the late Latin *circāre*, to go round, which comes from Latin *circus*, meaning circle. (That tells me why our circuses are composed of rings.) And you can see this derivation in a line *The Oxford English Dictionary* quotes from Sir John Maundeville's *Voiage and Travaile*, written about 1400: "I . . . have . . . cerched manye fulle straunge places." It seems appropriate that on Source Day a circle of people should be circling your topic so that you can cerche it better. If you help others, they'll feel like helping you. Be a spring, a fountain of information and tips, a support or underprop. Help others' projects rise on the wing.

In my most recent I-Search class, Mary Palenick announced she was going to write a paper entitled "Is West Point for Me?" A couple of days later I noticed in the local paper the names and pictures of three young people nominated for acceptance to West Point. One was a high school girl I'll call Melanie Schmidt. I told Mary about Melanie but she wrote her paper without consulting the girl. I asked her why.

"I called the newspaper and they gave me Melanie's address," she said, "but not her phone number. Her name wasn't listed in the telephone book nor was a number listed under her father's name."

"If you had her address, why didn't you go to her home?"

"I never thought of doing that," she said.

These stories about John and Mary show how some of us let the notion of authority frighten us. We forget that we're all authorities on something, if only our own lives and needs. If we set out to learn on our own something that counts for us as Benjamin Franklin or the novelist Jack London did, instead of waiting for a teacher to hand us a list of books, we can do the job. We were all born detectives. At the age of six months when we encountered unfamiliar objects we knew how to sniff and chew on them.

Mary Palenick was so disappointed with herself for not talking to Melanie Schmidt that she chose to do her second I-Search Paper on the same topic as her first and expand it. Here's some of what she wrote in that paper:

> I called the paper, they gave me Melanie's address, but not her phone number. Her name wasn't listed in the telephone book, nor was a number listed under Pete Brannam [Names have been changed in this paper], her father. There wasn't much to go on, so in desperation I called another Brannam on Melanie's street to ask if they knew her. They did, even though they are not related. I gave her a call and we set up an appointment to meet. She advised me to call Will Clymer, another nominee, and also Mr. Clyde, her counselor-recruiter.
>
> Will was on campus the day I called, so we got together at Gaspare's tavern. I was surprised when he ordered a Sprite, he looked much older than 17. He had played football for several years, and if he is any indication of the men at West Point, wow! they sure are tough.
>
> Will said that he is really looking forward to entering this fall. The structure and routine are a prime incentive for him joining West Point. He has been taking extra math and science courses for what he terms the hardest part of the academy life—the studying. He isn't worried about the harassment at all. After eight years of football coaches breathing down his back, he says he is ready for a tough, gruesome [grueling?] training program, and I think he can handle it. . . .
>
> My interview with Melanie was on the same day as the one with Will Clymer. I took a taxi to her house that evening.
>
> Melanie was nothing like the girl I envisioned—a huge woman capable of lifting a tank—rather she was petite, blonde with dark circles under her eyes. No outstanding muscles were to be seen, instead she has a very thin frame.
>
> Her story was also far from what I expected. Instead of a highly competitive woman with a desire to triumph over men, I found a sensitive, mature person.
>
> Melanie never considered the military as a child. She was raised by very strict parents, who kept her secluded from the male-oriented world—no hiking, baseball, or football. She was even forced to drop out of physical education classes.
>
> Then, she says, she met Annie Sorm, a tomboy with a great mind who *always* did her own thing, whatever the

consequences. Annie is currently in West Point and really loves it.

Melanie became interested in the military life in her freshman year of high school. She investigated at first the Coast Guard and then West Point because as she puts it, "I always feel cheated if I go second best, even buying tennis shoes and cords."

She had many conflicts with her interest at home. Her parents were set against it. All her mail from West Point was tossed out. She says that she doesn't wish to condemn her true parents, but just says that her plans and ideas in life are not their plans and ideas.

Finally Melanie moved into a foster home where she is comfortable and can train for her career. Three miles a day, handball, running five circuits of stairs a day, and swimming are on her list of exercises and activities.

She says that her main reason for wanting to be an army cadet is an identity search, a need for stability and structure in school and life in general. I asked her whether it would bother her to be structured to the extent the academy goes. She felt that while the academy strives to mold your thinking, they are trying to train you to think right, but let it be your own thinking. "You are educated in your own right, rather than with the regurgitated mess high school leaves you with."

Melanie finds out if she is accepted at the end of May. She has already turned down chances for scholarships at State, Western, and Albion, and is set for West Point. She is looking forward to life as a Plebe and isn't really worried about the harassment. She doesn't feel that it's enough to make one fall apart. The seniors, she told me, are not required to harass the underclassmen. It's their choice, but if they don't, someone else will. It's a "do extras" process so the cadets can learn more.

As I left her house, she handed me some literature a postgraduate picked up for her. *Listen to West Point,* one of the pamphlets, is excellent. It has a lot of candid material. The pamphlet entitled *Information for Women Candidates* is also very good. It has several pictures of women working out along with men, and some of the opinions the women have about West Point. A few good ones are, "I'm not at West Point to prove a point, I'm here because West Point

is a school that offers what I want," [2] and "I love it here, it's
so different and I am always busy, and I feel secure. There
are so many people around and I feel like we're all a team—
I just feel better than I've ever felt in my life." [3]

Personally, I salute Melanie. She is an exceptional person, but I am not sure I can join the ranks of women like
her. I would have to start now by setting up a rigorous training program and enroll in more science and engineering-
related courses. There are also a few books I would like to
read on the subject, like *The Military Academy as an As-
similating Institution,* written by Sanford Dornbush, once
a West Point cadet.[4] My brother used to read me passages
from another book written very negatively about the academy that I would like to find.

Academy life will be tough to prepare for and endure,
but somehow the advantages outweigh the disadvantages.
The cadets look so sharp marching in formation with their
fresh, crisp, handsome uniforms. I would like so much to
join them. It would be a great challenge, one with many re-
wards—a chance to travel, develop leadership, and become
a more self-disciplined person.

Now the first thing I must do is to write to my congress-
man for a preliminary application, fill it out, then . . . .

And so, right there in the city where Mary attended college was a
young woman who had already gone through some of the steps that
Mary would have to go through to get to West Point. The only better
source would have been a woman who had already spent some time
at the Point as a cadet. And if possible, a number of such women.

Mary was wisely concerned about Melanie's character—was she interested in going to a formerly all-male school simply for the glamor
of it? Was she attracted to the Point out of weakness or strength? In
asking these questions Mary was acting naturally, putting herself up
against Melanie and testing herself as a possible candidate. Could she
trust Melanie's opinion of the West Point experience for women? To
answer that question she had to judge not only the opinion but the
person who held it. And so Mary thought a lot about Melanie's character. There is no more basic question in carrying out a search: can
I trust my sources? And if two sources disagree, which should I believe?

In any town or city experts or authorities are at work. The chances
are high that one or more of them can help you answer your questions. Think of students or other people you already know as possible
sources. You can talk to them easily. And teachers, who are profes-

sionals. They've read a lot and may be up on the latest work in their field. And experts outside school in the community. Don't forget that the other members of your class or group make up a resource pool. When they together consider your search, what one suggests may energize another's memory, and soon suggestions will come in from all sides.

Because school customarily expects you to leave your personal life outside the classroom door, you're apt to think too small when you begin a search. Keep your expectations high. Remember John investigating the mediation in Indonesia. He neglected to seek out the leading expert in the world, who lived just down the street. One of my students wanted to find out more about the then new sport of hang gliding. He could find only one book in the university library on it and that book was out, but he kept asking everyone he met for printed material. Eventually he came upon a student whose former roommate had left behind a couple of magazines on gliding, and he bought them from him for a dollar. Most remarkable among his discoveries was that in the sociology department of his university worked Dr. Richard MacDonald, who was listed as director of Studies of High Risk Life Styles. Here's what Scott Reed wrote in his I-Search Paper about meeting Dr. MacDonald:

> I thought if anyone could help me understand why someone would want to jump off a mountain while harnessed to an oversized kite, he could. When I arrived at his office in Sangren Hall, I was really surprised to see that the door was open and lights were on. I had heard that this particular professor was a very busy man, and that to find him available on the first try could be compared to hitting a hole in one the first time golfing.
>
> For the initial moment after I entered his office, I thought that the figure at the desk was a student. "Excuse me," I stammered, "are you Dr. MacDonald?"
>
> "No other than," he replied, as he swung his chair around to face me.
>
> My question of doubt was understandable when you consider I've always thought of college instructors as being dignified, upper middle-class, gray-bearded gentlemen wearing herringbone plaid suits; and now here is this "Doctor" wearing old faded jeans, a red flannel shirt with rolled up sleeves and worn-out Converse tennis shoes. His informal, outgoing style made me feel like I was in his living room rather than in his business office.

"Have a chair, and tell me what I can do for you today,"
he said in a raspy voice. I sat down in a chair by the side
wall and explained that I needed some information on hang
gliding. "Ya, I us'ta have a friend who did a lot of hang
gliding," he explained, "'till one day he ran into the side
of a mountain and killed himself.'

He explained that there's not all that much that goes into
gliding other than riding on a thermal of hot air. "Gliding
appeals to people on the same level as mountain climbing
or downhill skiing, or white water canoeing. People like it
because of the excitement and adventure." [1] It's just like
Henry de Motherlant (a French writer) said, "If your life
ever bores you, risk it." [2]

MacDonald said . . . "People have abandoned the specta-
tor role to pursue the active mastery and natural highs to
be found elsewhere."

Unfortunately, just at that time MacDonald noticed that
he was late for class; but before he left, he gave me a paper
he had written entitled *Danger and the Pursuit of Pleasure,*
which he said should really be useful to me. I thanked him
for his help and was reminded that if I were ever to try
hang gliding for myself, I should remember it was he who
first told me that hang gliding is the most dangerous sport
in the world. . . .

Scott Reed neglected to say in his I-Search Paper how he had found
that Dr. MacDonald was an authority on the motivation and consequences involved in such high-risk sports as hang gliding. But he
found him, and on the very campus that Scott walked every day. Dr.
MacDonald handed Scott his latest writing on the subject, before it
was put into magazine or book form. When you meet authorities in
person, you encounter their latest thinking and can judge its validity
partly by estimating their character as you observe it.

Scott and John in Chapel Hill both feared that the expert they
wanted to interview would be too busy to talk to them. A reasonable
worry. Put yourself in the place of the authority you're approaching.
I remember *not* doing that in the year after my graduation from college. I decided to visit several outstanding printers in the East and ask
them about a career in typography, the craft of choosing and arranging type for the printed page. I had spent a whole summer on
my own studying the history of printing types; I was consumed by
the subject, in love with type styles. In the back of my mind was the
hope that if I showed my interest in printing, one of the great typog-

raphers that I interviewed might offer me a job. That I possessed limited knowledge about types and no experience were facts I chose to bury.

I wrote ahead and made appointments—the first one with the director of the Yale University Press. When I asked a secretary if I could see him, she phoned, and out of his glassed office came the director, a sheaf of papers in hand.

"You wanted to see me?"

"Yes, but if you're busy—"

"I'm always busy, but here. Sit down. What did you want?"

I was so embarrassed about asking him if he was busy that I could hardly talk. It was a short interview. I didn't know exactly what I wanted to ask him, and so he couldn't focus his mind on my needs.

Think about interviewing persons expert on your topic. What would be the best way to approach them? Through another person who knows them? Directly, by telephone or letter? Find out what their lives are like. When would they be most likely to have time and inclination to talk to you? Do you need an introduction of some sort from others?

If you're worried about stealing experts' time, you might begin by asking them where you could look for more information and advice about your topic. What's the best book or magazine article they know? Not—what are *all* the works they've read on the subject. Then if they don't want to talk at length or haven't time, they can refer you to another source or expert.

As you search, think of yourself as Sherlock Holmes rather than a student following the requirements of researching laid out in a composition handbook. Use the phone book, the white and yellow pages. Use the atlas of maps and indexes of cities, the city directory, maps of the city, directories posted in office corridors. Find what you can on your own. Come to an interview prepared to ask questions that will help you. Don't ask the leading authority in the world on your subject how to get to the bathroom, unless she's an architect and you're both interested in the layout of office buildings.

∞ **DOING THIRTEEN:** Come to Source Day with your topic for the I-Search Paper clearly in mind so you'll get the maximum help from the others and won't waste your time.

chapter 9
tell it
as story

THE MOST FUNDAMENTAL MODE of human communication is telling stories. When Father comes home and Mother asks, "How did your day go?" he doesn't say, "Well, the salient characteristic of my day was frustration. I was frustrated with my fellow workers, with my employer, and with our customers," but rather, "It was rotten. First I ran into Harry and Ben, who said the pump had broken down. We went out into the plant, and there the damned pump was, spitting steam from a busted valve, and clumping. So I said to Harry—you know he's the one who always has an excuse—'What happened?' and he said, 'John, the pressure was left on high last night by someone . . .'"

If Mother's been out working and comes home to Dad, who's cooking dinner, she tells him the same kind of story. If she's been home all day, she says, "It was O.K. Tim fell down and tore a hole in his new pants, the expensive ones we just bought last week, and then he . . ."

When I was in college in the 1930s and in graduate schools in the 1940s and 1950s, my professors were influenced by a philosophy which said that nothing human beings did was "natural"; all was acquired from or determined by the social and physical environment. And the acquiring we students would do would take place in their classrooms, under their direction, where we would learn from the wisest thinkers, whom the professors would introduce us to.

Discoveries were being made in anthropology and sociology that supported this belief, but it was oversimplified and needed to be put on the Moebius Strip so that people could be seen as creatures both learned and learning. Students may be beginners in writing, engineering, or mathematics, but they're not beginners as human beings. For example, as you've seen in this book, they come to school already language-using creatures. Built into their nervous systems and/or brains are language circuits they've used thousands of times before arriving in the classroom. They're accustomed to communicating with words, not like my Siamese cat, who raises her paw tentatively toward me to say she wants to be friendly and sit in my lap, or yammers when she wants food at her dinner time. They do something she can't do—tell little stories to each other. The stories provide listeners with things they need to know or are delighted by. And, I must say, things they don't need to know or are bored by.

Contrary to common belief, we often think by speaking or writing. "Think about what you're going to say," is sometimes good advice, but often we talk and write our way into understanding, especially when we tell a story of human action: relating how and where it happened often shows us why, and with what significance.

> *What Marcia would have expressed orally at the time . . . was different from what she later developed on the page. Reflection and discovery through several drafts led to depths of perception not possible to reach through immediate conversation.*
>
> DONALD H. GRAVES

For the listener or reader, story often reveals where the teller's attitudes and judgments came from. To abstract or pull out of a complex human event a few conclusions often produces nothing more than resistance and animosity among listeners or readers because they haven't shared the experiences which gave rise to them. That's why so many lectures and textbooks are dry—they lack the blood, muscle, rain, and dust of stories, the sound of individual people speaking, that life-giving, dramatic resource of the storyteller.

When you were five and your mother asked why you were crying, you said, "Rickie called me a fatty, so I hit him, and then my nose began to bleed . . ." And it's *story*, this time perhaps missing a few crucial happenings, but the context is suggested, and will be filled out by Mother asking, "So Rickie called you Fatty. What did you call him?" And the story unfolds and the facts come forward, as they usually do in a court of law. Situation, motivations, consequences.

During the industrial and scientific revolutions of the last several centuries, in an effort to become more objective, physical and social scientists tried to become more detached from what they were studying. They invented impersonal means of measuring materials. They isolated rats in a cage and reduced the number of what they called "variables" between two individuals or groups so they could study one aspect of behavior. For example, two groups of rats were put in the same frustrating situation, three doors between them and food, and only one that they could push open. Then one group was denied food altogether so the scientists could see what effect starvation would have upon their ability to figure out how to get to the food. Often such studies were described in numbers—of heartbeat rate, of attempts to open doors, etc. Story was not a convenient mode of communicating such information; so it was largely abandoned in scientific reporting, except by a few researchers who used the case-history method.

For the most part exposition became the accepted form of communication in the scholarly world. It ordinarily takes up less time and space than story, but often at the sacrifice of context, which supplies so much meaning. Isolating one element of an event or situation helped scientists concentrate on it without being distracted; but the greatest discoveries come to human beings working on the Moebius Strip, both detached and attached. Observers who scorn story as a means of reporting may be preventing themselves from understanding in context the things they're observing, and reducing the chance that their readers or listeners will see what is going on.

The I-Search project asks you to scratch a genuine itch until you've quieted it. You're invited to go on an adventure, an odyssey that eventually brings you home. And then to tell the story of the trip, as Homer's hero did. In this way you'll enable your readers to judge the validity of your searching and finding. They'll know your predilections and purposes and be able better to judge the quality of your observations.

A natural way to begin an I-Search Paper is to tell readers *What I Knew* (or *Didn't Know*) and *What I Wanted to Know*—in story form. You don't have to write an essay or a pretentious declaration, just tell the story of how you got into the search. You can write an opening and present it to a group of searchers for their reactions before you begin thorough searching on your own. Here's such an opening:

> A few weeks ago a friend from Chicago Heights, Myles, called me to talk about business. Myles's business, customizing cars, was going slow, which made his bankroll low and in need of some quick cash. Myles recalled my interest in buying his motorcycle and asked, "What's the best offer you'll give me for the Norton?"

His Norton Commando was the smoothest riding and best performing street bike I ever rode when it was new, so I gave him an offer and got a Norton.

Last spring Myles rebuilt the suspension, replaced the tires, and put an oversize sprocket on the bike. After getting it together and trying it out, Myles said, "You won't believe how fast it's running." Riding a rebuilt bike makes me feel like a test pilot looking for trouble points. I rode around getting used to it before testing for unbelievable speed. The bike rode tight like when it was new, but it wasn't, just rebuilt. Cruising down a country road I came to an intersection with a four lane highway. The highway looked as good a place as any to check out the acceleration. Moving onto the highway, I gripped the handlebars tight, ready for a hundred mph wind. Rolling the throttle open started a rocket-like ride. The front wheel lifted off the pavement as first gear wound up. Shifting to second forced me back farther on the seat. My eyes teared from the wind. The dashed white line blurred into a streak. Third pulled smooth and strong up to 70, 75 going for 80 mph. The smooth ride ended. The handlebars started to shake back and forth fast, with increasing frequency. I gripped the bars tighter for fear of my hand being thrown off. Pulling back on both bars didn't stop the shake. All I wanted was to stop. "Get me off." Before ceasing my grip on the throttle, I was traveling 85–90 mph, too fast for conditions. The shake slowed down as the bike did and stopped around 60 mph. At a complete stop I couldn't stop shaking for a while. I checked the tires for a flat, the wheels to see if they were loose, but nothing was wrong that I could see. I knew the bike had a problem and told Myles 'cause it was his, not mine. He never found a cause for the trouble before I bought the bike, so searching for the cause is my problem now.

Wayne Jaedtke's opening to his I-Search Paper is a little story. By saying that this was "the best performing street bike I ever rode," he established that he'd had experience with motorcycles. And the way he referred to parts of the bike and how he had handled it on the test ride—without making the point explicitly—further suggests that Wayne knows what he's talking about. In a simple, natural way, Wayne has told the reader what he knew about motorcycles and what he wanted to know about the one he had bought. Because he told the story of his test ride without first announcing its outcome, he

created suspense in the reader and fulfilled what the British critic
E. M. Forster said was the first requirement of a good novel—it makes
you want to turn the page.

Here's another opening to an I-Search paper:

What I Know

> My mother and step-father went on a trip to Hawaii for
> their honeymoon eight years ago. I've wanted to take a trip
> to Hawaii since they got back.

What I Want to Know

> I want to find out how much money it would cost to go to
> Hawaii for two weeks. How much it would cost to fly there,
> how much for sight-seeing, hotels, food, etc.

Nothing in that I-Search Paper opening about Hawaii suggests there
was an itch to find out something. When I first read it I suspected
that the writer hadn't let a good topic come to her. She might have
been slightly interested in Hawaii, I thought, but felt no consuming
need to travel there. Note that her opening is not told as a story.
When we have a strong itch, we usually feel compelled to tell others
how we got it—in strong form—"You should've seen the size of that
striped yellowjacket! I heard it banging at the inside of the window
and forgot it. Remembered only when I put the triangular pillow behind me and leaned backward . . ." First the bite, then the itch and
the need for scratching.

Here's the rest of the paper on Hawaii that followed that opening:

> I can remember the excitement I felt when my parents
> told me where they were going. At that time I couldn't un-
> derstand why they wouldn't take a young daughter along!
> They quickly set me straight on that!
>
> My father is a camera nut and he took hundreds of beau-
> tiful slides and movies. Mom said that she thought he was
> interested in the scenery more than he was her. They both
> agreed that it was the prettiest place they had ever been to.
>
> They loved Hawaii so much that plans were started for
> the whole family to fly out that summer. I was really ex-
> cited and couldn't wait for school to end.
>
> One thing Mom and Dad didn't plan was the unexpected
> news from the "stork" that a baby was coming in the near
> future!
>
> With the added expense of a new arrival to our family
> we had to cancel our plans.

The years have gone by and we still haven't gone, but a dream remains in my mind to visit the islands that my parents loved so much.

I went to a Travel Agency a few weeks ago and talked to Miss Gordon. She gave me a colorful brochure on Hawaii and said that all the information I'd need would be inside. I quickly left and returned home itching to look inside. I read through the booklet and was really surprised at all the different tours that were inside.

It was hard to decide on the tour that was right for me. The prices range from $1,170.00 to $354.00 per person. Depending on the type of tour you'd like to take and how many days you wish to stay. I feel if you want to do something which is important to you then you may as well do it right. I chose the second most expensive tour because of the things it had to offer. I want to stay for two weeks and I'd like to visit more than one island. I thought that this tour sounded the best.

The tour is as follows:

1st Day: Honolulu, 4 nights
2nd Day: Luau, a Hawaiian Village Luau
3rd Day: Pearl Harbor Cruise
4th Day: City tour
5th Day: Fly to the Island of Kauai for 3 nights.
6th Day: Helicopter Ride
7th Day: Day of leisure
8th Day: Fly to Maui for 3 nights
9th and 10th Day: Days of leisure
11th Day: Fly to Hilo
12th Day: Kona
13th Day: Cruise
14th Day: Day of leisure
15th Day: Day of departure
16th Day: Back home

This tour features Hilton Hawaiian Hotels: 4 nights Honolulu; 3 nights Maui; 1 night Hilo; 3 nights Kona, Lei Greeting; Introductory Breakfast; 3 Dinner shows, including Hawaiian Village Luau; 26 Meals; 10 sightseeing trips. Cost of tour: $1,075.00.

I live near North Bend, Illinois, so I would fly out of the North Bend Airport. This is not included in the cost of the tour so I have to add $422.04. I will also add $65.00 to cover

the cost of flying from one island to the other. The total
cost of the trip will be $1,562.04. I'll also need spending
money so I rounded the figure to approximately $2,000.00!

That is an awful lot of money but to me it would be
worth it. Hawaii here I come? I hope so, but I think I'll
wait for awhile.

Brochure: Cartan Hawaii 1977
Discussion with My Parents, Mr. and Mrs. Kevin Nergard
[fictitious name]

When the author presented that opening to the paper, the seminar
members said it didn't do the job. They couldn't see anything in
Hawaii or in the writer's experience that was pushing her to make
such an expensive trip. Why did she want to go? Her original hope,
disappointed because of the arrival of a baby, was understandable because she was then about ten years old. But what now, when she was
a freshman in college, made her want to go to Hawaii? Did her father's
slide show create an irresistible desire to go surfing? Did the moun-
tains mesmerize her? Which memories recounted by her parents
caught her? She said she was *"really* excited" and *really* surprised"
but didn't demonstrate how she and Hawaii might meet each other
on a Moebius Strip.

When the writer presented her final version of this paper, she had
revised the opening, but it was still unconvincing. Perhaps she never
had allowed her "I" to get into the search. Maybe she went to
a travel bureau, grabbed a brochure, and wrote down verbatim some
details and schedules. Apparently she didn't read up on any of her
special interests in Hawaii, if she had any. Or talk to the dozens of
people at her university who knew Hawaii, some of whom I know had
lived there for a number of years.

In public and university libraries available to this writer resided
dozens of books that could tell her what she would find on Kauai or
Hilo or Kona, the islands on the tour she said "sounded best." A person hooked on Hawaii would naturally tell us what looked good to
her beyond twenty-six meals and ten sightseeing trips. In this paper
we never learn the "I's" interests, so we can't judge her assertions
about Hawaii.

When I say that writing an I-Search Paper or an opening to one in
story form is a natural human act, I don't mean that a person with a
good search topic can't goof up and write unnaturally. I mean simply
that it's possible for you to allow yourself to approach the act naturally, to think consciously about where the journey took you but to
let yourself tell the story. Don't plan a lecture to your readers. Take

them on a journey. Here's the opening to a paper that becomes fascinating once the writer begins telling his adventures as a story. But his opening is hard to follow and not as enticing as it could be—because it's not in story form.

What I Know

As the old saying goes, "All a person ever has to do is die and pay taxes." When a person dies, if he leaves family or friends alive it generally follows that they'll pay their last respects by giving him a funeral. A funeral can end up being a financial burden on those left behind, which only adds to the pain they're being put through.

What I Want to Find Out

I'm mainly interested in looking at the different choices a person has in being buried. I'd like to focus mainly on the economic alternatives. There are some other things I'd like to explore. I've been to two funerals in my life. Both were the type where you plop them in a box, say a few nice words, put them in the ground, and then go party. I know there are other choices like cremation or being put in a mausoleum. I'd like to see why other people take these choices.

I'd also like to find out what people who believe in reincarnation and those who believe in regeneration through the earth believe should be done with the body after it dies. My own feeling on religion leans toward atheist and so the religious aspect of the funeral wouldn't matter to me, but perhaps one of these other types would follow my own thoughts on death. One that I'm thinking of in particular is regeneration through the earth. I'll have to do some searching and see what I can find.

From that opening I couldn't tell what led the writer to the topic. He speaks of a funeral being "a financial burden." Maybe someone he knows suffered under that burden, but he doesn't tell us. Where did he first learn about "regeneration through the earth"? Couldn't he tell us a little story about one of the funerals that apparently disappointed him? From reading a number of his papers in a seminar, I know he's a perceptive observer—and I think you'll agree when you read the following excerpt from his paper—but his opening was lacking. He could have made it powerful by simply telling us in story form how he came to be so interested in burial ceremonies that he wanted to write about them. Here's more of his paper:

Mr. R., the minister, handed me *The Cokesbury Funeral Manual* printed in 1933. He told me he has used this manual since he was first ordained. He just recently bought a new one, *The Cokesbury Funeral Manual* printed in 1973. He told me there was little difference in them; it was just that his old one was getting too worn out.

Mr. R. sat down and drew an outline of how he writes out his funerals. He starts out with introductory Scripture sentences. The manual had one chapter full of these. They're about a page long. They deal mostly on death and forgiveness of sins. The next step is to give the obituary. Here he tells of a person's life, their marriage, kids, and accomplishments in life. The obituary is followed by reading of Scripture lessons. These too are found in the manual. After the Scripture lessons, Mr. R. gives a message in which he tries to do three things. H tries to pay whatever tribute he can to the deceased. Often this is harder than it seems. He told me that many times he's found a person that lives such a plain life you just can't find anything to say about him. The second thing he tries to do is give comfort to the bereaved. He uses the manual for this too. It has a chapter called "Comforting Passages." The third thing he does in the message is try to say something beneficial for the living: try to call attention to the seriousness of life and death. Here a minister has to be careful not to be too condemning. It's not the purpose to make the people at the funeral squirm. The message is followed by prayer and benediction. The whole ceremony lasts around 45 minutes.

During his explaining Mr. R. kept trying to show me how to make each funeral unique and interesting. He cautioned on not using the same Scriptures over and over because you're performing funerals in the same congregation or town. Mr. R. wasn't too convincing. He rattled off this outline very quick. While doing it, he would write down particular Scriptures from memory, saying, "This one is really good" or "I've often used this one." His manual was full of little stars and underlining. Beside a lot of Scriptures he wrote "very good" or "remember." The impression I got was that his funerals were the same structure with different Scriptures he could plug in and out. He tended to think this made them unique. I didn't. . . .

John Dirkman, who wrote that I-Search Paper, made his case against commercialized funerals in detail, delivering his evidence in deadpan fashion, much as Charles Dickens made fun of such insincere businessmen in his novels. Among seminar writers in my experience, John was one of the few who had sharp perceptions to report but expressed them in unnatural, heavy sentences. Yet I always learned from reading his writing.

But the opening to John's I-Search paper doesn't project his independent mind, his respect for his own feelings, and his determination to place them on the Moebius Strip along with the established ways of society. He carried out a Homeric or Dickensian search, yet opened his paper weakly. But how easy and natural it is to open the story of a search with the story of the roots of that search! More and more professional writers who aren't novelists or short story writers are beginning their books or articles in this way. I think of the book on the Attica Prison rebellion in New York written by Tom Wicker of *The New York Times* (New York, Quadrangle, 1975). In his review of it in *The Times* (March 6, 1975) Christopher Lehmann-Haupt calls it "History as a novel," and says:

> When called away from a sumptuous lunch in Washington by the news that he has been designated an observer by the Attica inmates, Wicker accepts the assignment on nothing more than a newsman's instinct to go where the action is. But as his involvement deepens—as he realizes he may be in over his head and sights as the island toward which he will swim, the objective that nobody [in the prison where the inmates are holding officials hostage] will get killed—he probes further and further into the personal history that brought him to Attica.

The opening to your I-Search Paper can show you probing "further and further into the personal history that brought" you to begin that search. Scientists, as well as news reporters, are increasingly using the I-Search form to report their work. Here's an article from the quarterly magazine *Terra* published by the Natural History Museum of Los Angeles County (fall, 1978): Note the opening of this We-Search Article: it perfectly answers the question, "How did we get into this quest?"

TYRANNOSAURUS REX AND THE AMATEURS

Mary Odano

How a plumber, some housewives, and a handful of high school students hunted down and restored the largest Tyrannosaurus skull ever found.

"Tyrannosaurus rex—why don't we have a specimen of Tyrannosaurus rex?"

I must admit my imagination was fired that day in 1965, when I
heard Mr. William Sesnon, a member of the Board of Governors of
our museum, ask that question of Dr. Reid Macdonald, our Senior
Curator of Vertebrate Paleontology.

Dr. Macdonald quickly replied that while *Tyrannosaurus rex* was
probably the most famous of the dinosaurs, and any small boy or girl
could tell you all about him, he was also one of the rarest.

The first and second specimens were both found around the turn
of the century by Barnum Brown and his party from the American
Museum of Natural History. They were looking for fossils in the Hell
Creek area of Montana when they came across this great carnivorous
beast. The second of the two finds was the most complete skull and
skeleton ever uncovered to date. Today, it is a prime attraction at the
Museum in New York City. Since then, other remains had been
found, but at best they were scattered, miscellaneous bones. In all,
there were in 1965 fewer than a dozen recorded specimens.

"Your chances of finding anything like the American Museum
skeleton are about as good as winning a million at Las Vegas, Mr.
Sesnon. Are you willing to gamble?"

Mr. Sesnon was not anxious to wager huge sums on such a remote
possibility, but he did agree to provide enough money to send a field
party to Montana for three summers. So preparations for the hunt
began at once.

The best fossil prospector known to the museum was Harley Gar-
bani of San Jacinto, California. Harley was a plumber by trade, but
escaped to the surrounding countryside as often as he could to in-
dulge himself in his favorite hobby, fossil collecting. For many years
he had supplied the museum with fossils from many localities.

When he heard of the proposed three-year search for *T. rex*, Harley
was easily persuaded to head the expedition. The party that would
accompany him included his wife Vi, their daughter Charlotte, and
Steve Wright, a member of the High School Workshop at our museum.
Thus, every member of this important expedition was an amateur—
but they were amateurs animated by a great enthusiasm for paleontology, and possessing a truly professional attitude about their work.

Harley was more than eager to get started, but there was one problem. His past discoveries had been almost exclusively mammals—
horses, camels, sloths, dire wolves, and mammoths. What, he wondered,
did the bones of *T. rex* look like? The museum had no collection that
could show him their size and shape, so the best we could do was find
books containing illustrations of the bones and duplicate them for

Harley to take to the field—not the ideal solution, but the only one we had.

The logical place for Harley to prospect was the same area in Montana where Brown had made his finds almost seventy years before. For two years, Harley scoured the cattle range badlands of Garfield County. He found many fascinating creatures—the skull cap of *Pachycephalosaurus* (a thick-skulled herbivorous dinosaur), two huge adult duckbill dinosaurs and one juvenile, some *Triceratops* skulls, assorted crocodiles and turtles, Cretaceous mammals with mouse-size jaws and teeth—but no *T. rex*.

From the beginning, the inside joke in the party was that *T. rex* would not be found until the last week of the third summer that Mr. Sesnon had agreed to finance. But during the third summer, as this possibility became nearly a reality, anxiety began to grow. What if *T. rex* didn't show at all? Although it was true that the dinosaur specimens found to date had more than made the trip worthwhile, the disappointment of not finding the big prize would have been great.

Harley covered most of Garfield County following leads from the local ranchers. He spent Saturday nights in the small town bars of Jordan, the county seat, talking to curious ranchers who wanted to be helpful. They told Harley about bones they'd seen on their ranches, and almost every sighting was followed up. Harley made many friends for himself and for the museum among these lonely, hardy people, with his friendly banter and his constant respect for their property . . . but no *T. rex*.

Meantime, a team of boys from the Museum High School Workshop had joined the field party. They labored to uncover the bones already found· by Harley and ship them to the museum while he continued to prospect for the big one. From time to time, hope was fanned by the discovery of an isolated tooth. But it was beginning to look as though *T. rex* himself was simply not going to turn up.

Then, on a hot afternoon in late August, 1968, Harley saw a toe bone—a big toe bone—protruding from the wall of a gully. It might just be big enough, he thought, to be a toe from the giant foot of *Tyrannosaurus*.

Harley carefully scraped away the surface of the ground for several feet around, digging down into the soil inch by inch. More and more bones began to appear. A huge vertebra, more toe bones, ribs, and mudholes with strange pieces of broken bone—all seemed to be leading into the gully wall.

Harley was not entirely certain he had scored. But, filled with excitement, he hastened fifteen miles to town over the rough dirt roads to call Macdonald in Los Angeles. Normally, a trip to town was made once a week to restock food, gas, and other supplies—but Harley was not about to wait. From the description of the bones that Harley gave, Macdonald agreed that it sounded like *T. rex,* and the tension and excitement began to grow among the staff members at the museum.

The field party, now consisting of Mike Grey, Sue Haley, and Steven Odano, were beside themselves with joy. They had been performing the not-too-glorious, back-breaking job of collecting the previous finds, and this new find was sure to mean more of the same. But this one was different, and everyone went to work with a will.

Each bone or group of bones had to be isolated on pedestals of dirt or clay shale by digging around and under them while they still lay undisturbed in the ground. Once each pedestal was completed, the bone was covered with several layers of wet newspaper. Then plaster of paris was mixed in large pails, and strips of burlap were saturated with it. These strips were applied in layers to the pedestal and the newspaper-covered bone. Once the plaster was dry and hard, the pedestal was cut, the block turned over, and the other side plastered. Thus the bone would be well-protected against damage during the long trip home to Los Angeles. Fragments of bones and bones pulled out of the mud-holes were put in bags and given numbers. The numbers were then written on a diagram of the dig, showing where each of the fragments had been found. All activity meaningful to the history of the dig was entered in a log book.

The bones found thus far indicated that this was indeed a huge carnivorous reptile. But no parts of a skull had been found, and so it was difficult to make a positive identification. The bone bed led back into the gully wall, and to remove the hard overlying material by hand would take more time than there was—a chill in the air was already signalling the imminent arrival of winter. The son of the ranch owner agreed to bring in a bulldozer, which would save the diggers many days of back-breaking work. Afterwards, the boys could excavate with small tools and paint brushes.

Several days later a huge jaw came to view. This was a day of celebration—but the party's joy was quickly quenched by the first snow flurries of September. The jaw was hastily excavated. The ground containing the rest of the bone was covered over with plastic sheets and dirt, to protect it as much as possible against snow damage until work could resume the following summer. . . .

Finally, all three bones were shining and sturdy. Working with a set of illustrations of the American Museum specimens, we tried to identify the pieces. I learned that many of the bones of reptile skulls are joined with movable joints instead of the rigid joints or sutures characteristic of mammal skulls. The correct matching of these joints was not apparent. But it was easy to identify the dentary (the tooth-bearing part of the jaw), as well as the surangular bone (a large plate-like bone that forms the upper part of the back of the jaw).

There was, however, a third bone no one could quite identify. It was large and sub-triangular. A portion was broken off the top, but how much no one knew. Since it was found under the jaw, we assumed it went with it. From the illustrations we had, in fact, it looked a lot like the half-hidden angular bone of the lower jaw. We were not quite satisfied that it was the angular bone, but we positioned it below the surangular and continued to ready the jaw for exhibit. Three years later, when we were looking for the second jugal—a cheek bone—we discovered that his jugal was our third bone! . . .

When there were larger and heavier bones to be joined, large sand-boxes were used to support the pieces of bone being glued. The sand held the pieces in position while the glue slowly hardened. Thousands of fits had to be made, and each fit had to be as perfect as possible or the final product would be distorted.

After many months in the warehouse, we were finally able to leave our chilly purgatory and transport the bones to the museum for further preparation. All of our work had resulted in thirty beautifully sculptured pieces of fossil skull. The problem now was to fit all of them together to actually form a skull.

The position of the bones in the block didn't help much—they were too scattered. A cast of the *T. rex* skull in New York was obtained, and along with Osborn's paper, it was of great help. But on the cast and in the drawings many of the bones were obscured by the over-lapping structures. Some of them I could figure out—the bones with teeth were easy—but others defied my imagination.

Since no comparative collection of dinosaurs existed at our museum, we now needed someone to help us who had seen a lot of carnivorous dinosaurs. We decided to ask the Zoology Department at the Los Angeles campus of the University of California for a graduate student who might possibly fill the bill.

Dr. Everett Olson, chairman of the department and a world-renowned paleontologist, put us in touch with Ralph Molnar, a graduate student in Zoology who was looking for a suitable project for his doctoral thesis. Ralph had been to all the major museums in the United States and had studied many of the camosaur remains found in this country. He gladly came to look over our specimens, and they proved to be as exciting to him as they were to us. The immediate task of identifying each bone became the object of his research.

Ralph's identifications indicated that we had about two-thirds of the cranium and almost all the elements for both lower jaws. All that was missing for a complete set of jaws were two very thin bones on the inner surfaces, and even they were represented by fragments.

Ralph came crosstown from UCLA several days a week to engineer the assembling of the huge reptile skull. He designed a rough base of styrofoam, and we began to attach the bones we had positively identified. They were secured with wire rods and wood dowels which were punched into the foam.

The fact that we did not have all the bones of the skull was by no means a disaster. It's very unusual to find a complete skeleton of any fossil animal. When a fossil animal is to be displayed to the public, the museum preparators must usually make up many missing parts. In this case, we were fortunate to have all the elements of the skull represented on one side or the other, so each missing piece could be made in the mirror image of its real counterpart. The duplicate parts were carved from styrofoam and textured like bone, then painted to blend with the real fossils.

Since carving is not easy, this took a lot of time. Modelling in clay would have saved us time, but we were concerned about the weight of the completed skull, so light styrofoam was better. While I was busy carving and preparing the new "bones," Ralph was researching the next steps for assembly.

Earlier, I mentioned the overlapping sutures which could slide a bit to give the skull mobility in life. These structures were of a very thin bone that proved most difficult to fit properly. During the seventy million years that the bones had lain in the earth, some of them had been deformed by the weight of the rock and soil which covered them. We were sometimes forced to carefully break and reassemble these bones to change the angle a little.

The exacting work of restoration proceeded day after day, week after week. We had to work very slowly and carefully, but we were enjoying ourselves so much that time flew by. Before we knew it, more than a year had passed.

At last, all the bones were fitted on the base, and the skull looked most impressive. It was huge—almost four and a half feet (134.6 centimeters) from the tip of the snout to the crest at the back. It was two inches longer than the specimen in the American Museum. The serrated, fang-like teeth extended five inches beyond the bone of the upper jaw.

We had our Tyrannosaurus. There he was in our preparation lab, looking fierce . . . and awesome . . . and beautiful.

TO OUR READERS

The successful collection of a vertebrate fossil described in this article was done by amateurs working in cooperation with a recognized scientific institution and under the supervision of professional paleontologists. We want to strongly discourage our readers from attempting to collect vertebrate fossils on their own. A great deal of valuable vertebrate fossil material has been forever lost to science because the collector did not know how to properly collect it, or did not report it to the professional scientific community. If you do discover vertebrate remains in the course of your collecting, we urge you to report it immediately to a professional paleontologist. In all probability, you will still get to assist in the collection of the material, you will learn a great deal in the process . . . and you may be making an important contribution to science.

For Mary Odano, the author of that article, the story form organized a mass of details and built suspense in her readers. How would the search come out? Could they round up a crew capable of doing the job? Would they find a *Tyrannosaurus rex*? If they found one, could they assemble its bones properly?

In the following I-Search Paper, hundreds of facts are necessary to answer the central question, and putting them in story form made them clear and logical to the reader. I don't see how the search could have been presented intelligibly any other way. Note again how natural story is as a form for opening the paper. The writer's first two sentences don't begin a story and sound cute rather than compelling to me. But once past them and into "A few weeks back on a lonely stretch of freeway . . ." the paper picks up my interest and holds me.

BUYING A HOUSE

Laura Guenther

Bad wiring, leaky roofs, old furnaces; the list goes on and on. These are some of the things I have encountered since I began my latest endeavor, "house hunting."

A few weeks back on a lonely stretch of freeway between Lansing and Kalamazoo, Michigan, my father suddenly remarked that he should buy a house in Kalamazoo. At the present time I attend Western Michigan University and live in a dorm. My father reasoned that if he bought a house and let me and a few friends live there, he could save a lot of money. He also told me he could use the property as a tax shelter and make further savings.

The idea of having a real home to live in as compared to a dorm room was instantly appealing. My dad and I discussed the idea and finally agreed that if I could find an older home, close to campus, within a price range of $25,000.00 to $30,000.00 he would consider buying, if the terms were right.

After returning to the dorm that same day, I brought up the idea with some friends. They really thought it was great, so much so that we all piled in the car and went on our first "house hunting" expedition. We looked at a variety of houses. Often times we were quite enthusiastic about a place at first glance. But when we looked more closely, we were generally disappointed. Bad wiring, leaky faucets, and sagging floors were extremely common. It was after these first few searches that I realized just how much I *didn't* know about buying a house. Right then I decided to write this I-Search Paper on what a person should know before buying a house and what to look out for when looking at a prospective house.

The Search

I have found that it's a good idea to begin interviewing people with which you are at least slightly acquainted with. My obvious first choice was Steve Christensen, realtor and my landlord for this spring and summer. Steve is a sharp young man who really knows his business. I suspected that he would be flattered to be interviewed. I was right.

The information Steve gave me was extremely helpful. It provided me with a lot of basic information along with quite a few helpful hints.

Beginning with the basics, Steve warned that many a problem arises when people "buy on emotion." He told me that many a sale is made on decorations, not the house. The buyers are displeased when the pretties are gone and the plain house is left. Steve told me to go through a realtor when looking for a house. "They're free and if they're good, you should get what you're looking for." He warned me of pushy salesmen who are only looking at *their* best interests. Many real estate firms will have a house inspected for termites and powder post beatles when they list the house. The inspection is paid for by the seller and if evidence of pests is found, the seller must cover the cost of any repair. A non-suspecting buyer could overlook the pest possibility and be stuck with a large repair bill later.

Steve also recommended that before one buys a home, she should have it checked for bad wiring, plumbing, leaky roofs and so on. He said for $30.00 the city would go through and check it out. The Federal Housing Administration (FHA) will also check out a house. "But," he warned, "don't take their O.K. as meaning absolutely no problems. They can and do overlook things." A person can also hire a private firm to go through and check out a house for possible problems.

"Before buying," Steve continued, "a person should go through a house *at least* two or three times. This helps to curb impulse buying. The first time you should just get the feel of the house. The second time you should look at the finer points such as how many electrical outlets are in each room.

After this, Steve and I discussed things to look for in older homes. He told me to look at the line of the roof—a straight line between the peak is what to look for. A sagging in the middle could mean problems with leaking and rotting wood under the shingles. Furthermore, look for any signs of "layered shingles." This could be a sign of past roof problems. . . .

As for insulation, Steve said in the winter look for houses with snow on the roof. "If you see a house with little or no snow on its roof in an area where most houses do have snow on theirs, this usually means a poorly insulated house." He also said to put your hand next to an outlet on an outside wall of the house. "If you feel cold air blowing in, you could have an insulation problem. . . ."

My next bit of searching was a fruitful trip to Western's Waldo Library. There I found a helpful article on the pitfalls of buying and selling a home. The article consisted of an interview with Robert W. Semenow, authority on real estate law. In the article, Mr. Semenow said many of the same things that Steve Christensen had said. They both agreed that going through a realtor was best and you will be more likely to get what you want. Mr. Semenow also explained the purpose of signing a contract when buying or selling. "The contract is a legal paper that fixes the rights and the duties of both the seller and buyer. It spells out the exact terms under which one party agrees to sell and the other party agrees to buy." [2]

Mr. Semenow also said to consult an attorney before signing any contracts. A poor contract could later lead to an expensive lawsuit which is a hassle. He further stated that contracts should spell out everything which is to be included in the sale such as lighting fixtures, awnings, and shrubbery. The article also briefly mentioned "latent defects." These are defects in a home which are hidden and not usually found by inspections. This covers the case where a lawyer questions perhaps the condition of the roof and is told it is good. If problems arise within a reasonable time, the buyer may hold the seller responsible.[3]

My last bit of information came from a telephone interview with Mrs. Ann Gerould, female realtor. Being extremely busy, she reluctantly declined when I asked for a personal interview. But she said she would be happy to answer any questions I had on the phone. I explained to her about my I-Search Paper and what type of information I was seeking. . . .

Mrs. Gerould said to know what you can afford or are capable of financing. She said realtors or bank loan officers can quickly look at one's assets and liabilities and tell you how much you can afford to finance each month.

She also told me to be very aware of the current prices on comparable houses in your price range. She said with a little studying, I could become an expert on the type of home I was dealing with. "Ask a salesperson to justify a price if you think it's too high," she cautioned. "If they can't, something's wrong."

Mrs. Gerould concluded by saying your biggest goal is to have confidence in your realtor. "Make sure they're reputable in every way." She then told me that if I was serious in my search for a house, she would be happy to help me by showing me houses which weren't listed and were what I specified I wanted. I thanked her for her help and told her I would get back to her after classes ended for the summer.

I feel I was very fortunate to talk to two such knowledgeable sales persons. Both helped me with their knowledge of home buying and selling. Their tips were priceless. I now feel I'm in much better condition to really search for a house to buy. I have decided to go through a realtor, possibly one of the two I talked with. I also feel I am now a better representative of my father's wishes in looking for a house in Kalamazoo that will serve both my needs and his needs.

Interviews

Steven Christensen, realtor. Kalamazoo MI, March 28, 1978.
Ann Gerould, realtor, Kalamazoo MI, April 3, 1978.

Sources

Buying or Selling a House—Pitfalls to Watch For. *U.S. News and World Report,* 1973, pp. 57-62.

Footnotes

[1] **Buying or Selling a House—Pitfalls to Watch For.** *U.S. News and World Report,* **1973, p. 61.**

[2] *Ibid.,* **p. 58.**

[3] *Ibid.,* **p. 62.**

That I-Search Paper contains mistakes and inconsistencies in grammar, punctuation, spelling, and documentation. I think the writer didn't bring her paper to the seminar on Editing Day and so got no help from another proofreader. A person who wanted to read the whole article "Buying or Selling a House—Pitfalls to Watch For" would have a hard time finding it in *U.S. News and World Report,* because the date of the issue isn't given. That might entail looking through fifty-two issues, because that magazine is a weekly. The writer must have been absent the day that information on documentation was passed out to the seminar, for she typed out the citation for the above article twice, in sources and footnotes, when she could have merely numbered it "1." as a source and in the text of her paper keyed all references to it like this: (1:61), (1:58), and (1:62). Such a method of documentation for short papers is used in Chapter 14 of this book.

I wrote the above paragraph as the reaction of a conventional English teacher trained to think of matters of form first. I'm proud to say that when I received that paper from a seminar student, my response before the group and in written comments to the writer was positive. I think it a remarkably useful paper, as tough in attitudes and facts as a căpable, hard-nosed realtor. As a father I would trust that young woman to use my money wisely. In the last several years my wife and I have bought and sold several houses. I'm embarrassed to say that I didn't employ one-tenth of the checks on those houses that the writer discusses, and I wish I had. In that long recital of things to look for, I found not one that seemed extraneous or trivial.

More than an article or an essay, story compels readers. This happened . . . and what will happen next? The place in which events happens is described. We hear people talking with their individuality. People control things or are controlled by them, as they are in life, and we see where their ideas and emotions come from. In the beginning of a story we meet people, and we like or hate, or feel ambivalent. We step into their shoes. They are more than ideas because they are people, who deal with ideas or succumb to them.

I don't mean to imply here that scientists or other people have just discovered story as a form for presenting their searches and findings. At all times in history discoverers have given in to the natural inclination to use story and to employ the word *I*—so that readers can judge the objectivity and subjectivity of the searcher. In 1839 Charles Darwin, the propounder of the theory of evolution, published his *Journal of Researches into the Geology and Natural History of the various countries visited by H.M.S. Beagle* [Now often referred to as *The Voyage of the Beagle*]. He opened his I-Search book with these lines:

> After having been twice driven back by heavy south-western gales, Her Majesty's ship *Beagle,* a ten-gun brig, under the command of Captain Fitz Roy, R.N., sailed from Devonport on the 27th of December, 1831. . . .

After three pages of "We saw" comments, Darwin introduced the word I and continued using it throughout the book:

> Judging from the appearance, and from similar cases in England, I supposed that the air was saturated with moisture. The fact, however, turned out quite the contrary. . . .

So make the opening of your I-Search Paper a story, of how your topic worked its way into your consciousness. And use the word *I* truthfully, in a way that allows you to see yourself at times as an object, a *me*.

∞ **DOING FOURTEEN:** Write a tentative opening to your I-Search Paper telling what you knew and didn't know about your topic when you began and what you want to find out and why. Remember, it's the beginning of a story. A page or two will probably be enough, but the story you have to tell should determine the length. If possible bring enough copies of the opening to distribute to the others in your group.

*But to have a full kit of auditory pat-
terns curved to real emotions we do need
to listen. We need to listen, with inside
matching on our own part, to those
whose phrases fit their inner state.*

SIDNEY COX

chapter 10
talking
animals

WHEN WE READ or hear words like
"Who's that?" we wonder who said them, what the answer will be,
and who will answer. We're talking animals. Whales croon and bellow,
seals bark, dogs whine, and Siamese cats yammer and howl—but without words. Animals can communicate with body language, as my big
Standard Poodle Ben does, agitating his pom-pom tail like a sema-
phore. But they can't generalize on the feelings or discuss plans
for tomorrow's picnic in Bland Canyon.

I'm sixty years old as I write this, and only in recent months have
I realized that when I sit down to write, I hear the words that are
forming the sentence I want to write. Too often I reject them and try
for something better. When I do, I break down, stutter, and contrive
a sentence rather than hear it take off and sing. More and more I'm
trying to let myself be played upon like a piano. Since it's writing
I'm doing, I've decided to submit to the piano player in my head
because after the words are down I can change them if I want to.
But if I don't give in, my unconscious ability to control sound and
meaning is damaged or destroyed, and my sentences are born with
squeaks and discords.

"Who's that?" says one person to another, and a conversation en-
sues and accelerates:

1

"Just me."
"Aren't you home a little late?"
"Why, what time is it?"

119

"A little past three. How was the party?"

"Oh, it was all right."

"Just all right?"

"Well, it was fun."

"Did they like the hors d'oeuvres you brought and I made?"

"Yes! yes! yes!"

"Did Sean have a good time?"

"Oh yeah, he was having trouble staying vertical. That's why I'm home so late."

"You don't look so vertical yourself."

"Well, the punch was good and did they have a nice Christmas tree."

"Why, what was it like? How big? What was it in? Oh, that lady does have good taste."

"It was in the living room and it was one of those other kinds of Christmas trees, not like ours. It must have taken six hours to trim."

"Didn't Sean drive?"

"Yes."

"Then how did you two get home?"

"I drove their wagon to his house and walked home."

"It must have been cold."

"Just a bit, about five below."

"Serves you right."

"I guess so. How's your back feeling?"

"A little better. But when I get up it starts up again."

"Did Dad say to get firewood tomorrow from the office?"

"Yes, and you better not forget like last year. Take my car."

"Oh, by the way, you wouldn't believe what happened to this one girl."

"Why? What happened?"

"I'm not so sure I should tell you this, but, anyway, this girl was standing by the fireplace right next to the punch bowl. I don't know how it happened but she slipped and her elbow went into the punch bowl which then brought the whole thing down on top of her. She was a sad sight. Oh man, was it funny."

"Sounds like a wild party. What are those girls' parents going to say?"

"Well, I'm gonna go to bed. Do you want the light shut off?"

"Yes, please. Goodnight."

"Goodnight, Mom."
"And don't forget the wood."
"Yea, yea, yea."

John Wrenner, who wrote that dialogue, tried for truth—to get down the way two individuals talked to each other. The result is that tension, understanding, love, and the differences between generations come out. Before one of the speakers was identified in the third to last line as "Mom," you probably guessed that one speaker was a parent and the other a son, or a daughter. These two *sound* like parent and child. Their speech carries revealing patterns. It is not a great, significant story or drama, but it rings true and begins to characterize two people without the writer ever saying anything directly about either one. The only unnatural line I detected was "Did they like the *hors d'oeuvres* you brought and I made?" It sounds more like an explanation to the reader than a comment by Mother, who probably would have said, "Did they like my *hors d'oeuvres?*" knowing her son would know that she had made them.

Dialogue Number 1 above was written in play form, as if for actors to read. The next one is presented in narrative form, like a story.

2

[One afternoon last November, my bell rang.] Standing on the porch, clad in a Kelly green snowsuit, was a barely school-aged-looking boy.

"Well, hi there," said my roommate Lisa, [opening the door].

"Hello. Could I please use your bathroom?"

"Why sure. Come on in."

I jumped off the couch. "Hi. What's your name?"

"Scott. And I can take my snowsuit off all by myself. I don't need any help."

"Oh, okay," said Lisa and pointed to the bathroom.

"Can you believe that, Lisa? He's such a little guy."

"Gutsy, too. I sure wouldn't go up to some strange house and ask to use their bathroom."

The bell rang again and in walked a friend of ours, Bill, on his way home from work. "Hi gang, what's up?"

"Bill, there's the cutest little kid in our bathroom now."

"There's a *kid* in your bathroom?" he asked, flopping on the couch.

"A little guy," I added. "Wait 'til you see him."

The door creaked a little and Scott peered from behind it.

"Come in here, Scott." Lisa motioned him into the living room. "Do you want some pop?"

"Yes, please. But then I have to go home."

Lisa walked into the kitchen. Scott looked at Bill, who was loosening his tie. "Are you the dad?"

"No, I'm the friend."

"Do you live here?"

"Uh uh. I just come over to use the bathroom."

"Oh." He turned to me. "Do you live here?"

"Yes," I told him.

"Do you got any little kids that I can play with?"

"Uh, no, Scott. Ya see, there's just a bunch of girls living here."

"But where's your mom?" [He looked bewildered.]

"We all go to college here and live in this house. But our moms are at home."

"And we all have different moms," Lisa said, handing him his Pepsi.

"Oh, I have the same mom and dad," he said with a nod and climbed up on the couch.

"Scott, is that your school—the one across the street?"

"Yep."

"What grade are you in?"

"Kindergarten," he replied, taking a final swallow of pop. "I have to go home now. Thank you for the pop."

"You're welcome, Scott," Lisa said as we walked him to the door.

"Come back and see us again, okay?"

"Okay, bye." He waved, rang the doorbell, then leap-hopped down the steps.

"Wasn't he a little doll? He's adorable," Lisa said as we sat back down on the couch.

Bill shook his head. "You guys, what suckers! He cons ya into pop and you invite him back for more. It's like giving a kitten a saucer of milk. He'll be on your porch every day."

"Oh, I'm sure! He came here to use the bathroom. I offered him the pop."

"Suckers!"

•   •   •

The next afternoon, the bell rang. Two figures stood on the porch. I opened the door.

"Hi," said Scott. "This is my friend Mark . . ."

Number 2 above is more than a dialogue and surprises more than Number 1—we are led to remember how naive we were as small children learning the world. And it has a beginning and ending that frame the story: Scott alone at the door, and later, Scott with Mark at the door. Nancy Trost, who wrote it, was wise not to use a lot of unnecessary explanatory statements which beginning writers often include. For example, when Bill says, "There's a *kid* in your bathroom?" Nancy could have added, "he said scornfully, indicating his superior attitude." but she left it to readers to infer what was in Bill's mind. And when Lisa said, "And we all have different moms," Nancy could have added, "said Lisa, accepting his confusion as natural," but she expected readers to interpret the motive behind Lisa's words, just as we have to do every day in conversations. Supplying the reader with frequent explanations in dialogue slows down the exchange and often takes the life out of it.

In this story Nancy might have cut the words that I've enclosed in brackets, and intensified the drama. When you write a dialogue, make sure you don't insult your readers by unnecessary comments. For example, when Nancy gives Scott the line, "But where's your mom?" she doesn't have to add that "He looked bewildered." The bewilderment is established by his very question. In writing conversations, try to avoid nudging your readers' elbows. Don't write, " 'You go to hell,' he said angrily." The word *angrily* is unnecessary. Occasionally someone may say "Go to hell" in a friendly way and then you'll need to add, "he said in a friendly tone."

Listen to the way people talk. If you're remembering their conversation on paper, each speaker should sound a little different, because all persons have their own ways of thinking, feeling, and putting words together. A word or expression is unique to them—maybe because they mispronounce it, maybe because in their family it was a homemade word, created out of a funny or sad incident that the family members never forgot. Get down on paper not only what they say but their individual way of saying it. You won't succeed completely because your own word patterns will intrude on theirs, but if you try for this truth to life, you'll fashion a stronger dialogue than if you attempt to sound literary or dramatic.

When you choose a moment of dialogue that struck you, angered you, piqued you, or delighted you, often it will make a little play, not exactly a one-acter, more a one-momenter. To get the individual flavor of people's language (what's called their *idiolect*), you may want to tape-record a conversation; but the feel of that moment, the truth of its character, is more likely to appear if you don't simply transcribe every word spoken in the conversation. Sounds strange to say that an actual, verbatim conversation may not convey the truth of the moment as well as your remembered, and consequently coarser, version will; but what was said before and after a piece of conversation you intend to use—the context from which you took it—often helps give it point or meaning.

And then there's the common human habit of saying more than is necessary. If you record everything that was said, your readers may not be able to hear the airplanes because of the wind. Here's a dialogue that could be called a *one-momenter* because the first speaker tells more about love than he realizes. It's a small self-portrait:

3

"I tell ya, Tom, I just never met anyone like her. She's different. That night we met we ended up talkin' all night 'bout all sorts a stuff. She's really intelligent. She told me all about white bread, Man, I didn't know that. She's always tellin' me 'bout stuff like that, ya know. I mean she's got her head together."

"You want a beer, Ed?"

"Na, that's O.K. I got one. I guess I just love her. I suppose that's why I feel so lonely, 'cause she's not here. Life's like that, I guess. You're just cruisin' around and all of a sudden, wow! you find you're in love. That's strange, isn't it? Just lookin' up and findin' you're in love. Well, I guess that's what I found. Wonder if she loves me? Do ya think she loves me, Tom? She's all I been able to think about. Ever since I met her I just been really confused. I guess that's what love's all about, ya know."

•   •   •

"You need a beer?"

"Na, I got one. Yea, we talked till 5:00 in the morning, just talkin', ya know. You really get to know someone by doin' that. That's why I know it's love. There's just so much more to her than her body. She even said she likes my green eyes. Wow! Most people think they're brown, but she knew. I mean she just didn't look at my eyes. Man, she looked at 'em. She's different like that, ya know . . . really intelligent . . . not like most chicks. . . . I wonder what she's doin' right now. Yeah, that's what—I'll call her."

"It's gettin' kinda late, Ed."

"I know, but I just want to see what she's doin', that's all."

• • •

"So how was your late night audio rendezvous?"

"I guess she was sleepin'. She got really pissed off and told me to shove it. Imagine that—I didn't even know she had a temper. Just goes to show how you really don't know anyone until you wake them up in the middle of the night and tell 'em that you love 'em. Well, that's the breaks, I guess. Life's been known to—"

"Ed!"

"—take a few turns now and then. Crazy how you can be so in love, and just have it fall apart in a few minutes. Yep, just cruisin' along . . . in love . . . out of love . . . strange, isn't it?"

"You sure you don't need a beer?"

When you transcribe spoken words to the page, you drop out the environment or context in which they were spoken. The physical moment surrounding the words is seldom evident in them. For example, if you read this exchange,

"I can't stand this any more."

"You're not going to die."

the words will carry a different significance if you know they're said at a street corner in a snowstorm or in a lifeboat in a heavy sea. That's why writers have always reached first for the form we call *story*, in which context is given and speakers identified.

The other major form of presenting dialogue is that used in plays, where merely the speaking lines of the actors are given, and the context for them is accomplished by the stage setting and the fact that two speakers stand before the audience in their identifiable individuality. But when writers use story form, they must remember audiences need help in order to keep clear who's talking, where, when, and why; so they follow a conventional, established form of presenting both the conversation and environment. If they don't, the task of readers may become too difficult and they may quit reading. Here, for example, is a conversation told as a story but not put down on the page in conventional dialogue form by the person who wrote it. You'll find it brambly reading.

4

My conversation is with a beautiful girl with a beautiful name, Annette. We've just bought two ham and cheese sandwiches from Kroger's. I ask her, "Would you like your sandwich heated up in the toaster oven?" "If you do." These are one of the answers I don't really like. This is a pet peeve to me. "What do you mean if I do. It's a yes or no answer. It's your sandwich. I'm not going to eat it." She laughs and repeats "if you do." I throw both sandwiches in the toaster oven and close the door. I open the refrigerator for something else to eat and spy a pack of Longhorn Colby cheese. "Would you like a piece of cheese, I'm having one." She gives me one of those shy grins and answers "You know I love Colby cheese." It's true I did know that. I put the sandwiches on the table, pour two glasses of Coke, cut a hunk of cheese, breaking it in two pieces, giving her one and keeping one for myself. I look over at Annette and she's sitting there laughing, and shaking her head. "What's so funny?" "You." "Well, what's so funny about me?" "Oh, you're so *macho*." Annette is Mexican and in Spanish *macho* means male chauvinist. Puzzled I asked, "What makes you say that?" Laughing she says, "Look at the cheese." "Look at the Cokes." "You always give me a smaller portion." "You figure I'm feminine and more petite therefore you give me a smaller portion." I look and sure enough her piece of cheese is ¼ the size of mine. Her Coke is only half full. I have subconsciously given her the same amount I'd give my niece or nephew. We both start laughing. I said, "That still doesn't make me *macho*." "Well, what about the fair when you played those stupid crank games. You get a dollar's worth of dimes and give me maybe a dime or twenty cents at the most. You think you're so superior and such a master of those and I just can't play them as well as you." When she says this I'm embarrassed in a way but laughing because it's true. When I go to the fair I usually spend three dollars on those cranks. I never really noticed that I'd always given her only 20 cents. I always thought I was a pro and would say, "Now *I'll* win you a *prize*." She had deflated my ego and we both laughed at how asinine I am at times. Later I tell her, "I'll change my ways. Be less *macho* and more equal to her." "You better not," she replies. "I love to have doors opened for me. I love to be treated special. I love to have you care for me and go out of your way because I'm a woman." We kiss and both laugh again. I had weighted the question. I knew she liked the things I did. I knew by telling her I'd change she'd give me some compliments and help ease my previous humiliation. I also knew it would

put her in a romantic mood that did follow. I'll end here because the rest of our conversation contained little dialogue.

As you probably realized reading that story, the conventions of
writing dialogue were established to ease the readers' job, to make
up for the fact that the speakers are not *seen* as in life, a movie, or a
play. Here's the way that story would be written by a writer familiar
with the conventional forms of presenting dialogue:

5

My conversation is with a beautiful girl with a beautiful
name, Annette. We've just bought two ham and cheese sandwiches from Kroger's.

"Would you like your sandwich heated up in the toaster
oven?" I ask her.

"If you do."

That is one of the answers I don't really like. This is a
pet peeve to me.

"What do you mean if I do. It's a yes or no answer. It's
your sandwich. I'm not going to eat it."

She laughs and repeats "If you do."

I throw both sandwiches in the toaster oven and close the
door. I open the refrigerator for something else to eat and
spy a pack of Longhorn Colby cheese. "Would you like a
piece of cheese? I'm having one."

She gives me one of those shy grins and answers, "You
know I love Colby cheese."

It's true I did know that. I put the sandwiches on the
table, pour two glasses of Coke, cut a hunk of cheese, breaking it in two pieces, giving her one and keeping one for
myself. I look over at Annette and she's sitting there laughing, and shaking her head. "What's so funny?"

"You."

"'Well, what's so funny about me?"

"Oh, you're so *macho*."

Annette is Mexican and in Spanish *macho* means male
chauvinist. Puzzled I asked, "What makes you say that?"

Laughing she says, "Look at the cheese. Look at the Cokes.
You always give me a smaller portion. You figure I'm feminine and more petite therefore you give me a smaller portion."

I look and sure enough her piece of cheese is ¼ the size
of mine. Her Coke is only half full. I have subconsciously

given her the same amount I'd give my niece or nephew. We both start laughing.

"That still doesn't make me *macho*," I said.

"Well, what about the fair when you played those stupid crank games. You get a dollar's worth of dimes and give me maybe a dime or twenty cents at the most. You think you're so superior and such a master of those and I just can't play them as well as you."

When she says this I'm embarrassed in a way but laughing because it's true. When I go to the fair I usually spend three dollars on those cranks. I never really noticed that I'd always given her only 20 cents. I always thought I was a pro and would say, "Now *I'll* win *you* a prize." She had deflated my ego and we both laughed at how asinine I am at times.

Later I tell her, "I'll change my ways. Be less *macho* and more equal to her."

"You better not," she replies. "I love to have doors opened for me. I love to be treated special. I love to have you care for me and go out of your way because I'm a woman."

We kiss and both laugh again. I had weighted the question. I knew she liked the things I did. I knew by telling her I'd change she'd give me some compliments and help ease my previous humiliation. I also knew it would put her in a romantic mood that did follow. I'll end here because the rest of our conversation contained little dialogue.

FRANK BARRON

That story is easier to follow. Who's talking or thinking aloud is made clear at all times.

The conventions for writing story dialogue are simple:

(1) Indent and make a new paragraph for words spoken or thought by an individual speaker, so as to separate them on the page for readers.

(2) Use quotation marks to indicate where one speaker's words begin and end. Don't, as Frank Barron did in the first version of Dialogue 4, put quotation marks around several sentences in a row spoken by the same person—"Look at the cheese." "Look at the Cokes." "You always give me a smaller portion." "You figure I'm feminine and more petite therefore you give me a smaller portion." Annette is speaking all those sentences; so Frank, the writer, should simply mark off the whole passage—with beginning quotation marks before *Look* and ending marks after *portion,* as I've done in the second version.

(3) Unless the meaning of what is being said needs a cue for the reader, start your conversational lines with the spoken words, not with your own statements as narrator. Better not to write as Frank did in the first version,

> I said, "That still doesn't make me *macho*."

but,

> "That still doesn't make me *macho*," I said.

so that the first words in the paragraphs as one reads down the page are the statements and responses of the speakers, coming at the reader as they do in real life, without "I said's," etc. preceding them. Such a form creates more of an illusion that the speakers are replying instantly to each other, as they do in real life.

(4) Put within quotation marks only the actual words a person speaks. Frank forgets to do that when he writes:

> Later I tell her, "I'll change my ways. Be less *macho* and more equal to *her*."

In fact Frank didn't say that to her, but rather,

> "I'll change my ways. Be less *macho* and more equal to *you*."

because then he was talking *to* her, not *about* her. Interesting that in the early days of novel writing, authors frequently wrote the way Frank did, and failed to differentiate between what was actually said —or would have been said—and the way a third party, the author, might use pronouns to refer to speakers.

What I've presented here has been dialogue written in forms that are conventional at the moment. Because dialogue forms are irksome to punctuate—particularly remembering closing quotation marks— some editors and writers have dispensed with quotation marks. They precede the spoken lines with dashes or they use dramatic form in the middle of a story—(John: I don't like you).

The New Yorker magazine for November 7, 1977, printed a story called "The Left-Handed Woman," by Peter Handke, which mixed forms in this way:

> . . . When they reached the phone booth, the father said, "I've got a quick phone call to make."
> The woman: "You can phone from the house."
> The father replied simply, "My companion is waiting."

I think that's sloppy and confusing to a reader, and it's further weakened by a whole string of repetitions of "The woman" or "The father" down the left-hand margin of a column. As I said earlier, naming speakers before giving what they say deadens conversation. You may be wondering why I bring up these new forms. Isn't it enough that you have to learn the norm without being confused by exceptions? I want to take that risk in order to show that language and writing conventions change constantly, like all conventions in life. That's a truth people have to learn to live with. If they don't, they become ridiculous conservatives unhappy with the way other people are conducting themselves, or they become mentally ill.

Forms of indicating speech have changed and will change in the future. But these matters are only formal and can be learned mechanically. The first point to remember about dialogue is to try to capture the true sound of individuals talking. The second point is to get a feel for when you should present people's own words and when you should say in your words what they said.

Howard Blum, a *New York Times* reporter covering a fire in Brooklyn in which six firemen were killed, decided to construct his story (August 3, 1978) mostly of spoken words because he wanted to show how much the death of firemen means to their relatives, and how those relatives view the job.

RELATIVES TOLD
THE SAD NEWS
AT A FIREHOUSE

The blond, long-haired youth pulls his souped-up Pontiac to an abrupt halt in front of the red doors of the firehouse on Geritsen Avenue in Brooklyn and, despite his crutches, rushes toward a uniformed fireman.

"I hate to ask, but I'm looking for George Rice," the youth says haltingly.

"No Rice here," the fireman answers immediately. "Wait a minute, did they send you here?"

The teen-ager nods.

"You better come in here," the fireman says in a soft voice. He puts an arm around the youth's shoulder and, with his free hand, he motions to Deputy Fire Commissioner Stephen J. Murphy.

Solace Is Rejected

The deputy commissioner, after taking a name from the boy, checks six small white pieces of paper that he is clenching in his hand. Then, quiet words, almost whispers, are spoken by Deputy Commissioner Murphy. The youth learns his brother-in-law is dead.

"Oh no!" the youth shouts at the top of his lungs. Both his crutches crash to the ground.

"Oh no," he repeats, rubbing the hair off his forehead and lifting his face to the sky. Then, quickly he grabs his crutches. A fireman tries to help him, but the youth pushes him away.

"This job stinks!" the youth screams as he hobbles to his car, his right leg covered with a white plaster cast.

"This job stinks," he repeats.

Getting into his car, he yells again: "The job stinks!"

"Shut up!" Deputy Commissioner Murphy calls back at him.

Then, leaving a track of rubber behind him, the youth screeches off in his car.

The deputy commissioner, a short, white-haired man wearing thick, dark glasses and a carefully pressed brown suit, continues to stand in front of the firehouse, home base for Engine Company 321. Just three hours earlier, at about 9 A.M., each of the firemen whose names are now written on the six pieces of paper he is holding was standing on the roof of the Waldbaum's supermarket on Avenue Y. Suddenly, with a loud roar, the roof crumbled.

Deputy Commissioner Murphy arrived at the supermarket about 15 minutes later, and now he is in charge of notifying the families of the dead men.

Chaplains Are Notified

Inside the firehouse, firemen in blue uniforms are manning the telephones as relatives of the 150 men at the fire are calling to find out the fate of their loved ones. And firemen from the 321 company are calling to find fire chaplains to notify the six families.

Minutes after the boy drives off, Fire Chaplain Alfred Thompson arrives. Earlier that morning he was dressed in a white fire helmet, a black rubber coat and boots as he went into the flaming supermarket and anointed the six dead firemen. Now he has showered and changed his clothes.

The chaplain and Deputy Commissioner Murphy are joined by a circle of men from the firemen's union. While the chaplain is given a white piece of paper, a fireman yells: "Does Hastings have any children? Anyone know his wife's name?" The chaplain folds the white slip once, then twice and puts it in his wallet as if to hide it from his sight and mind.

Suddenly there is a commotion at the front of the firehouse.

"I just want to know if my brother . . ." a woman with red hair is saying through her tears.

"Maureen! Maureen!" shouts a fireman rushing from the circle of men around the deputy commissioner.

"Oh Frankie, oh Frankie, you're alive," she says and then breaks into full tears as she hugs her brother-in-law.

Meanwhile, the fireman who is to accompany Chaplain Thompson to the Hastings residence has changed into a clean white shirt.

"I don't want to go," the fireman in the white shirt complains to Deputy Commissioner Murphy.

"You're a big boy," the deputy commissioner tells him. "I did this 17 times in one year."

And then the Deputy Commissioner walks away, standing alone in the front of the firehouse, still holding his pieces of white paper.

When I first started teaching, trained as I was in the Errors Approach, my first response to that story might have been, "It's a good report, but I found an error. The term *the Deputy Commissioner* is capitalized in the last paragraph and elsewhere in the article is in lower-case." Today when I got to the line, "Oh Frankie, oh Frankie, you're alive," I cried, and that response told me how good a story Howard Blum wrote and how much power he gained by quoting what people said. He chose well which parts of the story to tell as narrative and which as dialogue.

∞ **DOING FIFTEEN:** Listen to or remember a conversation between two or more people that fascinated or moved you. Get down what they said to each other as truly as you can. Be faithful to how they spoke as well as what they said. Don't nudge your readers: put down the spoken words you consider most significant. If you strive for the truth of this talk, you'll probably find the conversation coming alive and writing itself. Use either story form or play form, whichever you prefer.

You can ask a baby frog if he remembers how you taught him to catch a fly, but there is no quest in that question.

chapter 11
interviewing

A BAD DETECTIVE interviewing on the two-sided loop says to the woman before him: "So you heard his footsteps in the hallway? And you took the gun out of that dresser drawer? And when he opened the door, you shot him?" All these things happened and the alleged murderer has to answer yes to each question because yes is the truth. A good detective says, "Tell me what happened that night, the events leading up to the shooting," attempting to put the alleged murderer and himself on a Moebius Loop, where he and she will meet as human beings living in the same world of pressures and motivations, although at the outset of their relationship they may have appeared to be foreigners, on opposite sides, one representing the Doers of Wrong and the other the Upholders of Right.

Certain facts suggest that this woman must have killed her husband with malice aforethought, but the good detective asks questions that allow her to tell her story: "He had beaten me for three nights in a row. I couldn't see out of one eye. He would be nice to me at dinner. Volunteer to wash the dishes, and then while doing them, he'd go out of his mind. That night, after being beaten in the kitchen, I crawled to his bedroom—the only one that could be locked. I heard him running down the basement steps and yelling he was going to finish me off with a broom, which would be an appropriate weapon, he said, 'because you never clean the house!' As I locked the door I could hear him sawing on the broom handle. And then I heard footsteps. He hit the door with his shoulder, again and again. I could see that metal thing where the latch goes into the door frame giving way with each blow. By the time it was torn loose and the door gave way, I had the gun, and just before he crashed into me, I pulled the trigger."

In the interview as well as in the courtroom, other questions need to be asked to establish each crucial fact solidly; but the story is different now. What the man and his wife did on that fatal night and earlier nights—according to her—is now also on a Moebius Strip. Each person comes to that encounter from a different side, and they meet. Since the man is dead, the detective can't hear that side from him, and will have to interview other persons and attempt to reconstruct— from the husband's experiences and point of view—what he did and was before that turn of events.

Here's an example of an interviewer asking open-ended questions that allow the person being interviewed to tell her story:

MARLENE SWANSON

Connie Schneider

Marlene Swanson is a 54-year-old woman. She works at the Kentwood Union Snack Bar. As a member of the American Businesswoman's Association, she recently received the Businesswoman of the Year award.

C: Could you tell me a little something about yourself? Your background?

M: Well, I graduated from high school at 16. I lived on a farm with my folks. My mother worked at the State Hospital. She was a nurse's attendant, something like a nurse's aide today.

C: What did you do after you graduated?

M: I couldn't go to college because we didn't have the money. We didn't have opportunities like kids today. There are grants, loans, and scholarships available now. So I went to work at the State Hospital. My mother used to take me to work with her when I was very small. I was only four years old. She'd ask me to help her with the patients sometimes.

C: Did the patients frighten you? [The hospital then housed mental patients.]

M: No, not at all. I was so young that I just never felt afraid. The people there never hurt me. I liked going to work with my mother. So after I graduated I got a paying job there. I took junior attendant training, so I had a lot of contact with the people. Some I worked with were violently disturbed. Others were pretty together, and didn't need so much help.

C: What do you mean "violently disturbed"? Is that like being mentally retarded?

M: No, it's more like being emotionally disturbed. These people needed help in their everyday world, to dress, to eat, to wash. That was my job. And to watch over them and help them when they needed me. My first night on the job I was supposed to be checking on a woman in her room from time to time, but I had fallen asleep in a chair in the hall. The woman got the sheet off her bed, put it up over a bar fixed to the ceiling, and tried to kill herself. Oh my . . . we did get her down in time, she was okay. But I almost got fired for that.

C: What other types of things did you do in the hospital? Did you say something about helping them to dress and eat?

M: Yes, with their everyday chores: we got them up in the morning, were with them all day, and helped put them to bed at night. I once worked with a young catatonic girl, 16 years old.

C: And what is *catatonic?*

M: The person is very withdrawn. This girl had no idea what was going on around her. She didn't seem to hear me. She would sit for hours and not say anything. If I put her arm up over her head, she'd hold it there forever if I didn't bring it back down. I helped her dress, I fed her, bathed her. I talked to her constantly while I was with her. We spent a lot of time together. It took her two years to recover, and today she is a very dear friend living in Lansing.

C: That's remarkable. And so good to hear. When did you quit at the State Hospital?

M: I quit in 1939 when I got married. I wanted to go back to the State Hospital after a few years, but I had to wait a few months to take a civil service test. We needed the money so I got a job in the Valley Dorm Snack Bar. I stayed there for several years. I never did go back to the State Hospital.

C: That must have been quite a change for you. Did you like working with the college kids?

M: Yes, very much. At this time the Valley dorms had just been built. There weren't any McDonald's or Burger Kings around, so all the kids would come to the snack bar. Today it's folding up, though, because there's not enough business. Then in 1964 I started working at Kentwood Union.

C: So you've been working with college kids quite a few years. I can tell you enjoy it by the smile on your face every time I come into the Snack Bar.

M: I enjoy this age group. I have three children of my own. The youngest is 24. Sometimes I'm a little shocked by what he and his friends do or say, but I never let on. I just go along. I can really keep up with the language. I can talk like the best of them. My son will just say, "Mother, you're gross." Now if I was anyone else's mother, it'd be okay. His friends think I'm cool, but he thinks I'm gross. (We both laugh.) I'm not afraid to try things. I was renting out a house to four students a few years ago. I went to collect the rent, and there they all were, smoking marijuana in the living room. They said, "C'mon, Mrs. Swanson, sit down and smoke with us." Well, I didn't know what to do. (We both laugh.) So I did! Sometimes I pretend I know what I'm doing when I don't! Smoking marijuana isn't bad, but I don't like it. At least I've tried it!

C: Who has influenced you the most in your life?

M: My mother, she was so lovely, gracious . . . witty. I loved her so. I wanted to fashion myself after her. After she died I was determined to do so.

C: You were quite young?

M: Yes, 24. My daughter was three weeks old.

C: What are a few essential things that you need to do your job well?

M: The need to communicate with others is one. It helps me to remember little things about the people I work with. Like "Good morning, Paul, how's the new baby today?" or "How did your test go yesterday, Julie? Pretty rough?"

C: Get kind of a radar system going, eh?

M: Yeah, put those antennas to work. (Laughter.) It's good to tune into people. I've been ill for two weeks with a cold. One day at work I was feeling sick, and getting cross, you know—

C: Yes, I was wondering if it's difficult sometimes for you to stay happy and smiley at work.

M: Heavens, yes. I didn't feel like working, and I didn't smile much. One of the girls had forgotten to put something away after she was done using it. It was in my way and I just got so mad. "Will you PLEASE put this away, Elena?" Her face was so shocked.

C: She'd probably never seen you that way before.

M: Well, not too often. I felt so bad about it later that I went back to her and apologized for being so cross. (She laughs.)

C: What else besides good communication is essential to doing your job well?

M: A pleasant personality.

C: *That,* you have.

M: Well (laughs), it never costs a thing to smile. I try to smile when I see someone needs it; it's not hard. I enjoy being pleasant to people. It makes my job enjoyable.

C: What do you like about working here as compared to the other places you've worked—Valley Snack Bar, Big Union Snack Bar, the State Hospital?

M: Kentwood gets the more mature students, the grads, and a lot of instructors. They're a different kind of people than the students in the Valley. The older kids are easier to talk to, and more willing to talk. We also get a lot of foreign students. They're hard to understand sometimes. One student always asks for "SHLAUS-KI-JES." That's sausages. Or they may not speak *any* English. They'll find out about one food and then always ask for it, like a hot dog. They'll ask for a hot dog at 7 o'clock in the morning. (We laugh.) We try to help, though. Teach them how to pronounce *bacon and eggs* so they can have a good breakfast for a change.

C: What do you have to contribute to people you see everyday?

M: Some people seem to need advice. And as a matter of conversation, I might give it if they ask. You can just about tell when somebody is uptight and wants to talk about a problem.

C: That radar system again—

M: Yes. And you know one thing I forgot. I think it's another essential thing—a sense of humor. (Laughs.) It's part of my lifestyle. They can take anything from me, but don't take away my sense of humor. My ex-husband was a very serious man. He drank a lot, hardly ever laughed. My daughter and I laugh at our own jokes all the time! I used to have supper ready for my husband when he got home every night. I wasn't going to be there one night, so just for a joke I emptied an open can of dog food into a plastic container and set it in the refrigerator. Well, he must have thought it was corned beef because he fried it up and ate it. (Laughs). He didn't talk to me for a week. My daughter and I still laugh about that one.

C: How do you feel when you're doing your job well?

M: I feel satisfied, in a good mood. Someone might say, "What is she? She just works in a snack bar." That's not the whole picture. I feel good doing my job. I feel happy.

To produce that interview, Connie Schneider didn't say to herself, "Well, whom could I interview? There must be somebody available around here." She gave a few minutes to her feelings—maybe while waiting in the dentist's chair or walking to school—so they could choose for her. Who amazes you? Who strikes you as unusual? Who keeps coming back strong in encounter after encounter? Connie had seldom, if ever, met a person in Marlene Swanson's kind of job who every day lifted the spirits of people she worked with and for. So there was a subject, and a question—"How did Marlene manage to be so friendly doing what most other people consider routine work?" In a sense, for Connie this was an I-Search interview.

Let someone slide into your thoughts and feelings until you have to respond. Such people will attract you because they're different from you in some ways, or you wouldn't admire them so much. Because they have skills or traits you don't have, most of your questions need to be open-ended, or like a schoolteacher you'll find yourself asking questions that draw forth answers you already know. Dull business.

Skillful interviewers make their subjects feel like opening up. They don't ask, "Did you start working at the snack bar when you were very young?" That's likely to bring forth a simple "Yes" and a pause anticipating the next question. Better to say, "Tell me something about—" as Connie did. Or "How did you get started in—?" Often the first attempt at an activity or job on the first day is significant, and prints itself on the memory of a person. Questions that can be answered yes or no should be used sparingly because they close off the flow of experience you want from your subject. Here are some remarks that are likely to lift the sluice gate:

1. How did you get started in this—?
2. Tell me about your first day.
3. If you were allowed to tell a beginner only one thing about how to do what you're so good at, what would it be?—the thing that counts most.
4. How do you feel at the moment when you're doing your best?

Marlene Swanson was easy to interview because she's irrepressibly friendly and positive. Some people you interview will be more shy and closemouthed. If, like Connie Schneider, you ask them to define a term you don't know—"What is *catatonic?*"—you may get simply "A catatonic is a withdrawn person." Then you'll have to say something like "Tell me about an experience you've had with one." What readers want is little moments of experience that do more than define; they dramatize, like Mrs. Swanson's simple but powerful picture of the catatonic girl she worked with: "If I put her arm up over her head, she'd hold it there forever if I didn't bring it down."

As usual, truthfulness is the fundamental in interviewing as in other kinds of writing. If you try to play the authority yourself, and talk as if you know as much or more than the experts you're interviewing, you'll probably stop them from opening up. From them you want truth that reveals things you have admired in them. You can establish the right feeling by yourself admitting when you don't know something. That doesn't mean you can't show your knowledge or insight—but both you and the person you're interviewing are most likely to stay with truth if you don't pretend. First-rate people are seldom ashamed to admit their ignorance, and are usually proud of their curiosity and eagerness to learn. "What do you mean 'violently disturbed'?" asked Connie. "Is that like being mentally retarded?"

> *Truth will steady you like the wings of a crow and the feet on a swinging vine.*
> LU PO HUA

Perhaps the Swanson interview should be shortened. It goes on a long time before reaching the topic of Marlene's job in the Snack Bar. Yet what she says about knowing the State Hospital since the age of four explains partly how she developed such empathy with other people. One way to cut it would be to use the Narrative-and-Dialogue method that is presented at the end of this chapter. It's the common way of saving space used by professional reporters.

Here I'm giving straight question-and-answer interviews so that you'll see how good interviewers draw out information and feelings from those they interview. Often when the person you're talking to begins spilling over, only a few words from you are needed to tip the cup, as in this interview:

DEBBIE NEWMAN

Keith Newman

Debbie, my wife, was frying chicken for Sunday dinner.

"Hey," I said. "I think you do a really good job."

She laughed. "At cooking?"

"No. Well, that too, but I mean as an elementary physical education teacher."

She laughed again. "What makes you say that?"

"Well, number one, whenever we drive through Bramwell it's like driving through the Rose Bowl parade on a float. Kids holler out to you and wave from the porches and sidewalks. And then, the stories you tell about Sammie Phillips and the scooter, or how Marcie reached into your magic pocket and found a tootsie roll, I can tell. Those kids like you a whole lot. I really admire that."

"What a lot of trash you talk."

"Oh no. Suppose you tell me how you got into PE in the first place."

"What are you doing with that pen and pad?"

"I'm interviewing you."

"Oh, come on."

"No kidding."

"I feel funny."

"That's all right, you're supposed to. Just tell me how it all began. How in the world did you get to be a PE teacher?"

"Oh geez. Well, remember back in high school when Grandma and Aunt Gen were hot for me to be a secretary? I took all those typing and shorthand classes. But I didn't want to be a secretary. About my senior year I made up my mind that if I was going to be something the rest of my life, it might as well be something I enjoy. PE was what I liked."

"Why did you decide to become an elementary PE teacher?"

"Because I didn't have to take swimming."

"Aw, come on."

"No kidding, really. The first semester I was at Western I took a swimming class and almost drowned. After that they wanted me to take diving. I said, 'Uh-uh folks, no more of this,' and the only thing I could major in without taking more swimming was elementary PE, so I did."

"Why that's a crazy reason."

"Well, you're a fine one to talk. Anyway, it worked out ok. I see now that I don't really have the personality to enjoy teaching middle or high school. Kids at that age are all the time causing you grief, coming to school crying with problems—heck, I couldn't take that. With the little kids, they play and I play and we all have a good time."

"You don't mean that little kids don't have problems."

"Oh no. Lord, you should know half of what goes on. Some kids have parents who beat them and burn them with cigarettes. One little girl lay in her bed for three days with a ruptured appendix before her mother took her to the doctor. Imagine! Another girl whose mother never married is taken care of by her older sister while her mother hops from bar to bar and shacks up with a different man each night. And now the big sister is starting to do the same. This little girl came up to me before you and I were married and said, 'You should go to the bar uptown and you could find a husband there."

"How are the little kids different, then?"

Well, they don't seem to be affected as much by the things going on at home. That little girl who told me I could get a husband in the bar played and had a good time in my class. By the time these kids are older they realize, hey, the things my mom or my dad do to me aren't right, and they're fed up with taking it, and they're looking for someone to help. When these kids come to me and spill out their troubles it just floors me. I'm not permitted to do anything, but these kids want me to help."

"What about your size? Has being such a little person ever bothered you teaching?"

"No. In fact it helps sometimes. Little kids don't see me as a true adult. My size is part of that. The other part is that I don't act like I'm an adult. I talk to them and treat them with respect. You know that Sunday school class I was teaching with Pastor Neal? He asked the kids to write down some things they didn't like about adults and three or four of them said they disliked being ignored. If they were talking to an adult and another adult came along, why the person they were talking to would stop listening while they were right in the middle of what they were saying and maybe start talking to this other adult. To me that's just bad manners and there's no excuse for it."

"What do you enjoy the most about teaching?"

"Oh, if you know you've got your lesson across. Friday I was teaching kindergarteners to skip. Well, some of them knew how already but some of them didn't. At the end of class three or four of these kids who couldn't at first, could. Or when kids who normally don't participate do. Or to have them respond to you as a person. Last year I had this little boy named Michael. Michael was my special friend. He was two-thirds the size of everybody else. One day he asked me to tie his shoe and while I bent over to do it, he kissed me right on top of the head. Another time this little girl brought me a tootsie roll pop because it was her birthday. Now that was something—I'm not a room teacher, and they're the ones who usually get those kind of things. If I get one it's really special. It means that little girl went home and said to her mom, 'Hey, I've got to have something to bring Mrs. Newman.' So when these kids respond to me as a person, that's what really makes working with them a joy."

"What does it take to be successful in working with kids?"

"Well, I think you've got to enjoy it. If it's not what you want to do, go find what you want to do and do that instead. If you don't, you might not like them, see, and that's important. You may pretend but the kids will see through you. You've got to have patience too. And a sense of humor. Now your dinner is ready so you'd better set that aside."

Keith, the interviewer, had his pen and pad out while his wife was making dinner. He captured her individual voice—an informal talker, lively and honest.

How should you record what people say in your interviews? And in your I-Search Paper? There's no one right way. Some interviewers take a cassette tape recorder along—being sure to inform their subjects that they are being taped. Other interviewers stick with the pen and pad. And still others record a few minutes of the interview in order to familiarize themselves with their subjects' style and idiom. In 1954 I followed Peter Kihss of *The New York Times* on one of his assignments. He's one of the most scholarly and thorough reporters of the last few decades. At a Senate subcommittee hearing he was covering, he took quick notes in a secretary's spiral notebook, and on the subway back to the *Times* office he began choosing what he considered the most newsworthy material and wrote it in a small, neat hand in that ruled notebook.

Most interviewers find that space limitations in their magazines or newspapers prevent them from using everything they heard; and ordinarily the ideas and experience that come out in such stories need organization and focus. What are you trying to get over to your readers? Choose the strongest parts of the dialogue and omit the weakest. That's not being dishonest. Your readers haven't contracted with you to deliver them the inconsequential or boring moments of an interview. Choose and discard. Better to score with a short, muscular interview than bore and lose readers with a long, flabby one.

Here's a long interview, but I think with no fat in it. If it had to be cut to fit a shorter space, it could be. The opening "editorial" remarks aren't necessary, but once John Jansen begins speaking, I'd like to see all his words retained.

JOHN JANSEN

Gail Leszinske

The main goal in life of John Jansen, a 19-year-old junior at Western, is to be independent and productive, a large task for anyone trying to achieve. But for the handicapped it's an unending struggle. John is blind.

In this interview, John speaks about his blindness and the everyday confrontations he deals with maturely and with an attitude of acceptance.

G: John, were you born blind?

J: No. When I was four, I fell off our porch. A piece of wood severed the optic nerve and lodged in my skull. The doctor didn't notice the splinter and he sewed up the cut with the wood still inside. A few months later, I was having problems standing up. I would get real dizzy. I was taken to the hospital and they found I had spinal meningitis. Then I was only blind in one eye. The other eye went blind when I was nine. It's called *sympathetic optic atrophy*. It was a slow process. From about September to December of that year I went blind. I was in fourth grade.

G: After you were totally blind, did you attend a regular school?

J: No, I went to Warren Consolidated. Kids from all over the county are bussed there. What they have is a resource room with a helper teacher who teaches you Braille and assists you with your other classes, helps you to take tests, and just talks to you. There are all types of handicapped people who go to this school. You still have a regular teacher to teach you reading and math. The helper teacher is just there for the rehabilitation.

G: How long did you go to this school?

J: For the rest of elementary school—to the sixth grade.

G: Did you like it there?

J: It was really hard to have friends. The closest one was about twelve miles from me. I would have to call them long distance and we couldn't get together that much. It was kinda lonely. I didn't have many friends then. I guess that's why I'm so outgoing. I never want to feel that way again.

G: Where did you go after Warren?

J: To junior high and to high school. It was nice to be out of the special program. When you're in a special room, people categorize blind people. They don't want to assist the blind. Kids tease a lot. They say, "Oh get out of his way, he doesn't know where he's going."

G: You accept your blindness so well. Was there ever a time that you didn't?

J: Yes, in junior high. I didn't know anyone or do anything. I was lonely then, too. It's an awful feeling—being alone when everyone else is going and doing things. I changed after junior high. I met a lot of people, had a lot of friends. I began to do things with my friends and they accepted me for what I am—John!

G: Do you ever have problems with people accepting you now?

J: If you and I should go to a restaurant they probably would ask you, "What does he want?" Sometimes I think people are afraid of me. But when I make a friend, that makes up for it all.

G: How do you feel when someone treats you like you can't make your own decisions?

J: Gail, I get really mad. You know, some people think I'm deaf, too. They shout at me. They give me more handicaps than I have. I feel like telling the person I know what I want—let me tell you. But you can't let it get you down. It's so common.

G: John, how do you feel and act toward others who are handicapped and tend to pity themselves?

J: I tell them, "Look, you can't feel sorry for yourself." You have to look at things realistically. Can't live in utopia. Some of my friends rely on sighted people too much. I find myself doing that sometimes too.

G: What are you studying?

J: Political science and communications.

G: How can you relate those two areas to your life?

J: I'd like to go to law school—maybe work for the IRS. There is a special school in Arkansas. They prefer people with a BA or BS—not directly out of high school.

G: John, can you name one influential person who helped you to accept and inspired you?

J: OK, my resource teacher, Mr. Carrick. He was my mobility instructor in junior high.

G: What did he do that was so different?

J: His mobility. He got us out of the school and into the city. He helped you to learn things that related to your life. He also went to Western, graduated from the Mobility Program. He always was so positive that I could get around on my own. Until then, I must admit, I doubted that I could.

G: Do you have any goals?

J: Probably just to get a job and work in regular society. I'd like to make it on my own.

G: How did your family handle your handicap?

J: They accepted it really well. Even my brothers and sister. They treated me like I was normal—I'm glad of that. We'd play baseball and all.

G: How did you play?

J: When it was my turn to bat they'd give me the ball. One of my team members would stand at the bases and yell at me, so that I knew where to go. I would usually be the pitcher—they'd stand at the plate and talk to me so that I knew which way to throw the ball.

G: How about your parents?

J: They accepted it pretty well. I was treated more and more specialer. (John laughs.) There isn't such a word, is there? They didn't treat me any different from my other brothers and sister. Boy am I glad I got that one out.

G: Did they have any grudges against the doctor?

J: Yea. My mom had a stroke the same time I was in the hospital. My dad didn't have any hospitalization and he had to pay for it all. It wasn't a problem, though. He ran a supermarket. My mother had a hard time. She couldn't be with me because she was in another hospital. During that time, I had to learn how to walk all over again. Everyone was so willing to help—so eager. Sometimes it bothered me that they were so eager.

G: What kind of things bother you?

J: When people are constantly asking me if they can help me to get somewhere even when I know where I'm going. Just last night, a girl walked me to my room from the cafeteria. I never say anything because I don't want her to feel bad. I'm not helpless.

G: I never see you depressed. Do you ever get down?

J: I try to be with people who are cheerful and easy going. I call them up and talk to them.

G: Is your family close? Would you be less close if you weren't blind?

J: Probably a little bit—because the only reason I think that is I never did the guy things like hunting, trapping, playing football—it seems to break you away from the family. Our family goes on hikes in the woods. I guess that's why I've made friends with people around me. To go on dates and football games. Asking a girl out on a date really bugs me, even now. She has to drive. I like this school. So many things are accessible, like the movies at Sangren. You can even get by bus here.

G: Do you ever want to get married?

J: Yes, definitely.

G: Would you ever marry anyone who is handicapped?

J: Let me clarify something, do you mean blind?

G: I guess so.

J: Not if they were handicapped from birth. I feel that there is a greater risk of having a handicapped child from a person who was handicapped from birth. I just wouldn't want to bring a child into this world handicapped. That's one reason I stopped seeing Ruth Anne (a blind girl he once dated). Besides, it would be too hard to get around, to read mail, go grocery shopping. You'd have to depend on friends. I'm very explorative. That's man's nature—to look around. I hope people don't mind. In the dorm the guys don't mind, the girls don't say too much. It's a blind person's nature to see how big a room is, what's on the dresser, what the room looks like. I'm also very punctual. It bothers me if other people are late—maybe 2, 3, 4, or 5 minutes late is OK, but 15, I don't know if they've forgotten me. Last winter I got a B in a class because the girl forgot me three times. The teacher said to me, "You wouldn't have gotten the B if you hadn't skipped those times." I didn't say anything. That's what I mean about depending too much on people.

G: Do you have any advice you'd like to give another blind person?

J: Live happily. Don't be afraid to meet people, to strike up friendships. OK, I get teased a lot. I hang around the receptionist desk a lot. I like to be around people. So, I'd just say be open to new friendships and don't always depend on others to find your way, but don't be afraid to ask for help to get where you want to go. I've seen too many blind people get lost and no one is around to help them. They should have admitted in the first place that they didn't know where they were going. You just end up being frustrated.

G: Are you ever curious about how people look?

J: One thing I don't know if I agree with or not is exploring other people with my hands. Sometimes I forget that people wear glasses. I was once sighted so that I can ask my friends what they look like and I can get a general impression of that from their description. I usually don't want to ask until I know the person really well. (John grins.) With a girl, I usually can tell when I dance with her, if her hair is long, what her build is.

G. What a sly dog.

J: A guy just wants to know. I'm blind, not dead.

If you're approaching your first interview, you may fear that when your subject begins talking, you can't keep up with what's being said. Don't panic. Think about what's being said, not about how to get it down; and you'll find you don't have to record every word that's spoken. If you don't hear or don't understand, you can say, "Will you repeat that?" or "I'm not sure I understand what you just said."

Listen for the things that count for you and they'll most likely count for your readers. You can let a lot of words go by without recording them. You don't have to act like a tape recorder. In a way, the fact that your writing can't keep up with the subject's speaking is good because it forces you to choose what's most valuable and best said.

Most people who have to write hurriedly—whether it's taking dictation in an office, taking lecture notes, or interviewing—learn an accepted shorthand code or develop one of their own. A simple way to speed up note-taking is to drop most of your vowels. (Example: 1 smpl wy to spd up t note tkg is to drp mst vwls.) Such methods you must work out on yr own. Don't ask me to giv you a code. If yr taking notes that force you to write the same long word again and again, you can develop a single letter abbreviation for it. For thirty years I've been an English teacher with certain interests. To indicate terms or words I have to write often, especially those with many syllables, I've invented symbols or single letters: English—E, language—L, literature—lit, individual—I, objectivity—ɸ, subjectivity—$, and for *characteristics* or *characteristic* I use a lower case c and curl its tail around itself much as *a* in the symbol for "at each" (@), which is used in price lists. Make up your own signs; they're for you, not me, so they don't have to make sense to me.

Interviewing is a basic human act of communication, like telling a story. To interview someone is to get her talking about herself and what she does or thinks. We do that every day with acquaintances and every other day with strangers. The question is only to choose which statements to put into writing. And to think of your readers. If what your subject said in the excitement of talking won't be clear to your readers, change it. For example, when John said,

> Yea. My mom had a stroke the same time I was in the hospital. My dad didn't have any hospitalization . . .

a reader might misconstrue his meaning and think that *hospitalization* there meant that Dad wasn't in the hospital; but reading on, the reader would see that the rest of the sentence—"and he had to pay for it all"—suggests *hospitalization* there refers to "hospitalization insurance." So the writer might add the word *insurance* to insure clarity as well as hospitalization. Most of us talk less exactly than we write, and as readers we expect more precision in statements than we do as listeners. As an interviewer, you can make up for that difference. Ordinarily your job is not to make a fool out of the person you're interviewing.

Many newspaper and magazine reports are fundamentally interviews. Some interviewers loosen up their subjects until they talk on and on brilliantly, without any jogging questions from the interviewer. When that happens, you don't need to ask questions. Sometimes a strict adherence to the question-answer format misrepresents the subject and stops his flow of words or ideas. There's no hallowed formula for presenting interviews; if the speaker is going great, let him roll. Break his talk only with occasional paragraphing to help the reader. When you do that, if you're using quotation marks as Keith Newman did when he interviewed his wife, you should know that the conventional way to punctuate that sort of speech is to use quotation marks at the first of several paragraphs spoken by the same speaker, but to omit the closing quotation marks on those paragraphs so as to indicate that the same speaker is still talking. Then at the end of the last paragraph, where the subject is, so to speak, signing off, use closing quotation marks.

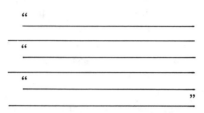

A good interview is usually not a word-for-word report of what two people said to each other, but rather a composing in which the interviewer studies his notes, chooses the best pieces, and puts them together to form a picture that makes sense to him, the person interviewed, and his readers. And so with reports that newspeople call "stories." Many of those that concern mainly one person's ideas, feelings, or actions are fundamentally interviews, with part of the subject's words translated into other words by the reporter in order to shorten or clarify the story. For example, in this report from *The Kalamazoo* (Michigan) *Gazette* for February 19, 1978, the reporter interviewed a citizen who had undergone radiation exposure. The reporter explained in his own words much of what his subject said in order to save space and emphasize certain points; but he included also a large number of the man's spoken words. If the reporter had told the whole "story" in his own words, it would have lacked the authority it gains from the sound of a man recounting his own experiences with feeling. I give short excerpts from a long article:

BOMB TESTS WITNESSED BY DELTON MAN
RALPH VARTABEDIAN, *Gazette* Staff Writer

Watching the detonation of an atomic bomb from a trench only three miles from "ground zero" in 1952 made William Leslie of Delton a wary veteran of the military.

Leslie, 47, considers himself no hero. "I was a guinea pig," he said. "And I've kept it pent up all these years."

Leslie, who works at Brown Co.'s Parchment plant as a maintenance man, is one of 300,000 people the U.S. Department of Defense wants to locate to gather information about the effects of early atomic blasts on participants. . . .

"Then we had to go to a place called a decontamination area—this is what really tore me up. It was an open canvas tent and I thought we would be given fresh clothes and a shower.

"But we were given a broom and told to sweep each other off. At the end of the line there was a guy with a Geiger counter. If you had too much radiation on you they sent you back for more sweeping.

"What could we do about it? We were told to do something and we did it," he said.

In retrospect, Leslie wishes a request he put in for Korean duty had been accepted. "I volunteered for Far East duty. I was never put on the list. One of the reasons they said was that I had a rare type blood AB negative." . . .

A good interview, enough of Mr. Leslie's own words to characterize him and enough of the reporter's narration—even in this short excerpt—to keep the report from becoming excessively long. As you can see, the reporting method here is in one way similar to that used by most I-Searchers. The reporter quotes only selected statements by the person being interviewed and in his own words keeps the story going.

∞ **DOING SIXTEEN:** For fifteen or twenty minutes, interview another member of your group and then let that person interview you. Find out something she or he likes to do, and get the waterfall of words flowing. Ask what is at the heart of this thing the person likes to do, and how she or he feels at the moment of doing it. Take notes. Inside or outside class, write up the interview.

∞ **DOING SEVENTEEN:** Interview someone outside of class whom you admire for the way he or she does something. Not somebody you think you should admire, but really do, a person you've observed several or many times. This person doesn't have to hold a glamorous or "important" position—might be the campus groundskeeper who picks up litter with a stab of a steel-pointed stick and talks charmingly to passersby, or the woman who runs the snowplow, or a coach you like, or the switchboard operator. Maybe it's your next-door neighbor who raises dahlias or studies cactuses on weekend field trips. Remember the interviews of Mrs. Swanson, Debbie Newman, and John Jansen.

You may write this as a straight question-and-answer interview or a narrative-and-dialogue story.

*Our friendship continued without inter-
ruption to his death, upwards of forty
years; and the club continued almost as
long, and was the best school of philosophy, morality, and politics that then
existed in the province . . . we acquired
better habits of conversation, every thing
being studied in our rules which might
prevent our disgusting each other.*

BENJAMIN FRANKLIN

chapter 12
i
and the
others

WE LEARN ALONE; and we learn from
others—most powerfully when they are learning from us as well. This
is not a guess, a theory, a hope, but a conclusion based on observing
thirty-eight groups of people meeting to write and respond to each
other's writings over periods of ten to fifteen weeks. I've watched
people for fifteen years in these seminars and seen them change as
writers and thinkers. When you know that what you write is going to
be listened to attentively by a number of your peers in a place where
the expectation of first-rate performance is high, both your conscious
and unconscious go to work for you with more power than usual.

School brings you together with peers but ordinarily only as listener
to a figure who delivers the authoritative word on every matter. But a
genuine seminar enables everyone to become an author and authority.
It's much like the clubs that people formed in the 18th century—and
still are forming today—to sharpen their minds by learning from each
other. When I was an instructor at a midwestern university, my office
mate, assistant professor Frederic E. Reeve, invited me to help him
form a book club. We asked ten other friends to meet monthly and
choose a book we would all read. Then at someone's house, with food
and drink to cheer us, we discussed our responses to the book. Each
month a different person was chosen to lead the discussion. We began

by reading some of the books on psychology that were being written for non-specialists.

Fred Reeve had just finished a two-year stint in Cleveland as associate editor of a refreshing new work aptly called *Webster's New World Dictionary*. In our club he read the books with remarkable comprehension, recalling every paragraph with a photographic memory that dismayed me. His performance at our meetings, whether as leader or supposed follower, was always leading; and at first it frightened me almost into silence. My ego was suffering. I had spent three years in the army during World War II, gone to graduate school in the South where I had worked with highly educated and thoughtful civil rights activists, and I expected to hold my own in a book club. Luckily, Fred liked me and never in those meetings turned his scorn or argumentative powers against me full force, or I would have quit the club and retired to my apartment to read alone. Several in the group did that, but a few of us gained confidence to speak out our responses despite the certainty that Fred would have thought past them and his remarks would reveal our shallowness.

When Fred's turn came to lead the discussion, we heard what was possible in such a role. He read more books as background, studied more of the history of the author and times, and had his remarks in better command than any of the rest of us. One day when he couldn't join me for a movie because the next day he was going to talk to a ladies' literary group about Dr. Samuel Johnson, I said, "Freddie, why do you worry about that? You know hundreds of times more about Dr. Johnson than those women do, and you know you can give a brilliant talk off the top of your head."

"Ken," he said, "when I contract to give a talk in public, to whatever audience, I believe I should give them my best. For that, I need to prepare thoroughly. A speaker owes that to any audience."

Despite Fred's domineering in that club, I saw what it is to study and give the best of one's mind and feelings to others without working under the external authority of a teacher. I think most of us did better than we had ever done in a classroom: as leaders, we made ourselves authorities because others depended on us to take more time than they were going to give to a book, and yet they were all reading it because they wanted to.

When I think about the person who hid in the bathroom and about others in our club—the man who was forever pontificating to us; the sweet woman who said often she had read only half the book, an excuse, we soon recognized, to cover her failure to understand or remember what was in it; and the man who talked on and on without giving others a chance—I'm reminded of Dr. Johnson's complaints about one member of his Ivy Lane Club, which he founded in 1749, during that great century of clubs in England. W. Jackson Bate, Johnson's biographer, reports that no one in the club liked John Hawkins. "Though sanctimoniously rigid in his outward religious attitudes, he was contentious, nit-picking, and chronically suspicious. In repressing or hiding from himself his own motives [I think of the woman who never read all of any one of the books we assigned ourselves in our club], he projected them on others." Hawkins refused to pay his share of the bill (it was a supper club), saying he didn't usually eat supper anyway. Dr. Johnson remained loyal to Hawkins as friend, but admitted to another person, "Why really I believe him to be an honest man at the bottom; but to be sure he is penurious, and is mean, and it must be owned he has a degree of brutality, and a tendency to savageness, that cannot easily be defended."

I bring up such difficulties with people in clubs, because in your group, inside or outside school, you'll encounter people you can't stand, but must stand, as Johnson and others did. Individuals must excuse some faults in persons they work with or regularly meet, or they'll not be able to exist in society. The fortunate thing about a class in school is that it will end in a semester or a year, and one need not pursue friendship or acquaintance with every member after that. And if the group is a self-formed club, it can begin with the intention of continuing for a year or two and then disbanding, perhaps to start up with a different membership at a later date.

This is a nagging difficulty in groups that meet regularly—what to do with irritating or sometimes warring personalities. Ben Franklin, who formed and sustained the most accomplished club in the western world—it lasted about forty years—early in his life faced the problem of discussing ideas without alienating people. When Ben was about twenty-six, he said that a Quaker friend,

> having kindly informed me that I was generally thought proud; that my pride show'd itself frequently in conversation; that I was not content with being in the right when discussing any point, but was overbearing, and rather insolent, of which he convinc'd me by mentioning several instances . . .

This said to a man who later was acknowledged in three countries as one of the most engaging, persuasive men ever to take part in social, political, and scientific affairs! Here's how he said he made the change:

I made it a rule to forbear all direct contradiction to the sentiments of others, and all positive assertion of my own. I even forbid myself agreeably to the old law of our Junto [his famous club], the use of every word or expression in the language that imported a fix'd opinion, such as *certainly, undoubtedly,* etc., and I adopted, instead of them, *I conceive, I apprehend,* or *I imagine* a thing to be so or so; or *it so appears to me at present.*

When another asserted something that I thought an error, I deny'd myself the pleasure of contradicting him abruptly, and of showing immediately some absurdity in his proposition. . . .

I've often been annoyed by persons who habitually say, "I'm sure you know a lot more than I do about this," or "I'm probably wrong—." But that wasn't Franklin. He wasn't apologizing or being hypocritical but simply avoiding rude and aggressive contradiction. In the group you become a member of, you'll encounter frequent disagreement, but the aim will be to countenance writers, not destroy them. If one person advances an idea or opinion different from yours, you can listen to it. There's no obligation for you to say whether or not you agree with it. You can occasionally let strong notions stand without direct contradiction. At that moment, or later, you may advance your notions without pointing out that they differ with someone else's.

> *As is often the case in debate, Foreman's arguments did more to strengthen the convictions of those already in sympathy than to convert those who were not.*
>
> MARTIN DUBERMAN

In 1727, when he was twenty-one, Franklin started the Junto Club. The men he gathered were not famous, but, as Carl Van Doren, one of his biographers, said, "solid, sensible, good-natured, ingenious. . . ." They were friends "with whom Franklin already liked to talk, and it was a kind of economy to meet with them all at once at a tavern every Friday night." Typically, Ben structured the meetings so they would work to the advantage of the members and the city of Philadelphia, which was then young and forming its character just as the Junto Club members were.

Customarily a Junto meeting began with twenty questions and a pause after each of them for members to respond if they wished. All point to action, unlike the questions most of us are confronted with in school. Here are two:

12. Do you know of any deserving young beginner lately set up, whom it lies in the power of the Junto any way to en- encourage? . . .

20. In what manner can the Junto, or any of them, assist you in any of your honorable designs? . . .

The members who listened to such questions represented a range of professions. Many groups in our society bring together only people of similar occupation or cast of mind, and thus reduce the chances for exciting exchange and learning. That's one of the virtues of classes in public schools—they're often made up of highly different people. The original Junto membership is here described in Franklin's words, a few of which I give because they are so concise and reveal both his affection and objectivity:

> Hugh Meredith . . . a Welsh Pennsylvanian, thirty years of age, bred to country work; honest, sensible, had a great deal of solid observation, was something of a reader but given to drink. . . . Stephen Potts, a young countryman of full age, bred to the same, of uncommon natural parts, and great wit and humour, but a little idle. . . . George Webb, an Oxford scholar . . . lively, witty, good-natured, and a pleasant companion, but idle, thoughtless, and imprudent to the last degree. Joseph Breintnal, a copier of deeds for the scriveners, a good-natured, friendly, middle-aged man, a great lover of poetry, reading all he could meet with and writing some that was tolerable; very ingenious in many little knick-knackeries and of sensible conversation. Thomas Godfrey, a self-taught mathematician, great in his way, and afterward inventor of what is now called Hadley's quadrant. But he knew little out of his way and was not a pleasing companion. . . .

Customarily, talk at the Junto Club resulted in action: Once Ben went to Boston to check out the firefighting clubs he'd heard about. He returned, reported his findings to the club, and they formed a volunteer fire company of thirty members, who not only fought fires, but met once a month to discuss how to do that as well as prevent fires. Others interested were encouraged to form other fire companies, and in 1736 Franklin formed the Union Fire Company of Philadelphia. In a few years the city became one of the safest from fire in the world. After Franklin read a paper to the Junto against the inequitable tax on citizens to support watchmen and policemen—a poor widow had to pay as much as a rich merchant—the club succeeded in reforming the tax law.

You may be thinking, "What do these 18th-century clubs have to do with me? I'm not going to join a group with members like Benjamin Franklin or Samuel Johnson." Behind my recital of these stories are several questions: In high school or college classes do you know the minds as well as the serious interests of the people who sit with you in the room? Have they and you brought out the best in each other? Do you realize that many of the people Franklin and Johnson knew in clubs were in their early years unknown and relatively unaccomplished? Are the people of your acquaintance bookards? Or is that something hard to perceive, given the nature of your school and social experiences with them? Have you been countenanced in learning since you stopped absorbing language at your mother's knee? Do you countenance the efforts toward learning of persons you know? Or are you aware of such efforts among friends and acquaintances? I think the answer to many of these questions may be negative because you aren't regularly thrown into situations conducive to the kind of learning Franklin and Johnson found so valuable. Thus, this countenancing book was written to emphasize learning on your own and in the company of peers, not just from one supposed authority called "teacher."

In the earlier days of the seminars, before I asked students to write I-Search Papers, occasionally I tape-recorded sessions in which we'd respond to each other's writing. I did the taping only toward the end of the course when we were relaxed. I wish I had taped more, and that I had done it for I-Search responding; but I didn't, so to give an idea of such responding, I'll have to reconstruct a session from memory.

After a week or so of searching, persons brought a trial page from their I-Search Paper to the group for response so they could get a feel for what they were going to write in their whole paper. Such a testing also helped them as searchers: they knew what kind of and how much information they might need when they got down to composing the whole paper. This is a way of finding out how your story is going to come across to readers.

Here's such a trial page from one paper. The class had already responded to the opening several weeks earlier, so the members knew what the writer was searching for.

1

I read an article in a local newspaper about the Chesaning Rest Home. It gave a list of the patients and a talent each one had. Myra Baker [name changed] was the home's "expert quilt-maker."

I'd never been to a rest home before, I had this vision of old, decrepit people who were just a little senile. It was something new and I was scared to go.

Myra Baker was ninety-four years old and as we walked to the game room she apologized for having to use a walker but "the age has gotten to me." She was a happy lady, the nurses referred to her as "our angel."

"I've made every kind of quilt possible, I couldn't count them." Her favorite was using small four-inch squares pieced together. "I think they're prettiest."

She suggested that all the pieces be cut on the same grain of the fabric and not to mix wools with cottons.

"I like to use sheets for the center's lining, it washes better without bunching up." I could see her point but I still want the thickness a cotton batting lining can give me.

Mrs. Baker started talking about how her mother, "the saint," could do anything, "she was the smartest lady. . . ." Her mind was starting to stray and the bingo cards were being passed out. I thanked her and she thanked me for visiting her, she asked me back. I walked away smiling, I'm glad I went.

RESPONSE

John: I like it. You built up my curiosity about what the old woman and the rest home would be like, and then I felt I really met her.

Gracie: I did too. Especially I liked the way you quoted her—very short quotes, but they brought her alive. That's kind of funny, isn't it? She was so near death but you brought her alive.

The writer: Yeah, she was very sharp when she had it all together.

Jane: I admire the way you got those little bits of conversation in there at the same time you were making points about quilting. That was good.

Carole: Little touches I liked, like here, "I thanked her . . ." I expected that would be the end of it, but you added, "and she thanked me for visiting her, she asked me back." That tells a lot, but you don't take a lot of words to say it. You could have gone on and on about what a charming old lady she was, but you got that over with very few words.

Kirk: At times you need to watch your punctuation. You don't seem to know when a sentence has ended. Like in that passage Carole was just quoting—"she asked me back" is a sentence and needs to start with a capital or else be joined to the rest of the sentence with "and." Same thing happens in the last sentence.

Brenda: Yeah, other punctuation things—when you quote what a person said and it's a sentence, it should start with a capitalized word, like in the last paragraph, "she was the smartest lady. . . ." Should be a capitalized *She*.

Teacher: I admire the page, too, for its conciseness. No wasted words, yet it's dramatic. If you can treat the rest of the people you meet in your search in this way, you'll have a fine paper.

That's countenancing—the positive things before the negative so the writer feels encouraged and willing to listen to suggested changes. And the teacher (or leader) waits for the others to comment first, so they'll feel the responsibility to comment and not leave the job all to him.

Here's another trial page from an I-Search Paper with the group's response. Think of Ben Franklin's resolution not to contradict others. And the feeling that ought to pervade meetings of a club where friends meet. Much care should be taken not to insult or cripple individuals whose work stands so vulnerably before the group. But a commitment to helping, to responding truthfully. Or else why meet at all?

2

As I walked into the room I caught the glance of a young field worker named Mary. I explained to her that I was writing a paper on my car engine; to understand how it operates. I asked if they had any pamphlets on file or if she could recommend any books. She seemed friendly and eager to help. She recalled seeing some dittoes in the file cabinet and started digging through the papers until she came across a short multiple choice test on "Identifying Your Vehicle." The ditto she gave me was pretty basic but at least it tested me on how much I knew. Mary was excited that they were starting a new library. The books were still packed away in boxes and the room was very congested. From checking in the card catalog she found that they had no books on cars. Her knowledge on the subject appeared to be very limited; she suggested that I go to Waldo library. I thanked her and was on my way.

My next stop was at Michigan News Agency. I liked the atmosphere of the store. The guys who worked there seemed very "down to earth" and neighborly. I walked directly up to the first salesman I saw and asked him, "Do you have any books on car engines?"

"What—did your car break down?" he asked. (That is a crazy question for him to ask! Does he think all females let their car go?)

"No, I'm writing a paper on my car engine and want to understand how it functions."

"Well, let's see. What kind of car do you have?"

"A Barracuda—Plymouth."

"Well, we have a book that has your model in it. Here it is, Plymouth—Tune up and Maintenance, 1967-76."

I looked at it for a while. It was packed full of diagrams and charts. The writing seemed simple enough to follow—so I bought it. He also showed me a book written by a woman for women. The book was called "Car Care and Repair" by Charlotte Slater. After skimming through the book I was amazed at how basic and almost dumb it was. A few examples of a typical chapter were; how to pump gasoline; a lesson on starting cars; clearing window fog; and better check anti-freeze.

After studying my book on Plymouth cars for a few hours I realized though it illustrated the parts and told how to analyze what is wrong with your car it did not tell how the whole engine operates. I could still use the book but would have to find another way to put the concept of the engine together.

RESPONSE

Lyall: I enjoyed it because I work on cars and was interested to see how a girl approached them.

Kirk: You got punctuation problems, too. You spray semicolons around as if they're commas.

The writer: What do you mean by that?

Dick: Let's get back to people's general response to the page. We can talk about punctuation later, or you and Kirk can go off in a corner at the break.

Kirk: Well, I was just trying to help her.

Dick: Yeah, but—

Deb: I thought it was great, but when I look back, I guess I'd have to say that part in the bookstore grabbed me harder than the stuff about Mary, the girl who was setting up the new library. I got a little lost there.

John: I think so, too. It seems to be more about the library than it does about car engines.

The writer: Well, I had to tell about why I couldn't get anything there. And we're supposed to tell the story of our search, aren't we?

John: Yeah, I don't know.

Elaine: As I look at the two parts, they're different. The stuff about the bookstore is like a conversation and the stuff about Mary is like an explanation.

Bill: Yeah, but if the first part were like the second it would be too long, and I don't think that much is accomplished there.

Teacher: One thing I want to say to you all is that it took me years to realize that in this situation I have an advantage over you because I've usually read the papers we look at before I come to class and you're seeing them for the first time. In my first reading I was also bothered by the first part of this page. What Elaine and Bill have been saying is beginning to show me why. I think maybe the first part about Mary could be shortened a lot—not so much about her feelings of confusion in opening a new library, although you might mention that if you want to. The two parts are radically different in form, probably because you wrote them at different times. The first is full of little details that don't advance your cause and the second never wastes a word. I think you could cut fifty words or more from the first part, easily. For example, you say, "She seemed friendly and eager to help." You could probably do without that sentence because the next one shows her doing the helping.

Pete: Well, I didn't find anything wrong with it. I thought it was great. I was right there with Helen all the time and I'm amazed that a girl could be so sharp about cars.

Sally: I'm amazed that any male would be so dumb as to say something like that.

That's not such good countenancing, although some of the remarks are probably highly useful to Helen. Kirk's early negative comment about the punctuation weaknesses apparently upset Helen and got her started defending herself rather than concentrating on what was being said that she might use to improve her paper. A group's responses to a piece of writing are valuable only if the writer will make them so. The first rule in listening to comments about your work is "Never defend yourself—unless you can tell that your critic has misunderstood something and will probably change her mind immediately upon being told of it." Listen. You're not on trial, your paper is; and you don't have to defend it. Simply listen to comments, then go back to your writing room and when you've cooled down and become more objective, decide whether or not you're going to act on the suggestions and criticisms that were made of your writing. Naturally you'll get angry during the response sessions when someone cuts down your paper. But anger isn't going to help that session. If you get angry enough and speak that anger, the responders may stop responding. Then you've robbed yourself of the function of such a club or group —to be a sounding board that will help writers.

This is easier for me to say than to put into practice myself when my writing is being criticized. As a professional, I send my book manuscripts off to an editor who finds faults in them. When I read his comments, I become angry. When I put them aside and look at them the next day, I agree with most of them and feel grateful I have such a helper. I know he's on my side. We both want the best book possible. As the members of your club or seminar move more and more toward that feeling—that you are all helping each other, all on the same side—you'll see everyone's writing improve dramatically.

But I don't want to leave my description of clubs in a sentimental glow. They're made up of people, and the best of people become foolishly belligerent at times. Here's that generous, experienced conversationalist Dr. Sam Johnson at a meeting of The Club where members began to argue about the advantages of drinking wine. W. Jackson Bate reports:

> Johnson—who, from abstaining from it so long, assumed everyone who drank wine was intoxicated—finally shouted to [Sir Joshua] Reynolds, "I won't argue any more with you, Sir. You are too far gone" (at which Reynolds actually made Johnson blush by saying, "I should have thought so indeed, Sir, had I made such a speech as you have now done").

∞ **DOING EIGHTEEN:** Choose a part of your search you have doubts about—for either your exploring methods or the way you write them up, and write a trial page of your I-Search Paper. You can imagine that it will occur at any point in the paper that you wish. Bring it to your group for response and help. Arrange to have enough copies of the page so that everyone in the group will get one.

All writing slants the way a writer leans, and no man is born perpendicular although many men are born upright.

E. B. WHITE

chapter 13
objectivity and subjectivity

MOST RESEARCH PAPERS written in high school and college are bad jokes. They're funny because they pretend to be so much and actually are so little.

According to *Webster's New World Dictionary* (one of the several good desk dictionaries useful to a searcher), research is "careful, systematic, patient study and investigation in some field of knowledge, undertaken to establish facts or principles." Those of you who've seen or done a research paper in school are probably laughing. More than half such papers are done carelessly, unsystematically, impatiently. A student waits till the weekend before the paper is due, rushes to the library, dips into a few books and magazines, takes a passage or two from each, strings them together with a few of her own sentences, follows the prescribed introduction and conclusion form, makes up a pretentious title like "Modern Psychology and the Problem of Drinking," and turns in a paper that doesn't in any sense *establish* anything.

To show how such a damnfool result emerges from such a high-minded enterprise, I'll tell a long story and explain a few things.

All students—being people—are curious. Don't give them a lot of credit for that: they were born that way, just as flies and chipmunks were. The whole caboodle—students, insects, and animals—are lazy: they like to sit in the sun and doze. English teachers, having committed themselves to the world of scholarship—mostly because they liked to read literature and wanted a job which would pay them for doing it —have been forced to learn the conventions or forms of their profession, things like how to make lists of books in the approved form, called *bibliographies,* and how to footnote scholarly papers according to a handbook of style published by the Modern Language Association. When they were in school as students, they were told to learn such things and often they didn't, because like many students they were lazier than curious, and the task of memorizing all the forms was boring. But when they got their graduate degrees and realized that in a few months they would be expected to teach others about footnotes and bibliographies, they went to work in the waning weeks of summer vacation and learned what they had failed to learn before. Once they had mastered these matters, they felt it their duty to put their students through the same rigamarole they had gone through, forgetting that when they were students the stuff had not *taken* with them.

A long story. One reason that research paper writing in schools is often a farce is that the notion of research as "patient study and investigation in some field of knowledge, undertaken to establish facts or principles" leaves out the basic motivation for the whole effort. The search should take place because somebody needs to find out something or wants to satisfy an itch of curiosity as insistent as athlete's foot. Somebody's got a question and wants to answer it. But that's not the way the project goes. It's more like the way the street in front of my house was resurfaced last year. It didn't need repaving, but the man in charge told my wife and me that other streets in the neighborhood had to be paved, and once the pavers got started they might as well do this one so they wouldn't have to remember at a later date that this one then needed it. And all those yellow monsters with their work crews were up there just beyond the intersection, and they had to have something to do.

My story really began in the 15th, 16th, and 17th centuries when people in the western world began to look at things in a way we now call "scientific." They made astonishing discoveries by attempting to separate—as the philosopher-critic Samuel Coleridge advocated—the perceiver from the things perceived. Instead of saying, "Isn't this ice shaped strangely?" they measured it on succeeding days and months and found it was moving. They gave it a distinguishing name, *glacier.* They devised measuring instruments and methods so they were able to perceive objects as separate, detached from themselves, the observers. Thermometers, rulers, scales, chemical methods of analysis. And so they developed precise descriptions of things formerly perceived only with the eyes and the other senses.

In the last part of the 18th century, the German philosopher Immanuel Kant began using the word *objective,* and later the British thinkers Coleridge and DeQuincey helped it along. The observer, or *subject,* was thought to be naturally subjective (prejudiced, partial, self-centered) and the observed, or *object,* was just there, challenging people to see it exactly as it was, nothing more, nothing less. When an observer supposedly saw it that way, he was being *objective,* letting nothing of himself interfere with or color the object.

After a few centuries of learning to control the physical world and to manufacture new products and machines out of its elements, people—mostly men, who were the prime movers in the scientific and industrial revolutions—got cocky about their ability to stand off and see things as they "really were." Such an improvement over the days when doctors used to apply leeches to patients and let blood from them so they'd get over their illnesses, or the days when fellows like Icarus, trying to fly with homemade feathered wings, crashed. Now, dreamers turned technologists conquered the air: the Wrights, Lindbergh, Boeing.

But in the 19th century, when men were bragging about their objective powers, a few people were beginning to say that maybe human beings couldn't remove themselves completely from what they observed. In 1896, J. T. Merz, a specialist in European intellectual history, said:

> A mind devoid of prepossessions is likely to be devoid of all mental furniture. And the historian who thinks that he can clean his mind as he would a slate with a wet sponge, is ignorant of the simplest facts of mental life. "The objectivity on which some of them pride themselves," remarks a caustic critic, "will be looked upon not as freedom from, but as unconsciousness on the part of, the preconceived notions which have governed them."

Despite warnings like that, scientists and technologists came to believe ever more strongly in their ability to be completely objective, and sociologists and psychologists, who couldn't measure human behavior with the same precision as geologists had measured the movements of glaciers, devised ways of counting human actions by what they called "quantitative methods," which they claimed were objective. At the end of their research reports they usually announced a statistically figured margin of error which they thought protected them from being charged with smugness. But in fact these margin-of-error formulas made some of their findings seem no more impressive than the "educated guesses" of people the scientists scorned because they failed to use quantitative methods.

In the last three centuries, the astounding discoveries and achievements of scientists and technologists have been due not only to increasingly objective methods of measuring but also to a habit scientists have institutionalized—of publishing their research findings to the whole world, so that other scientists can both use them and examine them for errors. In recent years this safeguard has been weakened because so many scientific researches have been carried out that no single person in one field can keep up with all that is being published. But the habit is basic to good inquiry. Most students' research papers in high school and college are bad jokes partly because they are not subjected to public inspection by a number of people who care about what they say: instead they're read by one person only, the teacher, who's thinking principally of how to grade them.

In these ridiculous research projects, students are trapped on a two-sided loop. Teachers assign them the job to teach them how to use the library and learn scholarly forms of documentation (hoping, usually vainly, that also the students will search for and find something valuable to them and others), and so the students produce papers no one wants to read. They're inside the loop with the teachers and their interest in *form;* outside the loop stand human beings who might be interested in the results of a genuine search. Since nobody apparently wants to know what is being *said* by the writers of these research papers, they say what amounts to nothing. And since their papers contain nothing, the teacher and other people see no reason for reading them for what they say. In such a trap, students concentrate their attention more and more upon taking sentences out of books and magazines and piecing them together (for the purpose of having something to footnote and bibliographize) in ways that have become increasingly meaningless. It's a great tradition of inanity, not far from that achieved by a professor in the Grand Academy of Lagado in Jonathan Swift's book *Gulliver's Travels.* He invented a contrivance so that anyone

> . . . with a little bodily labour, may write books in philosophy, poetry, politics, law, mathematics, and theology, without the least assistance from genius or study. He then led me to the frame, about the side whereof all his pupils stood in ranks.

There, on bits of wood linked by slender wires, were the words of the language of Lagado, said Swift.

> The pupils at his command took each of them hold of an iron handle, whereof there were forty fixed round the edges of the frame, and giving them a sudden turn, the whole disposition of the words was entirely changed. He then commanded six and thirty of the lads to read the several lines softly as they appeared upon the frame, and where they found three or four words together that might make part of a sentence, they dictated to the four remaining boys who were scribes. . . . the professor showed me several volumes . . . of broken sentences, which he intended to piece together, and out of those rich materials to give the world a complete body of all arts and sciences. . . .

Writing in 1727, Swift had the objectivity to see how we can delude ourselves into thinking that machinery and detachment can do away with the need to be constantly aware of the way subjectivity and objectivity must be related on the Moebius Strip. In this discussion, I don't mean to imply that there is some easy, foolproof way to truth. But the effort to simplify the matter has gone on year after year. In 1940, S.I. Hayakawa published a bestselling book on semantics (the study of meaning) called *Language in Action,* in which he stated, "A report must exclude all expressions of the writer's approval or disapproval of the occurrences, persons, or objects he is describing." But the difficulty is that reporters may communicate their disapproval of what they're writing about in such subtle ways that they're not aware of doing it. About ten years later, the Columbia Broadcasting System radio commentator, Edward R. Murrow, who became famous as a reporter during the Battle of Britain in World War II, said:

> It is not, I think, humanly possible for any reporter to be completely objective, for we are all to some degree prisoners of our education, travel, reading—the sum total of our experience.

There's the object out there, and here are we, the observers. Can we see it for what it actually is, so others can trust our perceptions? That's the simple question investigators and philosophers used to ask. If the observers cared passionately about the object, their vision might blur, or their hand tremble as a surgeon's would if while operating on a child's brain, he thought of how endearing a human being she had been when he visited her in the ward the day before the operation. For the surgeon, detachment is necessary, but not so much that he doesn't care at all what happens. Some sense of urgency and value must be felt in the operating room. S. Ramon Cajal, an internationally known investigator of organic tissues, once told medical people that doctors should make their work square with "objective reality," but added:

> We should pervade the things observed with the intensity of our emotion and with a deep sense of affinity, making them ours as much where the heart is concerned as when the intelligence is involved. Only thus will they surrender their secrets to us, for enthusiasm increases and refines our capacity for perception.

Always the act of perception or investigation seems double-sided, as can be described accurately only in terms of the Moebian Strip. As Dr. Cajal says, when we are enthusiastic, or attached, we see things we otherwise miss; for example, lovers see things in their loved ones that others do not perceive. But at the same time, they're often blind to blemishes and faults in their loved ones that are obvious to others. One of my professors in graduate school at Columbia University, Herbert Hyman of the sociology department, used to say that apparently people reach their greatest ability to perceive subtle differences when they're neither completely uninterested in an object nor completely immersed in it.

> *The press continually reminds us that students can no longer punctuate, use proper grammar, spell correctly, or write legibly. But the crisis in writing goes beyond these visible signs. People do not see themselves as writers because they believe they have nothing to say that is of value or interest to others.*
>
> DONALD H. GRAVES

As observers we need to stand off from what we're observing so we can see it for what it is. To find it wholly, at times we must lose ourselves in it, as well as let it enter us. Are we it? Is it us? Albert Einstein went so far as to say that the observer is part of the observed. In the I-Search Paper about captive wolves, which appears at the beginning of this book, Kirk Moll admitted that for years he had been in love with the animals, but he managed to be both subjective and objective in his search. He found wolf breeders who admitted that wolves might attack their owners; in fact one of them reported how she was bitten by her pet, but Kirk discovered that these very trainers, so realistic about their animals, at the same time loved them and enjoyed being with them because they were so intelligent. The wolves were not naturally aggressive toward their owners but became violent only when they misperceived a situation. And these misperceptions could be avoided or lessened by owners who got to know their pets well. Another relationship that is best described when put on a Moebius Strip.

A person who writes an I-Search Paper can be both subjective and objective, as was Carmen Rivera [name changed] of Rochester, New York, when she wrote the following paper. Her mother adopted a baby who was physically and mentally disabled. At first Carmen felt revulsion. But as the baby grew and prospered within the love of the new family, Carmen came deeply to love her adopted sister. That was her subjective self at work. Yet it was not enough, thought Carmen. Some day she wanted her sister to know the conditions of her adoption and early childhood. So she began searching them out and recorded them in her paper. This was an effort toward objectivity. Here is the result, which I consider truly Moebian:

A LIFE

To Jennifer, love always. Carmen

1

About a year ago my mother decided that she would like to bring up another child. She could no longer have children of her own. My father agreed; he liked the idea. My mother had worked several times, and keeping herself occupied was no problem, but she no longer held a job because it had begun interfering with her personal life with the family.

A few days after she had made this decision, she noticed a newspaper article about Mandato Center, which was a state facility that placed special children with families instead of in institutions. The children had physical or mental problems, or both.

My mother applied at Mandato Center and an interview was scheduled. The social worker assigned to the case asked my mother her reasons for wanting a child. She also asked what sex my mother preferred—male or female. The social worker then asked about our living conditions and inspected our home to make sure there was enough room for another child, and to see the conditions in which the child would be placed. Finally, the social worker found a child who she thought would be suitable for our family. My mother was asked to go and see her, and one of my sisters went with her.

When my mother first saw her, Jennifer had bed sores on her face and weighed approximately seven pounds. She was the height of an average one-year-old, although she was four years old, soon to be five in November.

My parents hesitated at first. They were afraid that my two younger brothers would begin to imitate her, that Jennifer would not be a good influence on them. That was their major concern.

A weekend visit was scheduled for Jennifer to spend with us as a trial basis. Everything went fine. Many of our relatives came to see her. She was readily accepted by everyone. Jennifer was to move in a week later, permanently. Permanently meant that we would keep her until her parents wanted her back. She moved in under the conditions that Jennifer's parents would take her home for a weekend once a month.

2

When Jennifer first came to live with us, I wondered why anyone would give up their child. As I began to love Jennifer, I doubted that anyone would give up a child like her unless they were insensitive people. That is why I am writing this paper. As Jennifer's sister I wanted to bring to life what was dead in Jennifer's little heart. I wanted to be able to explain that it was of a kind nature that she was given away, not because she was hated by anyone.

Jennifer had many beautiful qualities that slowly began to develop as her stay with us became a natural for her. In my mind, I wondered why Jennifer was progressing now after four years of little mental and physical growth with her parents. I wondered why Jennifer had weighed seven pounds at age four. She came to live with us then. In less than one year she gained thirteen pounds.

These are the major reasons why I am writing this paper. I don't expect to have all my questions answered, but I expect to understand the situation a little better once I am done.

3

The Search

Jennifer's mother had visited us for the first time when Jennifer was placed with us on a trial basis. After that we saw her occasionally when she came to pick Jennifer up to take her home for a weekend. I had no formal interview with Jennifer's mother. I could rely only on these few visits. Here is the story of Jennifer's first five years of life as told by her mother:

Jennifer was born after nine months of discomfort and anxiety for me. Every day I'd awakened and said my prayers. Like every mother, all I wanted was a healthy baby. I didn't care which sex it was.

I didn't get to see Jennifer until the next day when it was time for feeding. I was still under the effect of the anesthesia when she was born. Later in the day I was visited by the doctor and my husband.

A few minutes after the birth she had gone into an epileptic seizure. [Severe epileptic seizure; convulsions, loss of consciousness, jerkiness, and stiffening of the body (1:946).] The doctor had controlled it, however (with phenobarbital and dilantin). She was a multiply-handicapped child. Jennifer was found to have *quadriplegia*, a tightness in her arms and legs. Later she was also found to have profound mental retardation, the lowet classification of the mind. I had asked the doctor what had happened. All I can remember of what he told me was that she had lost oxygen, "a transient decrease in the amount of oxygen reaching the brain (*hypoxia*) during labor or delivery" (2:43). He wasn't really sure.

Jennifer was hospitalized for two weeks. Then she was sent home. After she had been settled in, the home worker was sent to visit us. She helped us learn the proper way to take care of Jennifer. She taught us the different exercises that would have to be done in order to keep the little muscle coordination that she did have from getting worse.

Jennifer started school at two. At the school they did exercises for her mind as well as her body. I visited the school once or twice before Jennifer was enrolled. It was a very colorful place. The teachers used various methods in order to reach each child. The whole place was very stimulating.

It was depressing, however. These colorful, stimulating rooms brought Jennifer closer to reality. I could feel her presence everywhere I went whether she was with me or not.

It became harder for me to handle Jennifer. Whenever I tried to do her exercises, she cried. I was afraid to even touch her. Jennifer was my fourth child. All the others were normal. Many times I cried because of my feelings, my reactions toward my child. Whenever it was time to go out, Jennifer was left behind with a babysitter.

After a while, I began to think about placing her with another family. Inside I felt guilty for her handicaps. I blamed myself and my husband. This guilt created a marital problem. I could not accept the responsibility of raising Jennifer. Indirectly by little hints I would blame my husband for the problems. I finally had to give Jennifer up.

I started looking at state facilities which would place children in with families instead of institutions. A social worker was sent to my house and I was interviewed for possible enrollment into Mandato Center. The procedure was simple.

As part of my I-Search, I decided I should interview Jennifer's social worker. She was very helpful to me and also I got to ask some questions about Jennifer that I had never dared ask her. She said:

Jennifer was born November 28, 1970. She started school at the age of two. Mandato Center is a state facility which places children like Jennifer with families to care for them instead of in institutions. In institutions the children outnumber the nurses 20:1. However in a family situation, it could be on a 1:1 ratio.

Jennifer came to the Riveras because her own family could not continue to have her in their home because of her severe mental retardation and physical handicaps.

For this paper I interviewed my mother and took notes to get her view of the experiences she had had. She said:

When I first saw Jennifer, she weighed seven pounds. Her right cheek was covered with bed sores. One cheek was slightly larger than the other, maybe because of the sores.

Her face appeared unproportioned.

Her body was that of a one-year-old. The top part of her had developed normally, but below her hips, she appeared distorted. Her legs and arms were stiff and hardly moveable. Her fists were clenched. Her body was faintly covered with hair. [Excessive hair growth on parts of the body on which it is cosmetically undesirable, especially on a little girl, is not an uncommon complication of dilantin therapy (2:117).]

Jennifer was trained to drink from a cup, but she didn't receive enough liquids. This caused frequent trips to the hospital. Jennifer suffered from a lack of sufficient amount of liquids. She also had eating problems. It would sometimes take two hours to get her to complete a meal because she would constantly spit out the food.

When it was time for her to sleep, Jennifer would not. Every time we entered her room to check her, she would be awake. After a few days, however, she began to get some sleep. For those first three days, Jennifer would neither sleep, eat, or show reactions to anything. At first we thought she didn't cry.

She stayed with us for one weekend on a trial basis. She was adorable. Everyone fell in love with her. By the end of the weekend my husband and I decided to keep her.

Yet my husband and I were a little hesitant. We were afraid that our two younger children might begin to imitate her. That was our main concern. Contrary to our expectations, the two younger ones fell in love with her and were eager to have her around all the time.

One week later, Jennifer moved in. My first attempts to handle her were unsuccessful. I couldn't get her to drink or eat. I started using a medicine dropper for her liquids. I proceeded to use a bottle. Spoon-feeding her was easier to cope with. As time went on, she began to spit out less food. Gradually she gained weight.

I was spending more and more time with Jennifer and neglecting my housework. My husband would sometimes become irritated when he came home and there was no food on the table. The kids were roaming free. I almost lost Jennifer; I was paying less attention to my own family.

Things began falling into place. Jennifer was progressing. Our major concern was her exercises. She seemed to sense when it was time for her exercises and start crying. At first we thought it was serious and we would take it easy on her, but when the social worker came over, we mentioned it to her. The social worker checked her out and found everything sound. It seemed that Jennifer was aware of the time for her exercises. She would cry in pain whenever we touched her and in hopes that we would pity her. She'd developed just fine.

Since the day she moved in, Jennifer has become a member of our family. She is no longer a foster sister to me or a foster daughter to my parents.

Jennifer has been living with us for a year now. In that year there have been many noticeable changes. She smiles. She doesn't know what she smiles about and neither do we. All we know is that something has touched her heart and made her see something beautiful. She especially likes to smile when there's screaming and loud noises around her. Jennifer drinks from a bottle and can be fed with a a spoon. When she first came, it took us hours to feed her because she was constantly spitting food.

So many things have changed in Jennifer's life during that one year. She can raise her head when laid on her stomach. She moves her arms. Before, her arms lay next to her with her fists clenched. Her arms could not be moved. She can be spoon-fed as well as bottle-fed. She can notice the difference between light and dark. After three days with us, Jenn had grown accustomed to sleeping with the lights on. If they were off she would cry.

But of all these accomplishments, one has really touched me deeply. When Jenn cries, she cries for "Mama."

Jennifer is so adorable. Just a few days ago, my mother went to the store and bought her some new clothes. They're gorgeous, she's gorgeous. She's outgrown practically all of her clothes that she brought with her. Her hair is down past her shoulders. Everyone says that Jennifer looks like one of my sisters. Some people even thought that Jennifer was mother's daughter. She practically is sister and daughter to all of us who share our lives with her.

4

What I Learned

I'm at the end of my I-Search. When I began I didn't know how to start, but it became so easy. Probably because Jennifer is part of my family. It's almost like writing about a part of myself.

Now I can honestly say to Jennifer, "You're part of our family. When you were small your mother decided that she loved you too much to see you suffer. She had to give you up so that you could enjoy the feeling of pure love, a love that was not mixed with guilt or pity or sorrow. It's because your mother loved that you can smile today. I love you, Jennifer."

By the way, my mother has decided that she would like to write down some of her joys of being Jennifer's foster mother. She would like to share with other people some of the memories and happiness Jennifer has given to us.

Sources

1. Cooley, Donald G., *Family Medical Guide* (New York, Des Moines; Better Homes and Gardens Book, 1976).

2. Lagos, Jorge C., M.D., *Seizures, Epilepsy, and Your Child* (New York, Evanston; Harper & Row, 1974).
3. *Encyclopædia Americana* (New York, 1958), pp. 616-617.
4. Interviews with Jennifer's natural mother, foster mother, and social worker, May 1976.

Carmen and her family gave Jennifer their love without qualification. That was a subjective act that arose out of feeling. Carmen had a genuine question bothering her: why did Jennifer's parents give her up? Also she knew that when the day came to tell Jennifer more about her natural parents, she wouldn't be satisfied to be told that they gave her up because they loved her. More objective evidence would be needed, more documentation of what all the people involved in her adoption actually had said. Some of the facts of that momentous time in her life would have to be given her in detail, and if possible, in the very words spoken by the participants; for human beings are comforted by, and are more likely to believe, significant events when told them in details that can be tested by common sense and past experience. So the paper about Jennifer, conceived out of love, was made stronger by Carmen's determination to make it objective as well as subjective. It could easily have been *sentimental*—full of feeling that for the reader was not grounded in fact.

> *Objectivity does not mean detachment; it means respect; that is the ability not to distort and to falsify things, persons, and oneself.*
>
> ERICH FROMM

The scientific revolution of the last several centuries eventually produced scientists who worshipped blindly what they called "objectivity." Now we need to employ a corrective that consists of working with both subjectivity and objectivity in a single endeavor. In general, professionals trained in research and professors who have idolized research without engaging in it themselves have become too detached from their subjects and society. In general, persons not acquainted with the great tradition of research have allowed themselves to perceive too subjectively, without checking their perceptions against those of others. They need to take on the researcher's habit of looking for authoritative statements on several sides of an issue, of submitting their findings to the criticism of their peers.

In your I-Search, you're expected to do that in the simplest investigation. If, for example, you're seeking to find which set of golf clubs is best for you—considering your game and money on hand—

you're expected to seek out salespeople and unbiased experts who recommended different brands of clubs, or at least two persons who disagree on one brand. Then you'll have not only extended your knowledge but forced yourself to compare the word of differing experts, a habit of thinking persons. On our Moebius Strips we need to place both doubt and belief. We need to learn the signs—how does a person speak and act whose enthusiasm in a cause or belief is well placed? Who needs double checking before we give our trust? Seems obvious that the clerk who stands to gain a commission by selling a car to us is one of those. And the nuclear scientist or bureaucrat who assures us that exposure to nuclear radiation is less dangerous than cigarette smoking. Those two stand to lose their jobs and perhaps their professions if they are not believed.

As searchers and readers we all need to make both doubting and trusting habitual in our lives.

∞ **DOING NINETEEN:** Look over what you've written so far for your I-Search Paper and ask yourself if you've given your readers what they need to know to judge your judgments. Are you objective or subjective at appropriate moments? Make whatever changes seem called for.

> *An excellent book that has in both its subjective and objective observations the complicated carillon peal of truth.*
>
> ANONYMOUS
> (reviewing *False Starts* by Malcolm Braly)

Instead of training only intellect and memory we consider the development of will, demonstrated in initiative and action, as our main task.

JOSEF ALBERS

chapter 14
four
i-search
papers

HERE ARE four I-Search Papers that meant a great deal to their writers and others who heard or read them. The first one, "Should I Become an Architect?" is the best I-Search Paper I've ever seen, in both form and content. After writing it, Karon Roach changed her life. I think it's a story that will excite many women who are thinking of making a career for themselves.

The next two papers, "The Flowers in My Family" and "Preacher Grandmother," were written by college fresh-women and had meaning for their families that can't be measured. I wish both writers had found time to tell the story of their searches as well as the results so that readers could appreciate how they located the facts they brought together into a narrative; but as I say in other parts of this book, the essential is that an I-Search Paper be valuable to the writer and her readers, not that the form of the paper fulfill the instructions of a teacher.

The fourth paper, "The Sound of My Life," was written by a community college student, one of those thousands of Americans who after many years of working go back to college and pursue learning with more zeal than ever before.

I have the urge to analyze these papers for their strong and weak points but I'm going to resist, so that you and your group, if inclined, can do that without being influenced by my opinions.

SHOULD I BECOME AN ARCHITECT?

Karon Roach

1

What I know is, I'm twenty-five years old and just starting college. I also know I have three children and if for some reason I have to support them by myself, I couldn't do a very good job of it. From these statements there are a number of options available. I could become a secretary or a dental assistant, even a licensed practical nurse. None of them require a lot of time and all provide a decent living. But, I don't want to do them. There isn't enough personal satisfaction to make them worthwhile.

Maybe my dreams should become a possibility. What did I want to do when I was in high school? Architecture comes to my thoughts right away. It's always been a love of mine. I remember houses I've lived in and visited, schools I've attended, churches I've sat in. Each building has its own effect on me, like a tranquil room in a Japanese shrine with rain sifting through the woods that crowd the windows or, a lousy kitchen my mother keeps griping about.

It would be exciting to create environments. To see something I had designed or worked on become a part of someone's life. I would like to try it. I come back to my first two statements. Architecture involves five to six years of education. At my age, people are starting to work at their careers. I'm just starting college. I'll be thirty-one before I can find a job. Three small children require a lot of time and energy; so does school. Will one have to suffer? Can I integrate the two or will the plan work at all? I wish I could say the probem ends once I'm out of college but it follows me into the career. Before I go any further, I need to ask questions and find answers.

2

How do I begin? My plans are to complete sixty-four hours in a Pre-Architecture curriculum at Western Michigan University. The next step for most people is to transfer to a four-year school of architecture. The University of Michigan accepts Western's transfers. It's the closest school of architecture, so I decided to start my search with an interview with the dean. I called and made an appointment with Assistant Dean Johe.

My best friend, Anne Lipsey, lives in Ann Arbor and is studying Urban Planning at U. of M. The interview gave me a reason to take a small vacation and visit with Anne and her husband. However, I couldn't just pick up and go. The kids had to be farmed out, so my husband, Jerry, could go to work while I was away. He was helpful with the arrangements and suggested it would be fun for our son to spend a day at work with him. We thought it would be good for the kids to have an independent weekend.

The whole thing was becoming a big deal. For the first time since I'd left high school, I was putting serious effort into something outside of being mother and wife. I was getting nervous. Jerry kept reminding me that it was important to use my mind. I wondered if I was making too much out of the trip. What should I ask? How would the interview go? I often felt like backing out and letting the entire search go. Fortunately I was curious enough to keep pushing.

The day of the interview was hectic. Anne had classes in the morning so we didn't have time to talk. My imagination got the better of me and I thought I would blow the whole thing. I dressed and wondered if I looked like someone who was serious about her search. Anne came home and we rushed through lunch. Then she drove me over so she could show me around the building.

I didn't think the school was very impressive from the outside. Too much glass and steel. Inside was different; there was activity at all levels of design and planning. People were busy working on all kinds of projects. I hoped I could be that involved someday.

The secretary announced my appointment to the dean and we began our talk with an explanation of my search and its purpose.

Dean Johe gave a general lecture of what architecture is all about. He stressed the wide range of occupations the field covers, like restoration, design, planning, budgeting, and management. It was an effort to impress me with the image of what an architect really is. He felt many people believe in a fictional type of character who's successful at designing jewel-like structures for everyone to admire. I agreed with him and got to my questions.

"What type of architect are you trying to produce?"

"We're working for an individual who has a well-rounded background. The college realizes the responsibilities a person must fulfill as an architect and we try to prepare him for it."

I was curious to see if I fit into a pattern of people who decided to follow the career. "Is there a particular type of person who decides to study architecture?"

"Well, I should say there are two types. One has thought about architecture since they were very young. Their main quality is that they like to create. Some are looking for individual credit. Most like to do things they can see. A building is a real statement of their creativity.

"The second group are what I call 'gropers,' people who are looking for careers. They start out in one and find it isn't what they want. Out of one hundred students who get in here, fifteen already have degrees in another field. They're dissatisfied for reasons like there wasn't enough creativity or tangible satisfaction in the career they started in."

It seemed to me, if someone just picked it out of a hat that maybe learning architecture was a snap. "How many make it through to graduate?" I asked.

Dean Johe pulled out some papers with numbers. "I estimate that one hundred fifteen start and eighty-one stick with it to graduate."

Later I figured it out: a little over a third don't make it. I continued to narrow down the statistics of success. "How many find employment in the field?"

He winced and answered, "That's the bad side to this. There's very little construction now. Mortgages are too high and businesses are holding onto their money, postponing expansion. Architecture is directly dependent on the construction industry, and if there's no building there are no jobs for architects. The field becomes flooded. I'm sure there are graduates out there driving taxis or picking up a new career that has jobs."

"Does that mean no one's getting hired?"

"I believe there's still a market for architects who are confident of themselves. People who are hardnosed and willing to put their head on the block. I don't think students who get all A's will succeed, though."

I took that to mean you have to challenge the system, not just sit back and fulfill the requirements without any question.

"How do you feel about women in the field?"

"We accept them here. And of course most places are hiring women. I think you have to prove your capabilities. So men will get beyond thinking of women as someone cute in their office."

I didn't want to hear that. "How do you get beyond that prejudice?"

"When they look at your portfolio they can see what you've done." He picked up one next to his desk. Inside was a resumé and many pages of drawings and projects the person had been involved in. "It's good to get exposure to all sorts of things, like community organizations or skills like photography. An employer can see the valuable resource you could be."

It occurred to me that unique skills would be a definite asset. Something that was in demand but no one had the skills for yet. I wasn't sure what it would be. Maybe my search would find something.

Dean Johe gathered copies of articles from architecture magazines. They were fairly general to give me an idea of what it's all about. I thanked him for his time and left relieved that it was all over.

While I waited for Anne to return, I thought about the interview. None of it was too depressing. Six years is enough time for the economy to change. Competition doesn't scare me either; it's just a matter of finding the right twist to things that make what I have to offer indispensable.

3

At Anne's townhouse, I read the articles he had given me. They explained the successes and failures of the past and the problems of the future. Good articles for developing a personal philosophy toward the field. They were useful because I realized I get excited about architecture and it's not a career I've chosen by the title alone.

One article was about flexible work schedules and this had real answers to how I could become an architect as a mother of three children. The article, "The Case for Flexible Work Schedules," in *The Architectural Forum,* came from discussions of women in Boston who realized the problem of working with families. They devised several types of arrangements for work schedules (1: 66). What it boils down to is, you don't have to work ten to sixteen hour days but contract for specific tasks or jobs. There are also situations where a person may only work a certain length of time and then take a sabbatical. You could also work with a partner, and between the two of you divide up the work normally set up for one person. The article also mentioned that since the architect is a "professional" person she should be able to do her work outside the office. These ideas allow all kinds of freedom and options so that family needs can be met and the woman can be active in her career. It's also beneficial to the employer because there isn't always enough work and he has to either lay them off or find "busy" work to do. An employer may not always agree to it, but I may be able to convince him of the logic involved.

The trip was a success. I came home ready to dig out more information for future planning. The kids missed me but had enjoyed their weekend away from home. Unfortunately there were members of my husband's family who didn't like what I was doing. They felt I wasn't taking care of my family and was putting too much pressure on Jerry. Obviously my place was in the home.

I had to think about my values and make a personal decision. There was no strain on my family—Jerry backs up what I'm doing. Cleaning, cooking, and being a constant companion to my children have been important. We are the ones to decide what's important for us, not everyone else. We choose our own lifestyle, not what our parents taught us to expect.

I decided to believe in me; consequently part of the family have stopped communicating with us.

4

More appointments were made, with architects Norman Carver, Jr., and Evie Asken. I wasn't sure of the questions I should ask, especially of Mr. Carver. He is strongly opinionated and although I want the controversy, I didn't want to be shot out of the sky.

Our appointment was at seven-thirty, and I had a hard time finding his house in the dark. I picked out what I felt should be the place and drove into the driveway. A wooden plaque by the front door, with the name "Carver" inscribed in both English and Japanese lettering, assured me I was right. A dog barked when I rang the doorbell and Mr. Carver answered. "Hi, I'll let you into the office and we can talk there."

He unlocked a door by the garage and I went in and down some stairs. We broke the ice by talking about Ken Macrorie, the instructor I'm conducting the search for. I noticed his books on Japan and told him that I had lived there for a year. Since we had lived on different islands we had different experiences to talk about. Mr. Carver had been to Japan on Fulbright Scholarships and had written a book from his experiences. While he was there he went every morning and took pictures of the Japanese architecture. After development he said he'd look them over, and decided on what he should do differently. Then Mr. Carver would go out again the next morning and take more pictures. This patient process eventually led him to a new way of photographing architecture. No one taught him what to do; he reasoned it for himself.

The conversation was going well, so I asked my first question, "Why did you decide to become an architect?"

"I never really thought about it," he answered. "I was always talented in art and the technical things weren't difficult either. It was a natural progression."

"What kind of work do you do?"

"I'm a designer, mostly homes. I've worked at a lot of other things and with other people but I find this kind of work to be worthwhile. What do you like to do?"

I wasn't ready to be questioned. "Well, my other love besides architecture is writing. That's one of the reasons I signed up for this different type of course. It's a lot more than just writing five term papers with footnotes and long bibliographies."

"You should work on it and incorporate the two. Very few architects can write as well as design. You could become a critic of architecture. There are very few people who can do that."

It was a direction I would consider. "What advice would you give to a person starting out in school?"

"You should be able to draw. Interpretation of what you see on paper. It's important to communicate this way. You need it as much as the technical skills you'll learn in college. The other thing is to get out and expose yourself to everything. Go, look at architecture, both good and bad. Then look at the surroundings and try not to get sick. Become critical of what you see. Does it provide an environment, or do people conform to it? All of this builds an architectural vocabulary that you can use later."

I left feeling inspired and ready to get involved. Norman Carver has taken a career in architecture and bent it to his personal needs. He travels, writes books, and earns a living that seems to keep his life full. There was hero worship, since I took every bit of his advice as the wisdom of a sage.

5

Later in that week I had my interview with Evie Asken and it helped pull my previous interview into better perspective. Evie gave me some of her background. She graduated from Kansas State. Her decision to become an architect came after talking to a physical education instructor about wanting to go into that field. At the time, there was no demand for teachers in Physical Education. So the instructor advised Evie to go into the other career she was interested in, architecture.

Evie didn't become an architect right away. She got married and had three children. When her husband was out of work she decided to get her registration. The children were at the ages of two, three, and five.

"Wasn't it hard on them?"

"Oh no, children are very flexible. They accepted it right away. The first year wasn't easy on the three-year-old but we all adjusted."

I wanted to hear more. "I have relatives telling me that I'm neglecting my family by becoming an architect."

She leaned back and said, "You know, those kids will be in school soon. Let me tell you, it's a long stretch during that time; if you're smart, you'll find something to do or go crazy."

"What happens while you work?"

"We tell the kids they have their work to do and we have ours. We get together at night and talk over our day. I believe it's the quality of time you have together, not the quantity."

This was the reinforcement I needed. Three children and a career working for one woman. I should be able to do the same.

All the hurdles had to be discussed, so I asked, "Have you had any experiences with sex discrimination?"

Evie laughed and said, "Oh yes! I interviewed for a position as a registered architect and they asked me if I could type. I'm glad I've never taken secretarial courses because someone would try and put me behind a typewriter."

I told her that I'd already decided to never admit to having secretarial skills.

She continued, "In the last firm I worked for I was the only registered architect outside of the principals. The other men were draftsmen or working on getting their registration. There was a reshuffle of employees and I was out the door with the youngest draftsmen.

"I'm sure what really upset me was when things got rough several times, I decided to stick it out with them. They couldn't stick it out with me, though."

"Why didn't you fight it?"

"I didn't want to burn all my bridges. I may want to use them as consultant, later. They did say things like, 'Aren't you lucky. Now you can be with your children.' It's tough convincing some men that you're serious about your work and that it's not just an extra income or a hobby."

I agreed with her and asked, "Do you think twenty-five is too old to start going to college to become an architect."

"No, you'll be more interested in it now and take classes because you want to, not just to get credits toward a degree."

We talked about school and Evie suggested I take some law and business. Again I heard advice about getting involved with people and exposure to everything I could handle. The message was being repeated too often to ignore.

Finding work was becoming my biggest concern. "Is there anything new happening that could possibly open up jobs?"

"One thing is beginning to happen that could save us all. Some architects are trying to get away from dependency on the building industry. They're forming teams of people who are not all architects, but say a sociologist or an urban planner. They do initial studies and budgets for planning purposes and then find people with a specific expertise for the job they're doing. There's one group in Grand Rapids and another in Kalamazoo." Evie pulled out a card that said, "Environmental Social Planners." "Derwin Bass is the architect but he's more of a planner than a designer. His wife, Kathy, is a sociologist with a specialty in criminology. Penal systems are undergoing a big change. You can see a group like this could have a lot of impact."

This was a new direction I could look into and I told Evie I would call them for sure. Evie wants me to keep in touch and has offered to help with anything except babysitting. When I left I knew I had made a friend.

6

The appointment was made with Derwin Bass and the following Monday I was driving down G Avenue looking for a business. What I found was a small modest house where they live and work. Derwin wasn't home yet so Kathy and I made tea. One of the things that continued to surprise me was that every architect I had met was relaxed and casual in their lifestyle. They were all very human and easy to relate to.

Derwin came in. We talked about the importance of architecture serving the people. Kathy jumped in with her feelings about its inadequacies, which brought us to the importance of their work.

Der explained, "Architecture is tied to the construction industry. We're breaking away from that. We see organizations that need initial research before going ahead; that's our job. Most of our work is the initial research, feasibility studies, budgeting and costs, land development, area impact. From what we find, an organization can decide if they should go ahead with construction, and to what extent. It saves them money and it makes us money. No architecture firm can do that."

"Would this be a new way for architecture firms to go?" I asked.

"No, because they wouldn't be flexible enough. They'd have the same architects and no way of getting specific expertise. It wouldn't work for us to staff architects, either. We'd be duplicating a service already available. We can use them and hopefully they'll learn to use us."

Kathy added, "For example, we're trying to break into penal systems and if we get the jobs we're after, there's a designer whose specialty is jails. We aren't tied to anyone, so it would be easy to contract him."

Der said, "Government already does this type of work for its projects. We're just using the same idea for everyone."

We talked about the problems of starting a new business. There are accounting problems and Kathy has problems with men not taking her position seriously. Der suggested we go to their basement office, where I could see an example of their work.

While I was looking through surveys and aerial photographs, Derwin told me I was welcome to come to the local chapter meeting of the American Institute of Architects. He added my name to the bottom of his mailing list and I realized I was getting hooked into a career.

7

The search is over for this paper. It's just beginning for my career. Important questions have been answered. Twenty-five is not too old. There is time for career and children. Our life will not be like Dick and Jane out of readers in my first grade class. This Mommy will not always bake cookies with baby Sally. For now the cobwebs will have to hang until semester break and the floors will just have to yellow. My children will learn how to blow their own noses and find their own interests. We'll eat out more often than the average family and someday I'll have to hire a housekeeper.

I'm looking for schools other than U. of M. I want to make sure I have the knowledge to give me what Derwin Bass calls "a high D and B rating" (different and better).

Some of it I won't find in school. For example this writing course is great. It would be even more valuable if I get through it as something more than a credit for graduation. That means I have to find ways to use writing outside of class to make it better.

There's a risk in what I'm going to do but I've eliminated some of the hazards. I can't say I'll make it all the way but I'll sure as hell work at it.

Sources

1. Women Architects, Landscape Architects, and Planners (WALAP) Contributing people: Andrea Leers Browning, Joan E. Goody, Lisa Jorgensen, Shelley Hampden-Turner, Sarah P. Harkness, Joan Forrester Sprague, Jane Weinzapfel, "The Case for Flexible Work Schedules," *Architectural Forum* (September 1972), pp. 53 and 66.

Interviews

2. Herbert W. Johe, M. Architecture, Assistant Dean of the College of Architecture and Urban Planning, University of Michigan, Ann Arbor.
3. Norman Carver, Jr., registered architect, attended Yale University; 3201 Lorraine, Kalamazoo, Michigan.
4. Evie Asken, registered architect, attended Kansas State University; 3707 Wedgewood, Kalamazoo, Michigan.
5. Derwin Bass, registered architect, graduated from University of Minnesota; 2834 East G Avenue, Kalamazoo, Michigan.
6. Kathy Bass, B.A. Sociology, specialty in criminology, Western Michigan University; home address 2834 East G Avenue, Kalamazoo, Michigan.

Man can only fully understand himself by fusing the objective knowledge which is gained by observation of the whole of organic nature with the subjective knowledge of individual experience. This can bring a new ease and self-acceptance, an innocence based on knowledge.

LANCELOT WHYTE

THE FLOWERS IN MY FAMILY

Violet Hawkins

I never thought very much about my heritage until recently when I watched "Roots" on television. Alex Haley wrote the novel which the movie was made from. It told the story of his ancestry, which began in Africa with a proud black slave named Kunta Kinte. The story was so interesting and exciting that I decided to find out more about my background.

Deciding that it would be too difficult to get information on my father's side of the family because all of his relatives live a great distance from me, I concentrated on my mother's side of the family. I wrote or called all of my living relatives who I figured would be able to help me. I soon began to realize my ancestors were not as dull as I had thought. They had led some pretty colorful lives.

•   •   •

My mother's grandfather, Orange Henry Flowers, was born on the Flowers Plantation near Hazlehurst, Mississippi, in 1859. He was the son of two slaves. When slavery was abolished he was about six years old. His family stayed near the plantation and sharecropped a piece of land.

In his early teens Orange Henry decided to attend school. After he learned the basics, he enrolled at Gamins Theological College in Northwest Mississippi. When he graduated from there he became a minister. During this time he met his wife, Addie Carrie Ashby, the daughter of a plantation owner and his black mistress. Addie was a school teacher. At this time you only needed a few years of school to become a teacher yourself, maybe four or five. But this was still a great feat for a black woman.

Shortly after they were married, Addie and Orange Flowers moved to Blayton Springs, Alabama. Here they homesteaded eighty acres of wooded land. The woods were predominantly pine trees. Orange cleared a large part of the land and built a log cabin. First, he was going to farm the land but later decided to make turpentine from the sap of his pine trees.

On that farm my grandfather was born along with six brothers and sisters.

Orange was doing well with his turpentine farm. It seems he was doing too well for a black man in the south. The white people in town didn't like to see black people so prosperous. So . . .

One day as Orange and his family were sitting down to supper, a black man came to the house with a message for him. He was to meet this white man down by the creek. He went right away. As he started to leave, he decided to take his gun just in case he saw a squirrel or a rabbit. As he was riding down the road to the creek, two white men came from behind the bushes. They had guns and looked hostile. They told my great grandfather that he'd better leave town before tomorrow because they wanted his farm.

Orange left town that night after talking it over with his wife. They knew that a black man's life was worth little to any white man. He was to send for his family as soon as he found a place to stay.

About two months later, Orange sent for his family. He'd found a place to sharecrop a piece of land in Mississippi.

Not long after the family moved to Mississippi, Orange decided that maybe he had acted too hastily in giving up his farm. So he sent his wife back to Blayton Springs to see if they could do anything about getting the farm back. He didn't feel the white people who took the farm would harm her but he knew they would kill him.

When Addie arrived in Blayton Springs, she found that their farm was being run by a white family and that there was no record of Orange Flowers ever owning it. Not willing to give up, she went to an attorney. He told her that he would like to help her but he couldn't, and no other lawyer in the south would either.

Orange was very disappointed but decided the best thing to do was forget it. He and his family sharecropped that piece of land until he died in 1922. Before his death Orange told his son Dell, my grandfather, that he wanted him to move the family up north to Chicago. He knew some people there who would take them in until they could find work.

Soon after arriving in Chicago my grandfather got a job as a chauffeur. He and his four brothers supported their mother and two baby sisters.

•   •   •

Robert Anderson, my own great grandfather on my mother's side, was born in New Orleans in 1869 to a Spanish mistress of a white ship captain. His mother died when he was very young and he was taken in by a black family named Humphrey. Although Robert wasn't black he was considered black because of his associations.

During his teens a man came to town to recruit men to work on his farm. He said that his men would get free room and board and a sizeable salary. It sounded inviting, so Robert signed up.

Once he arrived on the farm it was obvious he had been duped. They were little more than slaves. There were armed guards and dogs everywhere and you could not leave. He worked from dawn to dusk every day and soon began thinking of escape.

Robert became good friends with a kitchen girl. She gave him extra food and agreed to help him escape. The farm he was being held on was near the Mississippi River. Robert figured if he could find out the boat schedule he could slip away and jump on a boat. His plan worked and soon he was back in New Orleans. The Humphreys asked him to come and live with them. So he did, and started studying music. Soon he was good enough to earn a living for himself.

In 1892 he met and married a very fair black woman named Lucy Bonner. They had two girls before Lucy died in 1896. Robert didn't want to stay in New Orleans after his wife's death, so he and his girls moved to Chicago. One of these girls was Violet Anderson, who was going to be my grandmother.

In Chicago Dell Flowers met Violet and married her. Not long after they were married, they had my mother.

There are many things I would like to know about my history that I didn't find in this search. I hope one day I'll have the time and money to study my past further.

Every heart must lean to somebody.
SAMUEL JOHNSON

PREACHER GRANDMOTHER
Lorraine Mitchell

What I Knew

It wasn't until last year when a very close friend—who is considered an aunt to the family—married my cousin that I found out she and my grandmother were both ordained ministers.

What I Want to Know

Ten years have passed since my grandmother passed away and now I would like to know more about her. I'm interested in her life and how she got into ministry. Did she have any problems getting into ministry? What kind of person was she like, and what were some of her views she stood by firmly?

In writing this paper I got most of my information from my mother, along with my Aunt Faith and Rita Miller, the close friend spoken of earlier.

This paper was not written in an interview form, but as a life story. I was given facts about my grandmother's life from my mother, the only child out of six who was left living with her, where the others were out on their own. Other bits of information were added by my Aunt Faith and Rita when possible.

While talking with Aunt Faith and Rita, I found out there was much information about grandmother they did not know themselves. I hope I've put all the pieces of her life together in a way that, for whoever reads this paper, they get a true picture of how she was.

Part I

It was a miracle with all the strength
of this woman, to serve the Lord like she had.

Grandmother Finley, Juanita Anas Foster, was born in Allegan county in 1893. She lived and went to school in Pearl, Michigan, where she graduated from the 8th grade.

After graduation, Grandmother Finley went to work as an apprentice to a beautician. She established the first beauty shop owned by a black in the South Bend area. The shop catered to only whites. A few specialties of her shop were rain water for shampooing, human hair to make her own hair pieces, and her own cold creams.

As years went on, Grandmother Finley became a nurse, studying under a German doctor. She became noticed when she took care of a very distinguished woman named Mrs. Pugh, who was burned in the Great Chicago Theater fire. Mrs. Pugh's hands were so badly burned that she lost the tips of her fingers. Besides nursing Mrs. Pugh, Grandmother made all of her gloves to properly fit her fingers.

In the following years, Grandmother Finley took advantage of any training and education she could obtain. For her time, she was a highly self-taught educated woman. She felt you should learn everything you could, and would encourage you to do so.

Shortly after Grandmother's marriage to Herman Finley, she became a Christian and a member of the Morgan Park Pentecostal Church.

Mom was an unexpected arrival when Grandmother was at the age of forty. The family then moved to Bangor, Michigan.

In 1941 while Grandmother was critically ill and not expected to live, Grandfather unexpectedly passed of a heart attack.

Not expected to live, Grandmother made a promise to the Lord, that if he would heal her so she could raise Mom, she would dedicate the balance of her life to him.

The Lord did answer Grandmother's prayer; though not completely healed, she was able to start her work for him after Grandfather's death.

While serving the Lord as a State-side Missionary, Grandmother and my mom traveled around the states, going to Chicago, Kentucky, Cincinnati, Indiana, back to Chicago again, and then settling in Allegan, Michigan.

While on her mission of serving the Lord, Grandmother and Mom lived in faith homes, rented rooms, over and behind churches, and in a remodeled chicken coop. Running water and other facilities were not always available. Often times Grandmother did not know where the next meal was coming from, and the Lord would provide. Throughout her lifetime, she lived the life of Faith, and was never paid a salary, but managed to get Mom through school and pay the bills.

> This great woman of Faith was called to Allegan back in the forties from Chicago, a faithful worker in the Morgan Park Pentecostal Church. She and her daughter, Erma, established residence in Allegan and began working and digging out souls for the Lord in this pioneer field. (1:15)

When Grandmother Finley first came to Allegan, she was involved with the Missionary Band sanctioned by the United Pentecostal Council of the Assemblies of God, Inc. She was ordained about ten years before her death by Bishop R. W. Sunday of the Church Council. There were no problems getting into the Pentecostal Church; or if there were any, they were never discussed by Grandmother.

Grandmother never made it known to too many she was an ordained minister. She opposed the idea of female ministers wearing man tailored suits and things like that. She maintained herself as being a woman, by dressing in a feminine way.

> A Bible in her hand and Faith in her heart, she labored faithfully, paying a tremendous sacrifice in country fields and the city's bright lights. At times her daughters would provide transportation so door to door visitation and prayer for the sick could be possible. Her labor of love was sometime met with embittered opposition, but nothing darkened her Faith in God. She was the finest example of a leader, teacher, pastor and Mother in the Gospel. Working up north in Holland, Michigan, she pastored the All Nation Full Gospel Church for a period of time. She loved the saints and pressed her way in all sorts of storms and weather.
>
> Sister Finley was very ambitious, fasted, prayed for a 32 mile radius around Allegan. Her vision was to build a House of Worship. Among her visions she desired to do missionary work in Africa, God didn't grant her crossing the seas, but laid heavy burdens upon her for the mission-

aries that were already laboring in the field. She and her daughters prepared boxes and great efforts were performed through this burden for Africa. (1:15)

As stated, Grandmother's vision was to have a House of Worship and also a home somewhere on a lake. To do Baptising in the water and provide a place where saints (members of the church) could come for a period of time and rest.

Grandmother wanted a Full Gospel Church in Allegan. A small group of people banded together to collect money for a building fund for the church, and money today is still being collected.

Because of Grandmother's promise to the Lord, she visited the sick and took care of cancer patients. She had a contact in getting hospital beds, wheel chairs, bandages, and any other needed materials for her cancer patients.

She spent her life working with unfortunate people and preached the Bible.

Part II

Grandmother Finley was a "determined headstrong woman"; the Bible was her "Sword of life."

She believed in the King James Version of the Bible (English translation of the Bible published in 1611). Her views on the Bible were you shouldn't take one part and reject the other. During her lifetime Grandmother always lived and studied by the Bible. Whatever she taught or preached to others, she did herself.

Grandmother believed there was a God who had a son named Jesus, who died on the cross. She believed there was a "Heaven to gain, and a Hell to shun," and strongly believed in the Ten Commandments.

It was in Grandmother's faith, that once you became a Christian, you should live a visible life to others, separating yourself from things that would be considered sinful to the Lord, such as drinking, dating, dancing, theater, smoking, makeup of any kind, card playing, and some types of fund raising projects. These were only a few beliefs she stood by. It was also in Grandmother's faith that when once "saved," your life had to be different than before. That being "saved" you were actually "born again," to live a new life and put aside worldly things.

Grandmother didn't believe in those ministers, regardless of being black or white, who manipulated and used minorities, taking advantage of the congregation and stripping it of its money. She didn't believe in those churches that weren't based on "sound religious beliefs" or those that were of a "store front makeup."

It was Grandmother's faith to believe in Divine Healing (healing of physical ills by God's direct intervention or the practice of seeking this healing through prayers and other expressions of faith; faith cured). Divine Healing isn't something where you lay your hands on a person and he is healed, it is soul-healing. If Grandmother were alive today, she would be very dissatisfied with some of today's Divine Healing on television.

Even though Grandmother believed in soul-healing for herself, she did believe in others going to doctors. When it came to death, she didn't believe life should be maintained by artificial means, such as some shots or intravenous feeding, given in many cases to keep life support systems going.

At the time Grandmother knew that she was going to die, she chose not to be put into the hospital, but to lay at rest in her own home until she passed on.

For people who are sick for a long period of time in their home and die there, it is sometimes difficult to obtain a death certificate with a medical doctor's signature. In Grandmother's case, Mom was able to make arrangements before she died with Mr. N———, a funeral director in town. He contacted Doctor B———, a local doctor, then came out to the house after Grandmother died and signed the death certificate.

Grandmother spent her life working for the Lord, most of which she sacrificed to help others. When her help was needed, she would always go, and many of these times she was put into difficult situations. Never would Grandmother refuse anything given to her; she would eat food passed to her, knowing that later she would be sick. Grandmother would always give up what she had to give to those in need.

It was well known that Grandmother lived a very private life, and never liked to live with anyone. But a young woman in Allegan named Rita Miller desired to live with her right after three years' training from a Bible Institute on the East Coast. The desire must have stemmed from practical training under this great Woman of Faith. Many a prayer was answered, various kinds in many walks of life. Grandmother was not only a great source of faith and encouragement, but a qualified Bible instructor. She knew her Bible well.

Up until the last two months before Grandmother died, she led a very active life, and was not one for boasting or making a great display of herself. After her husband died in 1941, she never remarried.

August 3, 1966, Juanita Anas Finley went home to be with the Lord. It was out of pain and sorrow that it took a "miracle" for her to take care of the sick, work for the Lord, and go through all the hardships that she had after 1936.

Conclusion

In writing this paper, I found out a lot about my grandmother that was never known to me or other relatives before. She was a great leader and influence to those she came in contact with and I wish I could have gotten to know her better.

I plan on making copies of this paper to send to various relatives, for the benefit of their own use.

Source of Information

1. Pamphlet: Fifty-Seventh Annual Convocation & Youth Congress for the United Pentecostal Council of the Assemblies of God, Inc. July 12-19, 1976.

Interviews (March 1977)

2. Erma Mitchell—mother
3. Faith Portrum—aunt (mother's sister)
4. Rita Miller—ordained minister (close friend)

> Writing develops courage. Writers leave the shelter of anonymity and offer to public scrutiny their interior language, feelings, and thoughts.
>
> DONALD H. GRAVES

THE SOUND OF MY LIFE

Carol Goncalves

What I Knew

I remember as a child spending many summer days swimming in the salt water at Fairfield Beach. At night, as I lay in bed, I could hear the sounds of foghorns even though we lived three miles away. I can't recall ever seeing the beach in the colder months and as the years passed by, Long Island Sound became just a memory for me.

One recent year in the past I had the opportunity to visit the coastal areas of Maine and Cape Cod. My curiosity was aroused and grew more and more as time went by. I sensed that there was something special about the seacoast.

What I Wanted to Know

I wondered what it was like to live on a New England beach year-round. What was it like in the crisp air of autumn and the bleakness of winter, after the summer people headed for home? What were the pleasures, as well as the dangers, of living near the sea?

Searching

I borrowed a few books at the Fairfield Public Library which I thought would provide me with some answers.

Beaches, by Robert and Seon Manley, contained a vast amount of information on all aspects of beaches. I read about many famous writers, musicians, and artists, and how the sea had inspired them to create masterpieces.

Henry Thoreau, the naturalist and writer, had trekked across the dunes of Cape Cod in the last century with an umbrella over his shoulder as the weather was cold and wet. "Every landscape," he said, "which is dreary or not has a certain beauty to my eyes, and in this instance, its permanent qualities were enhanced by the weather." He was convinced that the best times to be near the sea were in the autumn and winter and especially during a storm, and wrote in his journal, "An outward cold and dreariness lend a spirit of adventure to a walk." (3:169)

I found a fascinating chapter on seacoast living in *Cape Cod and the Offshore Islands* by Walter Teller. It was all about Henry Beston, a man who built a cabin in 1927 on the dunes of Cape Cod. He spent a year living simply and alone and wrote a book called *The Outermost House.* Twenty years later, Mr. Teller interviewed Henry Beston who recalled that lonely year on the beach. On some wild nights a single wave would shake his house but it was a very happy year for him, a time of great awareness and discovery. As an old man seated in his Maine country farmhouse with the author, he said, "Now that autumn is here, and the skies have cleared and gone cold, it is the great sound of the surf I hear in my inner mind. . . ." Henry Beston died in 1968 but his beloved outermost house is still there on the Cape, moved back three times from the advancing sea. (5:76)

I could picture him out on the moors fifty years ago and could almost feel what he had felt by reading his observations.

Most of the books in the library were written about Cape Cod and Maine and other beautiful areas along the Atlantic Coast. I wondered if anyone ever wrote about their experiences on Long Island Sound. I found a book called *The Inland Sea* by Morton Hunt. The author traveled in a 33-foot sailboat, stopping along the way at many towns and cities located on the Sound. He came in the early 50's and again ten years later, writing down his experiences in a diary. Long Island Sound is the most heavily traveled body of water by pleasure craft in the world, and Morton Hunt loved it, although he was saddened by some of the changes that had taken place.

One night, while anchored off Milford, Connecticut, as he lay in his bunk reading, he became aware of "a steady, whining, grinding noise, somewhat like a factory or a piece of machinery. It was the basic chord struck by the Turnpike, its component notes being the broiling noise of tires, the roaring of motors, the snarling of truck gears and the rush of turbulent air. In scores of beach resorts and quiet coastal towns where human beings once slept in blessed native silence, there now is never real silence." (2:132)

After reading that paragraph, I realized that I hadn't heard any foghorns in years, but the noise of the Connecticut Turnpike came through every night, loud and clear.

The author also noticed that the air surrounding the cities, such as New Haven and Bridgeport, appeared gray and hazy from his boat on the Sound.

I couldn't locate any books about people actually living on the Sound, but I knew that a study had been done recently by a committee. I went back to the Fairfield Library and found a draft of the study entitled *People and the Sound: A Plan for Long Island Sound*. It contained numerous recommendations for conservation, zoning, ferry service, fishing, etc. and was very informative.

The Southern Connecticut coastline is heavily built up and most of the land is privately owned. Several flood-prone areas are listed, and the study recommends that the state buy properties in these areas and expand its beaches for the public. The Federal Flood Insurance Program discourages rebuilding if a major storm should result in heavy property damage. The government would like to see these low-lying areas become open space once again. The study goes on to say that 85% of coastal erosion damage is beyond practical remedy in environmentally, economically, or socially acceptable ways. "Floods, storms, and erosion can take an enormous toll on lives and property. The region hasn't had a major flood or hurricane in 20 years and our memories have faded. But the fact is we've built on a lot of land that belongs to the sea. And someday, inexorably, the sea will take some of it back." (4:15)

I set the study aside and opened a book called *The Nature of Violent Storms* by Louis J. Batten, which had a chapter on hurricanes. The wind in a hurricane striking coastlines can reach 100 to 150 m.p.h. and generate huge waves. It can blow over houses, rip down high tension wires, and carry away cars or anything else not securely lashed down. (1:123)

It sounded a bit frightening, and I wondered what happened at the beaches when Hurricane Belle struck this summer. I remembered hearing the police on the radio requesting the people in low-lying areas of Stratford, Fairfield, and Milford to evacuate.

I had read about the pleasures of the coast as well as the dangers and I decided it was time to ask a few questions of someone who lived year-round on the shore.

Interviewing

I spent one afternoon discussing my topic with a friend, Mrs. Carole Alexander, who had moved to Lordship in Stratford from Fairfield four years ago. I asked her how she felt about living in a beach community. She spoke of the Sound in glowing terms. As far as she was concerned, the pleasures far outweighed the dangers. There was more corrosion due to the salty air and her house had to be painted more often. The soil was sandy and poor for gardening and no one had a great deal of land, but she couldn't picture herself living anywhere else. She is very ecology-oriented as are many residents of Lordship, always fighting against expansion of the airport and for preservation of the Great Salt Marshes.

The earth is three-fourths water and so are our bodies. "We are tied to the sea," she said, her voice filled with emotion, "and if we destroy it, then we destroy ourselves." The mention of a major hurricane didn't bother her at all. If a storm came, then the airport would fill up with water and Lordship would become an island and maybe float out to sea. Some of the erosion was due to builders knocking down sand cliffs and tampering with nature just to make money. Hurricane Belle had changed Russian Beach a block away, removing rocks and leaving gorgeous white sand in their place. Carole sits down there and writes letters as the sea inspires her. In the cold weather, people sit on the beach wrapped up in blankets. "When I've had a boring or depressing day," she said, "I put on my coat, walk down to the beach, and I'm alive again." Well, it was my turn to put on my coat and go home, so I said goodbye to my sea-loving friend. (6)

While reading *The Bridgeport Post* I noticed an advertisement by a book store in the Connecticut Post Shopping Center in Milford. It's called *A Wind to Shake the World*, by Everett S. Allen and the ad describes its contents—"Factual narrative of 1938 hurricane, crowded with tales of horror and heroism gleaned from diaries, letters, personal interviews and endless research amongst the files of newspapers and libraries." I'm going to buy this book and learn exactly what can happen in a major hurricane, but I can't include it in my I-Search paper as I'm running out of time.

I decided that the best way to find out about seacoast living was to move there and find out for myself. And that's exactly what I did.

Personal Experiment

Here I am, living in a winterized one-story cottage at Bayview Beach in Milford, Connecticut. The owner, Mr. Saul Englander, lives next door the year-round so I asked him a few questions just before I moved in. What happened when Hurricane Belle arrived this past summer? He told me that the residents in this beach area had to evacuate by 9:30 p.m. that night or risk being dragged out by the police. His redwood deck overlooking the water was carried out to sea by the waves, but the people were lucky as the storm struck two hours after high tide. Belle and previous storms were the cause of a lot of erosion as the sand was six feet higher at one time. Now the beach is very rocky. He added, "It's an exciting place to live!" My curiosity would finally be satisfied, I had thought to myself, so I paid the rent and thanked him. (7)

The front of my house is built on cement piers, so the floors are very cold, even with heavy carpeting. The sand is underneath the house as is the water. I noticed that the concrete seawall next door was knocked down. My cottage has no seawall; the waves go under the house, and I'm sure it would be frightening during a hurricane. At low tide people walk across the sandbars along with strange-looking birds. At high tide the waves crash against the neighboring seawalls, and the Sound is so rough that it looks like I have the Atlantic at my door.

What I Learned

Many of the direct waterfront homes are rented to college students in the winter and vacationers in the summer, although more and more people are buying these homes to live in year-round. Waterfront property has skyrocketed in price and is too expensive for an investment.

This certainly is the best way to learn about living on the beach and perhaps the only way. I can't hear the noise of the turnpike here, only the sound of the sea. I found out that those white lines streaming from the sun in religious pictures are real. The water sparkles unbelievably in the strong sunlight and I can heat the house during the day with solar energy. On some nights, the wind blows fiercely and makes creaking sounds in the attic, as though there was a ghost present. Yes, I'm learning more and more as the days go by, just by keeping my eyes and ears open.

Tonight I'm gazing through the picture window, a huge moving painting on the wall of the living room. I'm hypnotized. The air is thick with fog and out there in the blackness, a ship is floating by, lit up like a Christmas tree. The smoke from my chimney is drifting across the window and the sea and wind together are making strange whistly sounds. And out there somewhere is the mournful sound of a foghorn, a sound I haven't heard in twenty years.

Sources

1. Batten, Louis J. *The Nature of Violent Storms* (Garden City, N.Y.; Doubleday, 1961).
2. Hunt, Morton. *The Inland Sea* (Garden City, N.Y.; Doubleday, 1965).
3. Manley, Seon and Robert. *Beaches: Their Lives, Legends, and Lore* (Philadelphia, Chilton, 1968).
4. New England River Basins Commission, Long Island Sound Regional Study. *People and the Sound: A Plan for Long Island Sound* (270 Orange Street, New Haven, November 1964).
5. Teller, Walter. *Cape Cod and the Offshore Islands* (Englewood Cliffs, N.J.; Prentice-Hall, 1970).

Interviews

6. Alexander, Carole, homemaker and Housatonic Community College student (Lordship, Stratford, Connecticut; November 30, 1976).
7. Englander, Saul, electrical engineer (Bayview Beach, Milford, Conn.; November 21, 1976).

> *If we had a keen vision and feeling of all ordinary human life, it would be like hearing the grass grow and the squirrel's heart beat, and we should die of that roar which lies on the other side of silence. As it is, the quickest of us walk about well wadded with stupidity.*
>
> GEORGE ELIOT [MARY ANN CROSS]

Whatever their weaknesses, their slips in grammar, punctuation, and format, these four papers are alive, and they have remained in my memory since I first saw them. I believe I will never forget them.

*Don't pass judgment on a manuscript
as it is, but as it can be made to be.*

M. LINCOLN SCHUSTER,
"An Open Letter to a
Would-Be Editor"

part three
becoming
an
editor

chapter 15
bad
words

ONCE WHEN I WAS PLAYING in the basement, a friend did something that outraged my seven-year-old soul—I don't remember what—and I yelled "Damn you!" That was the first time my mother had heard *damn* roar from my lips, and while, surprised myself, I was listening to the reverberations, she stomped down the stairs, shook me by the shoulders, and said, "Don't you ever say that word again!"

In the next fifty-four years I've said those words to a number of persons; and since then, Puritan mothers like mine have increasingly had to listen to such words in public, read them in books, and hear them at the movies. In my childhood fifty cents bought two movie tickets or ten candy bars, and *darn,* a soft way of saying *damn,* was considered by schoolteachers crude, or at best, slangy. Language usage changes.

With words, Mother was timid but not un-human. Unconsciously she knew, as we all do, that every family and society has its taboo words which are not to be spoken or written without incurring disapproval from people in power or the censors in our own heads. When Mother said, "Darn!" she probably was as shocked as I was when I said "Damn," and in fact she was saying the same thing. In all activities we must have limits—to ensure that others will act somewhat according to our expectations, so we'll live in civilization rather than chaos. But the rules change as circumstances change: people get bored with the old ways, and think up new taboo words when the old ones have been used so often they no longer carry any shock. When we need to express deep frustration or outrage, taboo words are available.

In our society most of the taboo words are connected to religion, sex, race, or the excretory processes. In most situations today when Americans say aloud "God damn!" others are not shocked, but a few people maintain that such a phrase profanes God, who should not be directed to damn someone or something by mere human beings. That feeling has persisted during the centuries that English-speaking people have invented and used what once were called "mincing" words that diminish the effect of such profane words by changing their form. *The Oxford English Dictionary* lists the following substitutes for the word *God*, which were invented to soften the word when used as an exclamation. In the G section of the OED (which takes up 532 pages, each carrying three columns), the editors have this to say in Meaning 13 of the word *God*:

> *By God* . . . From a desire to avoid actual use of the sacred name come various distorted or minced pronunciations of the word; see *COCK, DOD, GAD, GAR, GED, GOG, GOLES, GOLLY, GOM, GOSH, GOS(ES), GUD, GUM: also ECOD, EGAD, ICOD, IGAD.* Of these forms only *Cock* and *Gog* are common before 1600; the others occur mainly in the 17th and 18th c. *Gar* is by the dramatists chiefly put in the mouths of foreigners. . . .

When I found that entry in the OED I was surprised. I had read the expression *By Gog* in Shakespeare and I knew *Gog* stood for *God,* but I didn't know that *gosh* and *golly* were so-called "perversions" of the word *God.* I had also learned from reading Shakespeare that *Marry* was short for "By the Virgin Mary." And *Zounds,* which my father correctly pronounced to rhyme with "sounds" when he read me *The Three Musketeers,* was in fact a short form of the oath "By God's wounds." I think it should be pronounced "Zoondz" to remind us of its original form, but apparently the softeners would prefer to forget. The same pattern was followed in moving from the expression *God's blood to 'Sblood.* The word *God* there stands for Christ, who gave his blood for the people.

In our society the common words for sexual parts of the body and sexual acts are usually replaced in writing by Latin words such as *copulation, intercourse, coitus, pudendum, genitalia,* and *phallus.*

They sound impersonal and scientific, as if they don't belong to human beings. And maybe the readers of those words won't know what they mean, so everyone will be safe.

Although the authors of the proposal leading to the compiling of *The Oxford English Dictionary* said that "The first requirement of every lexicon [dictionary] is that it should contain every word occurring in the literature of the language it professes to illustrate," the people who collected the uses of words for it avoided certain Elizabethan poems and other subsequent writing that employed so-called "vulgar" and "common" sexual language. If any of the sub-editors at the time would have liked to shock readers by printing such words, they would have been vetoed, I believe, by the editor-in-chief, James A. H. Murray, who was essentially a reserved, religious, deeply formal man. But as more and more of these taboo words began to appear in "respectable" books and magazines, and a new work entitled *The American Heritage Dictionary of the English Language* published them in 1969, the OED changed its policy. In the 1972 OED supplements bringing the dictionary up to date for words beginning with the letters A through N, the editors cited uses of sexual words appearing in English works of the 17th and 18th centuries as well as American works of the 20th century. In the 1972 supplement, the editor, R. W. Burchfield, had this to say in the introduction:

> . . . whereas in 1956, when we began our work [on the supplement], no general English language dictionary contained the more notorious of the sexual words, '*nous avons changé tout cela*' [we have changed all that], and two ancient words, once considered too gross and vulgar to be given countenance in the decent environment of a dictionary, now appear with full supporting evidence along with a wide range of colloquial and coarse expressions referring to sexual and excretory functions.

That act was evidence of scholarly or scientific objectivity; the editors said to themselves and their readers, in effect: "We don't like some of these words. We're not comfortable with them, but we print them here as part of the record of how American-English words were being used in print in the 1970s because that is our obligation as compilers of a dictionary based on historical principles."

The power of the taboo against certain words is evidenced in the January 1979 issue of the scientific magazine *Human Nature,* in which two researchers report their thorough study of the gas produced in all human bodies from eating food—hydrogen, carbon dioxide, and sometimes methane. In their article entitled "Passing Gas," they use the Latin term *flatus* for gas, and *flatulence* for passing gas. They found that passing gas is a normal, natural bodily function but that repressing it—as our etiquette prescribes—may be dangerous to health. Although their article is, I believe, the first in a general magazine to discuss passing gas seriously, the authors don't use the word for it common in informal talk, but taboo in most magazines, until the end of their article. They report that a Canadian doctor wrote them saying that he and his students were now using the word in clinical discussions. In their last sentence the authors say, "In Canada, at least the fight for the fart has been won." It's still a dangerous word to use in such a publication.

[When I typed the next to last sentence above, I found the keys had printed the last word as *one* rather than *won,* another instance of the power of sound in writing. My unconscious was typing for me and typing wrong.]

Language is human behavior—I'm consciously repeating that statement several times in this book—and words should be treated as potentially highly explosive, respected for what they can do. "I don't know who the hell stole our garbage can" spoken angrily to a neighbor may imply something altogether different from "I don't know who stole our garbage can"—perhaps "You've always been a rotten neighbor and I wouldn't be surprised at anything you did." I would say that the *hell* in the first sentence is a bad word and might better have been left out, especially if the speaker doesn't know who stole the can.

In this textbook I would like to show how the editors of the OED have made the recent supplements to the dictionary more genuinely historical by introducing sexual terms they did not print before, but because this is a textbook that will be passed on by school boards and boards of trustees, I'm not going to risk printing those words. I don't want the whole program in this book rejected because of a couple of words not essential to the writing program I present in it.

I've jokingly titled this chapter "Bad Words," to show that I think other words, thought entirely decent by everyone, are often used badly or weaselly. In the absolute sense no word in our language is "bad"; always there is some context in which it may be used rightly and wisely.

Now I'm going to talk about *my* bad words, which are often used weakly, softly, or unnecessarily. I think you should use them in your writing, but only when they don't infect your sentences with gout or elephantiasis. I haven't quarantined all of them in this chapter. As you read, you'll think of some of them I've missed. You can make your own list.

THE REALLY BAD WORDS

That's another joking title, for *really* is one of the baddest of my bad words. Another is *little*. I've just interrupted my writing of this chapter to take a teapot and two cups out to men building a wall outside my house. It's noon, and I said to them, "It's a little late to be bringing the tea," and heard how phony my statement was. I was not a little late, but about two hours late. My *little* was not so much a description as an apology for my forgetting. I would have done better to have said, "I apologize for being late with the tea." So often we use the word *little* apologetically, demeaningly, or sentimentally that we usually improve our sentence if we strike it out.

Note in this chapter that I'm never saying that any one of the *bad words* in my list can't be used well. Here's John Miller, who lives on the Outer Banks of North Carolina, telling about surfing in the ocean:

> I was roller coastering up and down the wave trying to pick up speed. I didn't think I was going to make it. Squatting down as low as I could, the wave curling over me, I knew right then I was in the tube. All I could see was a *little* hole in front of me; the wave sounded like an earthquake rumbling. Finally I popped out, the rumbling gone.

John needs the word *little* there: he's talking about a wave big enough to envelop him but the hole looks little in the big wave. A careless writer might have stuck a *little* into that passage where it weakened the writing—saying "the wave sounded a *little* like an earthquake rumbling." That *little* would have made the earthquake sound foolish.

The worst use of *little* as a bad word ordinarily occurs when it's an adverb:

> Afterwards, paddling around and waiting for some waves to come, we never failed to get on the subject of sharks, and I would get a little tense and just look down into the dirty water and say, "Don't get me now."

A good ending to the sentence, looking down into the dirty water and saying, "Don't get me now." But a *little* tense? The whole passage from which this excerpt is taken is about the boy's fear of sharks. I believe he was *tense*, not a *little* tense, whatever that means. The difference here between *tense* and a *little tense* is not made significant. Maybe another boy in the group was more tense than the writer; but if so, the writer could have shown the difference by contrasting some reactions or comments of the boys rather than by using the word *little*.

Little is a *diminisher,* like *somewhat* or *rather.* It's supposed to soften or diminish the strength of the word it modifies, but some people use it so often that they forget its function and it seems to issue from a mealy mouth. *Rather* says little [There's a good use of *little!*] or nothing as a modifier. Even if you're speaking [Note that *even;* it could go also] rather than writing, it says no more than *somewhat,* which is a pale word with no kick in its tail. Maybe a swish at the most, as if the tail is made of taffeta. But when *rather* is used as in my next-to-last sentence above, meaning "in contrast to," it's almost always a good word performing a necessary function.

Watch out for words with *somewhat* or *something* meanings. Usually they are better replaced by meat and potatoes statements:

Original: I felt somewhat nauseated.

Revised: I felt nauseated.

Nauseated: head spinning, stomach gulping for release. A strong word, doesn't need *somewhat* modifying it. If the writer felt only the beginning symptoms of nausea, he might better have said what they were. Consider replacing diminishers with facts, as in this example:

Original: It was rather hot.

Revised: Sweat was forming in a pool above my belt.

Diminishers:

little	rather	sort of
a little bit	somewhat	kind of
slightly	something like	

I had forgotten to mention *sort of* and *kind of.* They're sort of bad words, too.

Here are words I call *intensifiers.* They're intended to charge up the words that follow them, but they seldom do:

real (-ly)	quite	very	deep (-ly)
actual (-ly)	sheer	too	especial (-ly)
complete (-ly)	big	even	special (-ly)
total (-ly)	important		tremendous (-ly)

Consider this sentence: "He was really crazy: he put both hands in his soup." That *really* is really unnecessary. It does nothing to help *crazy.* The hands in the soup suggest the man was eccentric at least, psychotic at most. But without knowing the situation, we can't be sure whether he's putting his hands in the soup jokingly or insanely. Whatever the truth of the matter, *really* could be deleted.

Actually is brother of *really:* bad writers use it because they fear their sentences carry no authority. They try to soup up the engine with emphasis words:

> I was so mad that I was going to kick her in the stomach,
> but then I found out she was actually my aunt.

That's a strong sentence, weakened by one word—*actually,* which must
go.

> She was *real big.*

Better to say, "She was six feet one, a hundred and eighty pounds."

Good writers as well as bad use these bad words I'm discussing.
Look back to the paper, "Buying a House," near the end of Chapter 9 in this book. In the fourth paragraph the writer uses four unnecessary intensifiers or qualifiers: *"Really* thought," *"quite* enthusiastic," *"generally* disappointed," and *"extremely* common." The
passage would gain, not lose, power if all four of them were dropped.

When I originally wrote the sentence on page 202 characterizing
Sir James Murray, I said he was *"essentially* a reserved, religious,
deeply formal man." *Essentially* was O.K. there because Sir James was
not reserved when he rode a bicycle, but otherwise could properly be
characterized as an essentially reserved man. When in this chapter I
put *deeply* on the list of intensifiers, I remembered using it in the
sentence about Sir James, and looked back. First reaction—"good word
there," because he was *especially* formal. But then I took out *deeply*
and found that *formal* was a strong word without it. Most people aren't
formal; Sir James was. Two lessons there:

(1) Take out a suspected bad word before you decide your use of it
is good. Then make your judgment whether or not to restore it.

(2) Consider the power of any modifier to overwhelm or weaken the
word it modifies.

If you've written a word with iron in it, like *honest* or *gobble,* you
don't need a modifier with it. The lesser word will draw energy away
from the head word.

Original: She walked two miles to tell me the milk she had sold me
was sour, a very honest person.

Revision: She walked two miles to tell me the milk she had sold me
was sour, an honest person.

If you had written that original sentence and thought about improving it, you might have gone further in cutting and written simply:

Second revision: She walked two miles to tell me the milk she had
sold me was sour.

Any half-awake reader would come to the conclusion she was honest.

Original: The bird gobbled the meat voraciously.

Revision: The bird gobbled the meat.

Gobble is a strong word. It doesn't mean *pick at* or *eat*. Let it stand by itself and gobble like my Standard Poodle eating his canned meat every night. Don't let your hand get in the way.

∞ **DOING TWENTY:** Write freely for half an hour on anything you're thinking about in connection with your I-Search Paper—an experience you had, a reaction to something you read, the feel of the search, the most surprising happening in it, whatever. Remember, try to tell truths, write so fast your hand aches, don't worry about punctuation, spelling, or grammar.

In this chapter I'm challenging you take on the self-discipline of the finest writers. If you pick up habits that give your words full weight, readers will pay attention to your writing. They may not know why your words are affecting them, but they'll enjoy reading because you write solid sentences, not strewn with packing straw or plastic pellets. That doesn't mean you're the equal of Shakespeare or Thoreau in characterization or thought, but why shouldn't you use their techniques of expression when you can?

The words on my list are more frequently used badly than other words, so they come out meaningless or wan. Or simply unnecessary. Should I have written "simply unnecessary" there? Why use *simply?* I recognize it's making a distinction, suggesting that the unnecessariness is further down the scale of importance from meaningless, but it's not a distinction worth making. Look at the revised statement standing by itself:

. . . so they come out meaningless or wan. Or unnecessary.

Nothing more than that *unnecessary* is necessary. When it stands alone, a reader is apt to give it the full weight of its meaning. *Unnecessary* is a good word, a strong word. *Simply* isn't going to help it.

Powerful writers seldom surround their good words with bad ones. As a writer you'll do well to strive to be one about whom readers say, "I pay attention to her. She means what she says." When you're writing well, in the truthtelling groove, you won't find many bad words in your paragraphs because your unconscious is zeroing in on the facts of the experience. You're relating what happened to the conditions out of which ideas and feelings arose. Here's a quick writing by Nick Semple, one of John Miller's classmates at Cape Hatteras School:

> **When I was in the second grade, I had a teacher who didn't like me. I think she actually hated me. I don't know why and don't care. I am left-handed and my teacher**

> didn't like left-handed students. She would give me a
> paper; I would put it on the left side of the desk, and she
> would come along and put it on the right side, and I would
> put it on the left side again. She did that every day. I
> would sit in class exhausted from moving my paper back
> to the left side, and I would daydream and she would come
> to me and shake me for about a minute. One day the boys
> in the class told me to hold onto my chair. When she came
> and started to shake me, I held onto my chair and she
> started to shake herself. It was so funny I could have
> laughed my head off, but I didn't. But that broke her from
> shaking me.

Nick had something to say and got it said without bad words, except
for that cliché "could have laughed my head off," which he might
have improved upon. The *actually*—ordinarily a bad word—in the second sentence makes a valid distinction, saying the teacher didn't just
not like Nick but actually hated him. It wasn't one of those dead uses
of *actually* like this one:

> I was actually smaller than my younger brother. He was six
> feet and I was five four.

which might better have been written like this:

> My younger brother was six feet and I was five four.

Readers like you and me can figure out the surprise in that statement
without having it pointed out to us. That's a fundamental about
writing: if your words explain what intelligent readers will understand
without explanation, they're bad words. Readers don't want your
meaning to be beyond them, but neither do they want to be treated
like dolts.

Because they look so innocent and useful, the words *even* and *all*
are two of the sneakiest words. The way to face them is to remove
them and see if your sentence improves. You'll write them—everyone
does—and often without noticing. "Take the plants outside, will you?"
—that sentence means "Take all the plants outside," not some of them.
So *all* isn't needed. "I like to walk before the sun is up."—I catch the
surprise in that statement without the writer saying, *"even* before the
sun is up." *Would* is another dangerous word:

> When we were kids we would go up by the river bank and
> fish. We would find worms and tie a string around their
> middle and then drop the line. But the fish wouldn't bite.

Would there means *often used to.* Once you establish the *would* notion, you can drop the word, don't need to repeat it. Many *would's* not only dull a story but often prevent it from falling into a *once* which tells an incident fully enough to develop suspense and point. If you write, "We would drown gophers and we would tease girls," you may have shot down two stories before they could show their character.

Another desperado needs here to be uncovered—*this particular.* "This particular guy needs to be murdered." He's a cousin of "the *exact same* guy." The word *this* points at someone or something particular, just as *that* does. *This* and *that* are weak substitutes for the name of a person or thing. If we don't know the name, we may properly use *this* or *that,* but never hooked onto the word *particular.* "That particular evening" says no more than "That evening."

> All of us guys would always play ball in the vacant lot next door.

There's a sentence with three bad guys in it—*all, would,* and *always.* The last fellow is a strong word. Not many things happen always, except perhaps the sun rises and sets every day, but you can't *always* see it because of clouds. "I always liked to go to the movies when I was a kid." Drop the *always:* sentence now says the same thing.

Then there's Whooery, Whichery, and Thatery, expressions that make prose sound textbookish. "He was a man who had gone far." Try it without the Whooery, and in this case, without the Mannery as well—"He had gone far." Does the job. Look at the free writing you did when you were reading the first part of this chapter and mark any uses of *who, which,* or *that.* Should you omit any of them?

Like all bad words on my list, *who, which,* and *that* are sometimes good words, or at least necessary, as in this sentence:

> That plan, which ended up on its head, was nevertheless my favorite.

Then there are squishy words that strand a reader in the Great Vague Swamp, which I believe adjoins the Great Dismal Swamp of New Jersey:

destination	situation	concerned with
predicament	thing	as far as . . . concerned
problem	process	phase
area	involved with	aspect

Avoid them. Strike them out. Think of what lies behind them and write words that open meaning to the air instead of smother fish, plants, and turtles in quicksand. Occasionally the best writers sink, as John Steinbeck did in this passage from his story "Beans" in *Tortilla Flat:*

> Teresina was a mildly puzzled woman, as far as her mind was concerned. Her body was one of those perfect retorts for the distillation of children.

Maybe a male chauvinist statement, but it could be better said:

> Teresina was a mildly puzzled woman in mind but her body was a perfect retort for the distillation of children.

Say goodbye to *as far as . . . concerned.* Say the farewell aloud so you'll remember you pushed it out the door with such limping phrases as

generally speaking	after what seemed like hours
all things considered	efficient and effective

BAD WORD LIST

I'll put down the bad words I've discussed and a few more, so you can see the rotten company together and maybe remember their faces. All of them are good words at times, but we succumb to them when we shouldn't. I'm sure that you can catch me in this book surrendering to them when I should have conquered them.

a little bit	effective	phase	somewhat
actually	even	predicament	sort of
all	exactly	problem	specially
always	frankly	process	surely
area	important	quite	(Thatery)
as far as . . . concerned	in fact	rather	thing
aspect	incidentally	really	too
at least	involved with	sheer	totally
big	just	simply	tremendously
certainly	kind of	sincerely	very
completely	little	situation	(Whichery)
concerned with	obviously	slightly	whole
deeply	of course	somehow	(Whooery)
destination	particularly	something like	would

Trouble with these characters is that they've bored us so many times that we wouldn't hear them if they said, "There's a nuclear accident in town and you better light out for the hills." Their past emptiness, their constant nothings have lulled us into ignoring them. I'll write a passage in this dismal language so you can get the effect of its vapors:

I wasn't exactly meaning to upset you totally by listing all the words again. Certainly you can always sort of stand just one more list, can't you? As far as using language is concerned, it wasn't an especially bad thing to do, was it? But I suppose it puts you in quite a predicament, really. After all [there's one I forgot] it's not a sheer waste of time because it's my special area, these ineffective words.

Several of the witnesses for the Watergate cover-up heard on television were addicted to *at this point in time.* Perhaps the phrase was appropriate: it was pompous and wordy and helped keep listeners from sensing that nothing essential was being revealed. The translation of *at this point in time* is "now," which the Watergaters were trying to avoid because it was both embarrassing and incriminating.

One last word—*it.* I can't stand to write at length about it, because it has so many ways of wrecking a sentence. It's so hard to get away from. Necessary at times, useful; but just watch it in your writing, will you? It can bring about *assification,* as *The Oxford English Dictionary* puts it.

∞ **DOING TWENTY-ONE:** Look for bad words in the free writing you did while reading this chapter. Mark with penciled brackets those words you want to delete, and write in any necessary additions. Bring them to the group so others can see what you did. Probably you'll have used bad words in free writing, where you're zeroing on truthtelling. A more likely place to find them is in papers you've written for other classes. Bring in also a page of your writing where you let yourself surrender to a number of bad words.

> *. . . but surely painting can afford to be done a little badly better than sculpture can. When I say "surely" I suppose it means that I am not sure about this.*
>
> SAMUEL BUTLER

chapter 16

getting
the
point

PUNCTUATION. How can so many Americans study it year after year—in elementary school, high school, and college—and not learn it?

Answer: (1) Most writing they do in school doesn't count in their lives and reaches no public, so they develop no motivation for presenting their sentences in accepted, professional form. (2) School is often a place for sitters and receivers, not searchers and learners. (3) In school, people are taught punctuation as they're taught spelling —by the Errors Approach, red ink in the margins and exercises in the drillbooks.

Most people who've mastered the punctuation system did it outside school, away from drillbooks and methods that set a pace for them not right for their bodies or minds. My experience talking to hundreds of teachers around the country and for three years editing a national journal for composition teachers tells me that most teachers didn't learn punctuation, and some didn't learn spelling, *as students.* When first hired to teach English, the week before school opened, they sat down with a book and learned punctuation because they realized they would be embarrassed in front of students if they didn't know it, and they feared they might lose their jobs.

To learn the system these people went beyond filling out exercise books and memorizing rules. They looked at American-English sentences printed in books, and they studied a textbook on punctuation. They placed the actual use of punctuation along with the traditional rules—on a Moebius Strip where the two met each other, and yet remained themselves, not always the same.

These teachers had to learn punctuation or be embarrassed out of their jobs. Jack London, author of *The Sea Wolf* and *Call of the Wild*, also had to learn it to succeed in his job. Here he is describing his hero in *The Adventures of Martin Eden,* a novel based closely on London's own life:

> He did not know how long an article he should write, but he counted the words in a double-page article in the Sunday supplement of *The San Francisco Examiner,* and guided himself by that. Three days, at white heat, completed his narrative; but when he had copied it carefully, in a large scrawl that was easy to read, he learned from a rhetoric he picked up in the library that there were such things as paragraphs and quotation marks. He had never thought of them before, and he promptly set to work writing the article over, referring continually to the pages of the rhetoric, and learning more in a day about composition than the average schoolboy in a year. . . . He never lost a moment. On the looking-glass were lists of definitions and pronunciations; when shaving, or dressing, or combing his hair, he conned these lists over. Similar lists were on the wall over the oil-stove, and they were similarly conned while he was engaged in cooking or in washing the dishes. New lists continually displaced the old ones. Every strange or partly familiar word encountered in his reading was immediately jotted down, and later, when a sufficient number had been accumulated, were typed and pinned to the wall or looking-glass. He even carried them in his pockets, and reviewed them at odd moments on the street, or while waiting in butcher-shop or grocery to be served.

If you want to master the punctuation system, look at how magazines and books are punctuated. (Not newspapers: they follow a different set of conventions from those for books and magazines. Most newspapers set their pages in type that doesn't have italics—slanted letters like these: *italics*—and so they can't signal certain things with italics that books and magazines can.) "This is already getting confusing," you may be thinking, "a different set of punctuation conventions for different kinds of publications!" No surprise there. We have a different set of conventions for dressing for church than for a formal dance or pool game. Punctuation is part of our language system, and language, as I've said before, is human behavior—varied and contradictory at times. You probably have learned part of your punctuation patterns from comic strips, which have a still different set of conventions, such as three to five exclamation points !!!!! to indicate emphasis, or a mess of marks to indicate a profoundly confused reaction—??!!#$%6&??

But enough of confusion. Look at semicolons ;;;;;;;;;;;;;;; and love them because they can be a master key to the American punctuation system. Consider this mark ; —a period above a comma. You'd expect it to be a stronger mark than the comma and it is. But how to learn its several uses? There are two commonly accepted ways of learning a system. (1) Find a person or book that will give you the system as experts have discovered or devised it, and memorize it. Probably you've already taken that way, or had it forced on you, and not learned punctuation. (2) Look at the actualities the system describes and try to figure how and why it works the way it does. The Moebian approach, as you might suspect, is a third way. It employs both (1) and (2). Until you examine punctuated sentences on your own, you'll probably not remember the "rules" of the system; for you won't have any principle in mind that ties your observations together. You need to Jack London it or Ben Franklin it. No teacher or book can finally learn it for you.

In this chapter I'll give the major uses of, or principles for, semicolons; but first you need to speculate on them by yourself.

∞ **DOING TWENTY-TWO:** On separate pieces of paper or cards, copy twelve sentences from printed pages that contain semicolons. You're most likely to find semicolons in formal or scholarly writing, for reasons that will become apparent later if you have the will to do this searching on your own. Now put in piles those sentences that seem to use the semicolon in the same way or for the same reason. Make up rules or generalizations that seem to cover these uses and compare them to those I'll present in the next paragraph. If you look at my rules first, you're cheating yourself once again out of learning punctuation. This is an exploring expedition, not an exercise that's going to be graded.

THE SEMICOLON

1. ————————————; ————————————.

Jack is a fellow without courage; Pete is foolhardy and lovable.

You go down to the supermarket; I'll stay home in bed with a book.

This first use of the semicolon is to join two major word groups that could stand alone as sentences. Note that each word group in the examples above could stand alone as a sentence. In the following sentences, the word groups on the right of the spaces couldn't stand alone, and therefore shouldn't be joined by a semicolon to the groups on the left.

This is a sorry mess   which I am not going to get into again.

Don't stay around here   pretending you are a big shot.

When I say "you can't" or "you should," I don't mean that I'm making up rules for you to follow. I mean that you "should" or you "can" punctuate in a certain way if you wish to observe the conventions of punctuation. The conventions are not laws passed by Congress; they are simply the practice of most published writers.

In order to understand the second use of the semicolon, you must first consider the pattern of two word groups that can stand by themselves but are joined by the common connectives *and, but, for, or,* and *nor.* Such word groups are separated by a comma:

———————————————, ————————————————.

The end of the world is not in sight, but I think it's just around the nuclear corner.

You should go to the movie, for it's the kind that will make you eat your popcorn fast.

Notice what confusion would occur if one or both of the word groups in these sentences had commas within it:

——————, ——————, ——————, ——————, ——————.

You wouldn't see quickly where the turning point, or pivot, of the sentence was:

Jack, a crazy guy, is my friend, but Pete may be an enemy.

The major word groups would be picked out more clearly for the reader if the sentence had the following punctuation pattern,

2. ——, ——————, ——————; ———————————.

Jack, a crazy guy, is my friend; but Pete may be my enemy.

The second world war, fought mostly by conventional weapons, was a horror; but if there is to be a third war, probably fought in the main with nuclear weapons, it will be even more inhuman.

The second use of the semicolon is to join two word groups, which are connected by *and, but, for, or,* or *nor,* but have internal commas within one or both of the word groups.

The third use of the semicolon is to separate a string of paired words or phrases when the members of each pair are separated by a comma.

3. ——————————, ——; ——, ——; ——, ——.

The teams' colors were red, blue; white, green; black, orange.

I went to Chicago, Illinois; East Orange, New Jersey; Mason, Michigan; and Manders Corners, Vermont.

You will seldom use the semicolon in this way, but you can see the logic of a pattern in which commas and semicolons separate parts according to their importance or sense.

The fourth use of the semicolon is an illogical one. It occurs between word groups that can stand alone as sentences but are joined by certain connectives (*therefore, consequently, moreover, yet, still, now, then, however,* and so forth) which are not as commonly used to connect word groups as are *and, but, for, or,* and *nor.*

therefore
4. ——————————————; **consequently** ——————.
(etc.)

The process of reporting is complex; therefore you may need a few years to master it.

He has gone all the way to the bottom of the well; now he has to come up.

You may quite logically say, "Why do these words take a semicolon before them when *and, but, for, or* and *nor* do not in the same circumstances?" The answer, "Because that is convention." Use 4 of the semicolon happens to be one of the punctuation conventions that doesn't make sense and isn't particularly useful, but you should follow it unless you want to make an issue of not doing so. You can wear a cabbage on your head instead of a hat, as did one of Gilbert K. Chesterton's characters; but like him, you may find it causes more reaction than you had anticipated.

To review, these are the four uses of the semicolon.

1. ——————————; ——————.

2. ——, ——————, ——————; ——————.

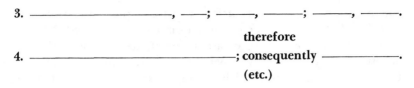

3. ——————————, —; ————, ————; ————, ————.

                                     therefore

4. ————————————————————; **consequently** ———————————.

                                     (etc.)

In all but number 3, the word groups on each side of the semicolon must be able to stand by themselves as sentences. Note again the kind of sentences that aren't made up of such word groups and thus can't be conventionally tied together by a semicolon:

He is   however   a person who will help you when you need help.

George and John   who were sick   went home together.

The fact that you now know the four major uses of the semicolon doesn't mean that you'll remember them and be able to put them into practice when you write. A child doesn't learn to use a napkin at the table by sitting in his room and practicing how to pick one up. He learns principally by observing others using napkins. Eventually he feels the pressure to mimic the practice or conform to it. Look in this book right now for uses of the semicolon. Ask yourself which one of the four uses each example represents. For several days, study the semicolons in magazines and books until you begin to realize in what kinds of word situations they are conventional. Two minutes or so every day will help. When you've mastered the semicolon, you can move on to the comma.

That's enough searching into punctuation for a while. Too much work of this kind at a time and out of exhaustion you'll give up once again on the learning task. In a day or two you can pick up your reading of this chapter once again, after these *bullets* [a printer's term for heavy dots used to emphasize or mark off].

•   •   •

> *1551 T. WILSON Logike (1580)70 When sentences be euill pointed, and the sence thereby depraued.*
> *1602 MARSTON Ant. & Mel. IV. Wks. 1856 I. 51 Weele point our speech With amorous kissing, kissing commaes.*
> OXFORD ENGLISH DICTIONARY

Punctuation wasn't invented to torture you. In backing up that statement I'll take most of my information on punctuation from an article in the 15th edition of *The Encyclopædia Britannica* by T.

Julian Brown, professor of ancient writing at the University of London, but I'll throw in modern-day examples of my own. I'm something of an expert on punctuation myself, having loved the forms of letters and the points and symbols that surround them ever since I was a boy who dreamed of becoming a typographer and later, one summer after graduating from college, spent a whole summer on a porch in Oberlin, Ohio, studying the history of printing types because I loved letters so much.

Julian Brown says that our punctuation evolved in this way: Greek inscriptions were normally chiseled out of stone in capital letters, without divisions between words or sentences. If these early Greeks had been chiseling out the Eighth Amendment to the United States Constitution, they would have presented that clear and succinct statement like this:

EXCESSIVEBAILSHALLNOTBEREQUIREDNOREXCE
SSIVEFINESIMPOSEDNORCRUELANDUNUSUALPUN
ISHMENTSINFLICTED

I don't know whether you could make out all or some of the words in that punctuationless sentence or not. You probably caught the first words because the opening space signals the beginning of the first word.

The next step by Greeks writing inscriptions in capital letters was to break up phrases with two or three dots arranged vertically, something like my using a colon to do that:

EXCESSIVEBAIL:SHALLNOTBEREQUIRED:NOREXC
ESSIVEFINESIMPOSED:NORCRUELANDUNUSUALPU
NISHMENTSINFLICTED

These stops help a reader. I'm not saying that there was a clear line of development in Greek or English punctuation from none to much, but rather a hit and miss movement from no punctuation to increasing punctuation. In the classical and medieval periods some nations and scribes (there was no printing then in the western world) used points (marks like periods, middle dots, straight commas, or *virgules*—which were shortened versions of our present-day slash mark [/]) to separate words, phrases, or sentences. Assyrians and Babylonians devised wedge-shaped characters and employed a word separator that looked like a tilted triangle with a tail on it.

> *The virgule, originally placed high, sank to the base line and developed a curve— turned, in fact, into a modern comma.*
>
> JULIAN BROWN

At one time in their history, the Greeks had moved all the way from no punctuation to putting a separator between each word as the Assyrians did:

EXCESSIVE·BAIL·SHALL·NOT·BE REQUIRED·NOR·
EXCESSIVE·FINES·IMPOSED·NOR·CRUEL·AND·UN
USUAL·PUNISHMENTS·INFLICTED

Some Latin books of the 6th century abandoned points and went back to continuously written words. During the 7th and 8th centuries, scribes began to put *spaces* between words as we do today. Up until the 13th century, prepositions were commonly attached to their head-words (in modern-day American-English that would be like writing *ondemand* as one word), a practice that to me seems helpful. Since punctuation has been used with roman letters, some persons who were concerned to help priests reading before congregations attempted to force the punctuation system more and more in the direction of indicating places where a reader should pause and take a breath, and others attempted to force the system in the direction of indicating relationships in meaning between parts of sentences. The latter group has now pretty much won out, but still some of our punctuation practices indicate pauses the speaker should take.

My purpose in presenting some of these historical details is to show that the conventions of punctuation and writing have been constantly changing over the centuries, and to suggest that you can expect further change within your lifetime. As in spelling, some people revert to, or stay with, earlier usage and others keep up with change, so that a confused practice results. Understandable. Punctuation is human behavior and some of us like to "get with it" and others prefer to stay with what we consider the "pure" or the "true." As new marks were invented, use of them increased, and by the middle of the 19th century, commas were used to separate almost every phrase in every sentence. Note the heavy punctuation in this paragraph from Henry Thoreau's essay "Walking," written in 1862:

> I think that I cannot preserve my health and spirits, unless I spend four hours a day at least,—and it is commonly more than that,—sauntering through the woods and over the hills and fields, absolutely free from all worldly engagements. You may safely say, A penny for your thoughts, or a thousand pounds. When sometimes I am reminded that the mechanics and shopkeepers stay in their shops not only all the forenoon, but all the afternoon too, sitting with crossed legs, so many of them,—as if the legs were made to

sit upon and not to stand or walk upon,—I think that they
deserve some credit for not having all committed suicide
long ago.

Writers today would probably not use eight of Thoreau's eleven commas in that passage, but he was following the custom of his day. At
that time phrases of interruption or further explanation were commonly marked off from the rest of a sentence by pairs of commas and
dashes on each side of them, as in Thoreau's first sentence; whereas
now either two dashes or two commas are customary. Seldom do
writers use double marks [!? or,—] except when quotation marks
or parentheses are involved [?" or .")].

The fashion now is to use punctuation that points up grammatical
relationships, grammar being in our language principally a way of
signaling meaning through word order. If a pause or separation is
needed to make a sentence clear, punctuation is used, but only as
much as is necessary.

•   •   •

When you look for uses of the comma in print, you'll find more of
them than you found for the semicolon. If you're bewildered, look at
the treatment of punctuation in the back of *Webster's New Collegiate
Dictionary* or *Webster's New World Dictionary* (College Edition).
There you'll find not only the conventional uses of the comma but
those of all other punctuation marks as well. If you own *The American Heritage Dictionary* (New College Edition), you'll have to look up
comma, or whatever other point you're interested in, among the words
defined in the main part of the dictionary. I'm asking you to consult
a dictionary for further word on punctuation for two reasons: every
bookard should own and use a good collegiate dictionary, and if you're
not willing to drop this book and go to another to learn punctuation, there's small chance that you'll master the system and large
chance that once again you'll have started to study punctuation and
given up. Emulate Ben Franklin: don't tell people about great plans
until you've carried them out.

Here are a few practices in punctuation that may reduce your
confusion as a reader and writer.

The British use different points for quoting than we do. For example, for a quotation within a quotation Americans write:

He said, "What do you mean 'crazy'?"

What the speaker (he) said is placed within double quotes ("——") and
the quotation ('crazy') is placed within single quotes. The British reverse this convention:

He said, 'What do you mean "crazy"?'

I like that practice better because it means that I'd be using single quotation marks more than double and thus expending less effort. But I'm not going British in punctuation; I want to be accepted by my countrywomen and men.

Commas and periods in our system always precede closing quotation marks (,") (."); colons and semicolons follow quotation marks:

He said, "Go home to mother"; I paid no attention to him.

Question marks and exclamation points should follow or precede quotation marks according to the sense of the sentence:

"Did anyone ever say to you, 'You have to be a slave'?"
Are you sure he said, "Turn them in tomorrow"?
"Watch out, you fool!"
"How frightful was that man who said 'swindling' "!

A minor matter that people often go wrong on: a parenthesis is never preceded by a comma but may be followed by one.

Wrong: This man, (he was the auditor), is the culprit.

Conventional: The steep ascent of the cliff was mastered by the four climbers (only two men had ever climbed a higher point in the Adirondacks), and now they were ready to descend.

When the newspaper columnist Don Marquis wrote his three books about archy the cockroach, which are collected under the title of *the lives & times of archy & mehitabel* (1940), he explained that the poems were set in lower-case type and without punctuation because archy, the cockroach who inhabited the office where Marquis wrote, was unable conveniently to operate the shift key on the boss's typewriter. Here's one of his poems. After reading a few lines I think you'll become accustomed to the lack of punctuation and enjoy archy's form of expression, a reaction which if true may suggest that we could do away with all punctuation with less harm than some people suppose.

CAPITALS AT LAST
I THOUGHT THAT SOME HISTORIC DAY
SHIFT KEYS WOULD LOCK IN SUCH A WAY
THAT MY POETIC FEET WOULD FALL
UPON EACH CLICKING CAPITAL
AND NOW FROM KEY TO KEY I CLIMB
TO WRITE MY GRATITUDE IN RHYME

YOU LITTLE KNOW WITH WHAT DELIGHT
THROUGHOUT THE LONG AND LONELY NIGHT
I'VE KICKED AND BUTTED (FOOT AND BEAN)
AGAINST THE KEYS OF YOUR MACHINE
TO TELL THE MOVING TALE OF ALL
THAT TO A COCKROACH MAY BEFALL
INDEED IF I COULD NOT HAVE HAD
SUCH OCCUPATION I'D BE MAD
AH FOR A SOUL LIKE MINE TO DWELL
WITHIN A COCKROACH THAT IS HELL
TO SCURRY FROM THE PLAYFUL CAT
TO DODGE THE INSECT EATING RAT
THE HUNGRY SPIDER TO EVADE
THE MOUSE THAT %) ?)) " " " $$$ ((gee boss
what a jolt that cat mehitabel made
a jump for me
i got away but she unlocked the shift key
it kicked me right into the
mechanism where she
couldn t reach me it
was nearly the death of little
archy that kick spurned me right
out of parnassus back into
the vers libre slums i lay
in behind the wires for an hour after
she left before i dared to get
out and finish i hate
cats say boss please lock the shift
key tight some night
i would like to tell the story of
my life all in capital
letters

archy

In German all nouns are capitalized. And for several centuries English people capitalized "important" words. Only a little more than two hundred years ago, formal documents in America showed traces of that practice, for example, *The Declaration of Independence:*

> . . . That whenever any Form of Government becomes destructive of these ends, it is the Right of the People to alter or to abolish it, and to institute new Government, laying its foundation on such principles and organizing its powers in such form, as to them shall seem most likely to effect their Safety and Happiness.

In Ben Franklin's paragraph quoted in the Preface you'll see the same profuse employment of capitals. Elsewhere in this book you'll find modern use of capitals because I've used sources that were modernized by editors.

But the trend is to less and less capitalization. You may wonder why I bring up such historical facts. What good are they to you? They suggest how to place your bets when you're writing and don't know whether or not to capitalize a word. If you're uncertain, bet on starting it with a lower-case letter. To know the drift of human behavior and the reason behind it is to feel less confused and overwhelmed. The general law in punctuation, as in spelling, is toward simplicity. For example, a term made up of two words begins like this,

air plane

and as it's used more often is punctuated like this,

air-plane

and eventually becomes

airplane.

The process takes years, sometimes centuries. Highland was once *high land* and *high-land* before it became *highland,* which as one word is pronounced differently than it was when two words. Writing this book I typed out *semi-colon* and my editor told me that the term is now written *semicolon.*

Our punctuation system is admirable because it helps us keep meaning clear and is highly consistent, easy to learn. If I write,

After home was a relief.

you might well infer I had forgotten to finish my sentence, but if I use a comma, the sentence is complete and clear:

After, home was a relief.

Another neat and logical pattern in the system is the one for indicating interruptions or explanations within a sentence. It calls for use of commas, dashes, parentheses, and brackets, in that order—according to how removed the interruption is in sense from the main part of the sentence. Here are examples. I'll put the interrupting elements in italics so that you can compare them easily.

1. John Butler, *the man over yonder,* is my second cousin.
2. John Abercrombie—*a man who likes Stroh's beer*—goes to work before dawn.

3. John Abercrombie (*of all the men I know the least likely to drink dangerously*) goes to work before dawn.
4. John Abercrombie [*That's a Scottish name that combines the names of the rivers Aber and Crombie*] goes to work before dawn.

What you see there between brackets is so removed in sense from the main sentence that it might also be set as a footnote. Commonly editors put their own remarks or explanations between brackets.

I've purposely kept this discussion of punctuation short and far from complete so that you'll realize that learning it is up to you. Punctuation is easier to master than golf or tennis, but no book can do it for you. You have to grab semicolons and commas by the tail and start swinging them.

As the last page in this chapter I'm reproducing a leaf from a famous grammar of the 18th century, Thomas Dilworth's *A New Guide to the English Tongue*, published in London in 1740 and reprinted and sold by Benjamin Franklin seven years later in Philadelphia. Reading it, you'll see that Dilworth believed punctuation should aid reading aloud as well as silent reading. I hope that after looking at my chapter you feel like joining me in the sentiment below and punctuating it with what Dilworth calls the Mark of Admiration:

Oh Punctuation! Beautiful Punctuation!

∞ **DOING TWENTY-THREE:** Look in your file of writings for one you like—an interview, a free writing, whatever—and try to improve its punctuation. Bring it to the next meeting of your group and for five or ten minutes discuss with another person any problems you had. Ask for help if you need it. Do the same for the other person's paper.

to the English Tongue.   95

Q. *What other Use does a* Colon *serve to?*
A. It is also used before a *Comparative Conjunction* in a Similitude.

Q. *Give an Example.*
A. As we perceive the Shadow upon the Sun-Dial, but· discern not its Progression; and as the Shrub or Grass appears in time to be grown, but is seen by none to grow: So also the Proficiency of our Wits, advancing slowly by small Improvements, is perceived only after some distance of time.

Q. *What is a* Period?
A. The *Period* is a full Point, thus (.)

Q. *Of what Use is the* Period?
A. It denotes the full ending and finishing of a whole *Sentence*, at the Conclusion of which, it is always placed.

Q. *Give an Example.*
A. There is no Man without his peculiar Failing.

Q. *What are the proper* Pauses *of these* Stops?
A The *proper Pause* or *Rest* of each of these *Stops* may be thus measur'd: The Time of stopping or resting at the *Comma*, is the Time of saying *One*; at the *Semicolon, One, One*; at the *Colon, One, One, One*; and at the *Period, One, One, One, One*, before you begin the next Clause or Sentence

Q. *Which is the Mark of* Interrogation?
A. The Note of *Interrogation* is (?)

Q. *What is the Use of this* Note?
A. To shew the Reader when a *Question* is asked.

Q. *Give an Example.*
A. What is the Use of this Book?

Q. *Which is the Note of* Admiration?
A. The Note of *Admiration* is (!)

Q. *What is the Use of this* Note?
A. It is used to express our *Wonder*

Q. *Give an Example.*
A. O the Cares of Mankind!

Q. *What are the* Pauses *of these Notes of* Interrogation *and* Admiration?
A. They are the same as that of the *Period.*

Q. *What do you call a* Parenthesis?
A. A *Parenthesis* has two crooked Strokes, thus ( )

Q. *What is the Use of a* Parenthesis?
A. It serves to include one Sentence in another, without confounding the Sense of either; and yet is necessary for the Explanation thereof: And should be read with a lower Tone of the Voice, as a Thing that comes in by the by.

When a child writes, "My sister was hit by a terck yesterday" and the teacher's response is a red-circled "terck" with no further comment, educational standards may have been upheld, but the child will think twice before entering the writing process again. Inane and apathetic writing is often the writer's only means of self-protection.

DONALD H. GRAVES

chapter 17
editing
day

IN THE FOUR YEARS that I conducted seminars in which members wrote I-Search Papers, my only large disappointment was the half effort many of them gave to helping each other on Editing Day. I understand why they weren't highly motivated to polish their own papers and help others polish theirs—they knew that most of the writing would not be published beyond their classroom. Because the papers were usually six to twelve pages long (in double-spaced typed form), they could not be practicably posted on bulletin boards and expected to be read by other students passing in the halls.

I typed and xeroxed copies of some of the best and worst papers and distributed them in seminars. Those copies were read with interest. Violet Hawkins's paper "The Flowers in My Family" was published in the student newspaper of Western Michigan University, which then had a press run of about twelve or fourteen thousand copies. That paper and "Preacher Grandmother" were circulated or published among the living members of the families the writers wrote about. I've passed copies of these papers out to teachers and students in many parts of the country, and this contextbook is doing that even more widely. But most I-Search Papers written in groups or seminars around the country have not gone beyond the eyes of those who joined together first to write them. We need to find more ways to publish these papers. The thought of publication goads writers to their best efforts. That's as it should be, for the purpose of writing is to communicate.

Your group can pull together and do first-rate editing. When you read the following account about a man who became an editor, remember that you're working in a situation he never enjoyed while he was young. Once again, I give you part of the life story of a person with will power: Frederick Douglass. Note the two s's on the end of his name. In your city there is probably a Douglass Center or a Douglass Street. You'll know whom it's named after when you see the two s's.

Douglass was born a slave in 1817, as nearly as he could remember. He was the child of a white father and a black slave mother, on the Eastern Shore of Maryland. At twenty-one, he escaped the plantation, traveled north, became a world-renowned writer, editor, and speaker against slavery. He was received with honor in Edinburgh—that great Scottish center of learning that is mentioned several times in this book. With the proceeds of two years of lecturing in Great Britain, he bought his freedom. Here's an excerpt from his long, stirring book called *The Life and Times of Frederick Douglass*. I own a paperbound edition published by Crowell-Collier in 1962.

> The frequent hearing of my mistress reading the Bible aloud, for she often read aloud when her husband was absent, awakened my curiosity in respect to this *mystery* of reading, and roused in me the desire to learn. Up to this time I had known nothing whatever of this wonderful art, and my ignorance and inexperience of what it could do for me, as well as my confidence in my mistress, emboldened me to ask her to teach me to read. With an unconscious and inexperience equal to my own, she readily consented, and in an incredibly short time, by her kind assistance, I had mastered the alphabet and could spell words of three or four letters. My mistress seemed almost as proud of my progress as if I had been her own child, and supposing that her husband would be as well pleased, she made no secret of what she was doing for me. Indeed, she exultingly told him of the aptness of her pupil and of her intention to persevere, as she felt it her duty to do, in teaching me, at least, to read the Bible. And here arose the first dark cloud over my Baltimore prospects, the precursor of

chilling blasts and drenching storms. Master Hugh was astonished beyond measure and, probably for the first time,
proceeded to unfold to his wife the true philosophy of the
slavery system, and the peculiar rules necessary in the nature
of the case to be observed in the management of human
chattels. Of course he forbade her to give me any further
instruction, telling her in the first place that to do so was
unlawful, as it was also unsafe, "for," said he, "if you give
a nigger an inch he will take an ell. Learning will spoil the
best nigger in the world. If he learns to read the Bible it
will forever unfit him to be a slave. He should know nothing but the will of his master, and learn to obey it. As to himself, learning will do him no good, but a great deal of harm,
making him disconsolate and unhappy. If you teach him
how to read, he'll want to know how to write, and this accomplished, he'll be running away with himself." Such was
the tenor of Master Hugh's oracular exposition, and it must
be confessed that he very clearly comprehended the nature
and the requirements of the relation of master and slave.
His discourse was the first decidedly anti-slavery lecture to
which it had been my lot to listen. Mrs. Auld evidently
felt the force of what he said, and, like an obedient wife,
began to shape her course in the direction indicated by him.
The effect of his words *on me* was neither slight nor transi-
tory. His iron sentences, cold and harsh, sunk like heavy
weights deep into my heart, and stirred up within me a
rebellion not soon to be allayed. . . . I am not sure that
I do not owe quite as much to the opposition of my master as to the kindly assistance of my amiable mistress. I
acknowledge the benefit rendered me by the one, and by
the other, believing that but for my mistress I might have
grown up in ignorance.

•   •   •

In ceasing to instruct me, my mistress had to seek to justify
herself *to* herself, and once consenting to take sides in such
a debate, she was compelled to hold her position. One needs
little knowledge of moral philosophy to see where she inevitably landed. She finally became even more violent in
her opposition to my learning to read than was Mr. Auld
himself. Nothing now appeared to make her more angry
than seeing me, seated in some nook or corner, quietly
reading a book or newspaper. She would rush at me with

utmost fury, and snatch the book or paper from my hand, with something of the wrath and consternation which a traitor might be supposed to feel on being discovered in a plot by some dangerous spy. The conviction once thoroughly established in her mind, that education and slavery were incompatible with each other, I was most narrowly watched in all my movements. If I remained in a separate room from the family for any considerable length of time, I was sure to be suspected of having a book, and was at once called to give an account of myself. But this was too late—the first and never-to-be-retraced step had been taken. Teaching me the alphabet had been the "inch" given, I was now waiting only for the opportunity to "take the ell."

Filled with the determination to learn to read at any cost, I hit upon many expedients to accomplish that much desired end. The plan which I mainly adopted, and the one which was the most successful, was that of using as teachers my young white playmates, with whom I met on the streets. I used almost constantly to carry a copy of *Webster's Spelling-Book* in my pocket, and when sent on errands, or when play-time was allowed me, I would step aside with my young friends and take a lesson in spelling. I am greatly indebted to these boys—Gustavus Dorgan, Joseph Bailey, Charles Farity, and William Cosdry.

In Boston, Douglass proposed to publish a newspaper against slavery. His friends were against the notion.

They had many reasons against it. First, no such paper was needed; secondly, it would interfere with my usefulness as a lecturer; thirdly, I was better fitted to speak than to write; fourthly, the paper could not succeed. . . . I can easily pardon those who saw in my persistence an unwarrantable ambition and presumption. I was but nine years from slavery. In many phases of mental experience I was but nine years old. That one under such circumstances and surrounded by an educated people, should aspire to establish a printing press, might well be considered unpractical, if not ambitious. My American friends looked at me with astonishment. "A wood-sawyer" offering himself to the public as an editor! A slave, brought up in the depths of ignorance, assuming to instruct the highly civilized people of the North in the principles of liberty, justice, and humanity! The thing

looked absurd. . . . From motives of peace, instead of is-
uing my paper in Boston, among New England friends, I
went to Rochester, N.Y., among strangers. . . . Of course
there were moral forces operating against me in Rochester,
as well as material ones. There were those who regarded
the publication of a Negro paper in that beautiful city as a
blemish and a misfortune. The New York *Herald,* true to
the spirit of the times, counseled the people of the place
to throw my printing press into Lake Ontario and to banish
me to Canada. . . . I had been at work there with my
paper but a few years before colored travelers told me that
they felt the influence of my labors when they came within
fifty miles. I did not rely alone upon what I could do by
the paper, but would write all day, then take a train to
Victor, Farmington, Canandaigua, Geneva, Waterloo, Ba-
tavia, or Buffalo, or elsewhere, and speak in the evening,
returning home afterwards or early in the morning, to be
again at my desk writing or mailing papers. There were
times when I almost thought my Boston friends were right
in dissuading me from my newspaper project. But looking
back to those nights and days of toil and thought, compelled often to do work for which I had no educational
preparation, I have come to think that, under the circumstances, it was the best school possible for me.

To reach a wide public, Douglass knew he would have to master
more than the plantation dialect he already knew. He would have to
become comfortable with what is called *Standard English,* the dialect
of the press, science, public affairs, and business. He learned it because he had need for it. That doesn't mean that he, or you, must
look down upon the language you learned at your mother's knee,
but that you should command at least two languages, your dialect
and Standard English.

I'd like to see more writing in the schools and in novels and short
stories done in black or Hispanic dialect. I envy Bernard Shaw, James
A. H. Murray, Frederick Douglass, and Bartolomeo Vanzetti for knowing how to write dialect, or what's called "broken English," as Vanzetti wrote it. But Standard English (with standard spelling and punctuation) is the language of economic, political, and scientific power,
and most persons who would be powerful and productive in this
country learn it.

•   •   •

If Frederick Douglass could become an editor for many years, you should be able to become one for a few hours in your seminar or club. On Editing Day, or Days, two to four people from your group can work with each other and offer suggestions for editorial changes in each other's papers. Then they can proofread them. You'll be asked to edit, not just play at editing. You'll all do better writing and editing if you believe there's a chance of your paper being published in some way, if only on a bulletin board in the hallway. Look for ways of circulating the papers. Xerox a few of the best. Place the liveliest in the school paper, or publish a few in a newsletter financed by your club.

RESPONDING

If you have time, meet in groups of four or more so that your paper can be read aloud and responded to by the others. I'm talking about the kind of response presented in the chapter "I and the Others." Did you like the paper that was read? Did it seem to do the job it set out to do? Can you suggest ways of improving it?—shorter or longer opening, or ending? Changes here or there to clarify meaning? Cut parts that seem off the point of the search? Is the writing style consistent, formal, informal? For example, are contractions like *don't, can't* and *didn't* used in part of the paper and *do not, cannot,* and *did not* in other parts? The criticism you offer should be like criticism of your paper you would find fulfilling and useful.

Always in such an ego-involved situation, some responders and writers will dominate or hold back. I think of the woman in our book club mentioned earlier, who was so shy she spent forty-five minutes in the bathroom while the discussion was going on. If our group had been a club that met over several years, we might have been able to help her step onto the Moebian Loop where she and the others could have met easily.

Essential to helping another writer on Editing Day is your thinking of how useful a certain remark would be to you as writer. You're not there to show your superiority, but to help. The most powerful aid you can give is to praise the parts of the work that you feel are strong. In your zeal to point out mistakes or weaknesses in a paper, you may forget that this response will be for many writers the only one given to searches that may have taken five or seven weeks of work. This is only one writing experience in their lives. They need confidence and strength as well as knowledge if they are to write well after they leave this group.

After the small editing sessions of four, when the large group comes together again, the teacher or leader might ask if people encountered papers they feel should be read to the whole group. That will be another chance for you to exercise your editorial judgment, employing both your subjective and objective critical abilities. You responded well to a paper—was that simply because the topic interested you? Or in comparison to other papers, including your own, was this one outstanding enough to deserve special attention and publication?

PROOFREADING

When you bring your next-to-last version of your I-Search Paper to Editing Day to exchange with another person, you'll each need at least fifty minutes to respond as editor and proofreader to each other's work. A good arrangement would be to spend an hour doing that and then trade papers with another pair of persons who give each paper a second proofreading. One reading—or as is customary in publishing, three or four—seldom catches all the typographical errors. Occasionally, the most egregious errors slip by. For example:

1. In the book *Caught in the Web of Words*, about J. A. H. Murray and the OED, K. M. Elisabeth Murray and the proofreaders of the Yale University Press let this passage be printed:

> In some directions indeed he found that his knowledge was superior to their's and he was in a position to help and even correct them. . . .

2. In a *New York Times* column following the third paragraph is a phrase which says, "3 bullets." That instruction to a compositor is to insert three large dots to mark off a section of the column from other sections. This phrase occurs twice more in the column. Someone forgot to put in the bullets and remove the reminder. In a later edition of the *Times* for that same day, the mistake was probably caught. Teachers and newspaper people often say that such errors are excusable because a newspaper must be published so fast. I agree, and believe that anyone who agrees must add that other people live under pressures also—for example, college students, who face a series of deadlines weekly in a number of classes. They, too, live a hurried life, and they aren't specialists in proofreading. We must allow ourselves and the professionals some errors. And try to find time and opportunity for several proofreadings so that those errors do not proliferate and take the attention of readers away from the sense of what they're reading.

3. Here's a line from an advertising brochure for solar homes passed out to people viewing one in the Southwest:

> Viga ceilings, brick and flagstone floors, hand-hewn lentils,
> and oak cabinets are only a few of the extras. . . .

Lentils? They're little bean-like vegetables that make good soup. You're hand hewing them? Man—or woman—you mean *lintels,* which are slabs of stone or wood that support a wall above a window or door. You put a lentil up there and you've got a wall as slushy as soup. But the words *lintel* and *lentil* are look-alikes, easily confused. The brochure isn't a failure because of one misspelling.

4. I noted two typographical errors while reading Herman Kogan's *The Great EB,* on pages 60 and 233. Not bad. I doubt there are many more, because being a bookard, a former editor, and the son of a librarian, I've got a falcon's eyes for punctuation and spelling errors, if I give myself time for two proofreadings, one moving backwards across the lines.

Proofreading Hints

1. Slow down when you come to words most likely to be confused with others—the sound-alikes and look-alikes—for example, *to, too; they're, their; lead* and *led* (the first is pronounced *leed* or *led* according to its meaning and the second *led*). Watch for plurals of words referred to as words: for example, "Don't use so many *and's* in your sentences." They take an apostrophe before the *s,* but most other words don't to make their plurals.

2. Read a piece of writing you're proofreading once for sense and once going backwards across each line for spelling and punctuation. Expect that every word will be misspelled and every punctuation mark incorrect. If you don't, you'll read with expectation of perfection and slide over errors. Proofreading's hard and boring work; I would understand if all professional proofreaders were alcoholics. Keep checking commonly confused words, no matter whose writing you're reading. Here's *The New York Times* for July 8, 1978, p. 19, in an article entitled "Down by the Louisiana Shore":

> Now I had to see what the night before I could ignore, or
> pass off as the lights of shrimp boats oddly stationery on
> swells.

Stationery is letter paper, *stationary* is standing still. *New York Times!* Don't you even know that? I hear the *Times* answering in low, embarrassed voice, "Yes, we do. We do."

Other common slips by writers and proofreaders occur because of forgetfulness, not ignorance. We intend to employ pairs of marks like ( ) " " or — —; but because our words spin out and we're thinking of meaning, we put down only the first of the pair. Once professional proofreaders see a parenthesis or quotation mark, or a dash, they train themselves to look for another, or closing, one. The dash is not always used in pairs, so it's a hard mark to get right. And so with underlining titles to indicate to the printer the words should be set in *italics*. After we've written the words in the title, we have to go back to underline them. Often we forget to.

As a proofreader you'll need a reference book in the place you work to check fine points of printing and publishing form. *The Manual of Style* published by the University of Chicago Press would be a good book to have available to your group. There are other such guides. The college dictionary you own—I'm presuming you have one by now —gives and explains proofreaders' marks in the back section (or under "proofreading" in the main text of *The American Heritage*). Usually, though, proofreaders' marks are employed only in correcting actual proofs that have been set in type by a printer and returned for corrections. In your group you'll be working with a manuscript, not a proof—the handwritten or typed original pages. Technically, you'll be copy-editing that, not proofreading. If you're a bookard, you'll appreciate the ingenuity behind proofreading marks; for example, the way a comma is differentiated from an apostrophe. A *v* is used to indicate an apostrophe and an inverted *v* to indicate a comma: ⱽ⋀ .

I'm not suggesting that professional writers and editors make the same number of mechanical or typographical errors as amateurs. In some seminars, writers turn in papers that carry ten or more errors or slips on one page of 350 words, while most newspaper articles that are badly proofread or not proofread at all seldom carry more than four errors in 600 words. A 350-page book with 450 words on each page (total of 157,500 words) may have only ten errors in it. My point is that professionals and amateurs are likely to make the same kind of mistakes and to profit from the same slow-eyed proofreading.

Above all, treat the manuscript you're reading with respect. Don't cross out words and write what you think are corrections or improvements between the lines. Maybe the writer won't agree with your suggestions. Maybe your corrections are wrong. Use the margins for suggestions. Write in light pencil. If you want to suggest cutting a word or passage, enclose it in penciled brackets that can be easily erased [erased]. A good editor points out and suggests, but doesn't command. The final authority for changes should be the author, except in cases where the lack of space dictates that the editor's wishes must be followed without question.

After your paper has been responded to and proofread, you'll have a chance to change it at the moment or take it home to ponder. If there's time to retype or rewrite in what 18th century writers called "a fair copy," do that so it will be ready for possible posting on a bulletin board or for xeroxing. But if not, turn in a version that makes clear to a reader which suggestions you have accepted from editors.

As editor, fundamentally you need to put yourself in the writer's place and avoid acting as Keith and Debbie did in the fourth-grade class I described in Chapter 1. In one college freshman I-Search seminar, a young woman I'll call Cindy from the first found fault with every paragraph—free or planned—written by the other students. She had nothing good to say about any of them. When a reader finished presenting one, she would pounce upon what she considered its weaknesses and errors. Often her criticisms were mistaken or trivial, and the other seminar members disagreed with them. When her writings were read before the group, the considered opinion was that her I-Search Papers were unacceptable—she had dreamed and hoped and pontificated instead of searched. Nothing she had done or presented constituted evidence. Both her I-Search Papers were entirely subjective. She had never climbed on the Moebius Loop. When she came to write the second paper she apparently had learned nothing from the seminar comments on the first. Her second paper she delivered late, so she couldn't get help on Editing Day. We hadn't helped her. At that stage in her life she probably couldn't have been helped until she relieved other pressures that must have been weighing on her. Her immediate response to the seminar seemed irrational, as if she considered herself wiser than anyone else when in fact she was doing the poorest work. But I would guess that her negativeness was a sign of repressed hostility against something or someone else in the world because it surfaced before anyone in the seminar had criticized her work.

In all the I-Search groups I've sat with, Cindy was one of the half dozen persons who acted so subjectively that they couldn't see the work of others and help them with it, and couldn't see their own clearly enough to use the comments others made on it.

If the job of editing fascinates you, try several of the books of the collected letters of Maxwell Perkins, perhaps the greatest helper of novelists in the history of our country. Here's a sample of the understanding and countenancing he provided his authors:

If you think you are not doing it well, you are thinking the way real novelists do. I never knew one who did not feel greatly discouraged at times, and some get desperate, and I have always found that to be a good symptom.

He was saying, "If we don't work to improve it, it won't get better," and also that frail human beings are engaged in the enterprise.

∞ **DOING TWENTY-FOUR:** Bring your completed I-Search Paper to your group and give it to another person for editing suggestions. Act as editor for the other person's paper. If you have time, exchange papers with a second editor. Remember, write comments and suggestions lightly in pencil. Use penciled brackets for suggested omissions. If you give the paper your best effort, your editor is likely to do the same for you.

*One of my students . . . was so con-
ditioned to research as rehash that he
couldn't see the possibilities of his subject in any other terms. I asked him to
BECOME an authority on his subject,
and told him that no doubt some day
other writers on it might make HIS article a footnote reference: "See Miller, p.
7." The finished article was quite satisfactory, if not definitive on the subject.*

SISTER M. PHILIPPA COOGAN
Professor, Niles College,
Loyola University, Chicago
[Letter to the author]

part four
looking
in the
cupboard

chapter 18
filled
with
books

ONE DAY walking by the university library, I heard a young man yell across the square to a friend, "Hey, John, you goin' skiin' with us tomorrow?"

"Yeah," yelled John, and paused. "Oh, I can't go! Got to spend the whole weekend in the damned library."

I walked on, thinking about that exchange until a voice in my head said, "We teachers have made students hate the library." How could we do that?—a place full of books and magazines all for free. With nobody to tell us which ones we have to read. Where we can look around and find what pleases us.

Always in my life, I thought a library a joyful place, like a basketball court or an ice-cream store. After school when I stopped at the public library to pick up Mother when she was through work, I would go down to the children's room and read any book that looked enticing on the shelves. At home as well as at the libraries where Mother worked during her lifetime, we read stories for fun. When I was in second grade Dad would come home on his lunch break and read me *The Three Musketeers* and *Robin Hood*. He loved the books and me, and I loved him and the books. If I didn't understand everything in the books—what matter? I liked the sound of the words rolling off Dad's lips. Several years later, with my buddy Sam Anderson, I play-acted some of the scenes—"You be Little John and I'll be Robin Hood"—a test of the book's magic powers and my ability to respond to them, but not multiple choice or true-false, and no grades, ever.

In our family when we wanted to know something, we looked it up in *Compton's Encyclopedia,* which we had at home, and if we needed more—at the library. Books filled immediate practical needs and everlasting needs to go inside other people real or imagined. They seldom failed us, but I know now we depended too much on books. I would, for example, get a book out of the library on how to make a birdhouse when I didn't know how to swing a hammer and might have done better to have walked down the block and got help in person from the old carpenter who lived on the corner.

> *Meek young men grow up in libraries,*
> *believing it their duty to accept the view*
> *which Cicero, which Locke, which Bacon,*
> *have given; forgetful that Cicero, Locke,*
> *and Bacon were only young men in*
> *libraries when they wrote these books.*
>
> RALPH EMERSON

I was a library child and never could have said, "I have to spend the weekend in the damned library!" But in high school and college when I was assigned term papers I lost some of that love. The teacher would write topics on the board and ask us to choose one. Then the instructions started: "Be sure to use at least three books, three magazines, and three newspapers or government pamphlets as sources. Put the call numbers on your 3×5 bibliography cards, follow the footnote form in the handbook, take your notes on 4×6 cards, and turn them in along with your paper. It must have a Statement of Purpose, an Introduction, a Body, and a Summary of what you found. . . ." The task was to follow instructions, not to find something I needed to know. Or something that would surprise the other students and the teacher and be useful to them. An exercise in dullness—for everyone, including me, full of do-this's and do-that's, although then I didn't understand the game. I just tried to follow the destructions, and they almost destroyed my curiosity forever.

Luckily, my other experiences in libraries were too pleasant to allow these assignments to damage my love for shelves upon shelves of books and magazines. I remember being thirteen when Mother was ordering books for a new library in a large junior high school. In August, she and I pulled new books out of cardboard boxes and she said, "Open the front and back pages and press down gently so you won't break their spines." The pages and illustrations looked so snapping fresh and clean that I felt like eating them.

Behind my mother, way back, was a fellow named Benjamin Frank-lin, who liked and profited so much from books that he devised ways to make them easily accessible. Here's part of his autobiography:

> From a child [he was born in 1706] I was fond of read-ing, and all the little money that came into my hands was ever laid out in books. Pleased with the Pilgrim's Progress, my first collection was of John Bunyan's works in separate little volumes. I afterward sold them to enable me to buy R. Burton's Historical Collections; they were small chap-men's books, and cheap, 40 or 50 in all. My father's little library consisted chiefly of books in polemic divinity, most of which I read, and have since often regretted that, at a time when I had such a thirst for knowledge, more proper books had not fallen in my way, since it was now resolved I should not be a clergyman. Plutarch's Lives there was in which I read abundantly, and I still think that time spent to great advantage. There was also a book of De Foe's, called an Essay on Projects, and another of Dr. [Cotton] Mather's, called Essays to do Good, which perhaps gave me a turn of thinking that had an influence on some of the principal future events of my life.
>
>   This bookish inclination at length determined my father to make me a printer. . . .

In 1723, at age seventeen, Ben became irritated working as appren-tice printer for his brother and took off from Boston for Philadelphia, where, he noted,

> I began now to have some acquaintance among the young people of the town, that were lovers of reading, with whom I spent my evenings very pleasantly. . . .

As you can see, early on this young man was a *bookard*. In his eighty-four years he had two of formal schooling. He learned greedily. His autobiography demonstrates that people become learned not by being exposed to knowledge but by going after it and using it. As a youth in New York, he said,

> . . . I found my friend Collins, who had arriv'd there some time before me. We had been intimate from children, and had read the same books together; but he had the advan-tage of more time for reading and studying, and a wonder-ful genius for mathematical learning, in which he far out-stript me.

True about math, which Franklin flunked in school under a good teacher. Later he mastered it on his own, as he did French, Italian, and Spanish—which he said made Latin easy for him—as a printer in Philadelphia when he needed these abilities.

In 1727, Franklin formed the Junto Club. Naturally all the members were bookards, with little libraries of their own at home. Ben suggested they put what books they could spare in one room for the use of all. His next idea was that Junto members should invite other citizens to chip in forty shillings for a starter and ten a year in order to buy books and set up a subscription library. They sent to England for books. A man was chosen to be librarian—2:00 to 3:00 every Wednesday, and 10:00 to 4:00 on Saturdays. Any "civil gentlemen" could read the books but only subscribers could take them from the library. As printer, Franklin offered to publish catalogues of the library's books and distribute them to Junto members. The library grew. When he lived in London from 1760 to 1765, Franklin acted as the library's agent in England. In 1769, the Library Company, as it had come to be called, absorbed the other subscription libraries that had sprung up in Philadelphia.

That's where libraries came from as we know them in the United States. The larger they became, the more difficult to find a book in them. In the basement of my house I have a library of about 600 books on metal shelves—my "stacks." In my study where I write, I have about 130. Those in the basement I've arranged by the last names of their authors, except for a few whose authors aren't familiar to me —they're arranged by subject. But upstairs the books I figure I need to use often are just there on shelves, in no particular arrangement. I have a terrible time finding a book I want in the 130 but an easy time in the 600.

What does a great city or university library do about arranging its books? I'm thinking now of Zimmerman Library at the University of New Mexico, whose collection and librarians have been of such service to me in writing this book. Zimmerman has approximately a million books. No user could possibly know the authors or titles of all those works. How are those books made findable?

In 1874, Melvil Dewey, the librarian at Amherst College in Massachusetts, evolved a system of classifying books by their subjects, dividing knowledge into ten main categories, such as,

000-099 General Works
300-399 Social Science
500-599 Pure Science
900-999 History, Geography, Travel, Biography

As work in various fields of knowledge increased, especially in the
sciences, the Dewey System became inadequate for large libraries,
most of which adopted the Library of Congress System, which contains twenty-one main categories, with call numbers that begin with a
letter instead of a number, for example:

A   General works, Polygraphy
G   Geography, Anthropology
H   Social Sciences (general), Statistics, Economics, Sociology
Q   Science
T   Technology

Many libraries haven't completed the change from one system to another; so, for example, in the University of New Mexico library I
found two books about the same subject, *The Encyclopædia Britannica*; one has a Dewey number and the other a Library of Congress number.

032   AE
K822g   5
             E44E4x
             1964

The books are:

Herman Kogan,	Harvey Einbinder,
The Great EB	*The Myth of the Britannica*
(Chicago,	(London,
University of Chicago,	MacGibbon & Kee,
1958)	1964)

I can guess that in the line K822g in the Dewey call number the *K*
stands for Kogan, the author, and the *g* for the first important word in
the title—"Great."

And I can guess that in the line E44E4x the first *E* is for Einbinder, the author. Maybe the second E is for the first word in the
name *Encyclopædia Britannica,* because I have another book from
that library,

John S. Morgan,
Noah Webster
(New York,
Mason/Charter,
1975)

which carries the call number

PE
64
W5M67

and the line W5M67 seems to be indicating with its *W*—Webster, the
subject of the book—and with its *M*—Morgan, the author. I may be

wrong about that but I'm not worried because I use the whole number only as a means of locating the book on the shelf. The librarian who placed that number on the new book after it was purchased by the library needed to understand the code, because that's his job. I'm trying here to get you thinking about what you need to know about libraries in order to use them efficiently and what you don't need to know. Learning all there is to know about a library like the one at the University of New Mexico is a task no single person has mastered, not even the head librarian.

The basic method of finding a book in any library is this: If you know its title or the author's name, look for that in the card catalog drawers. Libraries will have a card for your book listed under the author's last name, another card for it listed under the first important word in its title [not *The* or *A*], and a third card under the subject. The Kogan and Einbinder books noted above would be listed under the subject heading "Encyclopedias," usually typed in red ink. If the library is small, it may have all three cards for that one book located in catalog drawers in alphabetical order. If the library is large, those cards will be located in different sections of the card catalog marked *Author, Title,* and *Subject.* In a large library you can come up with nothing if you look up the author's name in the section of drawers marked *Title.*

When you're hunting for books on your subject and don't know the author or title of any of them, you've got a tougher job. Kirk Moll would have looked up the subject "wolf" or "wolves" and hoped to find cards indicating the library had some books on his subject. A small library might list its books on wolves under a wider topic heading such as "Animals, carnivorous."

Once you've found a card for a book you'd like to inspect, write down the call number and look around for a posted plan of the library which tells the location of stacks or shelves that carry books marked *AE,* for example, if you're looking for the *The Myth of the Britannica,* mentioned earlier. In a small library you may be able to see all the shelved books before you; but in a large library you may have to journey to another floor or, as in the University of New Mexico Library, to the stacks in the seventh floor of a tower.

Libraries can be pleasurable places to search if you have plenty of time and the librarians and customers have handled and shelved books with the love for order that characterized my mother as a librarian. But even she occasionally made errors, and might have put your *AE* book with the *AB's.* Although everyone has been meticulous with the books in a library, you may arrive at the place on the shelf where your book belongs and it isn't there. Another customer withdrew it yesterday. Patience. Be slow to burn. By their nature libraries are going to frustrate as well as delight you.

While writing this textbook I never damned the University of New Mexico Library because I almost always found what I wanted there. Incredible to me that this library had not only several editions of *The Encyclopædia Britannica,* which I was interested in, but three books *about* it. When I entered the library I had no idea that any books had been written on the *Britannica.* I was hoping maybe to find a magazine article or two on it, but I knew they would be harder to find, for reasons you'll discover in Chapter 20.

I'm talking about my search for material on the *Britannica* because it may help you develop a solid idea of what a library is if you don't already have one. Remember the Junto Club's first library—it consisted of books members thought they could spare from their personal collections. They were to be placed in one room for the use of everyone in the club. Not many books ended up in that room. The library didn't grow substantially until Franklin made it a subscription library by asking for funds from other Philadelphians besides members of the Junto.

Libraries have to buy books, and some are poor and some are rich. Only one library in the United States largely fulfills the notion that it will have *all* the books published—and that one has only all the books published in the United States that have been copyrighted since 1846. It's the Library of Congress. In 1800 Congress passed an act to establish it and bought Thomas Jefferson's personal library of 6,457 volumes as a starter. Jefferson was a friend of Ben Franklin's and, as to be expected, a bookard of the first order. The Library of Congress was founded to make books available to members of Congress for use in their work, and to form a national library. What makes its holdings so numerous is that the 1846 law on copyrights [a way of registering a written work so that others can't reprint large parts of it without paying a fee to the publisher or author after securing permission] stipulated that in order to copyright a book the publisher had to send two copies to the Library of Congress. Now that's the way to build a large collection of books—don't pay for them, make publishers send you free copies. Trouble is that the Library of Congress has no copyright jurisdiction over books published in England and other countries though they may be printed in the English language.

> *To the Librarian of Congress:*
> *You will receive my library arranged very*

perfectly in the order observed in the
catalogue, which I have sent with it. . . .
On every book is a label, indicating the
chapter of the catalogue to which it be-
longs . . . although the numbers seem
confused on the catalogue, they are con-
secutive on the volumes as they stand on
their shelves, and indicate at once the
place they occupy there.

THOMAS JEFFERSON

After writing my last paragraph, I was told by my wife that an item in the Sunday newspaper supplement *Family Weekly* for July 22, 1979, quoted the Librarian of Congress as saying that the Library decides which of the books sent to it will be placed in its collection. It doesn't put all the books it receives on its shelves.

But it's a great assemblage of books there in Washington, D.C., and the basis for all other libraries in the country. For example, when it decides to add a book to its collection, the Library of Congress sets in type a catalog card for it, and many libraries around the country buy these cards for their catalogs. Recently the Library of Congress has encouraged publishers to find out before publication the call number to be assigned to a book and include on the reverse side of the title page the information that goes on a catalog card. If you'll look on the copyright page of this book, you'll find that information. This practice makes the job of librarians around the country easier. They can copy the cataloging and publication data and type up a card for the book, certain that the classification by number of that book into the subject heading system will be the same everywhere in the country.

Speaking of copyrights, I should say that whenever you use ideas or words from copyrighted books you may have an obligation to the persons who own them by virtue of having written or published them. Ideas that are old or widely held naturally don't create such an obligation.

In the colonies in Ben Franklin's day, Americans commonly pirated books published in England. When Franklin took over a newspaper from another printer who had been running in serial form parts of Chambers's *Cyclopædia,* one of the first formidable encyclopedias published in England, he stopped printing excerpts from it. In the 18th century many printers did such printing without paying the author or original publisher for the privilege. Persons making their living by writing or publishing rightly considered such an act theft, just as you and I would if a dealer in California took a new General Motors car off a delivery truck, sold it, and never sent GM any money for it. I don't know why Franklin removed the *Cyclopædia* excerpts from the columns of his newspaper, but I hope it was because he felt he was re-establishing the newspaper's morality.

Related to such pirating is unauthorized borrowing of shorter passages from copyrighted books. It's called *plagiarism* and is, like *libel,* a difficult crime to define. You can perhaps get the feel of the act if you imagine another person has taken a page from the best section of your completed I-Search Paper and put it into his without acknowledging where he got it. But that's an extreme case—one in which intention and crime are plain. More often writers, professional and amateur, like something they've read and copy it down in a notebook without indicating with quotation marks that it's taken verbatim [word for word] from a printed, copyrighted source. Then when they go to write their paper, they use that material verbatim, thinking they had originally put the ideas into their own words as notes. I may have made such errors in writing this book, but I've tried to avoid them. I show my debt to other authors by listing the sources of my borrowing of ideas or words in the back of this book, and acknowledging in the front permissions I obtained—and sometimes paid for—from publishers so that I could reprint long passages of copyrighted material.

If you're announcing or using someone's idea, discovery, or work that you found in copyrighted material, you'll make that clearest to your reader by saying, "As Ebenezer Smith found (or said) . . ." right in the text of your paper, rather than depending on a reference to a footnote—(Smith [1])—or reference of the kind most I-Searchers use to indicate a numbered source they list at the end of their paper, along with the page numbers on which they found what they're using— (1: 13-14).

Paraphrasing means to put in your own words what someone else has said. That's not plagiarism unless you pretend the ideas are yours. Bookards can often spot plagiarism because they have developed an ear for the sound of a writer's sentences. If a writer of a research or I-Search paper is going along in a vocabulary like this:

> I learned a lot about veterinary medicine from the book *All Things Bright and Beautiful,* but not much that was technically useful.

and then suddenly slides into language like this:

> So while the book is neither hortatory nor admonitory, it delivers a sprightly lesson on the care and feeding of both animals and human beings.

they know something is fishy.

Significantly, few I-Search Papers out of the hundreds I've read have plagiarized. The form and approach, the urge, of an I-Searcher is not to try to look learned by exhibiting other people's knowledge, but to answer a need. And once into the search, the writer keeps track of who's saying this or that because she has listened to a number of the authorities speak in person.

What's unethical or illegal use of printed material is often hard to say. Like *libel* (saying something in print false or damaging to a person's reputation), plagiarism sometimes can be determined only when the matter goes to court and a judge decides. A rule of thumb is never to take more than seven consecutive words from a printed source without acknowledging them. And to refrain from using distinctive and unusual expressions of an author unless you put quotation marks around them. From this discussion, you can see the need for care in taking notes from printed sources and making clear in them which words are yours and which someone else's. Also the need to note precisely the name of author, publishing information, and the number of the pages from which you took material: for example, Jones, Herbert, *Jazz Revisited* (New York, Wentworth, 1980), pp. 14-15.

If, in a short paper, you present long quotations from sources you've consulted, those passages will stand out and suggest you have lost command of the expedition. When I say that, you may feel like replying, "But in this book you print long quotations!" True, but this is a whole book, and my comments greatly exceed those of persons quoted. Also, one of the purposes of this book is to examine and elucidate I-Search Papers which I didn't write, so I had to give them in full, and when I did, I paid the writers a permission fee. If you were to write a long I-Search Book like Carl Becker's great study of how the *Declaration of Independence* was written by Thomas Jefferson with the help of a committee made up of Benjamin Franklin, John Adams, Roger Sherman, and Robert R. Livingston, and the editing of the Continental Congress, you would naturally be quoting the *Declaration* and its revisions again and again.

When you use other people's words or ideas don't let them take command of your narrative. For example, instead of saying:

> His personal friend describes him as: "He is no ignoramus, no fool, no idiot."

say:

> His personal friend describes him as "no ignoramus, no fool, no idiot."

And when you're quoting an author, don't say:

> For example, one quote of Smith states: "Veterinarians work indefatigably, sometimes in the middle of the night."

Say:

> For example, Smith says: "Veterinarians work indefatigably, sometimes in the middle of the night."

You're quoting Smith. [Suddenly, I realize I'm committing that tiresome sin of a textbook writer. I've imagined someone writing things improperly and then wished that act upon you by saying, "You're quoting Smith." You haven't written anything wrong. You're just reading this book. I'll try it a different way.] The imaginary writer I was talking about was quoting Smith. A quote doesn't state. A quote is a quotation of a statement. The word *quote* is most often useful when a person is talking and doesn't have the aid of quotation marks to indicate to an audience where his words end and another person's begin. If he's speaking, he might properly say,

> *Time* magazine says, and I quote, "Sadat is making concessions to bring about peace."

The *I quote* in the remark shows that the speaker is giving *Time*'s words verbatim, not paraphrasing them. But if a person is writing, and has the aid of quotation marks, he need put down only,

> *Time* magazine says: 'Sadat is making concessions to bring about peace."

These are niceties, or fine points, of search writing. If you carry out a valuable search and mess up on one or two of them, don't feel disgraced. A paper that reports an exciting, useful search will make most readers forget little blemishes. But—the English teacher is coming out in me again—if you remember some of these techniques, you'll do your good I-Search justice, and readers will be more likely to think of what you're saying than how you're saying it. The last example: In a paper, when you're quoting, instead of saying,

> In the book *The Holocaust* it says . . .

you can write,

> The book *The Holocaust* says . . .

and get rid of an unnecessary *it*.

I've been talking for some time now about your relationship as a writer to sources you use. Writing an I-Search Paper will make you an authority in one sense—no one else can be as much an expert on your search as you'll become when you have reflected upon and recorded your adventure. The relationship between you and your topic is unique. You'll be a searcher, not a borrower or thief, and so you probably won't come to believe, as some student writers of research papers do, that the authors of books and magazines they consult learned first-hand everything they have put into print. You'll see that writers are always in debt to others. They build upon facts, ideas, and experiences others have written about or told orally. As a person who's becoming an authority, you'll admire and respect those who have written before you. You'll see that some of the things you've learned from them are erroneous, narrowminded, or foolish. And when you look back upon your own writing you'll see where some of it too is erroneous, narrowminded, or foolish. All of us writers work in a great company of phonies and strivers for truth. Any library is full of lies, half-truths, truths, and guesses.

In this book you're reading I've furnished facts and opinions about such works as *The Encyclopædia Britannica*, dictionaries compiled by Samuel Johnson, Noah Webster, Sir James A. H. Murray, and Frederic E. Reeve, as if I knew these people and had watched them work. In fact, I knew none of them except Fred Reeve, who happened to be my office mate and friend in the 1950s. I've got my information about the work of these people from books written by persons who have a passion for truth, but truth as they see it, affected by the experiences that made them the persons they were when they wrote those books. In their writing, I'm sure, they've been objective and subjective, like all human beings. What I wrote a few pages earlier about the Library of Congress was taken from a short entry in *The Oxford Companion to American Literature*, 1941, by James D. Hart. Maybe James or a printer he worked with made an error in the year the copyright law required publishers to send two books—Oh, no! As I look back at that entry in the *Companion,* I see that I misread it. Hart says, "After 1846 the copyright law required *one* copy of every book copyrighted in the U.S. to be deposited in the library, and since 1870 *two* copies have been required." So I misrepresented Mr. Hart's fact—and at the very time I was thinking of such errors! So it wasn't until 1870 that *two* copies were sent to the library, not an essential point in my discussion, but nevertheless an error that I almost let slip by. If I had failed to notice it, another author might have read my book, taken my mis-statement as fact, and published it more widely. It's safe to say that all books have errors of that kind in them. We writers owe it to each other to doublecheck what we borrow, but we can't expect perfection from any writer.

Before I leave Mr. Hart I must say that I admire his book. Since 1946, when I bought it, its short entries about people and events that have affected literature and writers in the United States have saved me hundreds of trips to a library. It stands on a shelf in what is the reference section of my library, close to my typewriter, where I can reach it, along with several small dictionaries, *The Oxford Companion to English Literature* (which I bought later), and a thesaurus. A few feet farther away in a separate bookshelf stand my fifteen volumes of *The Oxford English Dictionary,* a work I coveted for many years before I had enough money to buy it.

All libraries, of whatever size, have such a section for reference books—maybe in a corner of a room, maybe taking up several rooms itself—where you can find indexes that will lead you to other books, and encyclopedic and dictionary-like works that present short entries on a multitude of subjects and persons in a given field. In large libraries, a librarian sits at the reference desk to help you in searches when you're foundering, not finding.

No point in trying to find out everything that is in such a department, but maybe a good idea to spend five or ten minutes walking around sampling its wares. You might also ask yourself, "Do I have a library in my room? Am I beginning to form a reference section within it? Am I going to read and read and read until I turn into a bookard?" You could. For that disease there's no Alcoholics Anonymous, but I'm thinking of forming Bookards Beautiful, with monthly meetings deep in the stacks.

I began this chapter with a person speaking of the "damned library," worked my way into stories about bookards who feel it's a blessed place, worried about the mistreatment of its treasures, and ended thinking of the library you are probably forming right now. See you—in a library.

∞ **DOING TWENTY-FIVE:** Go to a library you'll use for I-Searching and look around for two hours. At anything that interests you. Pick a book or magazine off the shelf whose title catches your eye. Stick your nose in where things interest you. There will be no test given on this tour. I'm extending an invitation like the one Walt Whitman gives in "Song of Myself"—"Loafe with me on the grass . . ."—only here it is, "Loaf among the books and magazines." Or check the microfilm projectors, or newspapers from all over the country or world. See if you can break school habits and relax. Go where your feelings take you. Look for pleasure instead of grades. Wander into parts of the library you've never seen before. Case the joint.

If something is bugging you right now, or tantalizing you—maybe which are the best places in the world to ski or swim, maybe a question that you always argue with your parents or roommate—look it up in the card catalog or one of the hundreds of indexes or dozens of encyclopedias in the reference section. (I'm imagining you in a large library now; in a small one you'll still find dozens of valuable reference books.) But you don't have to do that. Follow a need or a whim. Or follow nothing at all, just cruise. This is that one assignment you'll have in school to do nothing the teacher or textbook prescribes. Those two hours in the library maybe you always wanted to take when you noticed something on a shelf and said, "I'd like to look at that, but if I do, I won't get my assigned reading done before the library closes." If you let this assignment take you, you'll find pleasure in the damned library.

> *Many a man lives a burden to the earth;*
> *but a good book is the precious life-*
> *blood of a master-spirit, embalmed and*
> *treasured up on purpose to a life beyond*
> *life.*
>
> JOHN MILTON

chapter 19
issued
periodically

KIRK MOLL, who wrote "The Captive
Wolf," which appears at the beginning of this book, cares a lot about
wolves. From his I-Search Paper you can tell his love affair is not going
to be a short one.

Kirk did a weak job of library searching and a great job of hunting
up people who could help him. Not always are books the best sources.
The Oxford English Dictionary, with its one limited definition of the
word *wolf* meaning the animal, would have been useless to Kirk:

> A somewhat large canine animal found in Europe, Asia,
> and N. America, hunting in packs, and noted for its fierce-
> ness and rapacity."

That definition demonstrates that a dictionary's job is not to tell all
about wolves or describe in detail the characteristics of one, but to
record with what meanings the word has been used by human beings
in print. It's the job of the encyclopedia and scientists' and naturalists'
reports in journals, magazines, and books to describe the wolf and tell
how it acts. A whole book on wolves can do a better job of that
than a relatively short encyclopedia article—although it might not.

If people's attitudes toward wolves are changing rapidly, a magazine
article may be the best source for Kirk, who knows something of
wolves already. An even more up-to-date source might be a report in
a newspaper or on radio or television. In the last few years, for exam-

ple, I've heard a number of radio talks about animals by Roger Caras, who impressed me as a person who knows wild and domestic animals in depth because he studies them objectively and communicates with them lovingly, Moebianly. If Kirk could have talked to Roger Caras . . . Or if not, if he could have read Roger Caras's words on wolves in print . . . Perhaps Roger Caras has written magazine articles?

How could Kirk look for words about wolves in print? Maybe something in nature magazines? Go to a friend who subscribes to *Field and Stream* or *Natural History* and ask him if he remembers any articles on wolves? One by Roger Caras perhaps? Maybe the friend saves old copies of his magazines and Kirk could look through a stack in the basement. At this point in my surmising, I should say that if you know about *The Reader's Guide to Periodical Literature,* you may be getting irked. You know there's a quicker, surer way of finding whether or not Roger Caras has written any articles on wolves. A look at *The Reader's Guide* for March 1976–February 1977, which would have been available to Kirk at the time he was searching, gives this entry:

> **WOLVES**
> Alaskan wolfkill. il Sci Digest 79:18-20 My '76
> Fear and loathing in wolf country. J. G. Mitchell. il. Audubon 78:20-39 My '76
> Recovery plan for the eastern timber wolf; with introd by E. H. Connally. L. D. Mech. il map Nat parks & Con Mag 51:17-21 Ja '77
> Showdown on the tundra. R. Rau. il Read Digest 108:147-50 F '76
> Wolf kill; signals between predator and prey. B. Lopez. il Harper 253:25-7 Ag '76
> Wolves: no refuge? timber wolves. il Nat Parks & Con Mag 50:26 Mr '76
> *See also*
> Coyotes

That first look at *The Reader's Guide* has already shown me that magazines called *Science Digest, Audubon, National Parks & Conservation Magazine, Reader's Digest,* and *Harper's* carried articles on wolves during those twelve months.

●   ●   ●

When as a child I first saw library reference shelves lined with fat indexes, I never thought of how they were created. I had the vague feeling that such volumes came with libraries automatically. Never occurred to me that once some person must have got tired rummaging through piles of tattered magazines and decided to do something about the problem.

In the United States, that person was William Frederick Poole, a charming man. Here's some of what he said in the preface to *Poole's Index to Periodical Literature,* 1802-1881:

> Thirty-five years ago, when a student in Yale College and connected with the library of one of the literary societies, I indexed such reviews and magazines as were accessible, and arranged the references under topics for the purpose of helping the students in the preparation of their written exercises and society discussions. I had noticed that the sets of standard periodicals with which the library was well supplied were not used, although they were rich in the treatment of subjects about which inquiries were made in vain every day. . . .

As a student at Yale, Poole was thinking for himself, not just attending lectures and taking notes. Like most people who live useful, productive lives, he began early. Apparently he looked at the situation and said to himself, "Here are all these magazines and a bunch of students who need to use them but no way for them to get to what they want. So I'll go through the magazines and list the articles and then arrange them under subject headings." It was that simple, but no one in the country had done it as usefully before. Poole wrote:

> My work, though crude and feeble on its bibliographical side, answered its purpose, and brought to me the whole body of students for a kind of help they could not get from the library catalogues, nor from any other source. My manuscript was in great demand [he apparently had written out one copy of a list, by hand, and it was passed around], and as it was rapidly wearing out, and printing seemed to be the only expedient for saving the work, it was put to press, and appeared with the title, "Index to Subjects treated in the Reviews and other Periodicals," New York, 1848, 8vo, 154 pp. The edition of five hundred copies was chiefly taken by other colleges, and soon disappeared. The little book is now a curiosity in more senses than one. For twenty years I had not seen a copy, when, in 1877, I saw it in the reading-room of the British Museum, with its leaves discolored and nearly worn through by constant handling.

Poole was born in 1821, five years before Thomas Jefferson died. [I say that to emphasize that it's good to connect people to a few other people or events that mean a lot to you. That's a way of putting history in its place and time, of remembering.] Poole lived to become assistant librarian at the Boston Athenaeum, one of the foremost American libraries of the time, and later helped organize the public libraries of Cincinnati and Chicago. Eventually he became head of the Newberry Library in Chicago, one of the most distinguished scholarly institutions in the world. This man, of such dignity in his profession, wrote the preface to his index in story form, telling his adventure in indexing, and employing the word *I* without apology. The article on him in *The Dictionary of American Biography* says, "An undisputed leader among his contemporaries, he was also a wise and patient counselor to his younger colleagues."

Poole's Index of Periodical Literature "covers" the years 1802-1906, as we say, but that doesn't mean it indexes all magazines and journals published everywhere during that period. To make an index of magazine articles a person must have in hand all the issues of the magazines he's going to index. Such a fact indicates the magnitude of the task. One person couldn't do it quickly enough to make it useful to readers needing the latest articles on their subject. The cost of purchasing all the magazines would be staggering. People kept asking Poole for new and enlarged lists of magazine articles, and in 1876 he finally proposed at the first meeting of the American Library Association that (1) he would send librarians a list of the magazines he thought should be indexed, (2) they would let him know which ones they had in their libraries, and (3) then he'd divide equitably the work between them, so each would index a certain number of the periodicals they subscribed to. Fifty librarians scanned the magazines they were assigned, sent him the material for compiling an index, and he alphabetized the listings under subject headings. Unbelievably, the plan worked. The librarians didn't fail to send material in, and didn't do a sloppy job. Next Poole went to England and won the agreement of a number of British librarians to supply material from eight British periodicals. His notion was to index magazines that would be used by general scholars or news reporters, not specialized journals like those in medicine, which were indexed separately by persons within the professions.

Such an endeavor may seem dull and routine to you. But it isn't. If it had been, people of Poole's caliber wouldn't have become mixed up in it. There were challenging puzzles to be solved; for example, some periodicals in those times customarily published articles without the names of authors, or with made-up names, as in our time *The New Yorker* magazine prints anonymous short articles in its "Talk of the Town" section. Good indexers try to find who wrote the articles that carry no author's names. They play detective and enjoy searching. For example, Poole found that in both England and America some people knew the names of authors who had written anonymous articles. Sometimes these names were revealed in letters or hints given of them in advertisements. British librarians had "scruples"—as Poole put it—about revealing these names, but Americans were more willing to seek out and publish them.

> *Every accessible collection of essays and miscellaneous writings which contributors have issued has been gleaned, and volumes of biographies and literary correspondence, without number have been examined. There was a fascination in the search which made it recreation.*
>
> WILLIAM FREDERICK POOLE

For all this work Poole asked of librarians in America and Great Britain, they received no pay. If he had paid them, he couldn't have published the index, because such projects, especially at their inception, are not money-makers. A library buys one copy only. In indexes, there's no such thing as a best-selling book like *Uncle Tom's Cabin,* which sold 300,000 copies in 1852, its first year of publication. Most indexes in libraries were put together and published by people who made little profit from them. They are completed because their contributors and editors are hooked on knowledge, as editors of dictionaries are hooked on words, and they do the job for pleasure and service. Poole reported that the copy [material submitted to be printed] for his index had to be constantly transmitted "to and fro between Chicago and Hartford," and went on to say, "When the manager of the Adams Express Company heard of the character of the work and its co-operative feature, he claimed the privilege of a contributor, and directed that all parcels relating to the work should be transmitted without pay."

As the number of magazines increased, the size and production cost of indexes became exorbitant, and still no good way to finance them. The libraries that bought them, especially the small ones, had little money. At that point, another energetic man came upon the scene, Halsey William Wilson. He was born in Vermont in 1868, twenty years after Poole had printed his first index to magazines. Both his parents died of tuberculosis when he was three. He was cared for by his maternal grandparents and then worked for his uncle as a farmhand in Iowa. Two years at Beloit College in Wisconsin, and he enrolled at the University of Minnesota, which was then itself but seventeen years old.

With a roommate, H.W. Wilson took on a newspaper route—up an hour before dawn, seven miles of walking, and then breakfast. Throughout one month of that first year, Minneapolis suffered below zero weather every day. Eventually, he decided to quit the university to become a church organist, but a year later re-enrolled in college and bought a printing press cheaply from the church. He and his next roommate borrowed money and opened a bookstore in their bedroom. Soon the university offered them a room in Old Main Building to house their bookstore. H.W. worked so many hours in that bookstore that he failed to earn enough credits to graduate in what was to be his last year.

Wilson was fascinated by bookselling, but soon found that his store and others in the country were hampered because there was no trade list of current books to which they could turn when stocking their stores or attempting to fill a customer's needs. Not that no one had ever published a list of books available—in 1564 a man had provided one for the famous Book Fair in Germany, and there had been many others between his time and Wilson's. But they didn't *cumulate*. They were lists of a single publisher or books in print at that very moment, but what had been printed in the past was not added to the list of what was being printed now. So booksellers had to save separate lists and go through them one after another in an attempt to locate a book they needed. In the 19th century attempts were made in America to fulfill such a need, but making such indexes took a great deal of time and money, and showed no profit. In 1898, while still running the bookstore at the university, H.W. published the first volume of *The Cumulative Book Index*. For a year his wife acted as editor of it, working in a room in the Wilsons' apartment; but the job was too much for her, and H.W. hired as the first official editor, Marion E. Potter, a graduate student at the university. She was so fascinated by the job that, as the story went, when she received her first paycheck, she said, "What is this for? Oh, I didn't know I was getting paid." Later when the company was larger and a heavy snowstorm blocked traffic and prevented most of the staff from reaching the office, the diminutive Miss Potter fought her way through five miles of snow to her job. She liked the work and stayed at it for some fifty years.

If you've never worked on a newspaper or other publication that has to meet regular deadlines, you probably can't appreciate how much pressure is put on writers and editors. Mistakes are always made in writing and editing, but those who work with short deadlines and small staffs are more prone to them because they have so little time for proofreading. In its first years, *The Cumulative Book Index,* still valuable to booksellers and librarians today, slipped occasionally and came out with such lines as

Baptists, see also Drunkards
Prince of Whales

Again, as for *Poole's Index*, the editors had to obtain their information somewhere and put it together. They were the people who had to work from scratch, and scratch was procuring the lists of new books being issued by publishers. That meant trying to find out the names of all publishers in the country and sending them requests for lists of new books. No way to force them to do that, or convince them they must act rapidly, or get into their heads the need for accuracy of information. Often publishers misspelled authors' names and book titles, changed prices without notice, and sometimes forgot to send the H.W. Wilson Company the needed information. But *The Cumulative Book Index* came out and, like other Wilson indexes, was not ditched after a few years when financing became difficult.

From the first, H.W. knew he was in the business of giving service to booksellers and librarians, who have to buy books and want to know what they're getting. In compiling indexes, he consulted his clients constantly. As a sober citizen motivated to improve the world, he made sure that the books and magazines he indexed were authoritative and valuable. He consulted experts, his editors studied the opinions of critics. He wasn't a flim-flam man out to bedazzle the country and empty its pockets. His work raised the standards of bookselling and librarianship in America. He lacked Ben Franklin's wit and charm, and Poole's grace, but he got the facts right and made them useful to all of us. In early days he posted a notice on the office wall which said:

> The company furnishes individual towels to each employee
> and expects that each shall hold himself responsible for his
> own towel. In case of loss, he shall pay the cost of the towel,
> which is eight cents.

As a worker, I don't appreciate statements like that, but I must say that I've worked for companies that furnished no towel to anyone. It's a man I'm presenting here, not a paragon, and his virtues of perseverance, patience, foresight, invention, and attention to detail were astounding.

> *We take your various indexes and bibliographies for granted, but when we think of what American libraries would do without them, we realize that it is not exaggeration to say that you [H.W. Wilson] have done more for libraries than any other living man.*
>
> PAUL NORTH RICE

Any person who year after year produced one cumulative index of the kind H.W. Wilson issued should be saluted, but in his lifetime the company put out an ever increasing number of them, and now lists among its publications, indexes of

General Science 1978–

Plays 1949–

Musicians since 1900–

Applied Science &
   Technology 1958–

Art 1929–

Bibliography 1937–

Biography 1949–

Biology and Agriculture 1964–

Book Review Digest 1905–

Short Stories 1900–

Business Periodicals 1958–

Education 1929–

Essays and General Literature 1900–

Poetry for Children 1970–

Legal Periodicals 1952–

Reproductions of American
   Paintings 1948–

Reproductions of European
   Paintings 1956–

Library Literature 1921–

General Periodical Literature 1900–

and dozens of one-volume reference works.

Wilson succeeded in producing such monumental and useful guides for searchers because he loved doing it. He enjoyed devising procedures that ensured a high level of accuracy and usefulness in reference works. He knew that magazines and books were increasing in number at an incredible pace and that if someone didn't furnish readers with ways of using them, the information and wisdom in them would go to waste. So he decided to fill that need. Every month, every year, he came up with new ideas to help the cause. And it was a cause to him: he knew he was helping America become a democracy in which ordinary people—not just a privileged class of scholars—would have access to the best ideas and information. But everyone before him had failed to sustain publication of their indexes and catalogues because they cost more money than the people who needed them could afford to pay. Challenges like that H.W. enjoyed taking on.

I'll mention two of the hard-headed strategies that Wilson thought up.

He had his printers set lines of type for an item, say a book or magazine article, with title, author, publisher, etc. for the monthly record and then file those metal lines of type away so they could be brought together again for the annual edition. Since these were cast lines of type, not printed proofs on paper taken by inking those lines, they sat on a table as metal lines that had to be read backwards, which his workers learned to do easily. Such a strategy saved people from having to take a print, or proof, on a piece of paper or card, work with it, and then reset the type lines again in order to arrange the newly enlarged list of items for the printing of an annual record.

In creating magazine indexes, his master strategy was to give up Poole's method of asking for librarians to compose the entries and send them to him for compilation. At first, the librarians were faithful and efficient, but as the job got bigger, the system broke down. H.W. saw that in order to be consistent, accurate, and up to date, indexes had to be created by a trained staff operating in one headquarters. He developed that staff and then charged libraries for his indexes on what he called a "service basis." The customers of large libraries, which subscribed to hundreds of periodicals, would naturally be using the indexes much more than those of small libraries, which subscribed to only a few dozen periodicals. So Wilson sold the indexes not at a fixed charge but according to how many periodicals indexed in his books were owned by each library. This was an audacious business arrangement; but it worked, and without it, we wouldn't have the indexes to library materials we now use throughout the country in libraries of all sizes and types. No matter how much libraries wanted or needed such indexes, if they couldn't pay for them, no company would undertake the tremendous task of compiling and publishing them.

Work on *The Cumulative Book Index* prepared H.W. for making *The Reader's Guide to Periodical Literature,* the most widely used index in American libraries. He was sure he could improve on Poole's index of 19th-century periodicals, which listed items only by subject, so that if you had the name of an author or a magazine article, you couldn't quickly look it up alphabetically and find where and when it had appeared. You would have to sift through subject headings until you found it. If you wanted an article on peanuts, you might have to start with agriculture, farming, food, or some other equally general subject. Poole's index also cited articles by volume number instead of date, and that meant trouble for many searchers. Now we have available H.W.'s *Reader's Guide to Nineteenth-Century Periodical Literature* and a special computer-made *Cumulative Author Index for Poole's Index, 1802-1906,* edited by C. Edward Wall, librarian at the University of Michigan Dearborn Campus. When I say "we have" I should be careful to say that these indexes are available only to libraries that can afford to buy them. Your city, high school, or college library may not have them. That's why it's a good idea to glance at your library's reference department to see what kind of indexes it carries in fields or subjects you're searching.

Having read this sketch of Poole's and Wilson's efforts, you know that no one could be expected in one work to index all the magazine articles ever published. If you know the magazine in which an article you're looking for is printed, you need to look in the first pages of an index like *The Reader's Guide* to find out whether it indexes that magazine. If it does, then you'll have to think of what years you're interested in. Magazine indexes are compiled monthly and yearly. If you're looking for articles on nuclear radiation, you'll probably want recent index volumes or supplements. If you want to see what people said about that topic, or didn't say, in the 1930s, you'll need to consult a volume for that time period. If you want a historical view, you'll look for the topic in both early and late volumes of the index. Searching of this kind can be fatiguing, and you may find yourself doing dumb things like looking in the latest monthly supplement to *The Reader's Guide,* finding nothing on your topic, and saying to yourself, "No one's ever written on this subject!"

Several chapters could be written in this contextbook on how to use indexes and other reference books, but you wouldn't remember or use the material unless you had need for it. Better here to give you a general notion of how reference books are made, and let you consult individual libraries for what is there. Look in the front and back of reference books for what each item in an entry means. Ask for help from a librarian if you're puzzled. There are traps in libraries that may fool you, but they weren't meant to be traps. The inconsistencies and awkwardnesses stem from problems that people like Poole and Wilson had to face. Generally, large libraries possess the indexes you'll need in order to lay hands on material in both popular and scholarly magazines, but be ready for the confusion that must arise because of changing needs of readers and the steady increase of publications in this country.

• • •

The indexes that cover general magazines (not highly specialized professional journals) are:

Poole's Index. 1802–1906 (arranged by subjects only)
Cumulative Author Index for Poole's Index. 1802–1906
Nineteenth Century Reader's Guide. 1890–1899 (author, subject)
Reader's Guide to Periodical Literature. 1900– (author, title, subject)

The professional journals, which cover subjects in more scholarly depth (and therefore are harder for general readers to understand), were first covered by the H.W. Wilson Company in

The International Index. 1907–65 (author, subject)

which was then continued in volumes called

Social Sciences and Humanities Index. 1965–1973 (author, subject)

and then divided into

Social Sciences Index. 1974– (author, subject)
Humanities Index. 1974– (author, subject)

Note the dates after the above four indexes and you'll see that together they make up one continuous index under different names. When you're looking for more learned or authoritative material than you can find in magazines indexed in *The Reader's Guide,* you'll need to choose which index covers the years you're interested in. Such changes can easily confuse you or cause you to miss entirely a guide that could help you. That's why if you're unsure in your search, you should ask a reference librarian which indexes are probably best for your purposes. For example, recently the H.W. Wilson Company began a new guide called *The General Science Index,* which starts indexing magazines published in June 1978 and onwards. For science information published before that, a general reader like Kirk Moll looking for articles about wolves should consult *The Biological and Agricultural Index,* which covers zoology, which covers wolves. That index was begun in September 1964 and continued through July 1978. In looking for magazine and journal articles, keep always in the front of your mind the dates they cover, for no index covers all subjects through all time.

You may be thinking, "I thought indexes and library reference materials were designed to ease the job of finding material, but they themselves sound like time eaters." True. That's why experts in a field can save you so much time by telling you what books or articles may be of value in your search. Karon Roach, who wrote the I-Search Paper "Should I Become an Architect?" found the perfect article when she interviewed the assistant dean of an architectural school. He knew the literature of the field and her special needs.

You'll do your best searching—whether it's for required school work or to satisfy your needs on your own—if you learn a library as you use it. Survey its system and layout. Every library has signs, instructions, and helpful handouts. And the books and indexes themselves are full of information on how to use them.

Now I'd like to imagine how Kirk Moll might have looked for articles on wolves. If he had gone to *The Reader's Guide* for the period in which he was working, he would have found the entry I reproduced in the first part of this chapter. It's full of abbreviations which Kirk might not understand. He should know that in almost all reference works the abbreviations used are explained in the front or back of the volume. In magazine indexes the names of the magazines indexed in those works are listed, usually in the front. Since these abbreviations differ in different fields, there's no point in your trying to learn all of them. When you use an index, look for its special codes. If you think such shorthand makes your task difficult, think what a reference work would be like that didn't use abbreviations and symbols —probably twice to five times as long and too heavy to lift. One of H.W. Wilson's early book catalogs weighed twenty-five pounds.

If you can't get in touch with experts who tell you of good things to read on your topic, often you can find lists of books and articles that experts recommend *in their printed works*. Note the full bibliographies given at the end of long articles in *The Encyclopædia Britannica*. If the book or article you read on your topic doesn't give the material you need, look in it for other sources the author mentions. They might carry what he didn't.

I think of Kirk Moll and the entry in *The Reader's Guide*. I've looked up only one article listed there, the one in *Harper's* magazine, "Wolf kill; signals between predator and prey," by B. Lopez. I chose that one because on television in the summer of 1978 I heard Barry Lopez talk about wolves. He spoke Moebianly, with an understanding of both wolf hunters and the remarkable intelligence of the animals. But I doubt that the *Harper's* article would have strengthened Kirk's I-Search Paper. It didn't center on his special interest in wolves. And the titles of the other articles cited in *The Reader's Guide* also looked irrelevant to me.

I was so impressed by hearing Barry Lopez on TV that I bought his book *Of Wolves and Men* (New York, Charles Scribner's, 1978), which came out soon after Kirk's paper was written. I wish it had been published in time for Kirk to use it. It's objective and subjective, as I believe Kirk is about wolves, and rich in history and understanding. Most valuable to Kirk would have been Lopez's eleven-page *annotated* [meaning with notes and comments] bibliography of books and articles Lopez has read about wolves. In that list of books I found this comment, which takes me back to my remark earlier in this chapter about the animal expert Roger Caras:

> Roger Caras tells the story of the Custer Wolf in *The Custer Wolf:* biography of an American renegade (Boston, Little, Brown, 1966).

There's the answer to my early question: has this animal expert I've admired so much written anything about wolves? I've looked in three libraries and found catalog cards listing books by Caras about animals, but never did I run across *The Custer Wolf.* That's an example of how a library may not furnish you with a publication that may be available in a bookstore or a larger library. If you want a book badly and can't find it in your libraries, ask a librarian for help. She can tell you whether it exists, and sometimes can get it for you from another library or recommend a bookseller who might have it.

But back to Barry Lopez. On page 280 in *Of Wolves and Men,* he has something to say to Kirk Moll:

> I am not an authority on wolves. I do not think my experiences are universal, and I do not wish to encourage other people to raise wolves. Wolves don't belong living with people. It's as simple as that. Having done it once, naïvely, I would never do it again. Most people I know who have raised wolves feel the same way. All too often the wolf's life ends tragically and its potential for growth while it lives is smothered. I am grateful for the knowledge I have gained but if I'd known what it would cost I don't think I would have asked.

That's how close Kirk Moll came to hearing this word from Barry Lopez, who later in the book recounts the story of how one of his two captive wolves was let out of a pen and shot by a neighbor. But *Of Wolves and Men* was published a couple of months too late for Kirk to find it. Perhaps he wouldn't have found it if it had been published in time. His search in libraries was not much of an effort. But the case of this book and Kirk's paper illustrates dramatically the nature of searching and researching. It's a hit and miss business even for the most committed inquirer. No matter how valuable a search paper is to the searcher, we should never take for granted that it says the last word on its topic.

•   •   •

That "damned library" that the student at my university mentioned in the chapter entitled "Filled with Books": its indexes can lead you to gold, or they can leave you cramped in the stomach with frustration. An example is *The Social Sciences Citation Index,* 1970–, a computerized work not published by H.W. Wilson Company. In it you can find not only the name of an article, and its author, on a certain subject, but mentions of that article or author or subject in social science literature. If you become interested, for example, in David Riesman, co-author of *The Lonely Crowd,* you can find in that index what other scientists have said about him in the years and periodicals covered by the volume you're looking at. It's a service made for detectives who want to trace the development of an idea or experiment and the evaluation of it by other workers—an amazing time-saver for a researcher or original worker in any field. Such a service would have saved William Bullokar in 1580 (whom I mention in the chapter on spelling) time, income, and embarrassment. In his preface to his *Booke at Large* he explains that when he began working on it he didn't know that two of his countrymen had already published a work that covered much of what he planned to take up, and when he found out, he felt obliged to change his manuscript, which meant a loss of two years to him.

But about this remarkable searching book, *The Social Sciences Citation Index,* I must add that though the editors say using it is a "relatively simple affair," I found its instructions dense and bewildering. I didn't want to spend a half hour learning how to use the index before I could find what I was looking for. But I love libraries. I'm a son of a librarian.

∞ **DOING TWENTY-SIX:** In this contextbook I've emphasized talking in person with authorities more than searching in libraries, because too much school research is library bound; but you owe it to yourself at some point in your searching to check periodical indexes for your topic. No matter how personal your need, some other human being may have felt it too and written something on it of value to you. Look it up. Even finding nothing may be significant.

chapter 20

a profundity of learning?

WHEN I WAS A BOY Mother bought my brother and me a set of *Compton's Encyclopedia*. They were red, and had a pebbly binding on their spines, which my fingers soon became familiar with. Another kid I knew had *The Book of Knowledge* at his home. I think it was blue. I liked those volumes because of all their pictures. As I've said before, my mother was a librarian. She knew *Compton's* was one of the better works for children, because she had looked up its rating in magazines published for librarians; but I think she believed in their unassailable authority as I did, mostly because they were in print and sat in reference rooms of libraries larger and more prestigious than the one she worked in.

From that set of *Compton's*—so massive to me—I gained confidence —false, I know now. Only one other kid on the block lived in a home stocked with an encyclopedia. I never thought much about where the stuff in the articles in *Compton's* came from. As I remember, they were pretty short, and at their conclusion, none carried those initials which I now know mean that the article was written by a leading authority on the topic. Things were relatively settled in the world then. In the late 1920s and early 1930s, for example, the map of Africa wasn't changing by the day as it did later on, and if *Compton's* said something, it seemed the Word to us, final and unquestionable. It was a set of volumes that belonged not only at home but also at school, where plainly books told us what was what, if we could just remember it. In the front pages of *Compton's* I saw the names of editors, but in those days had no idea that books were written by human beings like those I knew, faulty, full of zeal and prejudice, curiosity and lust.

In early childhood my notion of authority was shockingly naive; that's one of the few things I blame my parents for. They had a child-like trust in whatever seemed established—the bank was trustworthy because it was made of heavy stone and had always been there; teachers knew what they were doing because they were supposed to; merchants and their high officers and clerks were honest because if they weren't, the world of money would collapse. Then came the Great Depression and my parents found that many people they had counted on had failed them. I believe now that a faith in people is justified if it is counterbalanced by an awareness that sometimes they slip, misrepresent, and go under when pressures become unbearable.

Once at Christmas season, my confidence in the authority and rightness of the adult world was jolted when one of my parents' friends, who had worked for years at the best jewelry store in town, was caught sneaking out of that store dressed in a Santa Claus suit and carrying thousands of dollars' worth of jewelry. A moment of weakness. Pretty freaky, I thought, but I saw that this ordinarily dignified man was an exception, not representative of the majority of proper people my parents knew, and surely not of the class that wrote the books I'd been taught to trust in.

My next experience with encyclopedias came when I was eighteen. In the college library I noticed a magazine called *The New Republic,* whose cover carried no pictures, only titles of articles. Strange, I thought, and opened it to find it full of writing that made me feel as if what was happening in Washington might be affecting my life. Later I discovered that George Bernard Shaw, the Irishman whose plays *Major Barbara, Pygmalion,* and *Saint Joan* had captivated me, was interested in politics and had written *The Encyclopædia Britannica* article on socialism. That jarred me, also. I had thought encyclopedia articles were written by authoritative automatons called editors. If anyone had asked me where the editors got their information, I would have said, "Probably out of their heads? Or from other encyclopedias published earlier?"

Once I found that Shaw wrote for the *Britannica,* I knew it was a great book. When I was young I'd heard about it. In respectful tones Mother had told me it was the book that educated grownups consulted when they had to know anything. Too expensive for us, but crammed with learning and authority. She believed the advertisements:

> How Can You Express the Inexpressible Love You Feel for Your Child? . . . Britannica is the symbol of knowledge—the accumulation of all man has learned since the world began.

At the library in college I looked around in the *Britannica* and found that other great men and women had written for it. I remember reading somewhere that the leading authority in the world on oriental rugs had written the *Britannica*'s article about them—distilled the experience and learning of a lifetime into a long article. I was awed.

> *1708 MOTTEUX Rabelais v. xx, In you are lodg'd a Cornucopia, an Encyclo pedia, an unmeasurable Profundity of Knowledge.*
>
> OXFORD ENGLISH DICTIONARY

Once in a while in the following years, I used the *Britannica* [from here on I'll call it the "EB"] and handled its pages with reverence. When I came to write this book, I thought I'd discuss the differences between such an elementary, editor-written book as *Compton's* and a great authoritative work like the EB. And then I thought, "What about the people behind it? Who were they? How did they begin?" I expected to discover another H.W. Wilson or Benjamin Franklin saving the world with knowledge.

In my search to answer these questions I looked for books—none on the EB in my city, at the Santa Fe Library, the libraries of St. John's College or the College of Santa Fe, or at the New Mexico State Library. I had no clues as to how to locate magazine articles on the EB, no idea of when they might have been published. To find them, I probably should have called the EB office in Chicago; but from what I've learned since then, I doubt that the editors would have told me of any sources but those that praised the EB.

At the University of New Mexico library under "Encyclopædia Britannica" I found three books. When I saw that one was titled *Misinforming a Nation,* I thought maybe there was a story I didn't know about. And then another, titled *The Myth of the Britannica*—I was on to something. When I came to the third title, *The Great EB,* I was excited. Apparently I could get con and pro. But a quick look into *Misinforming a Nation* and I wasn't sure. Willard Huntington Wright, the author, in a magazine article had characterized the 11th edition of the EB as "a narrow, parochial, opinionated work of dubious scholarship and striking unreliability." In his book he complained about articles being too short or long, the failure of EB to cover two hundred names he considered important, and what he called partiality to British events and people over American, German, and Russian. I considered his criticism unimpressive. Because of its nature, wide-ranging and comprehensive, an encyclopedia is going to be open to such charges. What I wanted was analysis of weaknesses in the articles the EB had printed, and I found little of that in Wright's book.

After dismissing *Misinforming a Nation,* I turned to *The Myth of the Britannica,* 1964, by Harvey Einbinder. In a "Personal Note" at the beginning—much like the openings of I-Search Papers presented in the chapter "Tell It as Story"—he said he was a consulting physicist who provides technical assistance to defense contractors in missile and space projects. In order to write a TV education program explaining modern science to the general public, he consulted the EB occasionally. He read there that Galileo had dropped weights from the Leaning Tower of Pisa in a famous experiment. Later he read another writer who said that this story was fictitious and scored the EB for printing it. Twenty years later, said Einbinder, the EB still carried the Leaning Tower story as uncontested truth. This experience led him to check the 1958 edition thoroughly. On many points he found it lacking. I was pressing to meet a deadline for this contextbook and didn't want to read all 373 pages of Einbinder's book, but I couldn't quote his criticisms without knowing whether or not he was a fair critic. I wished that he had said in his "Personal Note" how much time he had put into examining the EB. I was forced to read the whole book. It was stuffed with specific evidence of weaknesses and omissions. For example, in its publicity the EB has always claimed it "keeps pace with the changing world," but Einbinder furnishes dozens of examples of dangerously outmoded articles in the 14th edition. In a footnote he wrote:

> The EB's negligence in dealing with modern music was confirmed by Paul R. Farnsworth in the *Journal of Psychology* in 1957. He examined the *Encyclopædia's* biographical coverage of 250 composers born since 1870. Although forty-nine of them appeared in the 1929 edition, not a single additional name was added between 1929 and 1950! And in the 1957 edition, only four new composers were included: Converse, Lekeu, Weill and Shostakovich.

On and on went Einbinder in his indictment, citing piece after piece of damaging evidence. By the time I was three-quarters through the book, he had convinced me, but I couldn't stop reading because I was hooked. What an I-Search he had done!

Among the hundreds of misinformed or weak statements Einbinder found in the 1958 EB, the most glaring to me was this passage about the people who live on the Malay Peninsula:

> The Malays are indolent, pleasure loving, improvident beyond belief, fond of bright clothing, of comfort, of ease, and they dislike toil exceedingly. They have no idea of money, and little notion of honesty where money is concerned. . . . They are addicted to gambling, and formerly were much given to fighting, but their courage is not high judged by European standards. The sexual morality of the Malays is very lax. . . .

I looked up Malays in the 11th *Britannica* myself and found the article suffused with a disgusting sense of superiority:

> The ruling classes among them display all the vices of the lower classes, and few of the virtues except that of courtesy. They are for the most part, when left to their own resources, cruel, unjust, selfish, and improvident.

Reading that passage, I thought I'd like to see a Malay characterization of the British ruling class, of which the writer, Sir Hugh Charles Clifford, was a representative. He was a British colonial official, and his article on the Malays for the 11th edition had not been changed in almost fifty years. Einbinder says that when the managing editor of the EB was asked by *Time* magazine about that entry, he answered,

> I wish to say we are embarrassed by the paragraph you quote. . . . It obviously should have been replaced long ago —and I cannot say why it was not.

A decent reply, but it didn't change the fact that while crowing about being up to date, the EB had not altered this article. In 1962 *The New Yorker* magazine said: "Boy, is the *Encyclopædia Britannica* in need of revision!" and spoke of the 1960 edition's article about the Masai tribe in Africa and their weapons—spears, clubs, and "a peculiar sword." *The New Yorker's* reporter interviewed a Masai studying in America who said his people were not allowed to carry spears or clubs any more except in ceremonies.

Many complaints about the 14th edition of the EB being out of date were made in periodicals. On October 25, 1929, *The New York Times* reported that the entry on South Bend, Indiana, stated that the city's major industry was the manufacture of "wagons and carriages" by the Studebaker Brothers. In *The New Republic* for February 19, 1951, Paul Nemenyi asserted that many entries in rapidly changing scientific fields were taken from the 1929 edition. He went on to suggest that each article in the EB should be dated, so the reader wouldn't be misled. Einbinder quoted Wilhelm Herzog saying in *Der Schweizer Buchhandel,* a Swiss magazine, November 15, 1947,

> It is to be regretted that the undertaking founded in 1768 seems to have lost in the last decade all power of differentiation. The ability to select and grade has apparently been lost. With tremendous expense a jumble of 37 million words is produced, newly published each year, so that every purchaser of the latest edition erroneously accepts it as up to date. But random tests show that the articles, being twenty and thirty years old, are out of date like refurbished bargain hats.

Walter Yust, then the editor-in-chief of the EB, replied,

> When [Herzog] states that *Britannica* is not up to date in every respect, he is quite correct. But his conclusion that this is evidence of incompetence, lack of scholarly integrity on the part of the editors is, to say the least, impertinent.

Watch out for people who reject their critics as being impertinent. It's the sort of response I expect from a bad schoolteacher or a nobleman characterizing the native Malays. Yust excused the EB's out-of-dateness on the grounds that World War II had interrupted the work, but failed to explain why many articles had been reprinted unchanged for decades. As I remember, World War II lasted only four years for Americans. Yust's reply to criticism was representative of the EB's responses. I'm sympathetic with those who work for the EB: the job of keeping it up to date by annual or, say, five-year revisions seems overwhelming, and finally impossible. An encyclopedia must make money as well as enlighten the world, or it will die. When I was asked to revise one of my textbooks—to satisfy school systems in states where by edict only recent editions can be bought—my first instinct was to write a new chapter or two but to leave most of the first edition intact so as to save work and money, thereby keeping the book profitable for the publishers and myself. And that's what I did.

Over a period of many decades no encyclopedia can keep up with changing events and thinking, and yet that failure may have serious consequences, especially when the sales and advertising departments imply or assert to customers that all the material in the books is modern and up to date. Throughout its more than two-hundred-year history, the EB editors have frequently been misrepresented by advertising agents and door-to-door salespeople, a circumstance that most authors complain about at some time in their careers. I've written books that were mis-described in advertising brochures or on books' slipcovers, not because the publicity writers intended to do so, but because they didn't know enough about the book or the field it was written in to see it in context.

At times the advertising for the EB has been deplorable—photographs of a little boy who couldn't possibly understand most of its articles, looking dreamingly into space alongside Mother, under a headline, "Are you giving your children more than you had?" The practices of some of the EB's door-to-door salespeople have been unethical. When my father died in 1930, my mother considered becoming an EB salesperson and decided against it because the push in the door and the flim-flam sales techniques expected of EB salespeople as explained to her were distasteful. I understand that the members of sales and advertising forces may misconceive the nature of the encyclopedia and their role in selling it; but the Board of Directors and the editors have a responsibility for stopping serious misrepresentation. Yet, that's a difficult task; and the first concern of these people should be to produce a great encyclopedia.

Although Harvey Einbinder's *The Myth of the Britannica* is readable and exciting, it isn't vague or sloppy. He documents his charges, quoting from the EB and other critics who discovered weaknesses in it. In his book I found the titles of many magazine articles that would have been helpful to me if I had had the time to consult them. That's a tip worth remembering for your I-Search. If you find a good book on your topic, look in it for mention of other books and magazines. The author is probably an expert and has done much of your reading for you—if you'll let him. Many books and encyclopedia articles contain bibliographies—lists of books and magazine articles the author considers valuable on the topic she's investigated.

Einbinder's references were always complete, citing dates and pages. This fullness reassured me of the validity of his case. I could tell he was fair-minded. After citing many weaknesses of the 1958 issue of the 14th edition, he gave credit to the EB for improving certain articles in the 1963 issue. He spoke not only of error and slovenliness but of strengths and improvements, and so his case against the EB was all the more convincing. On every page his book demonstrates how thoroughly he had read the EB. For example, after praising the book for removing some incredible legends about Columbus, he pointed out that it had inserted a new one.

> *Encyclopædia . . . The spelling with æ has been preserved from becoming obs. by the fact that many of the works so called have Latin titles, as* Encyclopæ-dia Britannica, Londinensis, *etc.*
>
> OXFORD ENGLISH DICTIONARY

When I turned to *The Great EB,* 1958, by Herman Kogan, I expected a book "puffing" the encyclopedia. It was written by a man who later was given a position with the EB and was published by the University of Chicago Press. The University of Chicago had been affiliated with the EB since 1943 and received many millions of dollars for lending its name and prestige. Appearing six years before Einbinder's book, *The Great EB* was not highly critical of the enterprise, but was so full and detailed in its historical record that I came to admire it. Herman Kogan was enough in love with truth that he presented many unflattering stories about persons who had worked for the EB since the publication of its first volume in 1771. His portrait of the first editor, a Scotsman named William Smellie—whose name and character seem borrowed from a Dickens novel—seems honest. I quote a few of Kogan's phrases about Smellie:

> [While working with the official printer for Edinburgh University, Smellie] was permitted to attend whatever classes at the university he wished . . . by the time he was nineteen, he was editing a literary weekly. . . . As devoted to whiskey as to scholarship, Smellie, when roistering, delighted in reciting tedious poems written in Latin by his father.

Kogan mentions that Smellie rounded up people to constitute "The Society of Gentlemen," who would appear on the title page as the makers of the encyclopedia. Einbinder points out that the Society was not an established functioning organization.

In the 18th century, publishing houses were small and flighty. Smellie made the encyclopedia principally out of bits and pieces taken from other works, as was the fashion of the time, cheerfully admitting that his method was to assign some articles to be originally written and that he took the rest from "the best books upon almost every subject, extracted the useful parts, and rejected whatever appeared trifling or less interesting." In his three-volume encyclopedia Smellie had the good sense to allot six pages to a discussion of Dr. Samuel

Johnson's dictionary and the stupidity and carelessness to give four words to the topic of

Woman—The female of man. See **HOMO**.

He described California as

. . . a large country of the West Indies.

and called Nigeria "Nigroland." It was a beginning that Einbinder might have said was the seed for the 14th edition with all its inaccuracies; but at the time it made its way with distinction among less well-done works. *The Britannic Hodgepodge* might have been a better title of this encyclopedia and its competitors of the time. A smattering of intelligent new articles, patches of borrowed wisdom and nonsense, sound and ridiculous notions, side by side.

For over a hundred years the EB was a Scottish book, connected with the thinkers collected in Edinburgh. A number of distinguished scholars wrote articles for it which were not only authoritative but represented some of the best thinking on the new frontiers of knowledge. Early in its life, the EB printed articles by famous and/or great figures: Sir Walter Scott, the author of *Ivanhoe,* wrote on chivalry and drama; Thomas Henry Huxley, the biologist, on evolution; Algernon Charles Swinburne, the poet, on John Keats; James Mill, the father of the philosopher John Stuart Mill, who is quoted in this book, on government; Thomas Young, a physicist, on Egypt; Thomas Babington Macaulay on Samuel Johnson; and William Robertson Smith, a Scottish professor and theologian, on religion. Smith was thrown out of his job at the Free Church College for writing the EB article on religion. Subsequently, he became joint editor of the 9th edition of the EB.

In 1911 the 11th edition appeared, which became so deservedly famous for its scholarly articles that many persons today have a set in their homes and many libraries carry it on their shelves next to the current edition. In the preface to the 11th, the editor, Hugh Chisholm, showed himself far ahead of most persons of his day in understanding the problem of objectivity:

> The object of the present work is to furnish accounts of all subjects, which shall really explain their meaning, to those who desire accurate information. Amid the variety of beliefs which are held with sincere conviction by one set of people or another, impartiality does not consist in concealing criticism or withholding knowledge of divergent opinion, but in an attitude of scientific respect which is precise in

studying a belief in the terms, and according to the interpretation accepted by those who hold it.

In his last sentence Chisholm is saying what John Stuart Mill advocated—studying controversial opinions by hearing those that hold them.

Like many editors of the EB, Chisholm was willing to print articles in which an authority took a strong position and advanced new views. He didn't want a neutral, colorless, and finally meaningless discussion of controversial topics. He expected writers to present the leading and divergent views of the time so that a reader would see that the topic was complex and stimulating.

•   •   •

With all that intelligence behind it, how then, could the EB contain as much wrongheaded, inaccurate, and out-of-date material as Harvey Einbinder discovered? The announced policy of the company was always to provide readers with up-to-date authoritative knowledge. Policies were set for constant review and revision of all volumes. Authorities in various fields were paid to inspect regularly portions of the EB assigned to them, to make sure they were timely and sound. Yet Einbinder was able to fill a 383-page book with instances of mistakes, omissions, and faulty opinions on the part of the writers and editors. Herman Kogan admitted that at times the "Great EB" had erred. For example, in discussing the 14th edition, which came out first in 1929, he said:

> William Cox [the publisher at that time] was greatly pleased with estimates from approving critics, especially so since few commented on the inclusion of a number of outdated articles.

Upon the publication of the 14th edition, in whose 1958 revision Einbinder found so many weaknesses, many prominent Americans praised it as a monumental achievement in scholarship that made the knowledge of the world available to ordinary citizens. Part of their reaction may have been due to the fact that this edition was dominated by American, rather than British, knowledge and viewpoints. A long time had passed since its Scottish beginnings in 1771. On the eve of the publication of the 11th edition, in 1911, the owners of the EB had succeeded in enlisting Cambridge University in England to lend its name to the work. In 1920 Sears Roebuck Company in Chicago had become the owner of the EB, and in 1943 General Robert Wood, the president of Sears, had given it to the University of Chicago, which continues to lend its name to the company that actually writes and publishes the work. When the book was published in England, Americans complained that it was too British in view; when it was published in the United States, the British complained it was too American in view. Throughout its history it has been a remarkably international work, printing articles by authorities from countries all over the world and attempting to cover the thought and behavior of all peoples.

In my search to understand and gauge the EB, the question that continued to nag me was, "How could such a distinguished effort, carried out and improved over a span of more than two centuries, be as faulty as Harvey Einbinder had shown it to be? How could so many leaders of opinion praise it? Was the whole thing a hoax?"

I've concluded that the answer is that no one except Einbinder had possessed the energy and knowledge necessary to make a comprehensive critical estimate of the work. It was too big. Over the years a few readers had written in to say they had read every word in the *Britannica,* but they were uncritical, apparently dazed by their feat rather than aware of what they had read. Many of the chief editors of the EB have admitted that they themselves have not read every word in the complete set, and I don't fault them for that. The size of a work or an enterprise inevitably affects its character, form, and quality. The EB apparently got out of hand and no one but Einbinder found a way to get hold of it critically. He knew a great deal about science and was knowledgeable in music and art. Apparently he spent years comparing the EB's treatment of topics he was competent to judge, and he compared hundreds of articles in different editions to see whether or not they had been brought up to date or changed in any way. In *The Myth of the Britannica* he included an appendix in which he listed the titles of 666 articles in the 1963 EB which were "taken from the ninth edition of 1875-89, the tenth edition of 1902-03, or the eleventh edition of 1910-11." All articles in the list occupied at least a half page in the EB. In his calm and fair way, Einbinder adds,

> Although occasional articles may be "classics" possessing an historical interest, it is difficult to understand why so many others have been retained. Therefore, this list may suggest the extent of obsolete material in the latest printing of the *Encyclopædia.*

Before I accepted Einbinder's opinions entirely, I thought I had better check some of those 666 articles in the 1963 EB which he said were ancient rather than up to date. I found that the entry on Henry Fielding, the author of that witty 18th-century novel *Tom Jones,* was a shortened version of an article in the 1911 edition, and that the article on "Inspiration" (in the religious sense of the "condition of being directly under the divine influence") was taken from the 1911 edition. As printed in the 1963 volume, the Inspiration article included a bibliography whose latest source was dated 1906. Six hundred and sixty-six articles out of date! That's a charge by Einbinder that I believe, because he seems on all counts that I have checked to know more about the book than anyone else in the world.

Next I moved to examine the 15th edition, which some people call *Britannica 3*, published in 1974. The first article that caught my eye was one on "Acting" by Lee Strasberg, director of the Actors' Workshop in New York City, which trained Marlon Brando, Geraldine Page, and others. I found it much more thorough, exciting, and readable than the same article in the 14th edition by drama critic Richard Findlater. It gave a dominating place in the history of acting to the works of the Russian director Constantin Stanislavsky, the patron saint of the Actors' Workshop, but I didn't mind because I respect Stanislavsky. Other articles I checked were shorter than those in the 14th edition, but lively and up to date.

I consulted H.W. Wilson's *Reader's Guide to Periodical Literature* and found listed an article by Geoffrey Wolff in *The Atlantic* for November 1976 about the 15th edition of the EB, which said that Harvey Einbinder had hailed it as "unmatched for convenience, freshness, and accuracy." He said, "It maintains a standard of excellence that renders other adult encyclopedias obsolete." I was stunned. Einbinder praising the EB for freshness?

Wolff said he found these opinions by Einbinder in *Bookletter* for September 16, 1974. I had never heard of such a publication, and neither had the reference librarian I talked to at the University of New Mexico Library. "We don't carry it," she said, and pulled Ulrich's *International Periodicals Dictionary* from the shelf, looked up *Bookletter,* and said, "It's published by Harper's." I went home, called Harper & Row in New York. The first two people who answered had never heard of it. I called again and got someone who said, "I think *Bookletter* is defunct. And I think it used to be published by *Harper's* magazine." So I called the magazine and found that the former editor, Suzanne Mantell, worked there and was out for lunch. One more call, my fifth, and Ms. Mantell told me that Harvey Einbinder had indeed written for *Bookletter* a whole article on the new EB, and she would send me a xerox of it. Two days later, I had the article "Old Salesmanship and New Scholarship" in hand. With his usual thoroughness Einbinder recalled some of the history of his investigation of the 14th edition, including this comment:

When I described some of these flaws in the *Columbia University Forum* in 1960, Robert M. Hutchins, chairman of the board of editors, dismissed my critique because only ninety of the Encyclopædia's 42,000 entries were criticized.

That may have been the EB's public response, but its private and, for a long time, secret one was to rewrite the work entirely at tremendous cost in work and money. In his *Bookletter* article, Einbinder finds in *Britannica 3* few flaws and many excellences. "The new set," he says, "is free from the bias and provinciality that marred the old EB." I rest content. On his judgment, I can recommend *Britannica 3* to anyone.

In the *Atlantic* article that I mentioned earlier, Geoffrey Wolff went on to document a finding of Ernest Barnes, an administrative judge of the Federal Trade Commission against EB salespeople for misrepresenting themselves to citizens in their homes. But I was more interested in the contents of the encyclopedia and was heartened to know that it had pulled itself out of the muck of the 14th edition, which was contaminated by all sorts of out-of-date articles and bibliographies borrowed from the 9th and 11th editions.

The new and completely rewritten *Britannica 3* is divided into three sections labeled fancily with inkhorn Greek terms thought up by its architect, Mortimer Adler: the *Micropædia* (short articles on all subjects), the *Macropædia* (longer articles on some of those subjects), and a special volume, the *Propædia* (an Outline of Knowledge), which Adler suggests outlines all the knowledge of the world in such a way that the alphabetically arranged articles in the EB can be brought together by subject by anyone who wants to make a course of study for herself on any large topic. The *Britannica 3* strikes me as authoritative, up to date, and comprehensive. Yet the job of keeping it timely remains overwhelming, and I suspect that in another thirty or forty years it may be as out of date as the 14th edition was when it was published.

From this discussion you can see that looking for a thorough, modern treatment of a topic in an encyclopedia is a chancey act. By their nature, encyclopedias are handy, relatively brief reference aids on any one topic. They can't treat a subject with the thoroughness of a book devoted entirely to that subject. In them, searchers can find overall views of complex topics that can lead them to other more satisfactory treatments. As I said, earlier, a short discussion may be what a searcher needs at a given moment in her search. I've written this chapter to show that the notion that a great encyclopedia like *The Britannica* will not, as claimed, give "comprehensive background information" that will make you "thoroughly informed on current events," and it will not give you "clear, complete and authoritative coverage of every subject." Rather it will present relatively short and highly abstracted pictures of the world of fact and thought, as seen by gifted, knowledgeable, naturally biased human beings capable of error and carelessness as well as brilliance and meticulousness.

And so there's my I-Search to find out whether the EB is a cornucopia of truth or a fraud. I found it was like a person with a long life. It always meant to be great, but at times it wore a Santa Claus suit, misrepresented itself, and stole a little. At other times it wore clothes that belonged to it, and spoke truth. If you use its 15th edition, called *Britannica 3,* you'll catch it at one of its best moments.

∞ **DOING TWENTY-SEVEN:** Look up in EB 3 something or someone you're greatly attracted to—for your own pleasure. Remember there may be two articles on the topic, one in the *Micropædia* and one in the *Macropædia*. While you're in the encyclopedia section of the reference section of the library, you might look at other encyclopedias on adjoining shelves. Maybe your topic is better covered in a more specialized encyclopedia that centers on religion, social sciences, or sports. If that's true, choose the best source. You don't have to read *The Encyclopædia Britannica*.

chapter 21
sam
and
noah

PART OF THE SEARCH in this chapter about dictionaries is to find how people evolve into bookards. Its roots may go back, as every matter that embraces words eventually does, to a mother—saying words to children and countenancing them when they grunt a sound that she wants to believe was a word.

For me the first feeling about books arose in the air of my home when I was two, crawling around in our dining room that was also our library room. The walls in my two-feet-high world were made of books, standing on shelves. I could poke my grubby fingers into almost anything in the room, but "Don't tear the books, Kenny." "And don't eat the pages." Not because they were taboo objects, connected with punishment, but rather treasures that would eventually make up a heaven, in which first I would see pictures, and later words, to be read with delight.

How do bookards begin to melt into books and books into them? Maya Angelou, the black poet and dancer, has told how that happened for her. Before I give her words, I'll sketch the setting in which I first encountered her. At the university where I was teaching in the Middle West, she came to speak to the two percent of the students who were black. She told them they could do almost anything they wanted to if they believed in themselves, used their capacities, and didn't lie or pretend to themselves and others. Her book, the first

part of a long autobiography, *I Know Why the Caged Bird Sings,*
she dedicated to

> My son, Guy Johnson, and all the strong black birds of
> promise who defy the odds and gods and sing their songs.

In over fifty years, I had never witnessed a person so persuasive. I
kept thinking, "She has this audience in her hand and they would do
anything she wanted them to do, at a word from her." Then as she
stopped talking and questions began, a young man ran into the meeting place and said, "I've just heard that one of our black sisters has
been raped somewhere in the city. What are we going to do about it?"
Ms. Angelou, a visitor for a day from the East, took one deep breath—
thinking, I suppose, of how she had just been telling these young people they must not allow others to treat them like second-rate human
beings—and said, in effect, "Brother, that's a familiar and moving
tale you've told. I want to say to all of you again that we're here in
our lives to stand up for truth and the rights of every person to justice.
If this act has indeed been committed, and you find that fact beyond
doubt, you should take steps to bring about justice for everyone
involved, but here, tonight, we must not act without the kind of knowledge that accords justice to all persons."

Later I read in Ms. Angelou's book her account of being raped at the
age of eight by a friend of her mother's. The experience stopped her
from speaking for a long time. When she and her brother moved from
St. Louis back to her grandmother's house in Stamps (I remembered
the town as being in Georgia), she was still silent. There a woman of
education named Bertha Flowers talked to her of words:

> Her skin was a rich black that would have peeled like a
> plum if snagged. . . . She was one of the few gentlewomen
> I have ever known. . . . She said, without turning her head,
> to me, "I hear you're doing very good school work, Mar-
> guerite, but that it's all written. The teachers report that
> they have trouble getting you to talk in class." We passed the
> triangular farm on our left and the path widened to allow
> us to walk together. I hung back in the separate unasked
> and unanswerable questions.
>
> "Come and walk along with me, Marguerite." I couldn't
> have refused even if I wanted to. She pronounced my name
> so nicely. Or more correctly, she spoke each word with
> such clarity that I was certain a foreigner who didn't un-
> derstand English could have understood her.

"Now no one is going to make you talk—possibly no one can. But bear in mind, language is man's way of communicating with his fellow man and it is language alone which separates him from the lower animals." That was a totally new idea to me, and I would need time to think about it.

"Your grandmother says you read a lot. Every chance you get. That's good, but not good enough. Words mean more than what is set down on paper. It takes the human voice to infuse them with the shades of deeper meaning."

I memorized the part about the human voice infusing words. It seemed so valid and poetic.

She said she was going to give me some books and that I not only must read them, I must read them aloud. She suggested that I try to make a sentence sound in as many different ways as possible.

"I'll accept no excuse if you return a book to me that has been badly handled." My imagination boggled at the punishment I would deserve if in fact I did abuse a book of Mrs. Flowers'. Death would be too kind and brief.

The odors in the house surprised me. Somehow I had never connected Mrs. Flowers with food or eating or any other common experience of common people. There must have been an outhouse, too, but my mind never recorded it.

The sweet scent of vanilla had met us as she opened the door.

"I made tea cookies this morning. You see, I had planned to invite you for cookies and lemonade so we could have this little chat. The lemonade is in the icebox."

It followed that Mrs. Flowers would have ice on an ordinary day, when most families in our town bought ice late on Saturdays only a few times during the summer to be used in the wooden ice-cream freezers. . . .

"Have a seat, Marguerite. Over there by the table." She carried a platter covered with a tea towel. Although she warned that she hadn't tried her hand at baking sweets for some time, I was certain that like everything else about her the cookies would be perfect.

They were flat round wafers, slightly browned on the edges and butter-yellow in the center. With the cold lemonade they were sufficient for childhood's lifelong diet. Remembering my manners, I took nice little lady-like bites off the edges. She said she had made them expressly for me and that she had a few in the kitchen that I could take home to my brother. So I jammed one whole cake in my mouth and the rough crumbs scratched the insides of my jaws, and if I hadn't had to swallow, it would have been a dream come true.

As I ate she began the first of what we later called "my lessons in living." She said that I must always be intolerant of ignorance but understanding of illiteracy. That some people, unable to go to school, were more educated and even more intelligent than college professors. She encouraged me to listen carefully to what country people called mother wit. That in those homely sayings was couched the collective wisdom of generations.

When I finished the cookies she brushed off the table and brought a thick, small book from the book-case. I had read *A Tale of Two Cities* and found it up to my standards as a romantic novel. She opened the first page and I heard poetry for the first time in my life.

"It was the best of times and the worst of times. . . ." Her voice slid in and curved down through and over the words. She was nearly singing. I wanted to look at the pages. Were they the same that I had read? Or were there notes, music, lined on the pages, as in a hymn book? Her sounds began cascading gently. I knew from listening to a thousand preachers that she was nearing the end of her reading, and I hadn't really heard, heard to understand, a single word.

"How do you like that?"

It occurred to me that she expected a response. The sweet vanilla flavor was still on my tongue and her reading was a wonder in my ears. I had to speak.

I said, "Yes, ma'am." It was the least I could do, but it was the most also.

"There's one more thing. Take this book of poems and memorize one for me. Next time you pay me a visit, I want you to recite."

I have tried often to search behind the sophistication of years for the enchantment I so easily found in those gifts. The essence escapes but its aura remains. To be allowed, no, invited, into the private lives of strangers, and to share their joys and fears, was a chance to exchange the Southern bitter wormwood for a cup of mead with Beowulf or a hot cup of tea and milk with Oliver Twist. When I said aloud, "It is a far, far better thing that I do, than I have ever done . . ." tears of love filled my eyes at my selflessness.

You may be thinking, "Why in this chapter about dictionaries are you presenting Maya Angelou eating tea cookies with Bertha Flowers?" As I said earlier, I'm asking how people become bookards. And I'm giving an instance, out of dozens I've read in stories by productive people about their lives, of how they learned unforgettably, usually outside school, from someone whom they made a model, someone whose influence never fades in their lives. Love is involved, as Ms. Angelou said, love for words and love for people who love them. Beyond that is the will, which says, "I will get to know words in the reading of them." When you give in to it, you'll find you have such a will.

Such countenancing is a Moebian happening and will not occur unless at the same time a person is being helped she reads or writes *on her own*. There is no reading or writing in the abstract. A Benjamin Franklin, a Jack London, or a Maya Angelou must do it on his or her own. The will to begin doing that manifests itself in persons of any age, in any place—at five or fifty, in a library or a jail.

•   •   •

Twenty-four hours after I typed those pages from Maya Angelou's book, the word *Flowers* came up in my mind. *Flowers,* wasn't that the name of Violet Hawkins's great grandfather in her I-Search Paper? I looked back to Chapter 14 of this book—yes, Orange Henry Flowers, "born on the Flowers Plantation." I had misremembered his story as taking place in Georgia and Maya Angelou's in Stamps, *Georgia.* When I checked the two stories again, I found that the Flowers Plantation was in Hazlehurst, Mississippi (apparently, as was common for slaves, Orange was given a last name the same as the white owners of the plantation) and Maya Angelou's town of Stamps was in Arkansas, not Georgia. I searched the picture of the United States in my mind, printed there from childhood where I played in that living-room library with a crossword puzzle of the United States, and saw that both Arkansas and Mississippi touch the Mississippi River. Maybe Stamps and Hazlehurst were not so far away? I checked my Rand and McNally highway atlas and found they are roughly two hundred miles apart. Could Bertha Flowers and Orange Henry Flowers be related? Could they both be descended from slaves who worked at the Flowers Plantation? Mrs. Flowers was highly educated; Orange Henry, born a slave, graduated from a Theological College—a family of bookards? I don't know, but now that the thought has hit me I'll try to get in touch with

Maya Angelou and Violet Hawkins and let them know that black people named Flowers figured in both their lives.

•   •   •

In my youth I don't remember a particular moment like the one Maya Angelou recounted, but there were many that helped me become a bookard. And once a bookard, moved by pages filled with words, a person turns to dictionaries, as Ms. Angelou turned to Mrs. Flowers, with love, not with the hatred and fear that children turn to a dictionary in school when it's the authority that decides whether they were right or wrong in a spelldown. When a bookard looks up a word in a dictionary it's not to help him pass a vocabulary quiz but to find out more about that unfamiliar face that appears in a sentence of a story he's enjoying. The word doesn't come from a list, but from a sentence (a *context,* as teachers usually put it, but which I prefer to call an *environment*). There in that sentence an unfamiliar word appears—as in a street, an alley, a woods, or an arroyo—an unfamiliar face of a person. This word may be a new person to us but we know that it belongs there in that setting, and the setting helps us guess its character, and the other faces around it give us clues as to its purpose.

That's the purpose of the I-Search I'm reporting in this chapter. Once in college one of the two great teachers I had in my eight years of higher education, Jesse Mack or Andrew Bongiorno, said something that led me to the then thirteen volumes of *The Oxford English Dictionary,* and I saw there, after almost every word, sentences from the past, dated, in which that word was used. The *story* of the word, its *history*. (Reading that great book the other day, I found that the word *aphesis* had no sentence illustrating its use in the past, and that was because the first editor of the OED, James A.H. Murray, had made up the word, he acknowledged, as a term for the shortening of such words as *history* into *story* and *esquire* into *squire*.) The purpose of this I-Search chapter, as I was saying, is to find out how in dictionaries the practice of citing the uses of words began, why? by whom? under the influence of whom? For forty years I've wondered, and I thought it time that I search for the answer. I knew that the OED was based on historical principles, but where did the editors get that idea?

You're reading now the sections of my I-Search Paper that should be entitled, "What I Knew" and "What I Wanted to Know." As a kid I loved dictionaries, but where did I get the urge, the need, to find out how they are made? I guess it was not until 1948 when I was thirty and met Fred Reeve, whom I talked about earlier as the leader of a book club. He had been one of the associate editors of *Webster's New*

World Dictionary. As I remember, he said that for four years he had labored in Cleveland with other people, putting together a work that in its college edition made the current *Webster's Collegiate Dictionary* (Merriam) look prudish and outdated. Fred had been associated with young people excited about the new thinking of psychologists, anthropologists, and political scientists; and he showed me some of the evidence in entries for words, all of which had been considered and written newly, not simply lifted from other dictionaries without review and thought, as had been the custom among lexicographers for centuries.

> lexico'grapher. *A writer of dictionaries; a harmless drudge, that busies himself in tracing the original, and detailing the signification of words.*
>
> SAMUEL JOHNSON, *1755*

For example, the eighth sense of the word *blood* in that handsome red-covered volume which Fred handed me in 1953 fresh from the press:

> radical heritage; race: loosely and unscientifically so used, for blood is not one of the ethnic differentia.

Reading that entry, I thought of how Charley Jones, a preacher in Chapel Hill, North Carolina, five years earlier had told me this story. "Ken," he said, "some white people will tell you that if a person has one-sixth Negro blood in him, he's a Negro. But they never would say that a person who had one-sixth white blood in him was a white." And I thought of passages from Violet Hawkins's I-Search Paper:

> . . . Addie Carrie Ashby, the daughter of a plantation owner and his black mistress. . . . Robert Anderson, my own great grandfather on my mother's side, was born in New Orleans in 1869 to a Spanish mistress of a white ship captain. His mother died when he was very young and he was taken in by a black family named Humphrey. Although Robert wasn't black he was considered black because of his associations.

Fred Reeve talked about dictionary making to me, but not enough. If he were alive today I would be searching him out for more words about words. He spoke admiringly of Dr. Samuel Johnson and his "great dictionary of 1755." "Read his preface," said Fred, and I read it and was amazed. What I was beginning to search for, back then twenty-six years from the moment I'm writing this, was "How and why does a person make a great dictionary that doesn't simply prescribe, but looks back at how words have been used through time?"

Could anyone know all those words? And, overcome by the thought, I believe I also asked subliminally, "How can I thank these people for giving me their dictionaries?" I'm trying to thank them now, in this chapter and the next.

At Princeton University, Fred studied Sam Johnson; and the longer I knew Fred, the more I saw how he modeled himself after that scintillating man. Fred was my live source; from being with him and observing his zest for living, for words, for eating good food, for humorous and well-phrased conversation—so like Dr. Johnson—I knew, incontrovertibly, that lexicographers were not dull and their occupation was bewitching. But to continue my search for the purposes of writing this chapter, I turned to books and magazines because I was pressed to meet a publication deadline. And already, from my years as an English teacher, I had learned the names of many persons to be trusted as authorities on language. In my own reference library there were books, *The Oxford Companion to American Literature* and to *English Literature* as well as *Webster's Biographical Dictionary,* and in public and college libraries, *The Encyclopædia Britannica,* which contained summaries of the lives of the men who made the three dictionaries I wanted to explore.

You might think of what's available to you. Do you need a short factual account of a person's life of the kind that appears in a one-volume work in a special field? Or a still longer one in an encyclopedia of many volumes? Or hundreds of pages in a book entirely devoted to her or him? You can waste time and become lost in the details of a long work, but you may need a detail that the short work can't offer. One solution is to find the long book devoted to your subject and look in the index—if there is one—to locate where it's discussed in the book. As the son of a librarian I was taught to do that. I'm not implying that such a step will always solve your problems. Searching is frequently difficult and confusing, sometimes because of errors committed not by you, but by the authority you're consulting. For example, when I checked the index in W. Jackson Bate's rich six-hundred-page life of Dr. Johnson for more about his friend, John Hawkesworth, whom I'd read about on page 267, I couldn't find his name. Looked up and down the columns of H's, and discovered that Bate or an editor had mis-alphabetized the H's, so that these three names occurred in this order: Hawkins . . . Henley . . . Hawkesworth. As I've said before, human beings write and put together books, and therefore books will never be perfect. Not much surprise in that statement, but an implication for teachers—if they expect students, who are only beginning to move toward authority in writing, to produce papers without error, they are cruel fools.

SAMUEL JOHNSON'S DICTIONARY, 1755

Writing this chapter, I've re-read **Dr.** Johnson's Preface to *A Dictionary of the English Language* and studied what people have written about him. And before that I talked to an authority on Johnson, Fred Reeve, for many hours. Only a little of all that can I give you here, to help set Johnson's life as a lexicographer. In his time he was the first man of letters in Great Britain, writing political articles, lives of great poets, and a charming, biting story called *Rasselas* (a young man who searched for utter happiness and found hardship, who was counseled by his philosopher friend Imlac, "While you are making the choice of life, you neglect to live"). Johnson wrote many other works besides these even while writing his dictionary, to which he gave about eight and a half years of his seventy-five.

Samuel was born in 1709 with a push toward becoming a bookard: his father was a bookseller and sheriff in Lichfield, Staffordshire, England. Sam says he roamed the shop and read books from the shelves. But his father, like many booksellers today, was not making enough money, and could afford to send his son to Oxford University for only thirteen months. So Sam, like Ben Franklin, was never fully conventionalized by college and went on to become ever an active rather than passive learner.

When he issued his plan for the great dictionary in order to interest London booksellers in supporting its publication, Johnson intended to read through literature and science and cull from authorities uses of words he would be defining in his dictionary. Several writers I read said that Johnson was the first lexicographer to print sentences from writers who had employed the words he defined. But I found in James Sledd's and Gwin Kolb's book, *Dr. Johnson's Dictionary,* that he was far from the first in Europe to do that. (I had reason to trust James Sledd, some of whose students have spoken to me with great admiration of him.) Greek, Latin, Portuguese, and French lexicographers had done that earlier. And the scholars of the Accademia della Crusca had given exact references for the books from which they took their illustrative quotations. They were a group working together on a dictionary; Johnson was one man aided by a few copiers. To have read widely and kept precise records of thousands of uses of words would have been impossible for one person to have done in eight and a half years while writing a dictionary.

What can individuals do, and what can't they do?—these are questions which this book you're reading asks and answers again and again. The great women and men you read about here carried out prodigious works, but all of those works were incomplete, inconsistent, and sometimes downright wrong. When you think of these powerful writers at work, you may be challenged by their courage and industry and comforted by their frailty. When he first thought of producing *A Dictionary of the English Language,* Samuel Johnson envisaged himself reading widely in all fields of knowledge and gathering from books passages that would illustrate the meaning of a word at a given time, and also impart knowledge and delight to readers; but, he said:

> When the time called upon me to range this accumulation
> of elegance and wisdom into an alphabetical series, I soon
> discovered that the bulk of my volumes would fright away
> the student, and was forced to depart from my scheme of
> including all that was pleasing or useful in English litera-
> ture, and reduce my transcripts very often to clusters of
> words, in which scarcely any meaning is retained. . . .

Further limiting an exhibition of the historical development of words was Dr. Johnson's policy of not quoting living authors (to protect himself against charges of partiality) and presenting mainly writing of the Elizabethan period, which he considered the best model. With customary truthfulness, he admitted occasionally quoting a favorite living author and at times quoting writers "in manufacture or agriculture" whom he didn't consider masters of style. He wasn't recording the historical use of words but mainly what he considered the best use of them.

Almost singlehandedly this son of a bookseller produced in 1755 the greatest dictionary of the English language up to that time. In many large libraries in the United States you can inspect that two-volume work (sometimes only after obtaining permission from a librarian to view it in a Rare Book Room). It was a powerful force in England. When members of parliament and other professional people said, "The dictionary says—" they meant "Johnson's dictionary says—"

Sledd and Kolb demonstrate with evidence that Johnson's dictionary was not original in any sense. In an essay on "The English Language" that appears in the first edition of *Webster's New World Dictionary* (which I always think of as "Fred's dictionary"), the linguist Harold Whitehall agrees with them. He says that before Johnson's great dictionary of 1755, Nathaniel Bailey in 1721 had printed quotations from authors illustrating uses of words, chiefly from proverbs. And before that, a number of writers had compiled lists of "hard" words with easier synonyms to aid the reader faced with the fancy, show-off language used by many "inkhorn" scholars, as they were called in the 17th and 18th centuries. Others had printed lists of simple words with fancy synonyms for those who wanted to write pretentiously. Like the great figures in dramatic writing and music, Shakespeare and Bach, Samuel Johnson didn't come up with entirely new ideas or compose highly original works, but produced something fuller, deeper, and more intelligent than those who had preceded him.

And like most great creative persons, Johnson was not pompous or full of brag. He discussed his job for what it was, proud of its excellences, not blind to its imperfections. In his preface he said:

> The work, whatever proofs of diligence and attention it may exhibit, is yet capable of many improvements: the orthography [spelling] which I recommend is still controvertible, the etymology [history of word forms] which I adopt is uncertain, and perhaps frequently erroneous; the explanations are sometimes too much contracted, and sometimes too much diffused, the significations are distinguished rather with subtilty [sic] than skill, and the attention is harrassed with unnecessary minuteness.

The vigor of the man who enjoyed life so much at dinner in the Ivy Lane Club and the Literary Club shows in the definitions he wrote for his dictionary. For example:

> **di'ckens.** A kind of adverbial exclamation, importing as it seems, much the same with the *devil;* but I know not whence derived.
> **cream.** (1) the unctuous or oily part of milk, which, when it is cold, floats on the top, and is changed by the agitation of the churn into butter; the flower of milk.

Occasionally Johnson could not suppress his feelings and wrote a highly subjective definition, like this, his most famous:

> **oats.** A grain, which in England is generally given to horses, but in Scotland supports the people.

At about age 45, when he wrote that definition, Johnson could not repress his habit of making fun of the Scots, those neighbors up north. Later he was to make friends with a number of Scotsmen, including James Boswell, who followed Johnson around and took hundreds of notes on what he said that eventually became his *Life of Samuel Johnson,* the most famous biography in the English language.

> *. . . the* English Dictionary *was written
> with little assistance of the learned, and
> without any patronage of the great; not
> in the soft obscurities of retirement, or
> under the shelter of academick bowers,
> but amidst inconvenience and distrac-
> tion, in sickness and in sorrow . . . if
> our language is not here fully displayed,
> I have only failed in an attempt which
> no human powers have hitherto com-
> pleted.*

SAMUEL JOHNSON

NOAH WEBSTER'S DICTIONARY, 1828

In this book I've not disguised my admiration for Samuel Johnson, nor can I disguise my dislike of Noah Webster, who wrote *An American Dictionary of the English Language.*

Born in Connecticut in 1758, Noah was a bookard. In a biography of him, John S. Morgan says that he "showed an academic bent early in his life, and his father frequently found the boy lying in the shade reading when he was supposed to be working in the fields." In school Webster used Thomas Dilworth's grammar, *A Guide to the English Tongue,* a page of which is reproduced in this book at the end of the chapter, "Getting the Point." But unlike Ben Franklin, Maya Angelou, Samuel Johnson, and the authors of the four I-Search Papers in Chapter 14, Noah seemed not interested in childhood beginnings, and although, as Morgan points out, he wrote a great deal during his lifetime, he never told us about his boyhood. I suspect something awful in it, like strangling his grandmother or murdering a possible rival in the spelling bee. Although my evidence for these acts is slight, or I might say nonexistent, the fact that he lacked a sense of humor points to terrifying failings. Joseph Friend, the author of *The Development of American Lexicography 1798–1864,* notes that Webster was forever alternating between praise and condemnation of Johnson's great dictionary, and yet he borrowed copiously from it, and outrageously used part of Johnson's crack against the Scots for eating oats as horses do, with this statement in his own entry on oats:

> . . . the meal of this grain, *oatmeal,* forms a considerable
> and very valuable article of food for man in Scotland, and
> every where oats are excellent food for horses and cattle.

Noah took Johnson's funny poke seriously. Joseph Friend shows his compassion by writing, "But lack of humor is scarcely a defect in a

lexicographer." Wrong, Joseph, wrong. Lack of humor is a grave defect in any writer and in Webster it was almost fatal, cursing his life
in a way that made him enemy upon enemy who could have been
friend. The basis of humor is incongruity—something occurs that
doesn't belong, that's twisted from its usual position, that's been
turned in a context or environment. And awareness of both the conventional position and the surprising change is necessary before a
person sees the humor. So—intelligence, knowledge, wit. A person can
be evil, like Senator Joe McCarthy, and have a sense of humor. I'm not
saying that humor excuses bad behavior, but people who are thought
of as intelligent and creative and yet lack humor are suspect—their
work may not be as intelligent as supposed. In Noah Webster we
have one of the rarest of persons—an intelligent worker, thorough and
productive, who made his mark upon the world while irritating many
persons he came in contact with.

It was not enough that this large- and small-minded man began as
a determined reformer of the spelling system, who put his own method
into practice in his writings, but to save poor spellers from disgrace
he had to go on to produce the little blue-backed spellers, travel the
country organizing spelldowns, and thrust American children into
eternal torture for not mastering a difficult and often contradictory
system. His superb dictionary sold poorly, but he made a name from
the widespread use of his speller in the schools. Two years after his
dictionary came out, Joseph Worcester published his *Comprehensive,
Pronouncing, and Explanatory Dictionary of the English Language,*
which Harold Whitehall says was "actually a thoroughly revised
abridgment of Webster's two-volume work of 1828" and better in many
respects. Worcester was more conservative and upper class in his treatment of language than Webster was, and a battle raged for many
years in America over which of the two dictionaries should be *the*
authority for writers.

Noah pushed himself on countless Americans, including George
Washington, Ben Franklin, and Thomas Jefferson. He needed money
and intended to make it by selling grammatical and spelling books
for the schools. He visited Mount Vernon to obtain a letter of recommendation for his book on spelling. In response to his request, the
General wrote this letter:

Mount Vernon, 6th Novr. 1785

SIR,

This Letter will be handed to you by Mr. Webster whom
I beg leave to introduce to your acquaintance. He is author

of a Grammatical Institute of the English Language—to
which there are very honorable testimonials of its excellence & usefulness. The work must speak for itself; & he,
better than I, can explain his wishes. I am &c.

G. WASHINGTON

If you've dealt with letters of recommendation, you can tell that this
one, addressed to the Governor and Speakers of the Virginia houses
of Legislature, was written in embarrassment by a man who didn't
want to praise Webster or his work. The general was willing to "introduce to your acquaintance" Noah Webster but not to say one good
word for him, not even that he was amiable, honest, courteous, or
well known. If anyone ever writes such a non-testimonial for you,
burn it.

When Webster had difficulty obtaining testimonials for his work,
he wrote anonymous letters to newspapers praising it. He struck many
of his contemporaries as insufferable. Joining the political opposition
to President Thomas Jefferson, he published writings in which he
charged him with "hypocrisy and deception," "imbecility and inconsistency," "vanity," "blind confidence," and an "intolerance des-
potic as it is wicked." This to a president who stood up under attacks
from the press and continued to support the First Amendment to the
Constitution guaranteeing the freedom of the press. Jefferson wrote
his friend Madison that Noah was a "mere pedagogue of very limited
understanding and very strong prejudices and party passions. . . ." That
was an intemperate and inaccurate statement. For his time, Webster
showed a remarkable understanding of language. That a man of
Jefferson's caliber would make it shows that Webster had an incredible capacity for assifying himself [I take that verb from *The
Oxford English Dictionary*, which marks it "jocular"].

As a lexicographer, Noah was a powerhouse. In 1828 at the age of
seventy, he finished his great *American Dictionary of the English
Language*. For several decades he had slurred Dr. Johnson's dictionary,
but he went on to produce a work himself more comprehensive and
accurate in definitions than earlier dictionaries and including more
scientific and technical terms. Here's part of Webster's entry for the
word *lane*—to my mind a model of clarity and distinctions in
meaning:

Lane. 1. A narrow way or passage, or a private passage, as
distinguished from a public road or highway. A lane may be
open to all passengers, or it may be inclosed and appro-
priated to a man's private use. In *the U. States,* the word is

used chiefly in the country, and answers in a degree, to an *alley* in a city. It has sometimes been used for *alley*. In London, the word *lane* is added to the names of streets; as *chancery lane*. [sic]

Webster rightly called his work an *American* dictionary, as you can see from the entry above. Americans needed a dictionary that presented the part of the English language particular to this nation. But as usual, Noah eventually made people sick—in this case, of his patriotism. It's delicious that his great predecessor, Sam Johnson, whom Webster spent so many sentences attacking, is known for the striking remark: "Patriotism is the last refuge of a scoundrel."

> ... *the principal differences between the people of this country and of all others, arise from different forms of government, different laws, institutions and customs. Thus the practice of hawking and hunting, the institution of heraldry, and the feudal system of England originated terms which formed, and some of which now form, a necessary part of the language of that country; but, in the United States, many of these terms are no part of our present language—and they cannot be, for the things which they express do not exist in this country.*
>
> NOAH WEBSTER

The key question I'm searching in this chapter and the next remains to find out how in dictionaries the practice of citing the uses of words began and of what value to us is a series of sentences that exhibit one word in action through the centuries. For an opinion I turn again to the judgment of Joseph Friend, not only because I'm impressed with the thoroughness of the evidence he brings to his comparison of Johnson's and Webster's dictionaries, but also because I remember Fred Reeve speaking of "Joe" with respect, as one of the two general editors of *Webster's New World Dictionary of the American Language,* and his boss for those years Fred spent in Cleveland. I trust Joseph Friend's inspection of the two books because it is more thorough than I have the learning, time, or inclination for; his comments about Webster are fair; and his book is published by Mouton, in the Netherlands, one of the most reputable publishers of books on linguistics in the world. He says that Webster quoted fewer uses of words than Johnson and that he apparently didn't appreciate how

such a listing of uses might speak to a lexicographer's task. Friend
quotes Webster's remark on the subject:

> One of the most objectionable parts of Johnson's Diction-
> ary, in my opinion, is the great number of passages cited
> from authors, to exemplify his definitions. Most English
> words are so familiarly and perfectly understood, and the
> sense of them so little liable to be called in question, that
> they may be safely left to rest on the authority of the lexi-
> cographer, without examples. Who needs extracts from
> three authors, Knolles, Milton, and Berkeley, to prove or
> illustrate the literal meaning of *hand?*

That remark indicates Webster didn't understand that to show the
uses of a word in several different centuries, however consistent, simple, or common those uses are, is as helpful as showing in a biography
of a person that he has remained much the same throughout his life.
In Friend's book and Sledd's and Kolb's, I found a surprising answer
to my question of how the practice of quoting historical uses of words
developed in the English-speaking world and eventually flowered in
The Oxford English Dictionary, whose first part was published in 1884
and last in 1928. These linguists say that Johnson's quotations were
sparse and undated, Webster's less impressive, less representative. And
so it can't be said that the two most famous dictionaries in English
before the OED, Johnson's and Webster's, marked high points in a
slowly developing realization of the usefulness of the historical
approach.

My search for who began a thorough historical approach in lexicography must continue in the next chapter.

> *In general, I have illustrated the signifi-*
> *cations of words, and proved them to be*
> *legitimate, by a short passage from some*
> *respectable author, often abridged from*
> *the whole passage cited by Johnson.*
>
> NOAH WEBSTER

∞ **DOING TWENTY-EIGHT:** Write freely for fifteen minutes (or
longer if you wish) on your early experiences with books or your love
(or hate) affair with words and their meanings. Was there a Mrs.
Flowers in your life? What's your *feeling* about dictionaries? Did the
basketball hoop or the dance floor call you more insistently? You don't
have to answer these questions; I ask them only to stir your memory.
Another entry for your journal, if you want to keep one.

Thus out of words, a puff of air, really,
is made all that is uniquely human.

LOREN EISELEY

chapter 22
historical
lexicography

THIS IS THE SECOND HALF of a report—
begun in the last chapter—of my I-Search to find out how dictionary-
makers evolved the idea of learning the meaning of words by studying
their use through history.

In reading of the great dictionaries by Samuel Johnson, 1755, and
Noah Webster, 1828, I came upon the name of Richard Chenevix
Trench (1807-1886), philologist [student of language] and archbishop
of Dublin. In 1857 he began the actions which answer my I-Search
question. Thinking how badly I searched for this moment in history,
I laugh at myself. In the 1950s when my friend Fred Reeve told me
to read the "Historical Introduction" to *The Oxford English Dictionary,* I did that, and was impressed. Since then, I've looked into
those pages several times, lately to read again how the dated quotations of words were collected for the dictionary. When in 1977 I saw
advertisements for a new book called *Caught in the Web of Words:
James A.H. Murray and the Oxford English Dictionary,* I was
ecstatic. A whole book on the OED and the editor who directed its
making for thirty-eight years, and written by his granddaughter, K. M.
Elisabeth Murray! [I liked those initials for a Scot.] I read that
book a year ago but had forgotten the two pages it contained on
Richard Trench, I suppose because most of the others were about
James Murray. Then at about the same time I began noticing references to Trench in the linguistic books I was reading. In their indexes
I looked up Trench and was convinced he was my man, but there was
not enough in any of the passages to satisfy me. At that point it was
time for me to turn once again to what I had saved for my last
study in this search—a re-reading of the "Historical Introduction"
to the OED. There I came upon better material on Trench.

I found that the Philological Society of England was composed of scholars grounded in a historical approach to language. They believed a new dictionary should be based on the work of the three great linguists of the early 18th century, Rasmus Rask of Denmark, and Franz Bopp and Jacob Grimm of Germany (one of the collectors of the fairy tales that bear his name), who made comparative studies of several languages that would have aided all the lexicographers mentioned so far in my I-Search report had they read them. (After such a grand statement, I should add that I haven't studied them either.) The members of the Philological Society, along with the Early English Text Society, had been working with British dialects and books written in early forms of English known as Anglo-Saxon and Middle English. Consciously and unconsciously these Britishers had been preparing themselves to produce a great historical dictionary of the language. At one of their meetings in 1857, Richard Trench read two papers jointly titled "On Some Deficiences in our English Dictionaries," and the movement that begins to answer my question was under way.

Elisabeth Murray says that Trench "adopted the historical principle in lexicography," which had been employed in *The Greek English Lexicon* of 1843, published in England. "The aim was to show the life history of every word, its origin and any changes of form and meaning." Trench told the Philological Society that

> A Dictionary . . . is an inventory of the language. . . . It is no task of the maker of it to select the good words of a language . . . He is an historian of it, not a critic.

In the last statement Trench was hitting Dr. Johnson and Noah Webster, both of whom, despite occasional statements to the contrary, were concerned about preserving the language at what they considered its best, Johnson going so far as to say in his preface that people should "preserve the wells of English undefiled." Later, the OED editors had similar urges to protect their readers—and themselves—against the dangers inherent in using "vulgar" or taboo words, as I have had myself.

The Philological Society pushed forward. In 1858 the first editors were appointed and in 1884 the first part of the dictionary, containing the words beginning with *A* through *Ant,* was published. In 1928, seventy years from its inception, the work was completed through *Z.*

When the project stalled and foundered, because of manifold causes, including lack of money, sickness, misunderstanding, and irresponsibility, the man who kept it going and maintained its high standards for the longest period of any of the chief editors was James A. H. Murray, a Scotsman, like me, a hardy person who had been sustained on oats. Naturally he was a bookard, but Moebian, interested in the plants, animals, birds, and geology of his native region as well as in its dialects. As a young man he toured parts of Scotland talking to the inhabitants and recording their speech. An I-Searcher by instinct, he was not content to spend all his time in libraries. His granddaughter says that one of the first questions he needed to answer was based "on a discovery he had made as a little boy that the boundary between England and Scotland is artificial, and he established that the border lands which were historically a province of England belonged linguistically to the branch of Anglo-Saxon once spoken . . . in a wide region." In a book called *The Dialect* of *the Southern Counties of Scotland* Murray recorded the languages of the region.

Although sound and solid in his linguistic studies, the young Murray spouted Engfish when he took to giving uplifting public lectures, a sample of which follows:

> Methinks . . . I see in that far-coming land, scenes more glorious, and enchanting than ever have painted the past. I can see that the monsters of Intemperance and War have left the shores of Old Earth, that Labour reigns in royal dignity, that Peace and Plenty dispense their blessings on Young and Old, that rich and poor strong and weak are bound together by the happy laws of indissoluble love, that Earth clothed in living glory has glided into the majesty and beauty of Heaven. . . .

His granddaughter reports that a reviewer criticized Murray the writer for "love of redundancy and empty phrases."

James Murray didn't instigate the system of voluntary readers who supplied the OED with its quotations of words listed in historical order. That had been done by the Philological Society before it hired him as editor. The collection was done in this manner: A list of books to be read was sent to the volunteers, who chose which they would read. On slips of paper they recorded the uses of words, following these directions from the OED editor:

> 1. Make a quotation for *every* word that strikes you as rare, obsolete, old-fashioned, new, peculiar, or used in a peculiar way.
>
> 2. Take special note of passages which show or imply that a word is either new and tentative, or needing explanation as obsolete or archaic, and which thus help to fix the date of its introduction or disuse.

3. Make as *many* quotations *as you can* for ordinary words, especially when they are used significantly, and tend by the context to explain or suggest their own meaning.

In May of 1879 the number of readers volunteering had reached 165. By 1881 there were 800 readers—some in America—and 656,900 quotations had been returned to James Murray. In the complete twelve-volume edition of the OED approximately 1,800,000 quotations were printed. The first set of wooden racks with pigeon holes for alphabetical filing was large enough to accommodate about 85,000 slips. And that was the way the speculation and actuality of making the great dictionary was to go for seventy years. "We'll have it out in ten years," or "another twelve," and the slips grew and the work mushroomed and the financial support became harder to get, until it was 1928 before what had been conceived in 1858 was completed.

Such an enterprise as the OED would have been impossible without the services of hundreds of volunteer readers over the world and dozens of sub-editors. In 1881 Murray noted that a sub-editor had spent forty hours arranging the fifty-one senses of the verb *set* and eighty-three senses of phrases like *set-out, set-off, set-down*. Murray said, ". . . the language seems not to contain a more perplexing word than *Set*, which occupies more than two columns of Webster, and will probably fill three of our large quarto pages." When the whole dictionary was completed, the editors wrote:

> When *Set* finally came to be done, more than thirty years later, it took nearer 40 days than 40 hours to digest the mass of examples which had accumulated by that time; the word occupies a column more than 18 pages of the Dictionary, and extends to 154 main divisions, the last of which (*set up*) has so many subdivisions that it exhausts the alphabet [as a marking-off symbol—a., b., etc.] and repeats the letters down to *rr*.

No one before had put together a dictionary that could compare to the OED in scope and thoroughness. Not only was the derivation or history of forms of the words and the definitions and quotations handled with scholarly care by the editors, but outside experts were frequently consulted before the entry on a word was approved for printing. In 1910 Chief Editor Murray had this to say about such methods. I quote him at length because the passage reads like one of the Grimm brothers' fairy stories:

> I write to the Director of the Royal Botanic Gardens at Kew about the first record of the name of an exotic plant; to a

quay-side merchant at Newcastle about the *Keels* on the Tyne; to a Jesuit father on a point of Roman Catholic Divinity; to the Secretary of the Astronomical Society about the *primum-mobile* or the solar constant; to the Editor of the *Times* for the context of a quotation from the *Times* of 30 years ago; to the India Office about a letter of the year 1620 containing the first mention of *Punch* [the beverage]; to a Wesleyan minister about the *itineracy;* to Lord Tennyson to ask where he got the word *balm-cricket* and what he meant by it, to the *Sporting News* about a term in horse-racing, or pugilism; or the inventor of the word *hooligan* in June 1898; to the Librarian of Cambridge University Library for the reading of the first edition of a rare book; to the Deputy Keeper of the Rolls for the exact reading of a historical M.S. which we have reason to suspect has been inaccurately quoted by Mr. Froude; to a cotton manufacturer for a definition of *Jaconet,* or a technical term of cotton printing; to George Meredith to ask what is the meaning of a line of one of his poems; to Thomas Hardy to ask what is the meaning of a word *terminatory* in one of his novels; to the Editor of the New York *Nation* for the history of an American political term; to the administrator of the Andaman Islands for the exact reference to an early quotation which he has sent for the word *Jute,* or the history of *Talapoin;* to the Mayor of Yarmouth about the word *bloater* in the herring fishery; to the chief Rabbi for the latest views upon the Hebrew *Jubilee;* to a celebrated collector of popular songs for the authorship of 'We don't want to fight, But by *Jingo* if we do', which gave his name to the political *Jingo.*

●   ●   ●

Until I shared an office with Fred Reeve and heard him talk of the ways of lexicographers, I had no notion of many questions that arise in such a job as expressing the meanings of words. In the making of a great dictionary the simple and apparently most obvious questions often yield complex answers. By its title, *The Oxford English Dictionary* suggests its coverage, but what is the English Language? James Murray's granddaughter says, "People spoke of it as if it were a known and well accepted mass of words which could be counted," and added that when James was asked, "How many words are there in the language of Englishmen?" he would answer:

Does it include the English of Scotland and Ireland, the speech of British Englishmen, and American Englishmen,

of Australian Englishmen, South African Englishmen, and
of the Englishmen in India?

The two supplements to the OED published in 1972 and 1976 show
a marked shift toward peculiarly American words, with their quotations, partly I suppose because the United States is a more powerful
country than it was in the 19th century and the British have borrowed
more of its customs and language. Always language changes and
grows. If it didn't, the recording of it wouldn't have interested such
men as Samuel Johnson and James A.H. Murray. Before his death
Sir James—he was knighted by the Queen for his work on the OED—
changed also. In his writing he divested himself of Engfish and often
wrote well, as the following passage from the "General Explanations"
at the beginning of the OED shows. To me it's written as skillfully
as a good poem, and its excellence suggests that when persons have
experienced deeply and over a long time what they're writing about,
they often compose eloquent sentences. I know that I'm presenting a
large number of long quotations in this chapter, but they zero in on
how persons have done great tasks exceedingly well, and that's what
I would be asking them if I could interview them in person. "What is
the essence of the thing you do?" Here's the passage:

> 'Old words' are ever becoming obsolete and dying out:
> 'new words' are continually pressing in. And the death of
> a word is not an event of which the date can be readily
> determined. It is a vanishing process, extending over a
> lengthened period, of which contemporaries never see the
> end. Our own words never become obsolete: it is always the
> words of our grandfathers that have died with them. Even
> after we cease to use a word, the memory of it survives, and
> the word itself survives as a possibility; it is only when no
> one is left to whom its use is still possible, that the word is
> wholly dead. Hence, there are many words of which it is
> doubtful whether they are still to be considered as part of
> the living language; they are alive to some speakers, and
> dead to others. And, on the other hand, there are many
> claimants to admission into the recognized vocabulary
> (where some of them will certainly one day be received),
> that are already current coin with some speakers and writ-
> ers, and not yet 'good English', or even not English at all,
> to others.

Looking again at that passage, I see why Fred Reeve was so anxious
that I read the "Historical Introduction" to the OED. If I had said to
Sir James, sitting in the Scriptorium—the greenhouse-like building in

which the quotation slips were stored and the editors worked—wearing his flat, ancient-scholar style cap, "What's it like, Dr. Murray, doing this crazy thing you and the others do here every day? Isn't it dull? Do you ever joke around?" I don't know what he'd have answered, being the dignified editor he was. But his granddaughter knew he had a sense of humor, unlike that self-righteous Yankee I wrote about earlier in the preceding chapter, and she gave evidence, such as this letter James wrote in 1876 to his friend and fellow philologist, Alexander J. Ellis. At the time, Murray was beset with problems in handling compound words for the dictionary:

> The other day I found myself *chairless,* in one of the rooms, and I am sometimes all but *bootless* and *shoeless,* before I can stir up the local shoemaker. We are not quite *tailorless* and not so obliged to go *trouserless,* like the thoughtless & careless if not quite shameless inhabitants of the *treeless, cultureless, gasless, Daily-paperless* & once *schoolless* regions of the north. The subject is endless & exhaustless, *boundless* & *bottomless* but the raising of it is not *purposeless* I assure you. Then must I not, if a place is *carpenterless,* at times wield the hammer *carpenter-wise* myself—or if my floor is *carpetless* spread it *carpet-wise* with something. . . . A great deal of this applies equally to -ful, -ly, -ism, -ize, etc. Think of this when *sleeplessly* tossing on your bed, or *carriagelessly* scuttling home in the rain. Yours truly, if *breathlessly,* JAHM.

"Dr. Murray, did any of your fun get into the OED itself?"

"Yes, my boy, but seldom. Sometimes, after wasting hours trying to find apt quotations from contemporary sources—you know we aimed to present uses of a word, whenever possible, from Anglo-Saxon days to the present—sometimes I simply had to fashion my own illustrations. Once at my wife's bedside after the birth of Elsie, I was correcting proofs and saw that an example was needed of the word *a* following an adjective preceded by *as.* So I wrote, 'As fine a child as you will see', and labeled it *Mod.*"

When Sir James said that to me, I thought of the problem I had with quotations in this textbook. Since for most chapters I had on file or readily accessible a number of quotations, I thought consistency required that every chapter be supplied with them, but for a few chapters I was wanting some. Thus, like Murray, I made up a couple myself and signed them "Lu Po Hua."

●   ●   ●

The task of reading books to find quotations containing uses that fill out a historical view of a word always has seemed a weird one to me. Sign up for a book, read it, not for sense, but to find words that for some reason the OED needs. I was pleased, therefore, when upon first looking at the 1972 Supplement A-G, I found the editor, R.W. Burchfield, saying that one of the readers who had sent in 100,000 quotations, Marghanita Laski, had written of the experience in *The Times Literary Supplement,* beginning with the issue of January 11, 1968.

Off to the University of New Mexico Library—an hour's drive from my home—look in the microfilm drawers, put the reel onto the scanner, and I learn from Ms. Laski. Interesting that she told her experience in story form. She read an announcement calling for readers to find uses of words that were new, or lacking in the original volumes of the OED. The first use of the term *alley cat* that the OED announced it had was dated 1946, and she thought of archy the cockroach (one of whose poems appears in the chapter "Getting the Point" in this book) and his friend, mehitabel the cat. So she filled out a slip that looked like this:

> 1927 *Don Marquis* Archy and
> Mehitabel iii 7.
> This is the song of mehitabel
> the alley cat.

and the OED sent her more words to look for and books to comb. When I checked my *A-G* volume, I found that other readers had pushed the date back further, to a use of *alley cat* in *The Atlantic Monthly* for 1904 and a Don Marquis use of it in 1916, eleven years before Ms. Laski's citation.

Ms. Laski said that she would never willingly read for the OED a technical book on a subject she didn't know because she would have no sense of what she was reading or any notion of which words might be unusual. Once, she started to read a book called *The Journals of Lady Charlotte Schreiber,* which she thought would be ordinarily autobiographical, but "it turned out to center on China collecting" and she quit reading it. She admits to being a poor speller and becoming lost in researching because once she has misspelled a word, she sometimes can't find the entry in the OED on it.

The thoroughness of James A.H. Murray apparently marks the work of subsequent editors, Henry Bradley, William Craigie, Charles Onions, and R.W. Burchfield. Today, the OED is asking voluntary readers for quotations for words not in the original volumes, for earlier quotations than the original edition carried, for later uses of words that were mistakenly labeled obsolete, etc. Ms. Laski found an example of the latter—*in the straw,* meaning "in childbed" dated 1844 when the OED's last quotation for it was dated 1832. The revisions, the questions, the searching go on. It's not a routine operation. Always decisions must be made that are forced upon the editors by questions such as that of determining "what is the living language" as Sir James asked it in the passage I quoted from him above. Ms. Laski says that there is a story in the OED offices of a man noticing a word card on an editor's desk some years ago, and saying, "I wouldn't bother with that—it won't take." The word, she said, was *brainwash.* The readers look at other things than books. As Ms. Laski says, "All is grist that comes to our mill—posters, packagings, catalogues, menus."

The knowledge that is accumulated by anyone who uses the OED is not merely of the history of words but of the history of things and events and human ways; for words are our names for things, ideas, and relationships, and their history gives us clues to the way human beings behave. From her work, for example, Ms. Laski learned that the "Black Death," as we have been taught to believe people called the plague in the 14th century, was first given that name in 1823. If these people didn't refer to the plague as the "Black Death," what did they think of it? The OED is a record of attitudes and it helps us answer such a profound question as Ms. Laski asks of past societies: "Who and when did they think they were and what did they think they were doing?"

•   •   •

One day I came to an I-Search seminar worrying about the tires on my car wearing out. I had heard from a friend that steel-belted tires would last twice as long as ordinary tires and help the car corner better. But I'd never thought of buying them—I was a child of the Great Depression and thought such purchases were nothing more than "conspicuous consumption," as Thorstein Veblen called it in *The Theory of the Leisure Class.* I told the group I had begun my search and been told by two tire salesmen that U.S. steel-belted tires were no good. Only foreign makes, they said, were satisfactory. So now I wondered. I asked the seminar if any members were authorities on tires, especially steel-belted radials. Three or four had had experience with them. One said his father worked for General Motors and regularly bought steel-belted tires for test cars driven to California and back to Detroit. He recommended one American-made tire as the equal of the foreign-made. I bought the tires he recommended and was amazed at the performance of my car—it cornered and steered as it never had before. Two years later, I must report, owing to a front-end mis-alignment, which no car doctor has been able to cure, one tire has worn badly, but not as yet blown.

While I was thinking about buying steel-belted radial tires, I looked up *tire* in the OED. Some of my findings: Used as a noun, one sense is:

Apparatus, equipment, accoutrement, outfit.

with this as one of the quotations:

1608 SHAKS. *Per.* III.ii.22, I much maruaile that your Lordship, Hauing rich tire about you, should at these early howers, Shake off the golden slumber of repose.

[To understand the abbreviations in any reference work, look for a section explaining them in the front or back of the work. In the OED the list of sources, with names of authors and titles spelled out, appears at the end of the thirteenth volume entitled *Supplement and Bibliography*.]

Sense 5 of *tire* as a noun reads:
A pinafore or apron to protect the dress.

And the next entry for the word as a noun reads:

[Probably the same word as prec., the *tire* being originally (sense 1) the 'attire', 'clothing', or 'accoutrement' of the wheel. From 15th to 17th c. spelt (like prec.) *tire* and *tyre* indifferently . . .]

and then appear these definitions, one after another, interspersed with quotations:

1. *collective sing.* The curved pieces of iron plate, called strakes or streaks, placed end to end or overlapping, with which cart and carriage wheels were formerly shod (now rarely used, and only for heavy agricultural vehicles, artillery carriages, etc.).
2. A rim of metal encompassing the wheel of a vehicle, consisting of a continuous circular hoop of iron or steel.

One of the quotations under that sense is:

1787 BRODIE *Patent Specif.* No. 1599. The tier [sic] is then heated a black red and put on the wheel.

And then the next sense of the word *tire:*

> b. An endless cushion of rubber, solid, hollow, or tubular, fitted (usually in combination with an inner tube filled with compressed air: cf. PNEUMATIC 1 b) on the rim of a bicycle, tricycle, or motor-car; now also often upon the wheels of invalid and baby-carriages, and light horse vehicles. In this sense now commonly spelt *tyre* in Great Britain (see TYRE); *tire* is retained in America.

The first quotation under this sense is:

> 8177 KNIGHT *Dict. Mech.* III. 2579 At the same time Mr. Dunlop patented a tire of annealed cast-iron, grooved to receive an india-rubber band. Various other patents followed, embracing india-rubber as a material to be used for constructing tires.

Surprising. Looking for a steel-belted tire in 1977 I found that in the 19th century Mr. Dunlop had put a rubber belt on an iron wheel. Dunlop? rubber? I was using Dunlop tennis balls at the time and had known that they and Dunlop tires were originally British. In my *Webster's Biographical Dictionary* I looked up Dunlop—John Boyd—and found, appropriately, that he was a Scotsman who had patented a pneumatic tire in 1888, but that

> The principle of the pneumatic tire had been patented in 1846 (See Robert William THOMPSON) but the company, which eventually became the Dunlop Rubber Co., was enabled because of accessory patents to establish rights to the invention.

That didn't sound so good to me—the old patent-swallowing act?—but I had learned, I think, how rubber tires evolved—not in an encyclopedia, but in *The Oxford English Dictionary,* which is, as the editors said, a history of things as well as of words.

> *Neither is a dictionary a bad book to read . . . it is full of suggestions,—the raw material of possible poems and history.*
>
> **RALPH EMERSON**

You'll be asked to use the OED in connection with your I-Search Paper. If Carol Goncalves, the author of "The Sound of My Life," had looked up *Sound* in Samuel Johnson's dictionary of 1755, she would have found this simple, short definition:

> Sound. [Sonde, French.] A shallow sea, such as may be sounded.

If she had looked up the word in Webster's dictionary of 1828 she would have found:

> Sound—n. [Sax, *sund,* a narrow sea or strait, a swimming; SW. Dan. *Sund;* Pers . . . *shana,* a swimming, L. natatio, Qu. Can this name be given to a narrow sea because wild beasts were accustomed to pass it by swimming? like *Bosporous;* or is the word from the root of *Sound,* whole, denoting a stretch, or narrowness, from stretching, like *straight?*]

Wild, Noah, wild, all those beasties swimming around, and stretching narrownesses. My first reaction was to say, "Carol Goncalves, don't trust him." According to many linguists the etymologies provided by both Johnson and Webster were often based on bad guesses rather than sound linguistic knowledge.

If I were Carol, I would have wondered about the verb *sound,* meaning to test the depth of a body of water. Time to turn to the OED.

There I find fifteen columns devoted to meanings of the word *sound.* Scanning them, I find material which shows that Webster had reason for being uncertain. So are the OED editors at times. Here are some of their pertinent entries and comments:

> I.1. The action or power of swimming. *Obs. a* 1300 *Cursor M.* 621 Fiss on sund, and fouxl on flight.
>
> II.4. A relatively narrow channel or stretch of water, esp. one between the mainland and an island, or connecting two large bodies of water; a strait. Also, an inlet of the sea.

Fits Long Island Sound, doesn't it, Carol?

> The first quot. may represent the OE. [Old English] *sund* 'sea, water', but the later use appears to be clearly of Scand. origin. Some writers, associating the word with SOUND *v.*[2], have attempted to limit the application to channels capable of being easily sounded.

You can be sure that the OED editors had consulted Samuel Johnson's dictionary and that he was one of those writers they alluded to. Here are some OED meanings of *sound* as a verb:

> 3.b. Of a whale: To go deep under water; to dive.
> 1839 BEALE *Nat. Hist. Sperm Whale* (ed. 2) 164 The whale suddenly disappears; he has 'sounded'.

4. *trans.* To investigate (water, etc.,) by the use of the line and lead or other means, in order to ascertain the depth or the quality of the bottom; to measure or examine in some way resembling this.

. . . 1762 FALCONER Shipw. II. 249 They sound the well, and . . . Along the line four wetted feet appear.

If Carol Goncalves had done this kind of sounding of the meanings of *sound* in the OED, she might not have discovered buried treasure. One can't know for sure until she tries for it, but in the act of looking she may learn other valuable things about the way words mutate.

•   •   •

After my I-Search for this chapter, I see how a dictionary may be genuinely historical, and illimitably fascinating and helpful. History. Story. The story of the words a dictionary is filled with. In collecting slips of word use for the OED, Marghanita Laski was acting not as drudge but as learner. For example, reading through the works of an author consecutively, and then other authors' works, she found that some writers start in youth with rich vocabularies and continue writing without adding new words to their store. Sinclair Lewis, the American author of *Babbitt* and *Main Street,* was one.

Ms. Laski's remark reminded me of the Great Year of Increasing My Vocabulary. It was in Pittsburgh, Pennsylvania, my first year out of college. I was working at office jobs for fifty dollars a week, going to night school at Carnegie Tech to study typography and printing; and I was full of zeal to improve myself—a veritable, but smaller, Benjamin Franklin. I had no television, I lived in a classic rented garret in a private residence, where the heat was inadequate. At night I would jump in bed, prop up two pillows, and read. My plan was to read good books with difficult vocabularies and look up and learn every unfamiliar word I came across, an excellent idea because I would be starting with words in real environments, in sentences where they belonged and were making sense, not in a list of words assigned for a test.

Sometimes I would forget to take my *Webster's Collegiate Dictionary* (Merriam's) to bed with me. Like a Hindu mystic I had disciplined myself—not to let a strange word go by unlooked up. Several times I remember staring across the cold floor at the dictionary in a bookshelf on the other side of the room, and debating. But with religious dedication, I always rose from the bed and retrieved it. I said to myself, "You will be more uncomfortable having failed to get the dictionary than you will be staying in the warm bed." The book that required the most trips across the room was Thomas Carlyle's *Sartor Resartus* (the tailor retailored). It's a funny book, but the fun depends on one's knowing Carlyle's large vocabulary—*prolixity, ineptitude, tortuosity,* etc. By dint of will power and bare feet on cold floor, I caught most of the humor in the book.

In that year, so crowded with work, I learned and retained the meaning of more words than I had in any other since being countenanced at Mother's knee. The point to the story is that I learned the words in green environments, in sentences I wanted to understand. These new faces didn't stand alone; they enjoyed helpful conversation with neighbors. A word is not itself except, Moebianly, with others. It has a place in each sentence it appears in, and that place affects, shifts, weights, transmutes, colors its meaning. I've culled from here and there in the columns on *sound* in the OED a number of uses of the word. I think they would speak to Carol Goncalves, who was so affected by Long Island Sound and its effect upon the noises she heard when near it. [The following are not presented in chronological order]:

> He will give you a sound beating.
> Their old theory, sound or unsound, was at least complete and coherent.
> Some night he begins to sleep sound.
> The trumpets sounded to horse.
> That sounds like nonsense, my dear.
> Their words are sounded rather like that of Apes then men. . . . [sic]
> Having previously introduced a metallic instrument, called a sound, into the bladder, and plainly felt the stone.
> He sounded Butler on this subject, asking what he would think of an English living.
> The sowne of swarming bees.
> Several little isles, divided by narrow and dangerous sounds.

In a great dictionary like the OED, each of the quoted sentences has a place among the other sentences that contain that word. Putting together sentences in historical order tells the life of that word through time, into our time. The word has meant different things in its lifetime; and we can respect its virtuosity; but when it occurs in a sentence that *we* write or read, it takes on a present meaning in us and because of us, as well as because of its past. Words take on their meanings from use, and we are their users. Another Moebian happening, whose significance arises at that instant when the old and new turn on the Loop and slide into each other.

•   •   •

Now for you and a dictionary. Wherever you are, locate a set of the OED. College libraries carry it and most public libraries, few high-school libraries. A two-volume, tiny-print Compact Edition, to be read by a hand-held magnifying glass is available as well as the thirteen-volumed, supplemented large edition.

But few students can afford the OED. On your personal reference shelf you need a one-volume college desk dictionary that's easy to handle. If you buy one, know what you're getting. And for that, a little story. The G. & C. Merriam Company of Springfield, Massachusetts, bought the unbound sheets of the 1841 edition of Noah Webster's dictionary from his heirs. That started a series of "Webster's" dictionaries that are still published today. The company eventually formed its own corps of lexicographers and, according to Harold Whitehall (another man Fred Reeve spoke highly of, who worked on *Webster's New World Dictionary*), produced in 1864 "one of the best dictionaries ever to appear." The sad thing about the legacy of Noah is that the books bearing his name have little if any connections with his great dictionary of 1828. And the amusing thing is—if you're not victim of the joke—that Webster's name has been placed upon all sorts of works that he had nothing to do with, and that in no way derived from his work. For example, G. and C. Merriam, having bought his dictionary, and knowing the value of the name that had been spread throughout the country by those blue-backed spellers, decided they had bought the name as well, to use as they wished. So they laid it on all sorts of their first-rate publications, including *Webster's Biographical Dictionary* and *Webster's Thesaurus*. For years lawsuits raged between Merriam and other companies over the right to use Webster's name on dictionaries. Today ignorant librarians—and I hate to use that adjective because most librarians I've met are a superior race of beings—often list those books and others under "Webster, Noah," in their card catalogs. Such a mislisting occurs even in the card catalog of my beloved Zimmerman Library at the University of New Mexico. And, even worse, "Fred's book," *Webster's New World Dictionary*, connects in no way to Noah Webster but there stands Noah's last name on the cover of the second college edition in yellow letters an inch and a quarter high.

Beyond all these misuses of Noah's name (which seem poetic justice to me for a man who puffed himself so hard during his lifetime) is the labeling of the superficial and carelessly put together and pirated drugstore and dime-store dictionaries that carry his name. Be careful when you buy a dictionary. The name *Webster* doesn't necessarily mean anything on it, but two of the best desk dictionaries carry it—*Webster's Collegiate* and *Webster's New World*. They and *The American Heritage Dictionary*, college edition, are scholarly works of the first order and in their opening and closing pages carry valuable discussions of pronunciation, spelling, etc. In *Webster's New World*, first edition, appears a thorough essay on the English language by Harold Whitehall, and in the second edition, one by Charlton Laird. The *American Heritage Dictionary* furnishes brilliant essays on language matters as well as a long listing of the Indo-European roots of English words.

∞ **DOING TWENTY-NINE:** Choose two or three key words or terms in your I-Search and look them up in the OED. For one of them record some of the things you found that interested or enlightened you, as I did in my search of the word *tire*—meaning changes, dated quotations, changes in forms of words, or whatever. If you're lucky you'll learn things that light the way of your I-Search. At the least, you'll find a line or a spelling that can ornament your paper. Bring the report to your seminar or group dittoed or xeroxed to share with others.

∞ **DOING THIRTY:** Think of someone you love, inside or outside your family, and of what they love—tennis? making pickles, cabinets, or philosophy? Whatever. In the OED look up a key word involved in that activity or the name of the thing itself and make a brief report for her or him on that word, as I did above for the word *tire*. Then send or hand the report to that person.

∞ **DOING THIRTY-ONE:** Spend a half hour wandering in the OED as you wandered in the library as described in DOING TWENTY-FIVE, without any purpose but enjoyment. Follow your interests through the words that name them, or follow nothing at all, just letting the pages fall open and your slow eyes look at that language as they will.

> *"Danny, don't say* ol' knight, *say* old
> knight. *Can't you see the* d? *You must
> learn to pronounce words the way they
> are written." The fact that even the
> teacher does not pronounce the* k, *the*
> g, *or the* h *in* knight *is seldom con-
> sidered at this point.*
>
> L. M. MYERS

chapter 23
spellynge
spellyng
spelling

WRITING AS WE KNOW IT is supposed to
be an alphabetical system representing the sounds of spoken words.

If you were a normal, thoughtful child, when you first encountered
printed words, you became upset when you found that the *ee* sound in
American-English is spelled in different ways: for example, *peak, peek;
believe, receive*. Or you became angry when told that one sound
sometimes has two different spellings and meanings, for example: *bred,
bread*. Or dumbfounded when you learned that the letters *k* in *knee*
and *p* in *psychology* aren't pronounced at all, along with all those
silent *e*'s at the ends of words like *bite* and *lope*. We have twenty-
six letters in our alphabet but forty some significant sounds, or
phonemes, in our spoken language. A phoneme is a unit of sound that
with other phonemes marks off or distinguishes one word from another. For example, the *th* in *thy,* a favorite word of Quakers, is
pronounced differently from the *th* in *thigh. Thy* is written with three
letters, *thigh* with five, although both carry only two significant
sounds—*th* and *i*. The word *them* carries three significant sounds. The
word *kick* also has three significant sounds, the first and third being
the same but represented by different letters—*k* and *ck*. These facts
spell t-r-o-u-b-l-e.

If you find our spelling system outrageous and feel defeated trying to get it right, know that you have had company. In 1580 a British school teacher named William Bullokar published a reformed spelling system, because, as he said,

> . . . the very voyce of children, who guided by the eye with the letter, and giving voyce according to the name thereof, as they were taught to name letters, yeelded to the eare of the hearer a cleane contrary sound to the word looked for. Heereby grewe quarels in the teacher, a lothsomenesse in the learner, and great payne to both. . . .

In 1768 Benjamin Franklin wrote *A Scheme for a New Alphabet and Reformed Mode of Spelling.* He thought letters, or graphemes, were needed, for example, for the two significant sounds represented by the grapheme *th.* Of his proposal for "rectifying our alphabet," he wrote a friend, "The true question then is not whether there will be no difficulties or inconveniences but whether the conveniences will not, on the whole, be greater than the inconveniences."

In 1783 Noah Webster printed in a textbook simpler spellings for English words. He talked with and corresponded with Ben Franklin about spelling reform, and himself advocated such spellings as *bred, hed, giv, brest, bilt, ment,* and *frend, skool, reezons, kee, tuf,* and *masheen.* But gradually he backed down from most of these reforms, publishing only a few in his great 1828 dictionary and fewer in its 1841 edition. A handful of his reforms have survived in American usage: for example, *honor,* for *honour* and *center* for *centre.*

In 1906 when President "Teddy" Roosevelt was approached by a group of reformers called the Simplified Spelling Board, he directed the public printer to employ three hundred simplified spellings, including such as *tho, thru, program,* and *whisky* for *though, through, programme,* and *whiskey.* For a number of years *The Chicago Tribune* used such simplified spellings.

In 1950 when George Bernard Shaw, the British music and drama critic, political reformer, and writer of plays such as *Saint Joan* and *Pygmalion,* died, he left a will providing money for the design and introduction of a new English alphabet whose individual symbols would represent all the phonemes in English words.

In 1961 Sir James Pitman introduced into English schools the Initial Teaching Alphabet, whose forty-four symbols reproduce all the phonemes, making it easy for children in the first year of school to spell. After they had used writing for communicating with other people rather than for fulfilling exercises in grammar and spelling, and after several years of reading, they were able to switch over to conventional spelling with much less difficulty than children who hadn't begun with i.t.a. An edition of A.A. Milne's *Winnie the Pooh* has been printed in the i.t.a. alphabet should you care to inspect it. The i.t.a. movement was launched also in the United States with considerable success, but it did not supplant the conventional spelling system.

All these spelling reformers, and several more I haven't mentioned, failed in their attempt to replace the standard system. A look back into history may show why.

In the Elizabethan Age dictionaries were common, but unlike our present-day ones. Most were specialized aids for a trade or profession, and those that were general were nothing more than lists of fancy words. A simple word was given and then a string of alternatives— for writers who wanted to sound superior or erudite. Other dictionaries listed the fancy words and defined them with simple ones, as in these entries from Cockeram's *Dictionarie* of 1623, which might be called a book for translating Engfish into English.

> *Indagation.* A searching.
> *Sorditude.* Filthinesse.
> *Collachrimation.* A weeping with.

Since there was no one authoritative book which listed and defined the majority of common and technical words, writers naturally spelled a word in different ways, just as long as its letters did a fair job of indicating the sound of the spoken word. Here's Shakespeare's Sonnet 56 as he, with the aid of his printer, spelled it:

> Sweet love renew thy force, be it not said
> Thy edge should blunter be then apetite,
> Which but too daie by feeding is alaied,
> To morrow sharpned in his former might.
> So love be thou, although too daie thou fill
> They hungrie eies, even till they winck with fulnesse,
> Too morrow see againe, and doe not kill
> The spirit of Love, with a perpetual dulnesse:
> Let this sad Intrim like the Ocean be
> Which parts the shore, where two contracted new,
> Come daily to the banckes, that when they see
> Returne of love, more blest may be the view.
>   Or cal it Winter, which being ful of care,
>   Makes Sommers welcome, thrice more wish'd, more rare.

Reading those words aloud, you'll hear that the spelling is representing the sound of the words faithfully: *alaied—allayed, winck—wink, cal—call.* How much fun it would have been to write in those days!

I'm a champion speller myself, but all the more reason for me to savor this I-could-care-less spelling. I like to see all the ways a word can be written and still indicate the sounds of speech. I doubt that anyone these days could get into college if he spelled the word *today* in the way Shakespeare did in Sonnet 56. Maybe a student could get away with *to-day,* but not *too daie.* And what an ignoramus Shakespeare was to put down *to morrow* in the same poem with *too morrow!* No consistency. But consider for a moment our spelling of the word *today. Day* is a noun denoting one of those parts of a week. What sense does *to* make in front of it? A look at *The Oxford English Dictionary* shows that authors like Thoreau and Emerson, writing in the mid-19th century, spelled the word *to-day.* And that *to* once meant "this." Apparently it was a common meaning for *to.* The OED lists the word *to-year,* now a dialect form, meaning "this year." In "The Wife of Bath's Prologue," ca. 1386, Chaucer wrote "Yet hadde I levere wedde no wyf to-yeere." ["Yet I'd rather not wed a wife this year."] Language changes.

I find even more delicious the spelling in a poem by John Skelton, published about 1650, after Shakespeare's sonnet. [Note: a marmoset is a soft-furred South American monkey.)

LA BELLA BONA-ROBA
I cannot tell who loves the Skeleton
of a poor Marmoset, nought but boan, boan.
Give me a nakednesse with her cloath's on.

Such whose white sattin upper coat of skin,
Cut upon velvet rich Incarnadin,
Ha's yet a Body (and of Flesh) within.

Skelton's spelling reminds me of a passage written by Kathy, a fourth-grader in the class I visited in the 1970s.

When I watered the calves I spilted the water on my self becose the two calves made me spell it and then I wen't up to tell my mom. The calves barn steks. And when the like you whith thay tung it tikls. And when they kike you it smarts. And when you feel then it fell's like bon's.

Some confusing spellings in that paragraph—*steks* for *stinks, then* for *them, the* for *they,* and *fell's* for *feels;* but generally the words are spelled upon Elizabethan or present-day patterns. Professor Yetta Goodman of the University of Arizona, an authority on children's language, calls this kind of writing "Inventive Spelling." It represents a child on the way toward standard spelling, guessing how to represent the sounds of the words she wants to use. The *ed* ending on *spilted* follows the pattern of *watered*. The ending of *becose* would rhyme with *Oz*. *Whith* is a logical way to spell *with*, on the pattern of *whither* or *when*. *Tung* and *tikls* look like Noah Webster spellings. *Thay* for *their* is close. The apostrophe before the *s* in *bon's* makes a plural like Skelton's *cloath's*. The final unsounded *e* in *kike* (kick) follows a practice of Chaucer's and Shakespeare's time. Note Skelton's *nakednesse*.

Once when I was reading a book called *The English Language: Background for Writing* by W. Nelson Francis, a scholar without pretension and with great good sense, I came upon this statement:

> In the seventeenth and early eighteenth centuries it was not considered essential even for people (especially women) of some position in the world to follow a consistent standard in their spelling.

I knew that shocking statement to be true because Nelson Francis had made it, and I suddenly remembered my surprise at reading some of the letters of Deborah Franklin, Ben's wife. Here's one she wrote to him on December 13, 1766:

> The Profile is Cume Safe and is the thing as everey one ses that has seen it I am verey much obliged to you for it every bodey knows it that has seen it. As to the Candil sticks and Corke Screw thay will doe when you return in the Spring. Be So good as to give my love to Mrs. Stephenson and her Dafter tell me is Polley is a going to be marreyed. I think you sed sum such thing sum time a go. When Shee dus I hope it will be to one that will deserve her. It Semes a dought with me wather Salley writes by this Ship as shee is setting for her Pickter for her Brother Shee is to be playing on the Armonekey. The vesill is gon down so I muste seel this all thow I have not got aresete [receipt] for the things. I am your a feckshonet wife
>
> D FRANKLIN

A lovely, relaxed letter. Two years ago I wouldn't have known that, before I taught myself (it involved a kind of unteaching) how to read an eccentrically spelled letter for meaning rather than spelling.

Deborah's letter is proof on Nelson Francis's side. What a rotten way of putting women down! To expect less of them in spelling. But I hear Deborah's letters rightly.

Today, kids in school who weren't born into bookard families—and some who were—have difficulty with spelling. When teachers who demand perfection deride them for mistakes, they sometimes block on the task so severely that they can't distinguish any sensible patterns in the system. I'm not exaggerating or imagining this behavior on the part of some teachers. And they've been joined by other bigots in our society for many years. In 1899, in *The Theory of the Leisure Class,* Thorstein Veblen wrote:

> English orthography [spelling] satisfies all the requirements of the canons of reputability under the law of conspicuous waste. It is archaic, cumbrous, and ineffective; its acquisition consumes much time and effort; failure to acquire it is easy of detection. Therefore it is the first and readiest test of reputability in learning, and conformity to its ritual is indispensable to a blameless scholastic life.

If Veblen's language throws you, let me say that he wrote that way on purpose, to sound formal and scholarly while making sarcastic remarks about people who enjoy putting others down.

Those who haven't learned to spell beautifully should take comfort in the fact that there are thousands of others like them in the country—so many, in fact, that a paperback is published by Random House called *The Bad Speller's Dictionary,* which helps you find a word if you don't know how to spell it. This book shows the patterns and their exceptions. We master spelling, as we do writing, to a large extent unconsciously. Many of us don't notice that our system does strange things, such as employing the letter *c* to represent the sounds *k* and *ess,* as in *dacron* and *Cynthia,* but we have no trouble spelling the words. Yet if we're demoralized by our spelling experiences in school, we may have trouble with every such inconsistency.

> *Some combinations of letters* . . . choak, choke; soap, sope; fewel, fuel . . . *I have sometimes inserted twice, that those who search for them under either form, may not search in vain.*
>
> SAMUEL JOHNSON

You may be wondering why all the efforts to reform the spelling system have failed. There are several reasons. Language is human behavior, and for one person to change the habits of large numbers of people in one sweeping action is rare in history. To create and use a new alphabet would require printers to buy new type and to reprint books, magazines, and newspapers already on file in libraries; for eventually the new spellers would lose the ability to read works set in the old spelling. Words in the new alphabet would look so different on the page that the great works of religion and literature might seem foreign to readers who had known them in their original form.

Beyond these objections to a new alphabet is the point brought out by Professor Wayne O'Neil of the Massachusetts Institute of Technology in his article "The Spelling and Pronunciation of English," in *The American Heritage Dictionary*. He says that despite its apparent inconsistencies, standard American-English spelling helps readers keep the meanings of related forms of words in mind and operates with a consistency so subtle that few people notice it.

For example, Professor O'Neil says, take the item (not the word) *telegraph–*. As a verb, *telegraph* is stressed on the first syllable. The adjective *telegraphic* is stressed on the third syllable. The noun *telegraphy* is stressed on the second syllable. Now I'm going to suppose that we spelled according to the International Phonetic Alphabet (which represents the sound of speech more faithfully than our present alphabet and is used in dictionaries to indicate pronunciation). We would see the basic item written this way, with the upside down *e* or *schwa* used to indicate the "uh" sound that *e* and the other vowels (a,i,o,u) sometimes take.

tel'ə graf

The adjective and noun built upon that item are pronounced with the schwa sound in different positions, so the basic item is lost to the eye:

tel ə graf'ik (adjective)
tə leg' ra fē (noun)

Many of our words follow similar patterns. The item *object–*, for example, is pronounced with different stress and sound in

əb jekt' (verb)
äb' jikt (noun)

If we spelled our words with the phonetic alphabet, we might not see that the word *objective* carries in it the item *object–*, because one was written with a *jekt* and the other a *jikt*. So, in one way, our standard alphabet makes spelling more difficult but reading more meaningful.

Despite its eccentricities, the standard spelling system is highly consistent and logical, and it can be learned by anyone who genuinely wants to learn it. Not to perfection—no one knows how to spell all the words in the American-English lexicon or keeps all the patterns straight.

If you want to improve your spelling, let yourself become attracted to the faces of words, as if they're the faces of people. Abandon yourself shamelessly to words. Stare rudely at them. When you sit before the television screen, gape at the words projected there. On the way to class, let yourself become hypnotized by the words you pass—on store windows, posters, car cards on buses, or billboards on the highways. Study the words on the spines of books in the office of a teacher you're waiting to see. Break them down into recognizable or familiar parts. Look for patterns. Before you begin reading an assignment at night, spend thirty seconds or a minute studying the spelling of words that appear strange to you.

If you make spelling a self-inflicted torture, you'll never stay at it long enough to improve in it. Spend many short intervals on a few words—perhaps five minutes three times a day—rather than long periods poring over lists of words that soon become confused in your mind.

Probably many people are poor spellers because they were not countenanced in school and didn't countenance themselves as learners. They and their teachers centered on the relatively few inconsistent or confusing spellings and the result was dismay and fright. "Cite, sight, site," said the teacher or the spelling book, and the child gave up. Suppose, instead, you start with common and consistent patterns.

All the words that rhyme with *at,* says spelling expert Ralph M. Williams, end with *at.*

And then there's this pattern, that you can figure out for yourself:

rate	rat	note	sit
rating	ratting	noting	sitting

Try it on other words that end consonant-vowel-consonant-*e,* or consonant-vowel-consonant.

relate	intermit	begin
relating	intermitting	beginning
stagnate	intermittent	sin
stagnating		sinning

Pronounce the words and study the spelling patterns. They're consistent. If you make up nonsense words on the same patterns as those above, you'll remember them better:

bipe	bip
biping	bipping
	bippen

For words that give you trouble again and again, no matter how many times you study them, invent devices for remembering their standard spelling. Memory experts say your devices should be personal, with meaning in *your* experience. Here are some I invented for four commonly misspelled words. They might help you, but don't use them unless they seem to stick in your mind. Invent your own.

1. environment, often misspelled "enviorment"; env *iron* ment
   I remember iron mines in the environment I once visited in Minnesota.
2. competition, sometimes mispelled "compitition" or "compitetion"
   The word *petition* is in there, and pet is the opposite of the competitive spirit.
3. conscientious, often misspelled "conscious"
   I know how to spell *con* and *science. Conscien*-tious.
4. psychology, usually misspelled "physcology" in imitation of *physics.*
   The heart of the word is *sych.* I know a man named "Sy." *Ch* often makes a *k* sound.

I've known a number of experts in language, who were interested in all aspects of grammar and spelling but not in making fun of people who have trouble with grammar and spelling. One, who enjoys studying the spelling system, wrote this to me in a letter the other day:

> The old way of remembering the spelling of *ie* words is wrong, and it was shown to be wrong in the 1930s (in a U. of Iowa dissertation), but it continues rolling merrily wrong and will no doubt do so till the end of the world (at least our world), and one may well contemplate why that is. Correct rule applies to over 100 words and has very few exceptions. When the sound is like *ee* then *i* before *e;* when the sound is not like *ee,* then *e* before *i.* Now here's the history. The rules were formed during a period of British history when pronunciation was different from now; hence, *seize* was pronounced *sez.* And of course *leisure* was *lehsure* and *either* was *i-ther* (just as the British pronounce them now). Earlier pronounciations [That's what he wrote, a misspelling of *pronunciations,* one of the most likely words to misspell] of *sheik* (shak) and *inveigle* (in va gl) also were different. These can be checked in the OED.

I think that's a delightful spelling discussion, by Professor William D. Baker of Wright State University, Dayton, Ohio. And it shows you that even spelling experts misspell.

The very mistakes that spelling purists say indicate illiteracy are made in the most distinguished publications. Because everyone who has gone through high school has been drilled on the difference between *their, they're,* and *there,* and *its* (possessive) and *it's* (it is), and *to, too,* and *two,* say the purists, no one past eighteen can be excused for confusing them in writing. On the contrary, such soundalikes are exactly the words that we should expect to confuse in writing, whether we are highly or lowly literate. Note:

Headline in The New York Times, *May 12, 1977:*

Professors' Association Criticizes
Way City University Cut *It's* Staffs

Announcement on a card sent to teachers across the country:

The Conference on English Education, an organization concerned with the education of teachers of English, publishes *it's* Newsletter . . .

From a book review in The Gazette Telegraph, *Colorado Springs, February 24, 1979:*

Who has the most liberal views on premarital sex? [and a few lines later:] In India, 73 percent said premartial sex should be avoided. . . .

That makes a good joke—premartial sex (*martial* meaning "connected with war"), but when the joke is on professionals, it doesn't seem a joke any more to the purists. Then they say, "Well, newspaper people are under such time pressures." And I say, "Students are under time pressures."

We all make errors, professionals and amateurs alike, and often the same errors—where confusion is most likely to occur. The point is not that we should excuse carelessness or error because we see them in professionals' work as well as our own, but that we should forgive each other our trespasses. We can expect higher performance from professionals than from amateurs, but perfection from neither. The practice, still followed by a few composition teachers, of failing a paper if it has more than, say, ten spelling errors, or five, or whatever, by its very nature suggests that perfection is possible. In publishing, it's not achieved, as I've demonstrated in the chapter on editing.

> *Never mind it, Sir; perhaps your friend*
> *spells* ocean *with an* s.
>
> SAMUEL JOHNSON

If you keep misspelling a word after the error has been pointed out to you, don't despair. Everyone does that at times, usually because they're being smart, following other patterns of spelling in the language. Six of the commonest misspelled words I've seen in thirty years of teaching are *separate, commercial, privilege, similar, writing,* and *procedure.* Three of them are usually misspelled inventively, on a pattern logical and phonetic:

separate (misspelled as):	seperate (on the pattern of):	operate
privilege	priviledge	ledge
procedure	proceedure	proceed

Commercial reminds some people of *numerical* and comes out *commerical. Similar* reminds them of *familiar* and comes out *similiar. Writing* reminds them of *written* and comes out *writting.* That last mistake is a dumb one, because *write* belongs to the group of words spelled like *lope* and *bite.* Often we find our pens or typewriters producing a common letter combination but in the wrong word, as if our fingers are not in our control.

The wildest graphemes in our language are probably *gh* and *ph.* The *gh* in *ghost* is pronounced like the *g* in *goes,* but the *gh* in *tough* like the letter *f.* In the headpiece of this chapter L.M. Myers points out rightly that the word *knight* isn't spelled phonetically. George Bernard Shaw said "The spelling l-i-g-h-t is simply insane." I agree with these men, who happen to be among the people I've most admired in my life. But persons setting out to improve their spelling might better say, *"Knight* and *light* are spelled ridiculously but on a pattern with a number of other words" [I've already used two of them in this paragraph]:

right	night	slight	wight
blight	sight	fright	playwright
might	flight	tight	bright

and so they're not alone out there and consequently hard to remember. In all these rhyming words the *gh* is silent, as it is in the words *ought, bought, sought,* and *brought.* And the silent *k* in *knight* has many comrades, in such words as *know, knowledge, knuckle, Knoxville, knot, knickers, knish, knit, knob, knave, knead, knee, knack, knell, knife.* Each of these *k's,* I note, is followed by an *n* that is the significant grapheme at that point.

In *pneumonia, pneumatic,* and *psychology,* the *p* is not pronounced. And the words are all derived from Greek, as your dictionary will tell you. I'm finding patterns for you now, but if you're going to improve your spelling, you need to find them on your own as well. Look in your dictionary or any printed pages for patterns. Say aloud words you know, and listen for patterns.

Think of beginnings and endings to words—prefixes and suffixes. All those knowledge words, for example, that end in *–ology* or *–ological*. Or the words that carry *gn* with the *g* not pronounced: *sign, align, assign, malign, design*. And those that carry *gn* not representing one phoneme, but two, and pronounced differently from those above:

signal	significant	signatory
signet	signature	

All of those words come out of or include the item *sign–*, but in them the *i* changes from long to short in pronunciation, another pattern for you to store away. You don't have to memorize such patterns or rules, just note them. Once you've made that sort of connection for yourself, it will print on your memory and emerge again at a useful time. If you look at the faces often enough, they'll become familiar and you'll think they couldn't look any other way than they do. For example, reading a child's paper written in the i.t.a. alphabet I found the word *once* spelled *wuns*. Not until I saw *wuns* did I realize how unphonetically standard spelling represents that word. I've seen *once* so many times that it looks right to me, although I doubt that anyone hearing it for the first time would ever put down *o-n-c-e* as a representation of its sound.

If you approach improving your spelling as a task that you must master or live in disgrace, nothing much will stick in your mind. But if you allow yourself to become interested in the way spelling has evolved into a more and more consistent system, you'll learn with little effort.

•   •   •

For several years I've believed that the cause of writing would be best served if we reverted to what I've sneakily termed "Shakespearean Spelling" (I could also call it "Mrs. Ben Franklin's Spelling") in which persons could write *boan* or *bone,* or *afeckshonet* or *affectionate,* without censure, as long as they came close to representing the sound of the word. But Wayne O'Neil's point gives me pause, for I see that the standard spelling system helps show the relationship of words or parts of words that indicate *meaning,* which is the fundamental in all writing and speaking. The spelling reform we now need, I believe, is a reform of teachers and people outside school who unwittingly use correct spelling as a weapon to keep other people down, as Thorstein Veblen suggested.

Some people learn spelling faster than others; but everyone can see the patterns in the standard spelling system, because they are there. And they can move toward mastering them, as Kathy was doing when she wrote that she "spilted the water." All of us—teachers, students, parents, and professionals—need to learn to read a badly spelled passage first for its meaning and second for its spelling. And then we need to countenance others and ourselves so that all of us improve in standard spelling. We need to understand that before Dr. Johnson's dictionary of 1755, the greatest writers, scholars, and religious leaders got along with a highly phonetic spelling that allowed variant forms for a word, and only as dictionaries and other printed matter proliferated did a single spelling standard emerge. Correct spelling has obsessed Americans ever since then.

Writing a whole chapter about spelling in this book, I'm running the risk of implying that writing exists for spelling rather than the other way around. One of the principal reasons Americans fear writing so much is that school has taught them that what they say on paper must be perfect in spelling and grammar or it's not worth anyone's attention. As Donald Graves of the University of New Hampshire has said, Americans are taught to believe that writing is more a matter of etiquette than of communication. Few of the closest students of language feel that way. Here, for example, is Professor Harold Whitehall summing up the point beautifully:

> Since English spelling is so completely arbitrary—irreducible to a correspondence of single sound to single letter as in Finnish or to recurrent groups of letters as in French—we are forced to rely upon an indirect and haphazard method of mastering it. But if the method fails and we still want to write, we should never let the feeling that we cannot spell prevent us from writing.

You can write any time people will leave
you alone and not interrupt you.

ERNEST HEMINGWAY

chapter 24
"can I
become
a writer?"

Dear Mr. Macrorie,

I AM A STUDENT of Bunnell High School [Stratford, Connecticut]. . . . I was hoping you could help me out by answering some questions.

(1) Did you attend a journalism college or major in journalism? If not, do you think a "writing" education is essential for success?

(2) Was writing always a set goal for you? If so, how old were you when you finalized this decision and what inspired you?

(3) Are there many job opportunities for writers in your community? In Michigan?

(4) Do you feel that a writer new to the field could support himself on writing alone?

(5) What inspires your writing?

(6) What are your motives for writing?

I would like to be a writer. . . . Your *Writing To Be Read* has helped me tremendously. . . . Thank you for realizing us. A lot of teachers seldom do.

Many Thanks,

/s/ CATHY SULLIVAN

Dear Cathy Sullivan,

I'm glad you wrote, because lately I've thought a lot about both what makes a writer and how to ask questions. What you sent me was an informal questionnaire. Seven years ago I quit answering questionnaires because most of them don't allow me to say what would be valuable to the questioner and me. So instead, I'll tell you a little story and make some comments.

Several years ago my wife (who has been a painter, etcher, metalsmith, and writer) and I sat down and asked each other, "What makes an artist?" A useful question because we, the answerers, were also the askers. It was not part of someone else's questionnaire into which we had to fit.

After an enjoyable half hour we agreed that "An artist is someone who can't keep from steadily producing art works." And so with writing. A writer is someone who writes—frequently, constantly (that doesn't mean continuously), not necessarily someone who goes to writing school or talks about becoming a writer. A *professional* writer is one who gets paid for writing.

I think the question you want to ask is, "Can I become a professional writer?" My answer is, "Sure. Anyone can who wants to strongly enough." But whether you want to strongly enough I don't know, and you don't know. Watch yourself and see.

Next week you might watch yourself writing an article that is accepted by *The Atlantic Monthly* or a play that is produced on Broadway. You might be that good and lucky. But chances are several million to one against such flaming success. More likely you will find out you are a writer if you—

(1) Get in the habit of writing of what you care about so much that you can taste it constantly on the back of your tongue as you walk through every ordinary day.

(2) Cultivate such a respect for truth and facts (whether you find them in Waterbury or dream them in Wonderland) that you feel sick when you start to write a false or pretentious phrase.

(3) Want so much to see your name and words in print that you immediately write works right for the publications nearest you: in school—the newspaper, the yearbook, the literary magazine; in the community—the shoppers' guide, the newspaper, and regional magazines. If the school literary magazine is phony and pretentious, you'll make it more honest, so it means something to readers. Or with other students you'll found a broadsheet of truthful writing that competes with it. Once you see your name and words in print—if you're normally, writerly insane—you won't be satisfied until you see them in print again and again. You won't be able to break the habit.

(4) Strengthen your stomach muscles so that each time you open an envelope containing a rejection slip your gut grows harder.

(5) Make your way. Investigate possibilities. What are you expert in? Do you raise sheep? Then submit articles to Future Farmer or 4-H publications, local or national. What's being done unusually well in your town? You can get to know that well because it's there, available. Maybe an old man has revived 19th-century cabinetry work. Maybe a great American woman lived or worked in your region. Maybe your town has built an enterprise on and out of somebody known around the world—say, a writer, like William Shakespeare. And *you* live in this Shakespeare town. Down the street, every year, you see his plays. And you read them at home. That's an unusual life for an American high-school student: you can tell the story to other people in the country.

(6) Remember that publishers have to pay their printing bills. So you'll study publications to see what's valuable to their readers. To the cooking magazine you won't send a poem about the loveliness of chocolate. You'll send a recipe. And not forget to mention the eggs and water. After you've shown readers how to make a chocolate cake, you may add a short, rich, nutty paragraph on the loveliness of chocolate. If the editor prints it, you'll be ecstatic; if not, you'll keep sending recipes. Because you want to write. And you keep writing.

(7) You'll love and collect people who'll help you make your writing better. Writers are like jazz musicians nurtured in New Orleans, Kansas City, and Chicago. (Note they didn't come from New York City; first they made great music at home in Manhattan, Kansas, and then that other Manhattan wanted them.) They always play the best they can where they are, and they constantly look to improve themselves. That's what an artist is: a person who produces art works continually and whose standards for her work keep rising.

Two things I forgot to say about writers. I liked one of your questions: "Do you feel that a writer, new to the field, could support himself on writing alone?" No is my answer. Not if you mean a freelance writer not working under wages or salary. Most freelancers need other jobs or sources of support to get along.

Today special interest magazines are almost the only possibilities for writers who want to reach readers in national periodicals. And there are many good ones, new and old. In the library you can consult *The Writer's Market* for names and statements of what the editors are looking for. Look in *Ayer's Guide to Periodicals* for newspapers. Otherwise you have to play detective and ask people who are experts in a field: "What magazine do you rock collectors read?" or whatever. Making these suggestions reminds me that the second principle of good writing (the first is telling truths) is that you must know what you're talking about. If you're not an expert in the general topic, you must get to know your subject deeply. Talk to people; draw them out; ask them to suggest other people who know what they're talking about.

Often today it's easier to get a book published than a magazine article. But thousands of bad book manuscripts are written every year by people who yearn to be famous but are unwilling to discipline themselves to write something people want to read. Better to begin your writing career with a letter to the editor that's printed than a novel you show to no one before sending it off to a publisher.

If you can become a reporter on a local newspaper or magazine— however small, maybe a club or church monthly bulletin—do so. You'll have to write truly about human beings in action, and face responses from readers who know those people. Nothing can do more to discipline you as a writer. When your first reader says, "You didn't spell my name right—it's Smyth," you'll begin to understand that writing is a relationship between people, not the creation of a final, authoritative statement on a page intended for people beneath the writer.

What I've said here is apt to discourage beginning writers. But if they're writers, it won't kill them off. Because writers are people who write constantly, and once published, get published again. There's no need that you or anyone else become a writer, except the need in you. If you're hungry enough to see your words in print, eventually you'll watch yourself eating.

Truly,
/s/ KEN MACRORIE

suggestions for teachers

Commonly, undergraduate research papers are farces because the writers haven't genuinely searched anything and the materials they've worked with are entirely foreign to them. To carry out a sustained project of high intellectual standard they need to be countenanced in ways new to them and their teachers. Few of us teachers realize how perfectly in so-called "research" projects we've been training people to act inanely and irresponsibly.

Those of us who have asked students to write I-Search Papers have discovered that above all we must protect our students' time, so they can conduct inquiries realistically—tracking leads, finding that many don't work out, and following up when things go right. They're taking other classes besides ours, and they're committed in many ways to life outside school as well as within it. For their I-Search project they need time to telephone and write people and get answers from those who don't reply at once. They need time to organize materials and compose a story of their adventure that's alive and fascinating. To do this they need a number of days unencumbered by assignments of any kind.

What I've just said may seem obvious, but isn't, I think, when one considers that we teachers often hope for professional performance from students who are never put in professional circumstances. Working researchers are given weeks, months, and often years in which to carry out a project. They live with an idea and nurse it, over many hours, at home, as well as at work. If they do well they are rewarded with more than an A or a B. I'm aware that many professionals work on assignment, with no choice of what they'll investigate, but the work is already in *their field,* which they have chosen. The I-Search project capitalizes on true motivation and asks a large effort from persons not accustomed to having their interests taken seriously. Their school-acquired habits of doing things carelessly and without commitment are likely to re-emerge unless teachers are careful to countenance the whole effort.

And so, this caution: *Nothing in the course must deny students the time to carry out a thorough search.* I've included in this contextbook a number of *doings* for students, but teachers should assign them only after fitting them into (or omitting some) a schedule that makes sense for their students and the length of the course. A paragraph from a letter to me by Jean Smith of Bunnell High School, Stratford, Connecticut, gives a notion of the realities of planning I-Search work:

> If at all possible, a day out of school is the best motivation. It means I trust students to use their time well. If they go on their own, it teaches them something about themselves in relation to the community. Then I can show them that anything is possible. Almost all successful adults love to talk about their work, and this is good for young people to know. I made up permission slips for the parents to sign, and arranged with the school to have students take individual Field Trip days. I'm pretty tough on this one. I can now fight with any Math teacher who feels that the sky will crack if Johnny doesn't attend Monday's 42 minutes of Algebra. But one has to be sure of the philosophy behind the I-Search project. (By the way, Ken, that would be my message to high-school teachers: Stop being scared, and don't look over your shoulder.)

College teachers have it easier, but they still face the task of making the I-Search project one that's genuinely respected by everyone involved. One way to do that might be to ask the campus or community newspaper to cover the work in an article or column.

Because some classes using this book will meet every day and others only twice or once a week, I can't propose a model schedule. I suggest that the course begin with students writing freely in class for twelve minutes or so, at every meeting for two or three weeks. And outside class as well, so they are writing four or five times a week. This is the practice used so successfully by John Bennett at Central High School in Kalamazoo, Michigan. John asks students to hand in the free writings as they do them; he glances briefly at them to see that they represent a true effort, signs his name at the bottom, and hands them back. He tells students that he's doing no more than that with their papers; they realize what their responsibility is. At the end of the week they choose the best writing (or several), amplify it, and bring it xeroxed or duplicated to the first meeting of the next week to be read aloud and commented on by the whole group and/or a small break-off group. This is similar to a professional's procedures—search, write up pieces of the work, bring them together, test them on colleagues, prepare a final report after taking it through several drafts.

In the last four years hundreds of first-rate I-Search Papers have been written in various parts of the country that scored with the writers and others. They were strongest in personal interviewing and weakest in library searching. None of the writers had available to them the chapters in this book that appear under the section heading "Looking in the Cupboard." I think those discussions will countenance students using libraries, but I don't want to stipulate how they should be used when I haven't yet used them myself in a course. I'd like to see students freed to read or consult them at what they feel are propitious moments. I'd be pleased to hear from teachers who have worked out optional uses for them by students.

Although this contextbook is designed to nurture initiative and will power, I feel that teachers in such a program should *require* that all students own a good college dictionary such as *The American Heritage, Webster's New World,* or *Webster's Collegiate* (Merriam's). This requirement, once so common in colleges, has been dropped in many schools today. I feel that a language-using animal without a dictionary is like a tennis player without a racquet.

Ordinarily if students have models of student research in their heads, they are models of bad borrowing or plagiarism. This book provides good models of I-Search Papers, but the most useful models in any teaching are those done by persons who worked recently in that very class and that very place. To some novices only those papers will seem convincing, reachable, and real. I'd like to suggest that teachers who receive good I-Search Papers in one class reproduce them for their next class, and invite the authors to be present when the papers are read so they can answer questions about how they did the work. A good way to prepare papers for reproduction is to type them on a carbon-ribbon machine, double-column, single-spaced, to save space and money. If xeroxing or other duplication costs block the teacher, he or she can collect a fee from students to cover them. Always papers may be posted on bulletin boards in classroom-building halls. The campus newspaper may be willing to print several papers that are widely appealing. There is no motivation like the possibility of being published.

When I taught a fifteen-week course wholly devoted to I-Searching, I found that asking for two papers, the first shorter than the second, resulted in the best work. It's only common sense to allow two chances at such a complex task. We don't expect a professional's first report to be as succinct and valuable as his later ones.

We expect both more and less than we should from students. The quality of thinking, the usefulness of the exploration, and the aliveness of the papers should be much higher in I-Search work than in ordinary school work. But the depth and authoritativeness of the knowledge should not equal that of most professional researchers who have devoted their careers to one field. Think of how much reading and valuable idle thought lies behind most original professional work. The topic is almost always with a professional, on weekends, in recreational moments, as well as "at work." The ruminating that goes on in odd moments enriches the enterprise. Deep familiarity with the tools and materials of the field is not likely to surface in student I-Searches. But at the same time, many papers will be more exciting to read than professional reports, because the searchers have divested themselves of Engfish and gone after something that has meant a great deal to them personally.

list of sources

NOTE: *Where frequently reprinted works are cited,*
I have not given edition or page number.

Page

ix *The Papers of Benjamin Franklin* (New Haven, Yale, 1961), III, 400.

1 William Carlos Williams, "The Beginnings of an American Education,"
The Embodiment of Knowledge (New York, New Directions, 1974).

2 Elbow, *Writing without Teachers* (New York, Oxford, 1973), 5.

3 Podhoretz, *Making It* (New York, Random House, 1967), 139.

6 Stafford, *Writing the Australian Crawl* (Ann Arbor, University of Michigan, 1978), 3.

8 McCarthy, in *Writers at Work: The Paris Review Interviews*, 2nd Series
(New York, Viking, 1963), 314.

9 Hall, *Writing Well* (Boston, Little Brown, 1973), 25.

10 Graves, "Balance the Basics," *Papers on Research about Learning* (New
York, Ford Foundation, 1978).

11 Nietzsche, *Beyond Good and Evil* (Chicago, Henry Regnery, 1955), 15.

12 Mead (Chicago, University of Chicago Press, 1934), 130.

13 Shelley, "A Defense of Poetry."

14 Emerson, "The American Scholar."

14 Partridge, *New York Times* (June 2, 1979), 1.

20 James, in Lane Cooper, *Louis Agassiz as a Teacher* (Ithaca, Comstock,
1945), 78-79.

21 Hazlitt, "On Familiar Style."

22 Graves, "Balance the Basics," *Papers on Research about Learning* (New
York, Ford Foundation, 1978).

23 Swift, "A Letter to a Young Gentleman lately entered into Holy Orders,
by a Person of Quality" (January 9, 1720).

25 "Blizzard of '78," Letter to the editor, *Kalamazoo Gazette* (March 24,
1978).

27 Johnson, in E.L. McAdam, Jr., and George Milne, eds., *A Johnson Reader*
(New York, Pantheon, 1964), 464.

27 Malcolm, "Mike Mansfield, the Ambassador, Doesn't Miss Senate One
Bit," *New York Times* (September 15, 1977).

28 Thoreau, "Life without Principle."

28 Ellison, in *Writers at Work: The Paris Review Interviews*, 2nd Series
(New York, Viking, 1963), 321.

32 Graves, "Balance the Basics," *Papers on Research about Learning* (New
York, Ford Foundation, 1978).

37 Chekhov to his brother Nikolay, in S.S. Koteliansky and Philip Tomlinson, eds., *The Life and Letters of Anton Tchekov* (New York, Doran,
n.d.), 80.

38 Emerson, *Journals* (April 25, 1831).

39 Nin, *Diary, 1931-1934* (New York, Swallow Press, 1966), 167.

40 Macrorie, "World's Best Directions Writer," *College English* (February
1952).

54 Lu Po Hua, *The Non-collected Works* (Santa Fe, Lost Books, 1980), 2.

62 Vivekananda, in *The Wisdom of the Hindus* (New York, Brentano's, 1921).

63 Agassiz, in Lane Cooper, *Louis Agassiz as a Teacher* (Ithaca, Comstock, 1945), 81.

65 Robinson, *The Mind in the Making* (New York, Harper, 1921), 79-80.

66 Thoreau, *Journals* (September 1, 1856).

72 Butler, *The Note-Books*, in *Works* (London, Jonathan Cape, 1926), XX, 102.

88 Thoreau, "Life without Principle."

98 Robinson, *The Mind in the Making* (New York, Harper, 1921), 58.

99 Graves, "Balance the Basics," *Papers on Research about Learning* (New York, Ford Foundation, 1978).

119 Cox, *Indirections* (New York, Viking, 1962), 131.

133 Lo Po Hua, *The Non-collected Works* (Santa Fe, Lost Books, 1980), 3.

139 Lo Po Hua, *The Non-collected Works* (Santa Fe, Lost Books, 1980), 3.

150 Franklin, *Autobiography* (New York Modern Library, 1950), 69, 103.

153 Duberman, *Black Mountain* (Garden City, Anchor Books, 1973), 182.

154 Franklin, in Carl Van Doren, *Benjamin Franklin* (New York, Viking, 1938), 74.

160 Bate, *Samuel Johnson* (New York, Harcourt Brace Jovanovich, 1977), 505.

161 White, "Letter from the East," *New Yorker* (February 18, 1956), 72.

163 Merz, *A History of European Thought in the Nineteenth Century* (1896), I, 7.

165 Murrow, in Charles Wertenbaker, "The World on His Back," *New Yorker* (December 26, 1953), 29.

166 Cajal, *Precepts and Counsels on Scientific Investigation (1951)*, 34.

166 Graves, "Balance the Basics," *Papers on Research about Learning* (New York, Ford Foundation, 1978).

173 Fromm, *Man for Himself* (New York, Rinehart, 1947), 105.

174 Anonymous reviewer. *New Yorker* (April 5, 1976), 138.

175 Albers, in Martin Duberman, *Black Mountain* (Garden City, Anchor, 1973), 323.

184 Whyte, *The Next Development in Man* (New York, Henry Holt, 1948), 223.

187 Johnson, in E.L. McAdam, Jr., and George Milne, eds., *A Johnson Reader* (New York, Pantheon, 1964), 453.

192 Graves, "Balance the Basics," *Papers on Research about Learning* (New York, Ford Foundation, 1978).

197 Eliot, *Middlemarch*, chapter 20.

199 Schuster, in Gerald Gross, ed., *Editors on Editing* (New York, Grosset & Dunlap, The Universal Library, 1962), 8.

200 Thoreau, *Journals* (January 26, 1857).

211 Butler, in A. T. Bartholomew, ed., *Further Extracts from the Note-Books of Samuel Butler* (London, Jonathan Cape, 1934), 183.

212 Brown, "Punctuation," *Encyclopædia Britannica*, 15th edition.

213 London, *The Adventures of Martin Eden*, chapter 9 and 23.

218 Brown, "Punctuation," *Encyclopædia Britannica*, 15th edition.

226 Graves, "Balance the Basics," *Papers on Research about Learning* (New York, Ford Foundation, 1978).

227 Douglass. (The three long quotations are from chapters 10, 11, and 7 of *The Life and Times of Frederick Douglass*.)

232 Murray, *Caught in the Web of Words* (New Haven, Yale, 1977), 72.

232 *New York Times* column, "Hers," by Linda Bird Francke (October 27, 1977), 44.

236 Perkins, in *Editor to Author: The Letters of Maxwell E. Perkins* (New York, Grosset & Dunlap [© 1950 by Scribner's]), 127.

238 Chaucer, quoted in an entry for the word "Library" in *The Oxford English Dictionary*.

239 Emerson, "The American Scholar."

240 Franklin, *Autobiography* (New York, Modern Library, 1950), 17-18, 33, 38.

244 Jefferson, Letter to George Watterson (May 7, 1815).

252 Poole. (All quotations from him in this chapter are from his preface to *Poole's Index to Periodical Literature*, 1802-1881.)

256 Wilson. (Material in this chapter about H.W. Wilson is taken from Lawler, *The H.W. Wilson Company* [Minneapolis, University of Minnesota, 1950] and Creighton Peet, "A Mousetrap in the Bronx," *New Yorker* [October 29, 1938].)

258 Rice, in Lawler, cited above, 83.

266 Agassiz, in Lane Cooper, *Louis Agassiz as a Teacher* (Ithaca, Comstock, 1945), 83.

267 *Encyclopædia Britannica*. (In this chapter discussion of the EB is based on my own observations and a reading of Harvey Einbinder, *The Myth of the Britannica* [London, MacGibbon & Kee, 1964] and Herman Kogan, *The Great EB* [Chicago, University of Chicago, 1958].)

270 Masai. "Talk of the Town," *New Yorker* (July 28, 1962).

280 Johnson, in E.L. McAdam, Jr., and George Milne, eds., *A Johnson Reader* (New York, Pantheon, 1964), 451.

281 Angelou, *I Know Why the Caged Bird Sings* (New York, Random House, 1960), chapter 15.

289 Johnson. (This and the next two statements about his work are from his preface to *A Dictionary of the English Language*, 1755.)

293 Webster, characterizing Jefferson, in John S. Morgan, *Noah Webster* (New York, Mason/Charter, 1975).

294 Webster. (His statement on "the principal differences between the people of this country and of all others . . . " and the next two quotations are taken from his preface to *An American Dictionary of the English Language*, 1828.)

296 Eiseley, *Propædia* of *The Encyclopædia Britannica*, 15th edition, 207.

298 Murray. (For this chapter, from K.M. Elisabeth Murray's *Caught in the Web of Words* [New Haven, Yale, 1977], I have taken the passages beginning (1) "on a discovery . . . " 83, (2) "Methinks . . . " 41, (3) "I write to the Director . . . " 201, (4) "People spoke of it as if it were . . . " 193, (5) "The other day I found myself chairless . . . " 192, (6) "a following an adjective . . . " 201. Most of the unattributed quotations in this chapter are from the Historical Introduction to the OED.)

306 Emerson, "Society and Solitude."

312 Myers, *The Roots of Modern English* (Boston, Little Brown, 1966), 6.

313 Franklin, in Carl Van Doren, *Benjamin Franklin* (New York, Viking, 1938), 425. (The comments about Roosevelt, Shaw, and Pitman are based on a reading of Abraham Tauber, *George Bernard Shaw on Language* [New York, Philosophical Library, 1963].)

314 Shakespeare, *Poems* (New York, The Limited Edition Club, 1941), II.

316 D. Franklin, *The Papers of Benjamin Franklin* (New Haven, Yale, 1961), XIII, 523.

317 Johnson, Preface to *A Dictionary of the English Language*, 1755.

319 Williams, "Spelling, Teaching of," *Encyclopedia of Education*, 1971.

321 Johnson, in E.L. McAdam, Jr., and George Milne, eds., *A Johnson Reader* (New York, Pantheon, 1964), 462.

324 Whitehall, *Structural Essentials of English* (New York, Harcourt Brace & World, 1956), 136.

325 Hemingway, in *Writers at Work: The Paris Review Interviews*, 2nd Series (New York, Viking, 1963), 223.

index